COMPUTER ASSISTED LEARNING

Selected Contributions from the CAL 91 Symposium

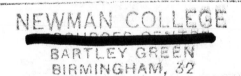

Titles of related interest

KIBBY	COMPUTER ASSISTED LEARNING: Selected Proceedings from the CAL '89 Symposium
KIBBY & MAYES	COMPUTER ASSISTED LEARNING: Selected Proceedings from the CAL '87 Symposium
SMITH	COMPUTER ASSISTED LEARNING: Selected Proceedings from the CAL '83 Symposium
SMITH	COMPUTER ASSISTED LEARNING: Selected Proceedings from the CAL '81 Symposium

Cover photograph: A Computers in Teaching Initiative Stand at CAL91
(photo: Michael R. Kibby)

COMPUTER ASSISTED LEARNING

Selected Contributions from the CAL91 Symposium

8–11 April 1991, Lancaster University

Edited by
MICHAEL R. KIBBY
and
J. ROGER HARTLEY

PERGAMON PRESS

OXFORD · NEW YORK · SEOUL · TOKYO

U.K.	Pergamon Press plc, Headington Hill Hall, Oxford OX3 0BW, England
U.S.A.	Pergamon Press Inc., 395 Saw Mill River Road, Elmsford, NY 10523, U.S.A.
KOREA	Pergamon Press Korea, KPO Box 315, Seoul 110-603, Korea
JAPAN	Pergamon Press Japan, Tsunashima Building Annex, 3-20-12 Yushima, Bunkyo-ku, Tokyo 113, Japan

First edition 1992

Library of Congress Cataloguing-in-Publication Data
Symposium on Computer Assisted Learning (1991: Lancaster University)
Computer assisted learning: selected contributions from the CAL91 Symposium, 8–11 April 1991, Lancaster University/edited by Michael R. Kibby and J. Roger Hartley.
   p. cm.
  Includes index.
  ISBN 0-08-041395-1: $110.00
  1. Computer-assisted instruction—Congresses. I. Kibby, Michael. II. Hartley, J. Roger. III. Title.
LB1028.5.S95 1991
371.3'34—dc20
                                  91-42861
                                    CIP

ISBN 0 08 041395 1

Published as Volume 18, Number 1–3 of the journal *Computers & Education* and supplied to subscribers as part of their 1992 subscription. Also available to non-subscribers.

Typeset in Great Britain by BPCC Techset Ltd, Exeter. Printed by BPCC Wheatons Ltd, Exeter

CONTENTS

COMPUTER ASSISTED LEARNING
Selected Contributions from the CAL91 Symposium

Computers Educ. Vol. 18, No. 1–3, p. ix, 1992
Pergamon Press plc. Printed in Great Britain

PREFACE

These Proceedings of the CAL series of biennial Symposia have a somewhat different origin to previous ones. The reason is that CAL91 had a somewhat different structure to its predecessors. The papers included here were not formally presented during the Symposium; however, they are all related to sessions held during the Symposium, reflect the contemporary concerns of participants and were refereed in the usual way. Some words of explanation regarding the content and stucture of CAL91 are necessary.

Regarding content, we believed it was important to identify a strong restricted theme rather than allow contributions to range too widely. A suitable theme emerged from the view that after 20 years of mainly pragmatic experience of using information technology to support learning, the time had come for an emphasis on hard research evidence, to which could be added what was judged to be substantially innovative explorations. Certainly not reports on the 501st good way to teach genetics! We also believed it worth experimenting with a new structure.

I remember some years ago being taught that one technique for checking the validity of a mathematical model was to examine its behaviour in extreme cases. Whilst many features of a model behave quite well in ways which seem to be reasonable in modest cases, it is rather complex to check general validity by such methods. Some quite useful and quick tests can be undertaken by examining the model's behaviour when it is pushed to the limit of some, even all, of the variables.

Our approach to CAL91 was a bit like that. We questioned the value of conventional sessions during which authors speak about, sometimes even read, their papers for 15–20 min and then respond to questions for 5 min or less. There was also a concern about the lottery involved in selecting plenary speakers (and whether the Symposium Dinner was going to provide better or worse, and more expensive, food than on other evenings!). We decided to experiment with another model for symposia and took an alternative model to the extreme. In doing so we hoped that the rather detailed evaluation, which was undertaken independently of the Programme Committee (and is reported in this publication), would show the strengths and weaknesses of the model and would benefit our successors. Nothing ventured, nothing gained!

After much debate, the comment of one member of the Committee gave us courage to stick to the innovative plan. We became convinced that participants would value a few substantive and interactive sessions rather than a larger number of passive, superficial ones.

So the model for CAL91 emerged, helped by the structure of the space to be used at Lancaster. Over 300 participants (nearly 400 attended for at least part of the time) in groups of no more than 20 people implied more than 15 parallel sessions throughout. It also implied 100 organisers of sessions, mostly of half-a-day. Such a structure depended very strongly on session leaders and their ability to engage participants in interaction on the theme of the session. We expected that the mixture of seminars and workshops of usually three hours duration would allow substantive debate to take place. In order to assist participants in making difficult choices, almost all sessions were provided with a "shop-window" in the form of a poster display. The displays were live at the opening of the Symposium and at advertised times later and in the evenings.

How successful where we? What lessons did we learn? Let me leave the reader to decide on the answers by reading the evaluators' report. Also, to wish the CAL93 Chairman with wisdom enough to keep most of the participants happy for most of the time!

PROFESSOR R. LEWIS
Chairman, CAL91 Programme Committee

Computers Educ. Vol. 18, No. 1–3, p. x, 1992
Pergamon Press plc. Printed in Great Britain

INTERNATIONAL PROGRAMME COMMITTEE

LANCASTER UNIVERSITY

Computers Educ. Vol. 18, No. 1–3, pp. 1–9, 1992
Printed in Great Britain

0360-1315/92 $5.00 + 0.00
Pergamon Press plc

REASONING SUPPORTED BY COMPUTATIONAL TOOLS

Joan Bliss,[1]* Jon Ogborn,[2] Richard Boohan,[2]
Jonathan Briggs,[3] Tim Brosnan,[2] Derek Brough,[4]
Harvey Mellar,[2] Rob Miller,[4] Caroline Nash,[2] Cathy Rodgers[1]
and Babis Sakonidis[1]

[1] King's College London, University of London, London WC2R 2LS, [2] Institute of Education, University of London, 20 Bedford Way, London WC1H 0AL, [3] Kingston Polytechnic, Penrhyn Road, Kingston upon Thames KT1 2EE and [4] Imperial College, University of London, South Kensington SW7 2AZ, England

Abstract—This paper sets out the work of the Tools for Exploratory Learning Programme within the ESRC Initiative Information Technology in Education. The research examines young secondary children's reasoning with computational tools. We distinguish between exploratory and expressive modes of learning, that is, interaction with another's model and creation of one's own model, respectively. The research focuses on reasoning, rather than learning, along three dimensions: quantitative, qualitative, and semi-quantitative. It provides a 3×2 classification of tasks according to modes of learning and types of reasoning. Modelling tools were developed for the study and descriptions of these are given. The research examined children's reasoning with tools in all three dimensions looking more exhaustively at the semi-quantitative. Pupils worked either in an exploratory mode or an expressive mode on one of the following topics: Traffic, Health and Diet, and Shops and Profits. They spent 3–4 h individually with a researcher over 2 weeks, carrying out four different activities: reasoning without the computer; learning to manipulate first the computer then later the tool and finally carrying out a task with the modelling tool. Pupils were between 12 and 14 yr. Research questions both about children's reasoning when working with or creating models and about the nature of the tools used are discussed. Finally an analytic scheme is set out which describes the nature of the causal and non-causal reasoning observed together with some tentative results.

INTRODUCTION

The Tools for Exploratory Learning Programme is part of the ESRC Initiative, Information Technology in Education, and is a development of work in the London Mental Models Group (see Appendix). The aim of the programme is to study children's reasoning when they are interacting with different types of computer tool. Their reasoning is examined through a series of tasks in which learners are asked to work in one of two modes: either to model a situation for themselves or to explore another person's model of a situation. So we were concerned with looking at: (i) whether interaction with tools containing representations of a domain could facilitate reasoning in that domain; (ii) whether learners can be helped to reason about a domain by representing and exploring the consequences of their own ideas about the domain.

The specific focus of the research is to examine how pupils reason in tasks using tools, which together require or permit quantitative, semi-quantitative or qualitative reasoning. We have chosen to study pupils in the age range 12–14 yr.

An approach to such questions requires analysis of:

learning and reasoning
the characterisation of different dimensions of reasoning
choice of, and distinction between, different types of tools
the research strategy

LEARNING AND REASONING

In our original proposal for the research[1] we had categorised tools as being either exploratory or expressive. Such a definition, however, became too restrictive. The focus needed to be on types of learning with tools, thus we now distinguish between exploratory and expressive modes of learning. Tools can be used in either mode. The Exploratory mode permits pupils to investigate

*Author for correspondence.

the views of a teacher or an adult about a given domain, views which will often be quite different from their own spontaneous ideas. The Expressive mode permits pupils to represent aspects of their own ideas about a domain, and to explore and reflect on these. In our earlier paper[1] we developed the characteristics of these two modes.

It seems to us to be a valid criticism of many studies of learning that they do not allow enough time for significant learning to occur. Learning of the kind discussed above seems likely to need weeks or months rather than hours. Our constraints prevented us studying children over such a period of time. It therefore seemed clearer for us to limit the scope of the study to an investigation of children's reasoning with tools. We have chosen to look at reasoning which would seem to be necessary to learning, and which can be seen as of value in itself, rather than to claim to be investigating learning.

Our research is thus based on specially constructed tasks designed to elicit and encourage kinds of reasoning which are relevant to learning. We have distinguished three types of reasoning with tools: quantitative, semi-quantitative and qualitative. A given task is designed to elicit one of these types of reasoning, although of course other forms of reasoning may be used spontaneously by pupils in the task. Thus when we describe a type of reasoning we are describing a task–tool interaction, in which the tool contains or allows the expression of, for example, a semi-quantitative model of a situation, and in which the cognitive demand of the task also requires the learner to use this same type of reasoning. We have created, therefore, three types of task–tool combinations which permit these three kinds of reasoning in both exploratory and the expressive modes. We now give a brief description of the three kinds of reasoning.

DIMENSIONS OF REASONING

Quantitative reasoning

Quantitative reasoning can involve a variety of aspects, from recognising simple numerical relationships, through working with sets of numbers and comparing sizes and magnitudes, to manipulating algebraic relationships. The problem may be to know how changing a quantity by a given amount will affect another quantity or quantities. Thus if the population close to the only large supermarket in a given area doubles, how may this affect queuing times in the store? Other quantitative problems can include questions about possible values variables can take, given constraints upon some of them (how can the price of a meal made from a range of ingredients vary if its nutritional value is to be more than a given minimum?), or they can be dynamic problems about the evolution of a system (how does the number of bacteria in yoghurt vary with time?). Our task–tool situations are limited to quantitative reasoning about variables linked by simple algebraic relationships $(+, \times, -, /)$, providing means for constructing and manipulating algebraic relationships between variables.

Qualitative reasoning

Qualitative reasoning involves making categorical distinctions and decisions. Thus it may require considering a set of choices or decisions and taking into account their consequences or, given a certain goal, formulating what is necessary to reach that goal. It may require noting and taking account of alternatives, weighing up evidence, or considering *if* a certain condition is realised *then* what follows, etc. In our qualitative task–tool combinations the reasoning concerns problematic situations, the actions which are possible in each situation, and the further situations and associated actions to which these might lead.

Semi-quantitative reasoning

It seemed to us that these two distinctions did not capture some essential aspects of reasoning, in particular reasoning in which the direction but not the size of effects of one part of a system on another is known. For example, Piaget's work[2] on causality showed that young pupils were capable of apprehending problems in this manner when quantitative methods eluded them. Recent work in cognitive science, for example, on mental models[3] indicates the importance of what is often called "qualitative" but is actually semi-quantitative reasoning: thus this type of reasoning involves seeing how in a complex system the rough and ready size of something has an effect on the rough and ready size of something else, which may in turn affect other things and might in the end feed back to affect the first quantity.

CHOICE OF TOOLS

The dimensions exploratory/expressive and quantitative, semi-quantitative, and qualitative produce a 3×2 matrix which allows a task–tool combination to be characterised (see our 1988 paper[1]). While some tools can be used in either mode of learning they usually require a specific type of reasoning. Quantitative tools are probably the most widely used. Those used in exploratory mode include simulations, while those able to be used in expressive mode include spreadsheets and modelling systems. Qualitative tools usable in exploratory mode include many expert systems, decision games, logic programs, data bases, and some simulations. Qualitative tools usable in an expressive mode include story-making programs, adventure game shells, data base shells and expert system shells.

Semi-quantitative tools are less known. Graphic structures for semi-quantitative models can be expressed in the modelling system STELLA but the tool itself is essentially quantitative. The Alternative Reality Kit (ARK) is another tool of this kind, but not one which is easily accessible. For exploratory mode we note that a number of simulations, in which the user askes for "more" or for "less" of (for example) water or a pesticide, have a semi-quantitative flavour. This flavour is usually introduced to simplify the simulation, but can be seen as valuable in focusing attention on the essentials of the quantitative relations without involving the complexities of the exact relationships.

Developments in hardware and software currently change faster than research can deliver results. For this reason, beginning in 1988, we chose to develop or experiment with software which might only be available to schools later, nearer the time at which our results and software would be ready. We chose to work with Apple Macintosh machines, in part because of the possibilities they offered for investigating tools with direct manipulation facilities, given the evidence that directly manipulating the icons representing primitives to construct models was likely to help children to learn the tool quickly and to grasp its nature.

The research programme is not intended to be either tool or task driven. We chose one tool for use in each of the areas of reasoning: quantitative, semi-quantitative and qualitative; these tools being designed to be able to be used in both exploratory and expressive tasks.

Quantitative tool

For quantitative tasks we developed a prototype tool which allows models to be built which use simple algebraic relations between variables. Quantities can be combined by addition, subtraction, multiplication or division, with consistency of units being partially provided for. Quantities can be given maximum and minimum values, so that variables can be altered in steps between these values by moving a graphic slider attached to the box representing the variable. If an independent variable is altered, the tool shows which variables will be affected, while calculating them. Graphs of values of any one dependent variable against any one independent variable can be obtained, thus enabling exploration of sections across the "space" of values of variables. In essence the tool is much like the Algebraic Proposer[4]. However, by using much of the code and facilities of our other tool IQON (see below), it works much more by direct manipulation. A Hypercard version was also used in some of the empirical work.

Semi-quantitative tool

No suitable practical semi-quantitative tool existed when we began the research. One source of ideas was the notion of causal loop diagrams, which form part of the metaphor used in STELLA and of the system dynamics thinking behind it[5]. Another more general source was thinking in Artificial Intelligence about qualitative reasoning about processes of causal change, as described by, for example, Kuipers[6], Forbus[7] and de Kleer and Brown[8].

A tool (IQON) was developed in Smalltalk for use with semi-quantitative reasoning tasks. IQON allows the user to represent a system in terms of interacting variables, specifying the relations between them. Variables are depicted as boxes and relations between them as arrows linking one box to another.

Figure 1 gives an example. All variables such as "nomad population" take semi-quantitative "values" of "above or below normal". A variable which is above or below normal drives another variable gradually up or down, depending if the first is linked to the second "positively" or "negatively". Thus in Fig. 1 a high level of "modern medicine" has driven down the variable "amount of disease". In turn, a low level of "amount of disease" has driven up "nomad population". The strength of the links affecting any one box may be varied relative to one another. As can be seen in Fig. 1, relationships can be quite complex, including interdependent variables such as cattle population and amount of grassland, or nomad population and food available. The whole diagram of boxes and links is animated, so that levels of variables can be watched rising and falling in response to each other's values.

Qualitative tool

We explored the possibilities of an expert system shell, Knowledge Pad[9], and a node and link story builder, LINX88[10], both for IBM machines, and built a Hypercard version of LINX. It proved more difficult than we expected to provide them with an appropriate content for use in exploratory tasks. The final qualitative tool "Explore your options" was a simplified and specialised Hypercard version of LINX. It provides for building a decision structure or tree, out of situations and a set of actions associated with each situation, each of which can lead to another situation. The tree is drawn graphically on screen. Situations and actions are entered as text, and no computation is done on them. The system maintains the tree and displays situations and actions as they are selected. Actions once taken can be undone, returning to an earlier situation to explore other courses of action. Thus in a task pupils are asked to think about a situation and to consider the possible actions allowed in that situation. They can look at all possible actions before deciding which to explore, or can follow up just one action.

It is possible for some of the alternative, different paths (arising from the initial situation) to converge on the same end point, whilst other paths give different results. Thus a task presents a starting situation, and a final goal, and the pupil has to consider alternatives among a set of coherent choices for reaching that goal.

RESEARCH STRATEGY

Research Questions

As mentioned previously, our two initial questions were:

> In what way can interactions with tools containing representations of a domain facilitate reasoning in that domain?
> Are pupils helped with their reasoning by representing and exploring the consequences of their own mental models of a domain?

These questions are elaborated in greater detail below.

Elements from which models are built.

> To what extent do pupils understand, think about and use the primitive modelling elements provided in the system (e.g. variables and links)?
> What kinds of interacting entities and connections do they spontaneously use?

Seeing a model as a whole.

> To what extent do pupils see models they are given, or the models they make themselves, as complex sets of interacting entities, with a structure seen as a whole?

Relationship between model and reality.

> To what extent do pupils treat a model as a formal structure with its own necessary behaviour?
> In what ways do they see the relationship between the model and the real world: for example is the model seen as predicting what will happen, or is the known behaviour of the world seen as testing the model?

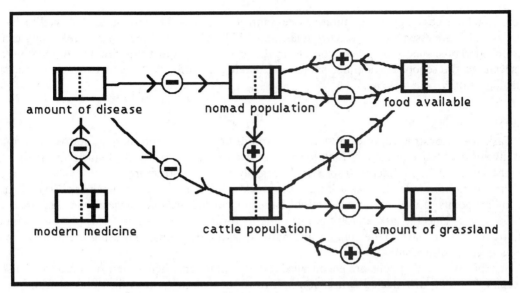

Fig. 1. A simplified model of nomad population, using IQON.

Modifications to models and evaluation of models.
Do pupils make modifications to models; what are the nature of, and reasons for, these modifications?
To what extent do pupils criticise models they are given, or ones they make?
Does working with the model lead to critical ideas about the task?
Learning potential.
Are there signs of pupils being helped (or hindered) in their thinking by the interaction with or making of a model?
Influence of the domain.
How far does the nature of the task and of the domain itself influence the pupil's reasoning?
Reasoning without the computer.
What do pupils think about the domain, before using any tool?
How do they reason about the domain: what kinds of arguments, elements and reasoning structures do they use?
Exploratory vs Expressive.
What can be said about differences in reasoning between these two kinds of task?
Quantitative, qualitative and semi-quantitative.
What can be said about similarities and differences in reasoning in tasks of these kinds?
Questions about tools.
Generally:

What are the essential features of tools used in expressive and exploratory modes?
What "vocabularies" do different tools provide? (where "vocabulary" means the primitive elements provided together with the metaphors they employ)

More specifically:

What are the operational and conceptual difficulties of a tool?
Is the "vocabulary" of the tool appropriate for the topic/task?
What "vocabulary" might be ideal for a given domain?
Is a close match between "vocabulary" of a tool and domain desirable?

TOPICS AND TASKS

Domains

Initially we had intended to investigate two contrasting domains: technology and systems of human relationships. This dichotomy tended to force the choice of tools, with quantitative ones being used in technology and qualitative ones in the humanities. Thus we decided instead to choose topics which are essentially cross curricular, and within which all three types of reasoning can be exhibited. Three such topics were chosen on the grounds of both being familiar to children and relevant to the school curriculum: shops and making a profit; traffic and congestion; diet and staying healthy.

Tasks

Tasks were constructed, of expressive and exploratory types, requiring quantitative, semi-quantitative or qualitative reasoning, each for at least two of the above topics. So far as possible, tasks of the same nature in different topics had basically the same structure.

In exploratory mode all tasks ask pupils to work in a "What . . . if?" framework. Several (three or more) points of view about what might happen in reality are put to them, and they are asked if they agree. Thus the tasks involve pupils thinking through a problem in terms of "what happens if you do this or that?", reflecting on alternatives, taking decisions, and using the tool to see the consequences of decisions.

In expressive mode pupils are encouraged, after having constructed their own model of a shop keeping in profit, of reducing congestion in a town, or of how to keep fit, to test it from several different points of view (e.g. "In your model, how can you keep profits up even if other things make matters worse?").

DATA COLLECTION

From December 1989 to July 1990 the main studies of semi-quantitative reasoning in both exploratory and expressive modes were carried out. Children interviewed were between 12 and 14 yr, the majority being from an outer London middle school, with a small number for the expressive tasks from an inner London secondary school. Forty-eight pupils were worked with individually, each for a total of 3–4 h, so that eight pupils were interviewed in each of the three topics in expressive or exploratory mode. Thus the time spent with any one pupil is fairly extensive, being spread through a series of sessions as detailed below, the schedule being similar in both modes:

 (i) reasoning about a task without a computer (approx. 30–40 min)
 (ii) introduction to the computer through a drawing task (approx. 30 min)
 (iii) learning to use the tool (approx. 60 min)
 (iv) carrying out a task (approx. 60/90 min)

Steps (i) and (ii) are carried out in the same session, with sessions (iii) and (iv) done separately but close to one another and no more than a week apart from sessions (i) and (ii).

With the Expressive tasks there is an additional session between steps (ii) and (iii), in which a small group of children (approx. four) are given a set of illustrated materials about the topic on which they will do the task (shops, traffic or health). The pupils read through the material with the researcher, discussing and asking or answering questions on the different sections of the material. Although most children will have some intuitive understanding of these topics we thought it important to provide at least a general overall awareness of the area in which they were going to be asked to develop a model.

Observation and interview data were collected, both in the interview (i) requiring reasoning about the topic without the computer, and during the performance (iv) of the task itself. All interviews were tape-recorded and transcribed *in toto*.

Data collection for the qualitative and quantitative task–tool situations took place during the Spring Term 1991. In each only two topics were used: congestion and traffic and shops and profits for the qualitative tasks, and traffic flows and health and diet for the quantitative tasks. The administration of the study follows the same lines as above. Numbers of pupils were also limited, with totals of 20 for both quantitative and qualitative tasks, equally divided between exploratory and expressive modes.

DATA ANALYSIS

An analysis of pupils' reasoning without the computer is being carried out and will, combined with results from the analysis of the tasks, be fed into a reasoning profile for each pupil. We will then want to compare pupils, and to look for similarities and differences across the three domains and between exploratory and expressive modes of learning. We hope to use the general features of this analysis to guide our approaches to the analysis of quantitative and qualitative tasks.

The data analysis scheme

The reasoning in the pupil's transcript is broken down into units which are then analysed along the following dimensions:

    relation to reality
    nature of outcomes
    description of model events

Relation to reality

There would appear to be three different relationships between the model and reality:

 (i) where the reasoning stays within the model
 (ii) where the reasoning refers to reality in order to substantiate or illustrate the model
 (iii) where the reasoning refers only to the outside world and not to the model at all

When the pupil's reasoning stays within the model the pupil can refer (a) to the content of the model or (b) to the representational level of the tool (nature or function of icons). In the latter case the pupil is in essence looking at formalism, whether the abstract formalism of the tool or its representation in the interface.

Nature of the outcomes

In each unit the child is saying something about the outcomes in the model or, in reality, which can be looked at in terms of the variables involved and the links between them.

Variables. What children say about variables is particularly important for the expressive tasks, since in these they are inventing them for themselves. In exploratory mode, however, we gain some insight into their understanding when they modify the given model, adding their own variables (for example, the politeness and friendliness of assistants in a shop).

Thus far we have identified three other types of entity used in place of a true variables which refers to an amount of some quantity: objects, events and processes. Pupils may go beyond the simple naming of an object, event or process and add to it a function or context, such as traffic lights for stopping cars, or an evening meal prepared for friends.

We also characterise these variables or entities according to whether they have already been used in the task or in a given model, whether they are a given element renamed or whether they are invented by the child.

Links. The pupil's description of links or relations can be either causal or non-causal, with causal links being seen as one variable having some sort of influence on another, whilst non-causal links are just co-occurrences of high or low values. Causal descriptions can be either direct, in which the relationship between two adjacent variables in the model is considered, or indirect in which pupils relate variables which are non-contiguous in the model.

Direct causal outcomes are simple, multiple or coordinated. Simple relationships are either connections where two variables are directly linked or chains where there are links across several variables, for example, a has an effect on b, and b has an effect on c and c influences d. Multiple relationships may concern one cause which creates more than one effect, or more than one cause creating one effect. Coordinated relations may involve simple feedback between two variables, articulated connections in which the pupil proposes that one connection functions because of other connections, or finally reasoning about the whole system of connections or a part of it.

Indirect causal outcomes may be single, in which pupils attempt to link two non-contiguous variables; or one to several, where one variable "influences" a series of other variables which are not actually linked to it; or global where one variable influences "all the others" or "everything".

Non-causal outcomes either mention isolated variables, or scan the model mentioning variables but not connections, or (by far the most frequent) concern sets of variables. Sets can be temporal sequences (children use temporal conjunctions such as *when, then, now, before, after, at the same time*), collections in which variables are linked by additive conjunctions (*and, also, but, in addition, as well as*), or lists where variables are just mentioned one after the other.

Sometimes when pupils are talking about what is happening with the model one of the links described is not in the model. This may be because the pupil has misread a link, has gone along it in the wrong direction, or has created a link that does not exist. We may not have evidence from the transcript to decide.

Descriptions of model events

In the task pupils are attempting to understand a dynamic model, and we are interested in how they describe the events happening in the model. There are two major types of descriptions: descriptions of states, or of the dynamism of the model. In the first, the system is talked about in terms of what has happened, as something finished and done. In the second, pupils talk about the system either in terms of prediction ("x will make y go up", "x should make y go up/down") or in terms of change ("x is going up, y is going down, z is going up and down").

CONCLUSIONS

Research which looks at young (12–14 yr) secondary school children's understanding of modelling is perhaps over-ambitious, especially if modelling were to be interpreted in the quantitative sense alone. However, we began with a belief that semi-quantitative reasoning, while being common to most adults when faced with complex systems, might also be a type which younger pupils might be able to manage. We can at least report that almost all our young pupils were able both to learn to manipulate the semi-quantitative tool IQON and to carry out the task, whether expressive or exploratory, at some level of success. In the expressive mode many of them could construct a model with three or four variables. Some models had complex interactions (i.e. structure) while others basically showed influences of several variables on just one main variable. Most pupils attempted to test the models. In the exploratory mode, although most pupils found it hard to cope with the model as a whole, many were able to deal with partial systems within a model. Also the exploratory tasks, with the different approaches to a problem, could elicit potentially valuable events for learning, when pupils were led to puzzle about the structure of the model until they could understand it.

The analysis of the quantitative and qualitative tasks has not yet started. One tentative impression is that performance on quantitative tasks has a very wide range, with some children finding the tasks extremely difficult while others coped admirably with parts we imagined might be difficult. On qualitative tasks, the alternation of situation and action leading to a new situation built into the tool seems sometimes to be an unnatural and inhibiting format. Actions seem easier to think of than the situations to which they might give rise.

The programme finishes at the end of December 1991 and the findings of the study will be disseminated both to a research and an educational audience.

REFERENCES

1. Bliss J. and Ogborn J., Tools for exploratory learning. *J. CAL* **5**, 37–50 (1990).
2. Piaget J., Bliss J., Chollet-Levret M., Dami C., Mounoud P., Robert M., Rossel-Simonet C. and Vinh Bang, *The Composition of Forces and the Problem of Vectors*. Centre for Studies in Science and Mathematics, University of Leeds (1990).
3. Gentner D. and Stevens A. (Eds), *Mental Models*. Erlbaum, Hillsdale, N.J. (1983).
4. Schwartz J., *Algebraic Proposer*. MIT, Cambridge, Mass. (1987).
5. Roberts N., Anderson D., Deal R., Garet M. and Shaffer W., *Introduction to Computer Simulation*. Addison-Wesley, New York (1983).
6. Kuipers B., Commonsense reasoning about causality: deriving behaviour from structure. Tufts University Working Papers in Cognitive Science, No. 18 (1982).
7. Forbus K. D., Qualitative reasoning about space and motion. In *Mental Models* (Edited by Gentner D. and Stevens A.), pp. 53–74. Erlbaum, Hillsdale, N.J. (1983).

8. de Kleer J. and Brown J. S., Assumptions and ambiguities in mechanistic mental models. In *Mental Models* (Edited by Gentner D. and Stevens A.), pp. 155–190. Erlbaum, Hillsdale, N.J. (1983).
9. Briggs J., Brough D., Nichol J. D. and Dean J., *LINX88*. PEG, London (1988).
10. Briggs J., *Knowledge Pad*. PEG, London (1989).

APPENDIX

The London Mental Models Group

The Tools for Exploratory Learning Research Programme for the ESRC Information Technology in Education Initiative was proposed by the London Mental Models Group. This group, established in Spring 1986 by Joan Bliss at King's College London, is multi-disciplinary, involving staff in science and mathematics education, cognitive psychology, educational computing, expert systems and artificial intelligence. It is multi-institutional, drawing members from four institutions: King's College London, Institute of Education, Imperial College and Kingston Polytechnic.

The research programme described in the paper is co-directed by Joan Bliss (King's College) and Jon Ogborn (Institute of Education) who together with Jonathan Briggs (Kingston Polytechnic), Derek Brough (Imperial College) and Harvey Mellar (Institute of Education) constitute the programme's management group. On the team are Rob Miller, Caroline Nash, Dick Boohan, Tim Brosnan and Babis Sakonidis. The London Mental Models Group is also collaborating with Jean-Blaise Grize of the Centre de Recherches Semiologiques, Neuchatel. The work of the programme is being developed in close collaboration with other members of the London Mental Models Group, and is seen as an integral part of the work of the group.

The group also has received an award from the EEC for the Basic Research Actions ESPRIT Programme as a Working Group together with partners in Paris at Université Paris Sud, Orsay, and with Jorge Jensen in Denmark. The theme of the work for ESPRIT is about the nature and form of children's and teachers' explanations and the gap between how we understand these and how computers might represent them.

Computers Educ. Vol. 18, No. 1–3, pp. 11–22, 1992
Printed in Great Britain. All rights reserved

OBJECT-LESSONS FROM SELF-EXPLANATORY OBJECTS

DON CLARK

The Open University, Institute of Educational Technology, Walton Hall,
Milton Keynes MK7 6AA, England

Abstract—Self-explanatory objects (SEOs) are based on objects found in object-oriented programs and object-oriented interfaces. In some object-oriented interfaces the functionality of the objects depicted can be discovered by exploration and experiment. However, users may not be able to identify an object's name, alternative views or representations of the object, its relations to other objects, its full functionality and/or the ways in which it was designed to be used. When a system has been programmed in an object-oriented style its coded objects may correspond with aspects of users' conceptions of the system and/or domain. Thus the form and operation of a program's code can represent a source of information which may be meaningful to users and which can be accessed and presented as explanations by a help system. This has been demonstrated by a proof of concept prototype and also by a second system, called Partickles. Some of the SEOs in Partickles offer explanations of their specific prospective functionality—indicating what they "would do" if activated in the current context. Partickles has been used to investigate when and how information from self-explanatory objects and other forms of help is used. The paper outlines the aims and context of the SEO project, describes the two systems and presents some of the results of the empirical studies conducted with Partickles. The studies showed that the Partickles SEO help facilities were used, though the usage often consisted of phases of contiguous help accesses which occurred while subjects were learning to use the system. The studies also revealed some factors, related to presentation and object-based help, that strongly influenced user behaviour. It appears that extra information from self-explanatory objects can assist users to understand and learn about systems and domains, but it may also accustom users to expect to be able to obtain extra information and challenge their existing learning strategies.

INTRODUCTION

Self-explanatory objects (SEOs) are objects within a system, some of which may correspond with objects displayed by the interface. A help system based on self-explanatory objects provides information about system objects. It also draws information from system objects and may provide access to their functionality. Though the information may be helpful to users it is the act of seeking information and what the existence of additional information implies about the users' role that may offer most educational value.

According to the Shorter Oxford English Dictionary an "object-lesson" is: "a lesson about a material object conveyed by actual examination of the object" or figuratively: "something that exemplifies some principle in a concrete form". The Self-Explanatory Objects section of this paper indicates that the extent to which objects lend themselves to "actual examination" is increased by a SEO system. Also, though the objects may be intangible, a SEO system can augment the information available about them—adding an extra and/or alternative dimension and hence providing a more substantial overall representation.

The paper presents the broad aims of the SEO project in relation to help-system research and in regard to its potential educational significance. It then considers interfaces, help systems and some currently available systems as part of the current context of information provision. This is followed by a brief examination of some relevant terms and concepts. After outlining the general principles of a SEO system, the two prototype SEO systems are described and then some of the findings of the empirical studies are presented. The paper ends with a discussion of some of the results and implications of the project.

SEO AIMS

Help aims

Duffy and Langston[1] provide a broad definition of the purpose of a help system: "The general goal of a help system, regardless of application, should be to provide the typical user with all the information he or she needs to efficiently operate the system".

A SEO system, like a help system, is a source of information additional to that provided by the main system's interface. A SEO system may also resemble a help system in both the content and presentation of its information. However, a SEO system is intended to augment the main system's interface and is not intended to replace all the functions of a help system. One of the aims of the SEO project has been to identify and suggest roles for help within the context of modern graphical interfaces.

Where levels of user expertise are accorded particular emphasis and/or user goals refer to the domain of the system, the goal of a help system may involve educational considerations. The SEO paradigm is independent of any domain and does not actively cater for variations in levels of user expertise. However, a SEO system may supply a framework to which descriptive and prescriptive knowledge can be attached, and its presentation may be varied in accordance with domain considerations.

Educational aims

The computer is a multi-purpose tool and its use requires the ability to adjust, and adjust to, its varied roles. Learners might benefit from the option to disregard the constraints of the interface environment and make any adjustments, or obtain any additional information, they wish—thus situating the program in a broader and perhaps more relevant context in which the educational considerations of awareness, choice, self-enablement and rehearsal are paramount.

In addition to assisting users to learn about a particular system and extend their exploration strategies, the SEO project has a meta-level educational objective involving users' expectations and awareness of their own capabilities. Users are not limited to, and by, the information available from the interface—because SEO provides alternative perspectives and additional information. Consequently users choose their own limitations and, in so doing, select how and when to learn. This crucial opportunity to choose would be eroded by a system that attempted to adapt its information to users' more immediate needs. "Intelligent" help might encourage questions such as "What do I do now?", to which the answer implicit in a SEO system is: "You are in control. You can experiment and decide". And, when the question is task-oriented, such as a "How do I . . . ?" question, the SEO information may be used for reference because it is consistent (except insofar as its reflects the state of the system) and users can learn where and how to find answers to their questions.

INTERFACES AND HELP SYSTEMS

Information from interfaces

Interfaces typically present and elicit information: maintaining and constraining an input-feedback cycle. Some of the less recent research on help systems, much of which is still cited, involved systems whose interfaces, and sometimes help systems, were of the textual, teletype form. Some of this research remains relevant, though the SEO project has focused upon object-oriented interfaces of the sort that are usually visual and iconic, which may involve WIMP features (i.e. windows, icons, menus and pointers) and which may allow the user to engage (to a greater or lesser extent) with the system by direct manipulation[2]. In such systems objects and the relations and functionality of objects may convey information by being apparent, active, responsive and so on. If they are labelled, as icons representing files and filing system directories commonly are, this may convey additional information and reinforce the information conveyed by the object. In some cases objects may imply information by use of metaphor and/or convention so that users may be able to draw on their previous experiences in other contexts in order to interpret the interface and select appropriate actions. Other features of the interface may convey information, such as: error messages, history traces, example files/sequences, undo/redo facilities, sound effects, and parts of the interface (e.g. dialogue boxes) which depart from the iconic format, central paradigm or metaphor.

One of the weaknesses of interface metaphors may be that—like painted scenery—they offer less functionality than their representations suggest. Conversely, the representations may not suggest the fully functionality of the objects they depict. The object may even contradict the metaphor and become magical[3]. In exploring an iconic interface there is seldom any acknowledgement that the process of discovering functionality is ever completed. Also, users may not be able to identify: an object's name, alternative views or representations of the object, its relations to other objects, its full functionality and/or the ways in which it was designed to be used. It is not suggested that the user should stop experimenting with the system in order to "find out the answers", but rather that at a certain stage experimentation becomes mundane and the limits of the representation become restrictive. When that stage is reached users should (figuratively) be able to pick up the object, view it from another angle, heft it in their hands, read what is on its bottom, check its entry in a catalogue and continue their investigations from there. This is not wishful thinking, for, when a system is programmed in an object-oriented style, much of this information is already contained within the system. For example, the system "knows" which objects can respond to a "do something" message and it might offer these objects as a list with the option of "doing something" to one of them.

Help information

Help systems can be broadly considered to be online facilities dedicated to the provision of information concerning the interface and/or domain of a main system. Help information may be of many types, e.g. advice-giving, tutorial, examples, rehearsals, descriptions of the system's functionality, procedural information regarding users' tasks, information that attempts to anticipate users' goals and/or to answer questions a user might ask. The presentation of help involves considerations such as: access, timing, quantity, levels, consistency, modality and intrusiveness, and it may take many forms such as: "canned", modular, context sensitive, textual and diagrammatic. Kearsley[4] provides a relatively up-to-date survey of design, research and implementation issues in the field of online help systems.

O'Malley[5] raises the question of whether it may be possible to "bypass the need for formal 'help' by making the objects in the user's task environment 'visible'", but she notes that object-oriented interfaces without formal help facilities do not provide task-based help. Bauer and Schwab[6] write that: "One modern statement of why help-systems are not built is that systems are self-explaining. But for most systems this is only true in part". Non-visible objects, relations between objects, partial or undiscovered functionality, the limits of metaphors and the restrictions of a single form of representation suggest that an online help system may have an irreplaceable role in augmenting the accessibility and expressivity of objects in an object-oriented interface in addition to providing information appropriate to users' tasks, expectations, experience and familiarity with the main system and/or domain.

Help systems have often failed to fulfil their potential. This is partly because their potential could be considered to include all the possible short-comings of main systems (and users!), and partly because, in the context of complete product development, help systems have tended to be marginalised. Borenstein[7] considers that: "Historically, little attention has been paid to on-line help mechanisms. They have been built, if at all, as afterthoughts, last-minute additions to complex software systems", and Trenner[8] attributes the poorness of many help systems to their low priority in system development.

Three of the principal approaches to the provision of online help are: online manuals which present previously prepared ("canned") and largely unchanging help information, context-sensitive help which modifies its information according to the state of the system, and "intelligent" help which attempts to modify its information according to the state of the user. An online manual obliges users to map between the information it provides and that provided by the system. Context-sensitive help may use parts and states of the system to reference its information. "Intelligent" help attempts to infer a user's requirements and use these as a means of referencing its information. Users of online manuals may have difficulty finding the information they require. Context-sensitive help is more difficult to implement than an online manual, and can fail to reflect the help system user's interpretation of the current context. "Intelligent" help systems may be impossible to implement successfully[9,10], and according to Trenner[8] may be undesirable. There are many variations on these themes (discussed in greater detail by Clark[11]) such as: user editable help, smart help, systems which provide means for refining users' questions, object-based help and systems (such as the Did You Know system[12]) which facilitate serendipitous browsing.

Some currently available object-based online help systems

MacroMind's Director program, which can be used for the creation of animated graphics, contains a facility called "Object Sensitive Help" which provides a question mark pointer, but can only be used to access descriptions of currently visible objects. National Instrument's LabVIEW provides a number of pointer types and shapes used in the construction of control applications. Its pointers include a magnifying glass which, when clicked on an object, provides context sensitive help and access to an online help documentation facility. Microsoft Word 4 is a word-processing program that provides question pointer entrance to its online help documentation facility (the question pointer is obtained by simultaneously pressing the command and question mark keys). Version 7 of the Macintosh System Software offers a modal bubble help option in which, when the arrow pointer is used to select a desktop object, descriptive and context sensitive information related to the object appears next to it in a pop-up bubble. All four of these systems offer a degree of object-based and context sensitive help and in some cases this has been combined with online manual help facilities.

OBJECTS, EXPLANATION AND SELF-EXPLANATION

What is an object?

Heidegger's discussions of "The Thing"[13] suggest that "the real world" is only subjectively, dynamically and pragmatically divisible into objects. For example: could a hammer be considered a single object, part of a toolkit, or a head plus a handle? Is a rock a hammer, and, if so, is a mountain? Winograd and Flores[14] refer to interpretations of hammers being drawn from experiences of hammering. It seems that objects are so called because they possess qualitities of disambiguousness—and that having been abstracted from our experiences they survive temporary expedience through repetition, negotiation and convention.

There are three reasons for questioning the nature of objects in this paper. Firstly, because object-oriented interface design requires consideration of the disambiguation of its objects. Secondly, because disambiguation seems to be a crucial and underemphasised aspect of learning. Thirdly, because if objects cannot be objectively defined then it is not clear how knowledge concerning objects can be represented in artificial intelligence programs—which is why the SEO project has been preferred to the pursuit of "Intelligent" Help.

This paper refers to two sorts of computer-related objects: "system" objects (which are specified by program code) and "display" objects (such as icons). When a system has been programmed in an object oriented style some system objects may be represented at interface level by display objects.

Explanation

The term "information" is used in this paper to imply organised (formed) data that can be accessed (for acts of informing). To explain means to make plain (meaningful/unambiguous). "Explanation" is the act of making information accessible (or, by extension, both the information itself and information which could be used in this way) in a transaction between an explainer (or medium of explanation) and an explainee. These roles apply when either or both parties attribute the explainee with a requirement for an explanation and consider that the information provided can fulfil that requirement.

Draper[15] points out that: "Explanation is sometimes wrongly considered only as a response to some explicit request, especially in the context of simple user-driven help facilities".

Self-explanation

The term "self-explanation" tends to be applied to situations, events, objects and abstractions from which an explanation may be constructed by an explainee.

Suchman[16] introduces two senses of the term "self-explanatory artifact". The first is that: "a self-explanatory artifact is one whose intended purpose is discoverable by the user", while the second, which is now being applied to computer artifacts, is: "that an artifact might actually explain itself in something more like the sense that a human being does". As the second sense of the term seems beyond the reach of "intelligent" help systems the SEO project involves developing the self-explanatory properties of computer artifacts in order to make their intended purposes easier for users to discover.

SELF-EXPLANATORY OBJECTS

A SEO help system is integrated with its main system, but once activated it may display its own interface, options and navigation facilities. As the information is based on objects, the information provided can be associated with objects, remaining modular and distributed—with interface objects providing a top level index of SEO information. For example, clicking on an object may provide information about that object and options to obtain information about related objects (some of which may not be visible objects or may not even be display objects). In this way SEO objects are used as a way of referencing information as well as providing a source of information.

Draper[17] writes: "A desirable facility would be to allow the user to point to a display object and ask where it came from. In a sense, this is a kind of 'help' request, but aimed at a display object rather than a system object . . . . This is based on a crude notion of a display 'object' originating at a statement". In a SEO system it is not expected that the user would, or should, be able to interpret such "direct" information. Instead, the information is made available to the help system designer who converts it to a form considered suitable for the user.

Help messages are selected and prepared for presentation by the help designer but this task is made easier because some of the data representing the interactions and groupings of objects contains syntactic structures in "pre-parsed" forms. This is because object-oriented programming is often a process of problem decomposition in which aspects of a program's functionality are represented by the forms, structures, behaviour and interactions of its coded objects. Programming in an object-oriented style does not require an object-oriented language. It is perhaps more accurately regarded as a method of solving programming tasks by dividing the tasks into implementable components (rather than steps) where the components represent elements of the task rather than of the functionality of the implementation language. Rosson and Alpert[18] recommend that "the objects chosen for computational representation should be the same objects comprising the task domain being modeled".

SEOs represent information, and, as they are not a detachable information component, they have potential immediate relevance. There is no form of help information that a SEO system can provide that could not be provided by any system employing a sufficient degree of context sensitivity, but SEOs can make the help system designer's task easier, and given the poor quality of many help systems this may turn out to be a crucial factor.

A SEO help system can access message sequences passed between objects, the history of object interaction and the current conditions of the help request, it can interrogate objects regarding their methods, attributes and states and it can send messages to objects itself. In addition, it has its own data: information about the sequences and data it can match, information about conceptually related objects, canned components with which to build explanations, templates for its parsing mechanisms and so on. A full SEO implementation might provide a prototyping environment for help designers, navigation facilities for users of the help system and a variety of forms of help message.

A SEO system brings information contained within the program to the surface of the interface. This information, which is reinterpreted for the user by the help system designer, relates to the object's identity, functions, attributes and states and its relations to other objects. Descriptive and prescriptive information such as: how to get started, options, overviews and advice, explanations of error conditions and so on, may also be deduced from, or attached to, SEO information. One form of SEO help (which does not appear to have been featured in any help system to date) provides information indicating what an object would do next (i.e. in its current context if activated). This type of SEO information has been called *specific prospective functionality*, or "*would do*" help.

First prototype—noughts and crosses

A simple proof of concept SEO prototype, based on a noughts and crosses (tic-tac-toe) game, was implemented to demonstrate that in a system written in an object-oriented style there can be information in the form of objects that may be meaningful to users and that it is both possible

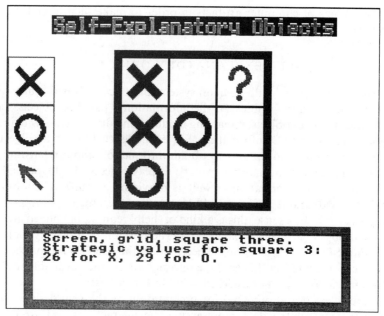

Fig. 1. The proof of concept prototype: noughts and crosses.

and practical to access and present this information. In Fig. 1, which shows the system in use, the arrow pointer has been exchanged for the question mark (help mode) and an empty square on the playing grid has been selected. The help message includes all the objects under the pointer and the help system has also accessed the unseen system object "auto-go" to obtain the current strategic values of the square for both X and O.

The SEO help system's question mark pointer can be used to select any onscreen object or combination of overlapping objects. In this simple prototype explanations are limited to text, all objects are identified (there has been no filtering of information by the help system designer), some objects have prescriptive information attached (e.g. "arrow—use to select X, O or ?, or to clear a grid square"), some have descriptive information attached (e.g. "text box—contains game information or self-explanations from objects") and some, in lieu of a user controlled navigation/ selection facility, can access information from unseen objects as shown in Fig. 1.

The noughts and crosses program was written in a partially object-oriented style which has some parallels with the Smalltalk language[19]. It can be regarded that each object that the help system designer considered significant contains a method that can list details of its methods and attributes. The SEO help facility is passed the identity of any object selected with the question pointer and it then asks the object for details of itself and parses these for the user. The proof of concept prototype was programmed in BASIC on an Archimedes. Procedures serve as method primitives or, with local data, as objects. In effect the only global variables are strings in which messages are passed and in which previous messages are stored (as a history trace). All objects are polled in sequence until the recipient of the highest priority message recognises it and responds. A SEO help facility can probably be based on any modular program which has structures (as objects) corresponding to aspects of users' tasks, goals and/or conception of the system, though it may be easier to collect information about objects if this can, initially at least, be indexed by the object rather than by the types of information.

Second prototype—Partickles

The second SEO system offers a variety of types of help so that the explanations provided by self-explanatory objects can be compared with those of other types of help. Like the noughts and crosses game this system is based on a game of strategy, but in this case the rules, goals and the objects involved are, initially, unfamiliar to users. In the second prototype the game is called Partickles and can be likened to a form of chess in which game pieces and their various functions can be combined. As Partickles is a research tool, its SEO facilities have been limited to provide

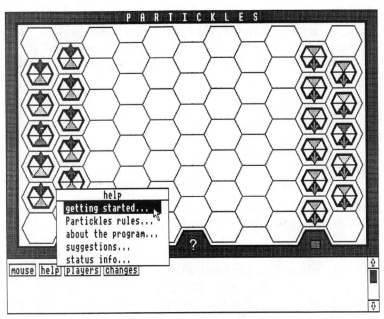

Fig. 2. The Partickles program with "traditional" help by menu.

exemplary evidence of the potential of a SEO system and because Partickles provides a number of different help systems. The menu help provided in Partickles is mainly in the form of canned text (with a few pictorial, diagrammatic and tabular elements). Only one of the menu options provides context-sensitive help because this would duplicate the context sensitivity of SEO help (leading only to a comparison of accessibility).

Three versions of Partickles were used in the empirical studies. The first and second versions were functionally similar, but, for the second version, the interface was simplified and some aspects of SEO help were made more prominent—e.g. by placing particle SEO information in "speech bubbles". The third version of Partickles was used during the last three (video) sessions of the final study and it included the question pointer as the default pointer and some extensions to the navigable SEO help facility. Figs 2 and 3 both show Partickles version 2.

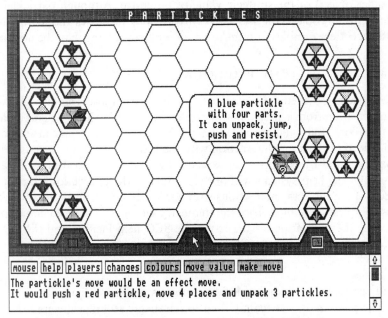

Fig. 3. The Partickles program with SEO partickle information.

In Fig. 2 the Partickles board is shown at the start of a game. The help menu has been opened and "getting started..." is being selected. There are four menu buttons. The "players" and "changes" menu-options alter game and system states while the "mouse" and "help" menu options produce windows of (mainly) canned text in the online manual style. The five help-menu options are as follows:

- getting started ...   pedagogical advice for beginners
- Partickles rules ...   the domain rationale
- about the program ...   system and operational details
- suggestions ...   pedagogical advice re. strategies and activities
- status info ...   shows states of play and of the system (tabular and context sensitive, but virtually superfluous in a visual interface).

The current pointer in Fig. 2 is the arrow pointer, but the question pointer can be seen in the centre of the lower edge of the game board frame. Clicking one pointer on top of the other swaps pointers.

In Fig. 3 a game is in progress and the question mark pointer has been used to select a partickle and obtain SEO partickle information. Descriptive information regarding the partickle's attributes has appeared in a bubble and information regarding the partickle's state (i.e. it is in effect-move mode) and its specific prospective functionality (what it "would do") is provided in the lower window. Three additional buttons appeared to the right of the menu buttons when the partickle was selected. These are the "colours", "move value" and "make move" hot-words boxes.

"Colours" provides access to the navigable SEO help facility which contains information regarding effects such as unpack and jump (represented by coloured triangles in partickles) that partickles may perform. "Move value" allows access to the computer player object which provides its assessment of the described move plus an assessment of the best move that the selected partickle could make in its current state. "Make move" would attempt to make the move described (or provide error messages) as though it had sent a message to the move object to perform its "make move" method.

Partickles was written in C on an Archimedes within the RISC OS Wimp environment. The most "significant" objects in Partickles are instances of classes which are represented by structures with implicit member functions (rather than explicit member functions as in the C++ language[20]). One particularly significant class of objects in Partickles is used to represent partickle moves. A move object contains a record of a partickle's state at the time of the move and details of all the changes that occur during a move. This object uses the computer-player function to provide an assessment (another object) of the strategic value of the move. Although partickles are probably the most significant display objects the user's tasks involve making moves and so this implementation probably provides a better example of object-oriented problem-solving than the noughts and crosses program.

THE EMPIRICAL STUDIES

The Partickles system provided the central activity in three empirical studies to investigate when and how help information from self-explanatory objects was used. The three empirical studies were the pilot study, the core study and the video study. A trace record facility in Partickles provided a time-stamped record of the user's interaction with the program, and this was used with the notes taken by the observer and transcripts of tape recordings (or video recordings in the video study) to assess the usage of the help systems within the context of the interaction as a whole. The most significant aspects of the subjects' interactions with Partickles were considered to be: the frequency and forms of use of question pointer help; the frequency, amount of use and choice of menu helps; the use, particularly the navigation, of the navigable SEO help facility; and the variation of help usage as subjects gained experience and knowledge.

The pilot study

The pilot study consisted of 9 sessions with 7 subjects studied individually whose ages ranged from 12 to 14. The pilot study was mainly used to iteratively redesign the empirical study and to adjust certain features of Partickles.

In the pilot study five out of seven subjects began their explorations of Partickles (the game) by exploring the interface and moving particles (playing pieces). One began by reading the help menu option: Partickles rules, and one explored the interface (but did not move particles) then read the help menu option: getting started. All the subjects tried using SEO particle help (some with prompting) but tended to prefer using help menu options and only one used the navigable colours SEO help facility successfully. None of the pilot subjects progressed past the stage of learning the game or won a game against the computer. However, all the subjects in the pilot study made progress during their sessions, and they were all willing to return for further sessions with Partickles. It was concluded that, although Partickles was suitable for users from the age of 12, older users would make more rapid progress and that the SEO particle information provided too much text with insufficient variation and lack of prominence so that after a first glance it was easy to overlook. Consequently, in version 2 of Partickles some aspects of SEO help were made more prominent.

The core study

The core study consisted of 6 sessions with 6 subjects studied individually whose ages ranged from 16 to 17. The core study used a consistent methodology and version 2 of Partickles in which the SEO particle information had been divided into two and placed partly in bubbles and partly in the lower window.

The core study subjects were older and had more computer experience than the pilot study subjects which may explain why all the core study subjects began their sessions with Partickles by reading help menu options and 5 of the 6 subjects began by choosing the help menu option "getting started". During the sessions 2 subjects used SEO particle information extensively, one avoided using any help facilities except at the start of the session, one was prompted to try using SEO help facilities and then used SEO particle information extensively and the remaining two occasionally used SEO help facilities and help menu options. All the subjects learned to play Partickles and some beat the computer player. Use of SEO particle help information was closely associated with success in game playing and speed of learning. The subject who began using SEO after prompting had won the fifth game he played but made no further progress and did not access any form of help in the next four games (after which he commented: "Seems to be getting harder"). His new learning strategy (using SEO help facilities) resulted in renewed progress, closer games and finally another win—which, this time, demonstrated his mastery of the game. Another subject was also prompted to use SEO facilities and did so in a contiguous phase (indicating that he was using this as a new source of information without adapting his learning strategies which were already adequate). In general, subjects seemed to use SEO particle information to extend/explain the representation of particles, they used the help menu option "Partickles rules" and observation of the computer player to learn the domain, and they used experimentation to learn how to operate the system and make particle moves. The help menu option "getting started" proved too general and verbose. Its information consisted of mapping a large number of initial states to a small number of goal states—and might have been improved if all the possible initial states had been reduced, by use of context sensitivity, to the one, current state. The navigable "colours" SEO help facility was hardly used, but its information duplicated some of the information in the help menu option "Partickles rules" and was only relevant in the early stages of learning. All the core subjects began their sessions by examining the help menu options and hence had already learned to find the information that was in the "colours" SEO help facility in "Partickles rules". Consequently more information was added to the "colours" SEO help facility in version 3 of Partickles—which was the version used in the video study. All the core subjects regarded the arrow pointer as the standard tool for manipulating particles and even after selecting SEO particle information with the question pointer they changed back to the arrow pointer in order to make a move rather than using the "make move" hot-words box. This attitude could have contributed a considerable bias against the use of question pointer help and hence the question pointer was made the default pointer in version 3 of Partickles. There was no evidence provided in the core study that the SEO help facilities were used to obtain information about the specific prospective functionality ("would do" help) of particles. Consequently the arrangement of SEO particle information in version 2 of Partickles which placed descriptive information about particles in the speech bubble and "would do" information in the lower window was swapped over for version 3 so that the "would do" information became more prominent.

The video study

The video study consisted of 3 sessions with 6 subjects studied in pairs whose ages ranged from 16 to 18. The video study was used to examine the findings of the core study (and, to some extent, to test the methodology). The video study used the third version of Partickles. Version 3 was built to see whether users would *opt out* of using SEO rather than having to *opt in*—and the navigable SEO help facility was extended to cover the essential details for getting started so that there was no *need* to opt out at an early stage. The video study subjects were studied in pairs so that their conversations could inform assumptions regarding their thinking and could provide evidence of the use of SEO's specific prospective functionality.

The video study subjects, like those in the core study, were older than those in the pilot study and showed a similar tendency to look first at the menu helps. This was in spite of the name of the help menu being changed from "help" to "info" in version 3 of Partickles. Also in version 3 a "help" hot-words box was introduced in place of "colours". Clicking "help" produced three options:

> "moves" (information about making moves),
> "? pointer" (information about SEO question pointer help) and
> "effects" (which was the same navigable SEO help facility as "colours" in version 2).

All the subjects read the "moves" and "? pointer" information but tended to be confused by the "effects" SEO help facility which could take up to four selections to obtain some items of information. The "effects" SEO help facility was seldom used successfully in the video study suggesting that it might be preferable to have SEO help facilities that allowed access to more traditional online manual facilities (such as those in LabVIEW and Microsoft Word 4). However, SEO partickle information was used almost continuously in the video studies. All three pairs experimented with changing pointers but indicated their preference for the question pointer—with which they had been initially presented and which may have gained in apparent significance by being the default pointer. When one subject changed pointers his partner responded by saying: "I think we need the question mark not the arrow" while another pair exchanged the following remarks:

> Subject A: It moved—why did it do that?
> Subject B: Go get your question mark.

The question pointer was used with the "make move" hot-words box though there was some reaction to the inconvenience of this double selection process. The video study subjects used "would do" help (in bubbles) easily and frequently. This form of help proved useful for cooperative work by separating the specification of an action from its initiation. For example, in one instance the subject read the bubble and, having assumed her partner had done the same, asked: "Do you want to do that?". However the video study subjects were less receptive to the descriptive partickle information presented in the lower window and instead of using that they sometimes accessed the "effects" SEO help facility in order to see what effects the colours represented. This was the opposite result from that observed in the core study and it demonstrates the power of speech bubbles as a means of presentation. Also, and most significantly for this project, exchanging the emphasis from descriptive SEO partickle information in version 2 of Partickles to the specific prospective functionality of partickles in version 3 showed that both types of information were used and that consequently it can be claimed that SEO partickle information was both appropriate and useful.

DISCUSSION

The empirical studies have suggested that question pointer help (providing both descriptive information and specific prospective functionality) can be very useful, that SEO-related information (from the "moves" and "? pointer" hot words boxes) is used, that initiating object actions from within a modal form of help (the "make move" facility) can be useful though the modality may lead to awkwardness and that other SEO facilities (such as the navigable help facility and move value facility) may be less successful.

In general, subjects seemed to operate in two modes: game playing and information seeking. SEO was mainly used when subjects were in information seeking mode. The subjects tended to use question pointer help in "chunks". Though this finding may be partially specific to this implementation it could support a view that one of the reasons for accessing help might be to reduce the future need for help. Help facilities tend to be modal, but even if help is provided concurrently with a main activity (e.g. by using non-overlapping windows to create a split-screen display) the evidence of chunked help accesses in the Partickles studies suggest that during a learning phase users tend to behave modally—i.e. engaged in either the main activity or in information gathering. However, in some cases the SEO help facilities acted as a bridge between the modes because it related directly to the objects of interest and it extended the domain representation. This occurred more frequently during the video study in which subjects generally elected to retain the question pointer (the default in the third version of Partickles) and hence they obtained SEO particle information before every move.

Partickles has proved effective in motivating users, encouraging extended use and in creating circumstances when help information is sought. However, SEO help facilities were only appropriate during the game learning phase. None of the menu helps, including the help menu option "suggestions" (which contained ideas for activities and advice regarding game playing strategies) were used by any subject who had learned to play the game. It may be that for players of strategy games like Partickles the point of playing, once they have learned to play, is to learn to play better without assistance. Nevertheless, the prominently displayed specific prospective functionality of partickles in the video study version of Partickles allowed subjects to play the game *while* they were learning it.

Specific prospective functionality provides a safety feature which is prospective rather than retrospective (as is the case with an "undo" facility). This differs from a "training wheels interface"[21] in which beginners use an interface with confusing or "dangerous" options blocked off. However, during the video sessions one pair of subjects was asked not to use the question pointer during their third game. When one replied: "O.K. That's not too bad 'cos we know what we're doing with it now" it seemed as though their training wheels had just been taken off. "Would do" help information may be sufficiently helpful for its usage to be included in users' usual procedures for operating a program, but perhaps only occasionally and optionally (unlike training wheels) during a learning phase or as a safety feature.

Selection by question pointer and the presentation of help information in bubbles may relate directly to a user's area/item of interest. However, one of the reasons that bubbles are prominent is that they intrude upon the main activity and they may distract the user and/or obscure other display objects. In Partickles, for example, a bubble may state that the indicated particle will push another particle but may actually be covering the particle that would be pushed.

There may be circumstances in which explicit and specific "would do" help information may conflict with a user's need to generalise (though this may be a broader criticism of object-based help). One of the core study subjects began a game by rotating most of his particles before making his first move. He was not wondering what each particle would do, but was (as he explained later) formulating his overall opening strategy. Once players have developed a repertoire of alternative types of moves they require game playing strategies to enable them to choose moves. The Partickles SEO help facilities did not provide goal related help of this sort (except for version 3 of Partickles which presented a brief description of the aim of the game when the "help" hot-words box was clicked). Object-based help does not seem to lend itself readily to the provision of goal or task-related help but this could be partly because display objects are not commonly used to represent processes. A particle is a display object but particle SEO help information is drawn from a system object that includes information about the particle but which actually represents the particle's move and therefore relates directly to the user's task of making a move. Making a good move may be a user sub-goal, but SEO's "would do" help offers only "one level of look-ahead" related to a single object. There are many ways in which "would do" help could be extended, but its limitations offer the advantage of simplicity. "Would do" help provides a fairly straightforward tool which could be used in combination with an undo facility to investigate prospective sequences of actions.

The SEO project may encourage program and help system designers to include SEO help facilities in their products because it attempts to deal with issues concerning information provision in object-oriented interfaces—which are becoming commonplace but still have many unexplored possibilities and problems. Some currently available systems already provide object-based help which suggests that program developers may be prepared to implement help facilities based on self-explanatory objects. However, it will always be easier for program developers to hang a screenful of help information onto a program than to take a more principled approach. Perhaps this situation will pertain until users have experienced principled help systems and begin to expect, and demand, that these be provided.

REFERENCES

1. Duffy T. and Langston M., On-line help: design issues for authoring systems. Communication Design Centre Report No. 18 (1985).
2. Hutchins E., Hollan J. and Norman D., Direct manipulation interfaces. In *User Centred System Design* (Edited by Norman D. and Draper S.), pp. 87–124. Erlbaum, Hillsdale, N.J. (1986).
3. Smith R., Experiences with the alternate reality kit: an example of the tension between literalism and magic. *CHI + GI Proc.* 61–67 (1987).
4. Kearsley G., *Online Help Systems: Design and Implementation.* Ablex, Norwood, N.J. (1988).
5. O'Malley C., Helping users help themselves. In *User Centred System Design* (Edited by Norman D. and Draper S.), pp. 377–398. Erlbaum, Hillsdale, N.J. (1986).
6. Bauer J. and Schwab T., Propositions on help-systems. *Angew. Inform.* **29,** 23–29 (1987).
7. Borenstein N. S., Help texts vs help mechanisms: a new mandate for documentation writers. *ACM SIGDOC Proc.* 8–10 (1986).
8. Trenner L., A comparative survey of the friendliness of online "help" in interactive information retrieval systems. *Inform. Process. Mgmt* **25,** 119–136 (1986).
9. Dreyfus H., *What Computers Can't Do: The Limits of Artificial Intelligence.* Harper & Row, New York (1979).
10. Dreyfus H. and Dreyfus S., *Mind Over Machine.* Blackwell, Oxford (1986).
11. Clark D., An on-line help facility based on self-explanatory objects. *Proceedings of the Symposium on Object-Oriented Programming Emphasizing Practical Applications,* pp. 244–257. ACM (1990).
12. Owen D., Answers first, then questions. In *User Centred System Design* (Edited by Norman D. and Draper S.), pp. 361–375. Erlbaum, Hillsdale, N.J. (1986).
13. Heidegger M., What is a thing?/Die Frage nach dem Ding (1936) or The thing (short paper).
14. Winograd T. and Flores F., *Understanding Computers and Cognition.* Addison–Wesley, Boston, Mass. (1986).
15. Draper S., The occasions for explanation. Paper presented at the *3rd Alvey Expert Systems Workshop on Explanation* (1987).
16. Suchman L., *Plans and Situated Actions.* Cambridge University Press (1987).
17. Draper S., Display managers as the basis for user-machine communication. In *User Centred System Design* (Edited by Norman D. and Draper S.), pp. 339–352. Erlbaum, Hillsdale, N.J. (1986).
18. Rosson M. B. and Alpert S. R., The cognitive consequences of object-oriented design. *Human-Comput. Interact. J.* **5,** 345–379 (1990).
19. Pinson L. J. and Weiner R. S., *An Introduction to Object-Oriented Programming and Smalltalk.* Addison–Wesley, Boston, Mass. (1988).
20. Stroustrup B., *The C + + Programming Language.* Addison–Wesley, Boston, Mass. (1986).
21. Carroll J. M. and Carrithers C., Training wheels in a user interface. *Commun. ACM* **27,** 800–806 (1984).

Computers Educ. Vol. 18, No. 1–3, pp. 23–28, 1992
Printed in Great Britain. All rights reserved

HOW CAN INTELLIGENT CAL BETTER ADAPT TO LEARNERS?

Gary McI. Boyd and P. David Mitchell

Centre for System Research and Knowledge Engineering, Concordia University, 1455 de Maisonneuve
Blvd West, Montreal, Quebec, Canada H3G 1M8

Abstract—Tutoring is assumed to be a conversational activity shared among the learner, the machine tutor and the educator/developer. The sort of student model that the machine should build, update and run simulations on, to help all three to be effective, is then derived. This derivation amounts to a demand for a new and different architecture for intelligent computer aided learning support systems. It is argued from cybernetic theory, and on the basis of empirical attribute-treatment results, that the student model must be a dynamic multi-level, and multi-personae model that also incorporates in rudimentary form the student's model of the teacher. Human tutors use multi-level models of learners' various characteristics to advantage. The promise of doing this in intelligent CAL systems is evaluated. Specific learner characteristics (including aspirations, expectations and cognitive style) are considered as elements of intelligent CAL student models. Since little is known yet about the moment-by-moment variability of many important learner characteristics, an intelligent CAL system is arguably a better laboratory for studying them. A formal connexion-matrix based language, and a fuzzy-logic based lesson planner, are advocated as a means for implementing and exploiting more adequate learner models in intelligent CAL systems.

INTRODUCTION

Our basic concern as educators is to be of long-term benefit to our students and the world. What is not learned is of no benefit. What is not deeply learned is a missed opportunity. What is not broadly connected into a coherent world-model by the student is unlikely to be used for long. If students do not believe what they are expected to learn is beneficial, it probably will not be. If students do not believe they can learn what is taught, success is unlikely. In short, students are the ultimate manager of their own learning and un-learning.

The Conant–Ashby law of cybernetics[1] states that an effective regulator must have (or be) a requisite variety model of the system to be regulated. An intelligent computer aided learning (ICAL) support system has four complex sub-systems: the student sub-system, the computer software sub-system, the target knowledge and skills sub-system and the educator–developer sub-system. These mutually regulate each other. Consequently by Conant–Ashby's law a good model of each of these sub-systems needs to be accessible to the others. In particular, students' learning is central to the enterprise of educating; therefore, an objective externalized dynamic model of the student as learner is even more important than the model of the subject matter in a conversational[2] ICAL system. A good student model can also be of great value, not only to the tutor and developer, but also directly to the learner.

These considerations suggest an architecture for intelligent tutoring aids which centrally involves a model of the learner, which secondarily is a planner and purveyor of teaching and learning strategies, and which is only tertiarily an embodiment of subject-matter knowledge and skills. By contrast, the majority[3] of intelligent tutoring systems (ITSs) seem to be characterized by subject-matter fetishism. The most notable exception is the work of Beverly Woolf[4,5] who has long been an advocate of student modelling that goes beyond overlays and bug catalogs. At this still early stage it is most important to get the overall architecture right. That means it should be centred on learner and learning-conversation not on subject-matter let alone machine-system factors. Artificial intelligence applied to augment computer conferencing may be the best route to follow. What is needed from the computer world to really improve education is quasi-intelligent machine assistance for *co-operative human* learning-teaching conversations—not automatic stand-alone teaching machines, however intelligent!

SYSTEMIC STUDENT MODELLING FOR ICAL

Given that one accepts John Self's argument[6] that student models for ITSs should be fully formalized, this does not mean that the student model has to be no more than a model of only what cognitive computer scientists are most comfortable with modelling—subject-matter knowledge domains. Anderson et al.[7] have already gone well beyond that by constructing "ACT*" learning models and "PUBS" performance models of how students actually execute target skills to be tutored. What is conspicuously absent are models of identity dynamics, motivation and learning styles. A formalized student model certainly need not be, and we argue should not be, just an overlay, nor even an overlay like Van Lehn's[2] with bug catalogs and mal-rules added on top of the "expert" (subject matter) knowledge base. ICAL support systems need to "know" a good deal more about a learner than just what mistakes the learner has made and which erroneous rules are probably being used to generate those mistakes.

If, instead of starting with conventional ITS architecture, we start instead with some basic questions, a better system can be designed.

The first question is: "What does a good human tutor need to know about each student to co-operatively plan and steer a conversational lesson?"; the answers, theoretical and empirical, should yield a specification for what ideally should be formalized in a really good ICAL "student model".

The second question is: "How can an ICAL system include such multi-level student modelling information?" The answer must be: by being loaded with a skeletal theoretical construction to be fleshed-out by asking, observing, testing and inferring operations such as those discussed by Murray and Woolf[5].

The third question then arises: "How can we formalize such as multi-level student model?" A tentative answer is: with Jaworski's 'info-maps'[9], suitably fuzzified and compiled.

The final question then remains: "What kind of ICAL systems are required to make use of more comprehensive student models?" Our tentative answer is: ones which use fuzzy logic[10] to make their strategic and tactical lessons planning recommendations to the machine-tutor, the student and the educator–developer sub-systems[11].

EMPIRICALLY IMPORTANT LEARNER ATTRIBUTES
SIX KEY COMPONENTS OF A STUDENT MODEL FOR TUTORING

An extended answer to the question "What does a good human tutor need to have by way of a student model, in order to support strategic and tactical lessons planning and steering decisions?", can be given in terms of six components:

● The first thing needed is the current identity of the student. Conventional systems usually take this as unproblematic, and simply ask the student to type in her or his name. However, as Pask[2] first pointed out, a given "mechanical" individual "John Brown" may actually operate in a learning conversation as one of several personae or participant "p" individuals (e.g. enthusiast, constructor, critic, integrator), possibly corresponding to Whitehead's three phases of learning; romance, precision and generalization, or possibly to the player protagonists in Kenneth Burke's[12] dramaturgical model.

One of the main weaknesses of personality typologies[13] when one tries to apply them to instruction is that a learner (or teacher) may switch personae during the course of instruction so that the assumed "personal style" may not be the one in use at all at some given phase of instruction.

In any case it is not enough to know that we have Mary Jones on the machine today; the question is: "Which of Mary Jones' personae is engaged in communicative exchange now?". That question can be answered both precipitatively and diagnostically, depending on the time and the intelligence available. Prescriptively the ICAL system can ask: "Do you agree to play the part of an (e.g. "editor") for five minutes?" and get a commitment from the student which is recorded in the student model. Diagnostically, conditions can be set up, and tested for, on the student input, to assess the probability that this student is acting as an "editor". The situation can be rather like that of a hockey coach or team captain who gets an agreement from each player to play a certain position and role while certain conditions prevail. The coach may find, however, that a goalie sometimes moves out to take a long shot unexpectedly, so that the role being taken needs to be monitored. (The situation is symmetric. The intelligent tutoring system may play different roles in turn, and actual students may try to guess what these are, in order to update their model of the current tutor-machine's personality.)

● Research on learners (adults in particular), e.g. Gilles Carrier[14], shows that the best predictor of their academic grade outcome is the student's expectation of achievement near the beginning of a course. We adjust our behaviour cybernetically to get the perceptions of the world that we have already decided we want—unless we are forced to change our expectations or aspirations. The most crucial components of a student model for a tutor are the student's course-related general aspirations, and anxieties, taken together with his or her current operating expectations (relationships or goals expected to be achieved in this phase of this learning venture by this operating "p" individual).

The goals of the ITS designer or curriculum planner are not necessarily the students' goals at all. As Noel Entwistle[15] found, students tend to fall into three classes with respect to their global goals for a course: (i) those who want as deep and thoroughly meaningful an understanding as possible; (ii) those who merely want surface knowledge and skills which they can reproduce as needed; and (iii) those who want only to get a certain grade by whatever game-playing means might suffice. These are a direct reflection of how the learner sees the teacher. If the learner sees the teacher as an opponent, gaming is appropriate. If the learner sees the teacher as just a source of useful facts and skills, then surface learning is appropriate. If learners see the teacher as a mentor who will help to re-create their identities then deep learning is called for.

Consequently if learners can be categorized in just these three ways, quite different instructional strategies should be employed for teaching each type of learner. Appropriate ventures and strategies also depend on whether one has the meta-goal of up-grading the learner's *modus operandi* from (iii) to (i) and/or also on changing the learner's notion of the tutor, e.g. from opponent to mentor (which amounts to much the same endeavour).

● The third key student characteristic for a tutor is the conventionally recognized one—the student's current model of the knowledge and skills of the domain. This often can be formally represented well in the conventional ITS manner as an overlay on an expert knowledge base, with a bug catalog, or a mal-rule catalog. At the very least, such overlay models should be augmented by models of the histories of past successful and unsuccessful student paths, as in some of Sleeman and Hartley's Leeds CAL systems[16]. This issue was raised by Genesereth[17] who framed it as a matter of determining the "students plan—the link between his beliefs about the subject area and his solution method." Genesereth's solution was a hybrid top-down/bottom-up plan recognition parser for the MACSYMA advisor. However it worked in a very narrow and minute area of algebraic problem-solving plans. Anderson's ACT*/PUPS only compiles possible student strategies for the currently assigned LISP programming problem[7]. Although their approach is capable of larger granularity, practical speed considerations restrict their current diagnostic student models.

For significant progress we need additionally to be able to infer the more global methods as well as the fine-grained tactics that a student may be using to solve complex series of problems. There is a question of subject-matter dependent cognitive style in strategic student plans which arises here. Sometimes students work with a variety of different kinds of mental models which are not conformable as variants on one expert model. For example, John Cowan's experiments[18], with students talking aloud while solving engineering mechanics problems, yielded three distinct kinds of student's preferred strategies: deflectors, forcers and mathematizers.

● The fourth key component of a good student model is information on the students' views of the working time available, which affects their perception of appropriate pacing and/or rate of achievement. The latter is of course correlated with the kind of achievement that the student is aiming for (as described above).

It is also related to reflective vs impulsive personality type, and the possibility of diagnosing that trait through latency (time to respond) measurements as has been done by Milos Lansky[19].

● The fifth key component in a good tutor's model of a student is information about the student's model of the tutor. If the tutor is seen as an antagonist to be beaten in a game, or as a drug pusher trying to seduce the student into an unwanted addiction, rather than a fellow seeker after understanding, then the nature of the tutorial exchange, and its outcomes, will be entirely different from what an unimaginative ITS designer might expect. Or less dramatically, if the student has a fixed model of one of the personae of the tutor while the tutor actually plays several different roles in rotation, e.g. planner, presenter, examiner, reflector, the student may be badly confused. This fifth component, perhaps first considered, as mentioned above, in Pask's work, or in Rapoport's game theoretic work, is one which we think is worth further exploration.

● Other components of the learner's psychostructure, such as affective states, e.g. high anxiety, and preferred modes of communication (audio, or visual, or even kinesthetic in the case of the deaf-blind) and cognitive traits, can also be of critical importance to the good functioning of an ITS for special learners, but will not be dealt with further here. Ideally the diagnostic section of the ITS needs to question and test for all six of these learner psychostructure parameters, and declare relations or set flags in the ITS student model accordingly. The strategic and tactical lesson planner/manager units can then use all this data in the student model as the basis for choosing among alternative ventures, tactics, messages and alternative moves.

QUESTIONING AND DIAGNOSTIC TECHNIQUES NEEDED TO BUILD LEARNER MODELS

We confine discussion to diagnostic techniques for determining the student's current model of the tutor because that has been altogether overlooked by most ITS designers to date.

The student's model of the tutor is usually an actor, trait and state model. That is, the tutor is seen as having abiding traits and also a current state which may be exceptional or may be predictable from a trait and the context.

● The three main kinds of actor which a student is likely to model the CAL tutor as being, in order of likelihood, are:

(1) goal-directed deterministic automaton/machine;
(2) game player (strategy-directed stochastic machine);
(3) performer (wanting an emulative student audience).

The simplest way to diagnose the kind of "p" individual actor the student believes the tutor to be is to ask a direct question. However, the game-player student, and the student who believes the tutor to be a game-player, may not answer honestly. Consequently some tests made by offering exercises with options for the student to take different kinds of initiative are needed.

● The two most instructionally interesting traits are, probably:

(1) the serialist or linear-sequential learning style trait;
(2) the versatile holist, or global spiralling learning style trait. These yield appreciably greater learning gains when they are matched respectively by (1) a linear instructional sequence, or (2) an open exploratory learning micro-world.

Low ability and high anxiety-trait learners are often also serialists (although some very high-ability students are also serialists).

Whether serialist learning is associated with field-independence and holist with field-dependence remains an uncertain question, as do the associations with Ference Marton's "surface" and "deep" learners. It is tempting to conflate all these into just two main traits, with a third situation being the "versatile" trait learner who can easily switch between serialist and holist approaches[20]. More research, which can perhaps most easily be done using ICAL systems, is needed to clarify this situation. Tests for these various traits have been produced as interactive computer programs. What is needed now is to incorporate them in an ICAL system.

ARTICULATION—HOW HUMAN TUTORS USE THEIR MODELS OF THEIR STUDENTS, INCLUDING THE STUDENT'S MODELS OF THE TUTOR

Some sets, possibly quite large sets, of condition-action rules may be adequate to describe the main uses tutors have for their understanding of how the student functions and also for how the student sees the tutor. These have the advantage of simple formalizability, and may be readily fuzzified to allow for uncertain possibilities and to resolve priority conflicts.

For example, consider that the student's model of the tutor's knowledge and skills may range anywhere from the notion of the tutor as an all-knowing infallible performer, down to that of a fellow blindman groping in the dark. The latter indeed may be very appropriate for learning with some ITSs, despite the designer having aimed for the former. Illustrative rules can be used:

Rule

If the tutor "knows" that the student believes the tutor is too wise, this error can be dispelled by bald statement, or probably by spontaneous inconsistent, or incomplete, output, or by incorrect diagnosis of student bugs.

Rule

If the student thinks the tutor is rather dumb then some nice diagnosis or problem-solving should be exhibited by the system to the student.

These rules may be formalized by using the very flexible connexion matrix language "info-maps" invented by Jaworski[9].

For the rest, detailed overlay investigation of agreements and distinctions between tutor and student can be worked through in the conventional ways developed by Pask and Mitchell in various conversation theory, and structural communication theory-based systems[21,22].

The problem of combinatorial explosions of possible permutations and combinations of all the possibly relevant learner attributes, states and actions, which can be related to instructional ventures, strategies and tactics will indefinitely remain with us. However this paper tries to argue that, by taking as options only, but also particularly, those attribute–treatment interactions which research on human tutoring has shown to be efficacious, the design problem may be reduced to a manageable size.

When options and classes are fuzzified, many theoretically distinct categories prove redundant, and deep reasoning chains are seen to be too uncertain to be worthwhile, so that a pragmatic simplification can be obtained which speeds up machine inference. The development of a fuzzy logic lesson planner which could be adapted to use sophisticated student models has been described by Liu and Boyd[10].

CONCLUSION

Even a brief foray like this into the literature on teaching and tutoring yields many learner attributes which are important to tutorial planning and decision making. Consequently we recommend that designers of intelligent CAL systems should consult the research on teaching literature, or better still work with educational psychologists, and educational technologists, who have studied learner attributes and conversation theory.

Acknowledgements—The questions and suggestions of the participants in the 9 April workshop at the Lancaster CAL91 conference have appreciably contributed to this paper. This work was partly supported by a grant from the Ministère de l'Enseignement supérieure et de la science du Québec, and the Social Sciences and Humanities Research Council of Canada.

REFERENCES

1. Conant R. C. and Ashby W. R., Every good regulator of a system must be a model of that system. *Int. J. Syst. Sci.* **1**, 2 (1970).
2. Pask G., Review of conversation theory and the proto-language Lp. *Educ. Commun. Technol.* **32**, 3–40 (1984).
3. Polson M. C. and Richardson J. J. (Eds) *Foundations of Intelligent Tutoring Systems.* Erlbaum, London.
4. Woolf B. and McDonald D., Building a computer tutor: design issues. *Computer* **17**, 61–73 (1984).
5. Murray T. and Woolf B., A knowledge acquisition tool for intelligent computer tutors. *SIGART Bull.* **2**, 9–21 (1991).
6. Self J., The case for formalising student models (and intelligent tutoring systems generally). In *Artificial Intelligence and Education* (Edited by Bierman D., Breuker J. and Sandberg J.), p. 244. *Proceedings of the 4th International Conference on AI and Education.* IOS, Amsterdam (1989).
7. Anderson J. R., Boyle F., Corbett A. T. and Lewis M. W., Cognitive modelling and intelligent tutoring. In *Artificial Intelligence and Learning Environments* (Edited by Clancey W. T. and Soloway E.), pp. 7–50. MIT Press, Cambridge, Mass. (1990).
8. Van Lehn K., *Mind Bugs.* MIT Press, Cambridge, Mass. (1990).
9. Jaworski W. M. and Grogono P. D., Info-maps: a pragmatic environment for seamless and non-deterministic software development. Computer Science Dept. Report, Concordia University, Montreal (1990).
10. Liu J. and Boyd G., Instructional planning based on fuzzy reasoning. In *Proceedings of the Sixth Canadian Symposium on Instructional Technology* (Edited by Association Committee on Instructional Technology), pp. 200–204. NRC Canada, Halifax (1989).

11. Mitchell P. D., Evaluation of understanding in intelligent interactive systems. *J. Interact. Instruct. Dev.* **1,** 7–12 (1989).
12. Burke K., The five key terms of dramatism. In *A Grammar of Motive and a Rhetoric of Motives*, pp. 17–25. World Publishing, New York (1962).
13. Burk K., Guild P. and Garger S., *Marching to Different Drummers*. Association for Supervision and Curriculum Development, Alexandria, Va (1985).
14. Carrier G., Student support and computer-mediated communications in distance education. Doctoral thesis, Concordia University, Montreal (1991).
15. Entwistle N., *Styles of Learning and Teaching*. Fulton, London (1988).
16. Sleeman D., Outline of the Leeds modelling system. In *Intelligent Tutoring Systems* (Edited by Sleeman D. J. and Brown J. S.), pp. 185–188. Academic Press, London (1982).
17. Genesereth M. R., The role of plans in intelligent teaching systems. In *Intelligent Tutoring Systems* (Edited by Sleeman D. H. and Brown J. S.). Academic Press, London (1982).
18. Cowan J., Individual approaches to problem-solving. In *Aspects of Educational Technology XI: The Spread of Educational Technology* (Edited by Hills P. and Gilbert J.), p. 242–248. Page, London (1977).
19. Lansky M., Automated adaptation to cognitive style in computer aided learning. Working Paper: Arbeitsgruppe Bildungsinformatik, (AGBI) am Fachbereich 17 (Mathematik/Informatik) der Universität Paderborn (1990).
20. Mitchell P. D. and Emmott L., Adapting to differences in cognitive style with computer aided learning. In *Proceedings of the Twelth Educational Computing Organization of Ontario Conference, and the Eighth International Conference on Technology and Education* (Edited by McKye G. and Trueman D.), pp. 284–286. ECOO, Toronto (1991).
21. Mitchell P. D., C/Caste: an intelligent multi-media, knowledge-based interactive system. In *Proceedings of the Sixth Conference on Interactive Instructional Delivery*. SALT Warrenton, Va (1988).
22. Mitchell P. D. and Grogono P. D., Modelling abstract concepts for conversation in an intelligent tutoring system. In *Proceedings of PEG91: Knowledge-Based Environments for Teaching and Learning*, Genova, Italy (1991).

Computers Educ. Vol. 18, No. 1–3, pp. 29–37, 1992
Printed in Great Britain. All rights reserved

MODELLING DOMAIN KNOWLEDGE FOR INTELLIGENT SIMULATION LEARNING ENVIRONMENTS*

Wouter R. van Joolingen and Ton de Jong

Eindhoven University of Technology, Department of Philosophy and Social Sciences, P.O. Box 513, NL-5600 MB Eindhoven, The Netherlands

Abstract—Computer simulations are an often applied and promising form of CAL. A main characteristic of computer simulations is that the domain knowledge is represented in a *model*. This model contains all necessary information to calculate the behaviour of the simulation in terms of variables and parameters and a set of *rules* or *constraints* which determine the changes to the values of the variables. In order to increase the learning effects of computer simulations additional support and guidance should be offered to the learner. This means that simulations should be embedded into a supportive environment, which we will call an Intelligent Simulation Learning Environment (ISLE). One of the basic components of the ISLE should be a formalised representation of the domain. In this paper the structure of this domain representation and its authoring will be discussed. It is argued that the simulation model is a necessary but certainly not sufficient source of information for building a domain representation for an ISLE. Besides a behavioural description as given by the simulation model (the term *runnable model* will be used) also a cognitive description of the domain is needed. This *cognitive model* forms the basis for a number of functions to be performed in an ISLE, like diagnosis, instruction and support. The current paper presents a framework which can be used to formalise the cognitive model. In particular the component of the cognitive model which contains a conceptual representation of the domain, the *conceptual model* will be discussed. An important element of the framework presented is a *relation typology* which describes the interrelationships between relations that are used for the construction of a cognitive model. This typology will be an important knowledge source for an ISLE and can support the author with constructing the conceptual model.

1. INTRODUCTION

Computer simulations are a promising application of Computer Assisted Learning because they enable *exploratory learning*. However, research has shown that this type of learning needs additional support for the learner to control and/or support the specific exploratory learning processes that are needed for successful learning. Therefore a supportive and adaptive environment should be built around a computer simulation[1]. A simulation embedded in such an instructional environment will be termed an Intelligent Simulation Learning Environment (ISLE).

The supportive environment can provide the student with additional instruction and learner tools for supporting simulation specific learning processes. To establish these facilities in a flexible and adaptive way the environment will maintain a learner model, containing information about certain attributes of the learner and about the current learner knowledge state. To enable all these functions the ISLE will need a formalised representation of the domain. This leads to a natural separation of the ISLE into four different modules: the domain representation, a learner model, an instructional strategy module and a learner interface module[2,3].

The aim of the current paper is the construction of a framework for domain representation for ISLEs as a basis for all domain related functionality of the ISLE. It will appear that the presence of a simulation model (we will use the term *runnable model*) has implications for the structure of the complete representation of the domain[4]. Therefore, the framework should take into account the simulation-specific characteristics of ISLEs (it should not be a generic framework for use for all possible types of intelligent tutoring systems).

The design of this framework is quite an ambitious task, therefore we do not claim to present an ultimate framework which is capable of describing all simulation related domains, our work

*The research reported was conducted in the project SIMULATE. SIMULATE is part of SAFE, a R&D project partially funded by the CEC under contract D1014 within the Exploratory Action of the DELTA programme. In total 17 partners are involved in the SAFE consortium of which Philips TDS is the prime contractor. The partners directly involved in SIMULATE are: Philips TDS (Fed. Rep. Germany), University of Leeds, University of Lancaster (U.K.), TIFSA (Spain), University of Amsterdam, Eindhoven University of Technology, Courseware Europe (The Netherlands).

is still under progress. The present paper is to be considered as a first step in the direction of a complete domain representation framework. We do believe that the proposed basic structures allow for a powerful extension towards such a complete domain description framework.

We will present our framework in a semi-formal form. Of course a truly formalised domain representation will be needed when our framework is to be included in an actual ISLE. However, the current status of research has not reached the state of actual implementation. Moreover the semi-formal approach used in the current paper allows for offering a conceptual view on the domain representation framework.

2. KNOWLEDGE RELATED TO COMPUTER SIMULATIONS

The first function of a domain representation for a simulation learning environment is to provide information for enabling the simulation of the real system which is the subject of instruction. The model that drives this simulation is called the *runnable model*, being the complete and runnable description of the domain as it is represented in the ISLE. This means that all important aspects of the domain are modelled in the runnable model, explicitly or implicitly. The runnable model is defined in terms of a *state* subject to change, due to a set of *state transition rules* or *constraints* [4,5]. The term "runnable" means that this description is unambiguous, in the sense that for each state, described by a set of variables, the transition to another state can be calculated in a unique way.

The completeness of the runnable model does not imply completeness in the sense that all knowledge required to allow teaching of the domain is available in the runnable model. There are two main reasons why this is the case:

- Much knowledge, contained in the runnable model, is only present implicitly, therefore unsuitable for direct use in teaching. To enable teaching about the domain this knowledge should be made explicit. Also the variables and parameters in the runnable model are meaningless entities, usually just numbers. This is illustrated by the fact that very often one runnable model can be used to represent a number of different domains. For teaching purposes a meaning needs to be assigned to these entities.
- Reasoning about a domain often takes place at a higher level than that of the runnable model by introducing higher order concepts, which are not represented in the runnable model.

These two reasons form the rationale for the introduction of a *conceptual reasoning layer* on top of the runnable model. This layer will have to enable reasoning at a higher, often qualitative, level than the runnable model.

Hartog[6] even argues that, considering the fact that reasoning about a model often takes place at a qualitative level, also the simulation itself should be qualitative, in other words that the simulation should be driven by the same model that the learner is to acquire as a mental model of the system, which should imply that the simulation should be performed qualitatively. We would argue that this is neither necessary nor desirable. The simulation itself should be performed efficiently and fast, something that is not always possible using qualitative simulation. Also, the results of qualitative simulation are not always accurate enough to allow for a faithful representation of the simulated system[7]. We do acknowledge a conceptual, often qualitative, representation of the simulation model should be present in an additional knowledge base. This statement does not mean that we want to exclude qualitative simulation for the runnable model in all cases.

Apparently there is a need for a supplemental domain representation besides the runnable model in an ISLE. Moreover, we argue that this domain representation, and not the runnable model, will be the *main* source of domain related information within the learning environment. This is true because the interaction of learners with the ISLE will be of a complex nature and will require monitoring and reasoning at a high conceptual level, a level which will not be supported by the runnable model. The different ISLE tasks that the domain representation should enable are the following:

Reasoning about the domain. Any intelligent learning environment should be able to model a domain expert. This functionality is needed in order to allow the environment to derive new relations about the domain when needed and, specifically for simulations, to draw conclusions from events in the runnable model.

Providing alternative conceptualisations of the domain. Often, in simulation-based learning, there can be several *views* on the same domain. Looking at a domain from different viewpoints can be useful in obtaining a complete conceptual representation of a domain. Also different views may be used to introduce different levels of complexity. One may start with a view which is in fact a simplification of the domain and move via one or more steps to a view which contains all important concepts of a domain. This would be a form of progressive implementation, which is a certain instructional strategy. White and Frederiksen[8,9] have implemented a learning environment in which this strategy is used.

Giving instruction about the domain. In order to enable instruction about the domain the domain knowledge base should contain instruction specific information. This would include information on how to manage different views and information on which concepts are central for learning and how concepts are dependent of each other. Also means for providing *examples* and information on *critical situations*, should be included.

Providing diagnosis. To enable intelligent instruction about the domain the learning environment should monitor the achievements of the learner and diagnose possible misconceptions. Therefore, a model of the learner's mental model about the simulation should be expressed within the same framework as the domain representation itself. Moreover, the domain representation should contain a description of possible and/or common misconceptions in order to allow for appropriate action if such a misconception should be diagnosed.

Guiding the interaction with the model. The interaction with the model takes place by varying variables and parameters. In general it will not be possible to vary all parameters and variables at the same time. Which variables can be varied depends on the *role* the learner plays at a certain moment. In van Joolingen and de Jong[4] the concept of *scenario* has been introduced as being the description of the possible interaction that can take place at certain moments. This scenario should be part of the domain representation.

The conceptual layer enabling all these functions will be called the *cognitive model*. It will include possibly overlapping submodels, each dedicated to one of the domain related functions mentioned above. The cognitive model as a whole will provide an expert teacher's view on the domain. The remainder of this paper will investigate the properties of these submodels, and of one of these in particular.

3. FORMALISATION OF DOMAIN KNOWLEDGE

3.1. Why formalisation?

Formalisation of knowledge is to describe that knowledge in a way leaving no room for interpretation. A formal description of some piece of knowledge should be done in a language with well-defined syntax and semantics. An example of such a formal language is predicate logic. Also a programming language is a formal language in this sense.

It is clear that eventually, when an ISLE is actually implemented, its functionality must be described in such a formal language, together with the information that should be contained in the knowledge base which serves the ISLE, but also earlier in the design stage a formal description of ISLE related information is necessary to enable the final implementation in a consistent way. Devising such a formal language is a major effort, which has not been completed at the current state of development. In this paper we will take the view on formalisation adopted by de Jong *et al.*[10], who strive at a semi-formal structural language for describing ISLE related information.

3.2. A model based approach

For the organisation of the knowledge base serving the ISLE, containing all relevant knowledge the ISLE needs, one may search for suitable decompositions of this knowledge base. For our purpose the knowledge base may be viewed as consisting of a set of, possibly overlapping *models*, for the domain, learner, instruction and learner interface, partly reflecting the traditional design of intelligent tutoring systems, using domain, learner, instruction and interface *modules*[2]. We add an extra flavour to this traditional design by showing the interdependencies between models and

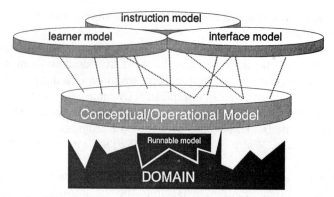

Fig. 1. Structuring of an ISLE knowledge base. The domain knowledge in the conceptual and operational models serves as a basis for the description of ISLE-related knowledge.

allowing overlap. This is illustrated in Fig. 1, there neglecting the overlap for reasons of clarity. In de Jong *et al.*[10] this model based approach, based on the KADS knowledge base development methodology[11], is elaborated further.

The basis of the ISLE knowledge structure models is formed by the *conceptual* model and the *operational* model. The operational model describes *tasks* that are associated with the domain, whereas the conceptual model is the knowledge base reflecting non-operational knowledge of the domain. Both static and dynamic properties of the domain should be included in the conceptual model.

The operational and conceptual models are *objects of instruction* for the ISLE[10]. We need additional models which enable us to use and teach this knowledge: the *instructional* model, the *learner* model and the *interface* model. These three dedicated models draw upon knowledge stored in the conceptual and operational models.

Every model will be constructed using *elements*, *relations* and *structures* as primitives. Knowledge is stored as relations between elements, organised into structures, defining logical chunks of knowledge. Cross model communication is furnished by allowing the various models to use structures of other models as elements. Especially, structures of the conceptual and operational model will serve as elements in the learner, instructional and interface models.

The model based approach described above will be reflected in the cognitive model. We can now define the cognitive model as consisting of those parts of the knowledge base models that contain domain-related elements, where notice should be taken that "elements" of the instructional, learner or interface models may be elements, relations or structures in the conceptual and operational models.

It will be clear that the conceptual and operational models will belong completely to the cognitive model, whereas the learner, instructional and interface model will partly belong to the cognitive model. For the part of the latter three models that are inside the cognitive model we will use new terms: the *diagnosis* model, the *instruction* model and the *interaction* model (see Fig. 2). These names

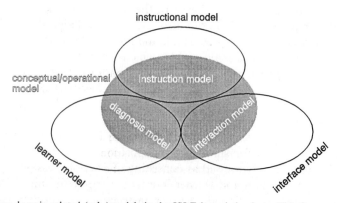

Fig. 2. The three domain-related (sub-)models in the ISLE knowledge base. This figure can be regarded to be a top-view of Fig. 1.

reflect the functions the three domain related (sub-)models should enable: diagnosing the learner's domain knowledge, giving instruction about the domain and guiding the interaction with the model.

The remainder of this paper will concentrate on the structural description of the *conceptual* model as an example of the structures used in our framework. The basic elements, relations and structures of this model will be defined and examples of ISLE functionality that is related to the conceptual model will be presented. In the current paper the instruction, diagnosis and interaction models will not be treated systematically. A more elaborate discussion of the complete cognitive model is provided in van Joolingen and de Jong[12].

4. THE CONCEPTUAL DOMAIN MODEL

4.1. Basic elements, relations and structures

In constructing a framework for a domain knowledge base for intelligent simulation learning environments, one should emphasise the nature of the simulation, reflected in the presence of a runnable model. This emphasis is necessary because of two reasons:

- The runnable model is a central source of information for both the student and the reasoning module in the ISLE. Therefore the structure of the domain representation should be such that fluent incorporation of the results of the simulation into the knowledge base is furnished, meaning that important aspects of the runnable model should be reflected in the conceptual model.
- For the author, developing a conceptual model, the structure of the runnable model itself is a source of knowledge. Consequently, the authoring process can be simplified by offering primitives that are similar to those that are used to define the runnable model.

On the basis of these two reasons a choice has been made for the primitives to use for the conceptual model description. Thereby, the runnable model is considered to be a collection or database of states, described by variables and parameters. State transition rules are the generators of this database, and need no further elaboration at the conceptual level.

The conceptual model (cf. Norman[13]) should give a description of the simulation model that emphasises the important features of the model, using only relevant information, while neglecting relatively insignificant model properties. The conceptual model will contain only the information to enable this kind of high level reasoning. This means that not all information contained in the runnable model will be represented at the conceptual level, which may restrict the scope of the conceptual level reasoning functions.

On the other hand the conceptual model may introduce new concepts, not represented at the runnable level. These new concepts may be used to state new relations which are, in principle, derivable from the runnable model. Therefore these relations will be called *implicit relations*. In our conceptual modelling framework many of these implicit relations will be stated explicitly in the conceptual model, because deriving them may be very hard or impossible for the ISLE. However, many implicit relations may also be derived at run time, using a built-in reasoning mechanism.

In the conceptual model the domain characteristics will be expressed in a more natural way than in the runnable model. As a consequence a description at the conceptual level will also (together with a theory on learning with simulations) give information on possible difficulties the student may have while learning the model.

4.1.1. Elements. The basic elements that will be used in the conceptual model framework are extensions of the basic elements of the runnable model: variables and parameters. In the conceptual model we will use the same names for the corresponding elements. When there is danger of confusion the term "conceptual variable" will be used, in contrast to "runnable variable". In the runnable model these elements just represent a value of some system characteristic, quantitatively or qualitatively. The conceptual counterparts of the runnable variables and parameters extend this meaning, the conceptual variables add an interpretation to the runnable model, often in qualitative terms.

The characteristics of a variable or parameter are largely determined by the relations it has with other variables. Not only the value of a variable is of importance but especially the position it has in the relational network of variables.

A variable or parameter is characterised by a range of possible values, by the fact that it may be dependent on time, which is an important characteristic if the runnable model is *dynamic*. An important characteristic of variables is that they can exist in an hierarchical structure. In the semi-formal conceptual model framework this is expressed by allowing *inheritance* between variables. A child variable does not only inherit the characteristics of its parent but also its position in the relational variable network. This enables the introduction of various levels of reasoning. Relations between variables high in the inheritance tree will be very global, but are representative for all lower variables, which in their turn enable more precise reasoning.

In a frame representation (see Brachman and Schmolze[14]), very much in the style of the data description language designed for KADS[15] a variable can be represented by:

```
variable ⟨name⟩ [inherit ⟨varframe name⟩]
range ⟨range⟩
time-dependency ⟨y/n⟩
initial value ⟨value⟩
```

4.1.2. Relations. The variables and parameters are still quite useless unless one can define relations between them. For our framework for conceptual modelling there was a need to extend the "traditional" relation concept (e.g. Cerri *et al.*[16]), because traditional relations are not suitable to express fuzzy knowledge like: "If A increases B also increases". Such a statement is not a relation between A and B but merely a statement *about* the relation between A and B without further specifying that relation. To cope with this kind of statements we introduce the concept of *generic relation* which defines a subset on the set of all relations that are possible between two variables. The subset contains all relations that satisfy a certain characteristic. Stating that a generic relation "holds" between two variables is equivalent to specifying a property of the relation that holds.

Relations can be expressed using a similar frame representation as for variables.

Generic relations allow the definition of a *relation typology*, a hierarchically organised collection of relations and generic relations. The major reasons for introducing this typology are:

- An author creating a domain representation can be supported by the typology in finding the relations s/he needs for expressing domain knowledge.
- The ISLE could use a relation typology to derive new domain relations from ones that are explicitly present in the conceptual model. This can be used for run-time reasoning about the domain.

We think of the relation typology as one of the most powerful elements of the conceptual modelling framework.

4.1.3. Structures. The relations and generic relations that are introduced in the previous section are still quite general. For example they are not typed, they can describe relationships between any kind of variable as long as the range of the variables is suitable. There is a need to combine the variables and relationships into structures, *models*, as we will call them. A *simple model* is a collection of variables, parameters and definitions of (generic) relations between them.

A model is a representation of a chunk of domain knowledge. It represents the characteristic of a physical or logical subsystem in the form of (generic) relations between variables. In that sense a model is a kind of inference rule or set of inference rules: it can be used to generate knowledge about variables on the basis of knowledge about other ones.

An important characteristic of the model structures is that they can be combined into *compound models*, which have all "outside" characteristics of a simple model. This means that they can be combined into even larger knowledge structures. This implies that the complete domain representation will have a granular structure, it will consist of a collection of interconnected models, each again decomposable into smaller units until the level of simple models has been reached.

In Fig. 3 the structure of the conceptual model framework is summarised. In this figure the main elements and features are drawn: the variable hierarchy, the relation typology, the model structure

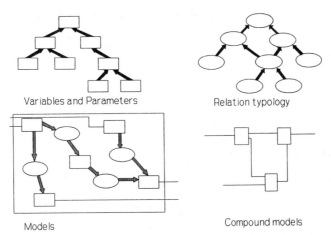

Fig. 3. Overview of the primitives used for representing the conceptual model.

(in which variables are represented both by lines and boxes) and the combination of models into compound models.

4.2. Functionality derived from the conceptual model

The conceptual model can only be useful when the ISLE is able to actually use the knowledge stored in it. This section will discuss a few examples of such related ISLE functionality.

A first function that can be directly based on the conceptual model is *generating predictions* of experimental results and, more important, motivating these predictions. This can be provided by using the relations in the model structures as inference rules. A prediction will describe all possible behaviours obtained from earlier experiments with the simulation.

Furthermore the conceptual model framework can be used to derive new relations between variables on the basis of the relation typology. The relation typology will contain relations between relations (meta-relations) to make this possible. The new relations can be used to derive extra information about variables, or to reason about them at a different level, e.g. a qualitative level.

A last example is the matching of learner *hypotheses* against the conceptual model. One can formalise a hypothesis about the model as a statement that a certain (generic) relation holds between two variables[17]. The hypothesis and the model match if the hypothesized relation can be derived from the conceptual model, the rules from the relation typology that have been used to derive the relation give extra information about the hypothesis, e.g. if it is more or less general than corresponding relations in the conceptual model. The information obtained from this matching can be incorporated in the learner model.

4.3. An example

We conclude this section by giving a small example. Suppose we want to model a physical system consisting of a number of particles. A runnable model which will be able to calculate the velocity and momentum and possibly the kinetic and potential energy of the particles can be defined for this system using the laws of physics.

On the conceptual level, new variables can be defined representing more abstract concepts used to reason about the simulation, e.g. a variable "energy". This variable can be used to express, say, the law of conservation of energy, using relations in the relation typology, meaning: the sum of the partial energies is a constant, when the system is closed. (The fact that a system is "closed" also needs to be expressed using variables and relations.) We may also create different *types* of energy, kinetic and potential energy, which will be subtypes of the energy variable. This is depicted in Fig. 4.

The conceptual model contains rules for reasoning about the model, e.g. predicting the future energy of particles or subsytems. This reasoning should use the information generated by the runnable model. Therefore at least some of the variables need to be defined in terms of runnable model variables. Establishing the link between runnable and conceptual model is called

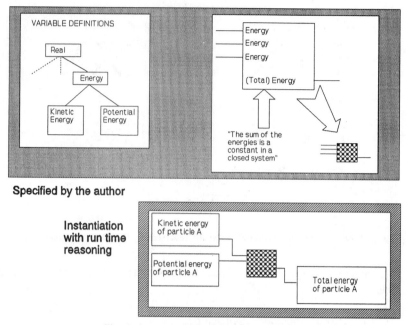

Fig. 4. An example model and instantiation.

instantiation. At which level this instantiation should take place is to be decided by the author of the domain representation. If the conceptual model should address properties of individual particles, these properties should be represented at the conceptual level. If the conceptual level reasoning only deals with more global concepts, there is only need for variables representing these, in one way or another defined in terms of runnable model variables. In the case of many particle systems this may even imply that the conceptual model only contains statistical relations between the newly defined variables, because not all deterministic information is used in the definition of these variables. In Fig. 4 the instantiation process is illustrated.

5. DISCUSSION

The framework for building a domain representation as described in this paper promises to be an effective way of describing knowledge related to computer simulations. Until this moment there are no actual implementations of ISLEs which use this framework, but as a theoretical object it can already show its value. For an experiment with a computer simulation about error analysis in chemistry, we used the framework for the analysis of learner hypothesis and experimental plans[17]. All inferences about the model were done by hand, but it would be little effort to formalise the assessment scheme that was used and to implement it.

Compared to traditional knowledge representation techniques it can be remarked that the framework offers some extras by introducing the relation typology and that it offers strong typing and classifications of variables. Both extras are introduced quite naturally and can support an author building a knowledge base and serve as a basis for intelligent reasoning about the domain.

An important feature of the presented framework is that it is *declarative*, meaning that the knowledge is stored independently from the context in which it is used. This implies that it can be used for several purposes, as indicated in Section 4.2.

The usefulness of the framework depends on possibilities to build interpreters for the proposed domain representation language. Since not even all aspects have been elaborated in a formal way it is too early to state that this will be possible, but the contemporary presence of qualitative simulation systems like QSIM[7,8] and the developments in the area of model based reasoning (e.g. [19]), which employ techniques that could be applied in the proposed framework, make it comprehensible that such an interpreter can be built. At the moment we are working on a prototype of such an interpreter.

A final feature of the conceptual model is its granular structure. This structure can be extended to the complete knowledge base of the ISLE, also containing domain independent knowledge. This would reduce the complexity of the authoring task, which may become a process of selecting, from dedicated libraries, tailoring and combining the structures, also called *basic building blocks*, into a knowledge base which the ISLE can use for generating support and guidance for the learner[10].

Acknowledgements—The authors would like to thank the partners in the SIMULATE project who have contributed directly or indirectly to the ideas expressed in this paper and also the participants of the session at CAL 91 for their input in the discussion.

REFERENCES

1. de Jong T. (Ed.), Computer simulations in an instructional context. *Education & Computing*, 6. Elsevier Science, Amsterdam (1991).
2. Duchastel P., Models for AI in education and training. In *Artificial Intelligence Tools in Education* (Edited by Ercoli P. and Lewis R.), pp. 17–29. Elsevier, Amsterdam (1988).
3. Wenger E., *Artificial Intelligence and Tutoring Systems*. Kaufmann, Los Altos (1987).
4. van Joolingen W. and de Jong T., Characteristics of simulations for instructional settings. *Educ. Comput.* 6, 241–262 (1991).
5. Zeigler B. P., *Theory of Modelling and Simulation*. Wiley, New York (1976).
6. Hartog R., Qualitative simulations and knowledge representation for intelligent tutoring. *Computer Assisted Learning. Proceedings of the 2nd International Conference ICCAL* (Edited by Maurer H.), pp. 193–213. Springer, Berlin (1989).
7. Kuipers B., Qualitative simulation. *Artif. Intell.* 29, 289–338 (1986).
8. White B. Y. and Frederiksen J. R., Progressions of qualitative models as a foundation for intelligent learning environments. Technical Report 6277, Bolt Beranek and Newman Laboratories, Cambridge, Mass. (1986).
9. White B. Y. and Frederiksen J. R., Qualitative models and intelligent learning environments. In *Artificial Intelligence and Education* (Edited by Lawler W. and Yazdani M.), Vol. 1, pp. 281–305. Ablex, Norwood, N.J. (1987).
10. de Jong T., Tait K. and van Joolingen W. R., Authoring for intelligent simulation based instruction; a model based approach. Paper presented at the *DELTA and Beyond Conference*, The Hague, The Netherlands (1990).
11. Breuker J. A. and Wielinga B. J., KADS: structured knowledge acquisition for expert systems. *Proceedings of the Fifth International Workshop on Expert Systems and their Applications*, Avignon, France (1985).
12. van Joolingen W. R. and de Jong T., An instruction related domain representation for simulations. Toward formalising the components of an intelligent simulation learning enviornment. Report SIM/19-20. Final report on formalisation. Eindhoven University of Technology, Department of Philosophy and Social Sciences, Eindhoven (1991).
13. Norman D. A., Some observations on mental models. In *Mental Models* (Edited by Gentner D. and Stevens A.). Erlbaum, Hillsdale, N.J. (1983).
14. Brachman R. J. and Schmolze J. G., An overview of the KL-ONE knowledge representation system. *Cogn. Sci.* 7, 171–216 (1985).
15. Schreiber G., Wielinga B., Hesketh P. and Lewis A., A KADS design description language. Deliverable B7, ESPRIT project P1098. Amsterdam UvA, Department of Social Science Informatics (1990).
16. Ceri S., Gottlob G. and Tanca L., *Logic Programming and Databases*. Springer, Berlin (1990).
17. van Joolingen W. R. and de Jong T., An hypothesis scratchpad as a supportive instrument in simulation learning environments. OCTO Report 91/103. OCTO, Eindhoven University of Technology, Eindhoven (1991).
18. Fishwick P. A., A study of terminology and issues in qualitative simulation. *Simulation* 52, 5–9 (1989).
19. Leitch R. R., Wiegand M. E. and Queck H. C., Coping with complexity in physical system modelling. *AI Commun.* 3 (1990).

Computers Educ. Vol. 18, No. 1–3, pp. 39–43, 1992
Printed in Great Britain. All rights reserved

0360-1315/92 $5.00 + 0.00

PEDAGOGICAL DECISIONS WITHIN AN ITS-SHELL

Julita Vassileva

Software Engineering Department, Institute of Mathematics, Bulgarian Academy of Sciences,
P.O. Box 373, 1090 Sofia, Bulgaria

Abstract—A unified, hierarchically-organized method of domain knowledge representation with teaching operators for an ITS-shell is described. It allows taking various pedagogical decisions at both a global level (instructional planning) and at a local level (instructional strategies and tactics). The main advantage is that the pedagogical component is domain-independent. It can take actual and useful decisions in any domain or level of articulation when it is activated with the corresponding set of teaching operators.

1. INTRODUCTION

For almost two decades the field of Intelligent Tutoring Systems (ITS) has been a subject of extensive research. Few ITSs, however, have been used in practice. We see two main reasons for this. First, the narrow subject domains in which the existing prototypes work and second, the implicitly built-in pedagogical principles of their designers which cannot be changed by teachers.

For more than 3 years we have concentrated our efforts on creating a domain-independent ITS shell whose pedagogical component can be tuned by the teacher. An experimental implementation of the system in the domain of elementary symbolic integration is now running on an IBM PC compatible. However, the system has not yet been tested in realistic conditions. This paper describes the theoretically possible pedagogical decisions that the system can take, and their dynamic management during instruction on the basis of the teacher's preferences.

There are many requirements to the pedagogical component in an ITS. Wenger[1] emphasizes its ability to take pedagogical decisions at both a global and a local level. That means that the system should be able first, to plan the sequence of teaching actions according to its knowledge about the curriculum in the given domain. Second, it should be able to decide when to interfere, what and how much to say and what presentation style to choose.

2. ARCHITECTURE

Our ITS-shell has a teaching operator-based architecture[2]. The different types of domain-specific knowledge, as well as procedures that diagnose errors in this knowledge, are organized at different levels of articulation and are represented in a unified way with teaching operators. That allows an invariant pedagogical component to take pedagogical decisions at a global and at a local level.

Our proposal of a knowledge representation scheme is based on the notion of "knowledge articulation"[1].

Knowledge articulation consists of:

(i) Decomposition of domain knowledge into elements with respect to: the curriculum, the stages in solving a given type of problem, the errors (misconceptions) that could be shown by the student, the actions (skills) that are needed, with respect to different viewpoints and solutions.

(ii) Configuration with respect to different links between the elements; e.g. links between subgoals, prerequisite or causal links, links of analogy, or of generality.

We define a level of articulation as the level of the elements of decomposition of the expertise. A lower level is a level which corresponds to a curriculum in the subject domain. For example, the elements of decomposition on the first level of articulation in our implementation are the names of the basic integration methods: substitution, integration by parts, or decomposition into partial fractions.

A higher level corresponds to planning a problem solution. For example, the elements on our second level of articulation correspond to different types of integrands that may be obtained during a problem's solution.

Some of the elements on this level may correspond to certain "bad-plans" in the student's solution. In our implementation if the student obtains an integrand of a type he has already obtained before, it may be a sign that the student is getting lost.

An even higher level will be that corresponding to performance of skills or elementary actions. In our implementation, the third level of articulation corresponds to performing a particular transformation—the elements correspond to different types of errors the student may do.

The architecture of a domain-independent ITS-shell contains five main components[2]. The Administrator is used by the authors for filling the ITS-shell with actual domain information. It is also used by teachers to tune the pedagogical component of the system according to their own pedagogical styles.

The domain-independent pedagogical component plans and leads instruction. It uses an explicit representation of the domain-specific curricular knowledge and teaching actions.

There are two types of student models—a domain-independent model of his individual characteristics, and a set of models of his domain knowledge for every level of articulation on which instruction is performed. A special student model is created for every domain or level of articulation. It contains a list of the names of the elements of the knowledge decomposition that are considered to be known by the student. (More about student modelling within this architecture can be found in [3].)

The domain knowledge base (DKB) is the core of the architecture. It contains the representation of the domain specific knowledge that is needed for instruction, and we shall concentrate on the structure of the DKB in the next section.

3. REPRESENTING DOMAIN-DEPENDENT PEDAGOGICAL KNOWLEDGE

The DKB consists of different sets of teaching operators. Every teaching operator is a structure, similar to a production rule. A set of teaching operators is in fact a production system that encodes a given level of knowledge articulation in a domain.

A teaching operator (TO) contains the following parts:

(1) Conditions, i.e. a set of elements in the domain knowledge decomposition that must be present in the student model at the current level of articulation to invoke the teaching operator.

(2) Effects, i.e. a set of elements that will be added to the student model at the current level of articulation after the application of the teaching operator.

[For example, at the first level of articulation, the conditions and effects of the TOs encode the curricular knowledge (the prerequisite links that must be followed during the study of elementary integration methods).]

(3) Action, i.e. a procedure that will "teach" the student the knowledge encoded by the effects. The procedure could be also a step in solving a particular problem. The action depends on the level of articulation of the teaching operator; in fact the action of a teaching operator reflects a link in the domain knowledge configuration. Usually the action involves asking the student to perform some task, e.g. to answer some question or solve a problem. It could also contain a recursive call of the system, with a set of TOs representing a different level of domain knowledge articulation.

For example, the actions of TOs at our first level of articulation are procedures which present textual explanations, and examples of solved problems or which present a sequence of problems to be solved by the student. Some actions invoke the system recursively at the second level of articulation in order to teach the student how to solve a particular problem. The action of a TO on this level is a procedure that displays the current integrand to the student and asks the student to choose from a list of possible transformations.

(4) Passing criteria, i.e. a list of procedures that check the correctness of the student's answer and try to diagnose the reason of his error (if any). A passing criterion can invoke the system recursively with another set of teaching operators to diagnose an error at a different (usually higher) level of articulation or from a different viewpoint.

For example, a passing criterion at the first level of articulation compares the student's answer of a given integration problem with the answer of an expert (the muMATH symbolic computations package). If there is a coincidence, the name of the current problem is added to the student model. If not (the student has made an error), the next passing criterion invokes the system on a second level of articulation to check the way the student solves the problem step by step.

(5) Evaluation criteria, i.e. a list of domain-independent parameters, describing the action of the teaching operator from a pedagogical point of view. They are used by the pedagogical component to create the individual student model.

In our implementation in the domain of integration, evaluation criteria are provided for the first level of articulation only. They denote the psycho-pedagogical types of the teaching actions as: inductive or deductive, need of concentration, self-dependence, and visual presentation.

Within this architecture a unified representation of knowledge from different domains and at different levels within a fixed domain is possible.

The teaching operators represent all of the domain-specific knowledge necessary for the (domain-independent) pedagogical component. The knowledge necessary for taking pedagogical decisions at a global level is encoded by the teaching operators at the first (curricular) level of articulation. In fact, the sets of teaching operators for all of the levels of articulation encode knowledge needed for instructional planning.

Domain knowledge that is necessary for taking local pedagogical decisions is encoded in two ways. The first is directly in the procedures of the teaching actions. This can be either direct instructional action at the given level of articulation or a demand for teaching at another level of articulation.

The other way is by a special type of Remedial operators that are used to recover from misconceptions or errors. Their conditions contain elements of domain knowledge decomposition corresponding to errors and misconceptions, and the effects include deleting (some of) the conditions from the student model. Their action is supposed to make the student see the reason of his error. Some remedial operators have a special element as a condition, meaning "undiagnosed error or request for help". Their action is an explanation or hint that will be issued if the student asks for help or if the diagnostic procedure cannot find the reason for the student's error.

For example, at the second level of articulation a remedial operator's action is to perform an appropriate transformation to obtain a simpler integrand and to explain the reasons for doing this to the student. The appropriate transformations for every type of integrand are defined in advance and there are remedial teaching operators for all of them. The set of all the remedial operators is in fact a transparent domain expert, based on Slagle's [4] rule-based heuristic symbolic integrator. If the student asks for help at every stage, he can see the full solution of the problem.

Another type of special domain-dependent knowledge is used to diagnose misconceptions or bad plans by analysing the structure of the student model at the same or at a different level. This type of knowledge is represented with diagnostic teaching operators. For example, a diagnostic teaching operator is used on the second level of articulation in our system to diagnose bad plans by finding cycles in the student model at the same level.

4. A TEACHER-MANAGED PEDAGOGICAL COMPONENT

The domain-independent pedagogical component contains the following sub-components: a Planner, an Optimizer, an Executor, a Statistical Mechanism for updating the individual student model and a Set of Adjustable Parameters of the Planner, Optimizer and Executor.

The pedagogical component can take decisions at a global and at a local level.

4.1. The global level decisions

These include ways of defining the resources of the instructional session (e.g. time, equipment) and decisions, concerning instructional planning. They are taken by the Planner and by the Optimizer.

The Planner can plan instruction dynamically for any level of domain knowledge articulation. It can generate sequences of TOs that lead from the current state of the student's knowledge to a goal state. During the teaching session the Planner can be invoked again to modify or change the plan according to the changing situation (e.g. goals of instruction and student's knowledge). There are several parameters which manage planning. One of these determines the type of instructional planning: automatic or not-automatic (i.e. the plan will be created by the teacher). Another parameter allows the teacher to denote certain elements in the knowledge decomposition at the level of planning, which will be given more attention during instruction. The teacher can participate in the planning of the time-schedule by assigning a given value of another parameter.

After the Planner has found all possible paths to the goal, the Optimizer is invoked to choose one of them to be the current plan (script). The Optimizer uses a criterion which can be chosen by the teacher from a given set. The optimization criteria match the characteristics, stored in the individual student model with the evaluation criteria of the TOs. They aim to find a sequence which has the most appropriate actions for the individual student. Once chosen, the script is followed until an obstacle in the student model or in the environment appears. Then the Planner is invoked again to re-plan.

4.2. The local level pedagogical decisions

The local level decisions of when to interfere, and what to say to the student are taken by the Executor sub-component. It consecutively executes the actions of the teaching operators which are listed in the script. However two types of unanticipated events may occur:

(1) an action of a teaching operator or a passing criterion may demand a recursive call of the system at another level of articulation for the purpose of teaching or of diagnosing an error;

(2) a student's error may be diagnosed and conditions for execution of a remedial operator may appear in the student model (remedial operators are never included in a plan or script; they are always "on-line").

When such an event that is not included in the script occurs, the Executor has to take a local-level pedagogical decision. The main alternatives are either to accept an opportunistic or a plan-based style of instruction[1]. An opportunistic style for an event of type (1) will fulfil the TO's query for recursive call. For an event of type (2) it will cause the system to react immediately to the student's error by executing a remedial operator.

A plan-based style will invoke the Planner to replan in case of event (1). In case of event (2) the system will silently follow the plan until a diagnostic operator finds a misconception underlying a sequence of errors. Then another local decision has to be taken, must it be treated at a different level of articulation, or does it require re-planning?

Diagnostic operators are executed repeatedly at a given period of time for every specific level of articulation. There are a lot of decisions connected with diagnosis, which the Executor should take. For example, what to do if there are two hypotheses for the reason of the student's error; after how many successful attempts is a given type of problem "mastered". These decisions are also managed by parameters which are given values by teachers.

Another important decision is what to do when two or more errors (bugs, bad plans, misconceptions) are diagnosed at different levels of articulation simultaneously. Is it better to execute a remedial operator for the lower-level error (underlying misconception or wrong method) first? Is it not more appropriate to execute a remedial for the higher level error to show the student that even if he has performed correctly the action (transformation) he would not obtain the solution? To decide such cases, a human-teacher needs to know more about the student's individual features, motivation, or need for criticism.

In general, intelligent leading of instruction needs to take into account the pedagogical style of the teacher, the individual characteristics of the student, the student's knowledge and the structure of domain knowledge. That is why whenever the Executor has to take a local decision, it uses several sources of information:

(1) the script, i.e. the TOs, included in it;
(2) the model of the student's individual characteristics;
(3) the parameters of environment (time, resources);
(4) the model of the student knowledge.

The decisions that an experienced human-teacher takes in a given situation are based on rather complex relationships between these types of information. In our opinion it should be possible to define explicit domain-independent rules that interpret different combinations of these data-sources in pedagogical decisions. This needs, however, a lot of experiment and a sound theory, which we still do not have.

That is why we decided to define different "characters" of the Executor. A character is a named combination of parameters that blocks or unblocks alternative pedagogical decisions when local events occur with different types of individual student models and environment parameters. For example, patient, critical, forgiving, helping, unobtrusive, friendly, competing. The teacher can choose between these characters and is not free to make arbitrary combinations. This is a serious limitation of the pedagogical capabilities of the system, but it is convenient for teachers too.

Many experiments can be undertaken with different "characters" of the system and different individual students. We hope that by using statistical mechanisms we shall find out some relationships that can allow us to formulate pedagogical rules and give the system a much greater flexibility. We believe this might be of interest for educationalists and psychologists.

5. CONCLUSIONS

The unified, hierarchically-organized technique of domain knowledge representation with teaching operators, allows taking various pedagogical decisions at both a global level (instructional planning) and at a local level (instructional strategies and tactics). The main advantage is that the Pedagogical Component is domain-independent. It can take actual and useful decisions in any domain or level of articulation when it is activated with the corresponding set of teaching operators.

An advantage of the pedagogical component is that it may be "tuned" by the teacher according to his own pedagogical style and knowledge of the student's individuality.

A domain-knowledge representation has been created for the domain of symbolic integration. it includes teaching operators at three levels of articulation, remedial and diagnostic operators. In this way the ITS-shell was used to create an ITS in the domain of symbolic integration. It is implemented on an IBM PC compatible and uses the muMATH package for symbolic computations as a domain expert.

Our future plans are to use this ITS as a tool for pedagogical and psychological experiments in drills and problem solving, and to create experimental implementations in other domains.

REFERENCES

1. Wenger E., *Artificial Intelligence and Tutoring Systems*. Kaufmann, Los Altos (1987).
2. Vassileva J., An architecture and methodology for creating a domain-independent plan-based intelligent tutoring system. *Educ. Train. Technol. Int.* **27**, 486–479 (1990).
3. Vassileva J., A classification and synthesis of student modelling techniques in intelligent computer assisted instruction. *Proc. of ICCAL'90*, Hagen, Fed. Rep. Germany. *Lecture Notes in Computer Science* No. 458, pp. 202–211. Springer, Berlin (1990).
4. Slagle J. R., A heuristic program that solves symbolic integration problems in freshman calculus. *J. ACM* **10**, 507–520 (1963).

Computers Educ. Vol. 18, No. 1–3, pp. 45–50, 1992
Printed in Great Britain. All rights reserved

A DIFFERENTIAL DIAGNOSTIC SKILLS ASSESSMENT AND TUTORIAL TOOL

Frank J. Papa,[1] Jon I. Young,[2] Gerald Knezek[2] and Robert J. Bourdage[1]

[1]Department of Medical Education, Texas College of Osteopathic Medicine, 3500 Camp Bowie Blvd,
Fort Worth, TX 76107-2690 and [2]Texas Center for Educational Technology/University of North Texas,
Texas, U.S.A.

Abstract—This paper reviews the progress made towards the development of an Intelligent Computer Assisted Instructional tool designed to function in a medical education setting. The tool, called KBIT (Knowledge Base Inference Tool) is an expert system-based instrument principally consisting of an assessment and a tutorial module. KBIT's sole purpose is to support the development and refinement of the differential diagnostic (DDX) knowledge and skills of medical students. The objective of the assessment module is to provide psychometrically reliable and valid measures of several DDS skills. The objective of the tutorial module is to create a learning environment wherein students make refinements in knowledge base (KB) constructs which result in progress towards the next level of DDX skills. KBIT's proposed educational approach is comprised of an iterative two-step process consisting of the assessment of several DDX skill performance parameters, followed by individualized formative instruction.

INTRODUCTION

This paper reviews the progress made towards the development of an Intelligent Computer Assisted Instructional (ICAI) tool designed to function in a medical education setting. The ICAI tool, called KBIT (Knowledge Base Inference Tool) is an expert system-based instrument principally consisting of an assessment and a tutorial module. KBIT's sole purpose is to support the development and refinement of the differential diagnostic (DDX) knowledge and skills of medical students.

DDX is the keystone intellectual skill of the medical practitioner. The objective of DDX is to determine which class of diseases best accounts for the patient's signs and symptoms. Medical practitioners initially use only the data obtained at the patient's bedside (i.e. historical and physical findings, not laboratory data) to reach a "clinical" diagnosis. However, diseases are rarely confidently diagnosed with such data. This is because disease states in general lack explicitly defined criteria for bedside-based diagnosis, i.e. a list of necessary and sufficient historical and physical signs and symptoms. Rather, the practitioner uses soft or fuzzy criteria to formulate a clinical diagnosis at the bedside. The practitioner subsequently attempts to confirm the clinical diagnosis with laboratory data. In short, the clinical (bedside) component of the diagnostic process represents decision making under uncertainty.

COMPUTATIONAL MODELS OF INFORMATION PROCESSING UNDER UNCERTAINTY

At least three general computational models of information processing under uncertainty have evolved[1]: probability, possibility (fuzzy logic or set theory), and certainty theory. The most widely utilized models are probabilistic, with Bayes' as perhaps the best recognized. Consequently, many researchers in cognition are not as aware of possibility and certainty theories as potentially useful information processing models in inherently uncertain decision-making domains. These alternative theories are sometimes referred to as deterministic theories. From the perspective of deterministic theories, the likelihood with which an exemplar is a member of a given class has nothing to do with the *a priori* occurrence of the given class in the population (as typified by probabilistic theories). Rather, a given exemplar is assigned, or determined to have, a "grade of membership" for each of several competing classes without consideration of each class's *a priori* occurrence. Without elaborating, Cohen[2] and Jungerman[3] have argued that probabilistic theories should not be unquestionably accepted as the only valid criterion for measuring the rationality or correctness of human decision making under uncertainty. Shortliffe and Buchanan[4] have gone further to suggest that probabilistic models such as Bayes' are not appropriate methods in inherently uncertain decision-making domains such as medicine. A deterministic computational model functions as a critical component within KBIT's DDX paradigm.

THE TENDENCY TOWARDS A DETERMINISTIC APPROACH TO DECISION MAKING

Deterministic models are theoretically and mathematically viable information-processing models. However, evidence that one actually attacks uncertain classification tasks from a deterministic rather than probabilistic approach is supported by the work of Kahneman and Tversky[5]. Their frequently referenced study suggests that people perform classification tasks based upon the extent to which an exemplar is typical of, or a member of, a class. This is contrary to mathematically correct or "normative" probabilistic theories. This deterministic approach to classification, i.e. classification via recognition of the degree to which an exemplar is similar to the typical class representation, is frequently termed the "Representative Heuristic".

CLASSIFICATION AND PATTERN RECOGNITION

The medical cognition literature embraces two primary theories of classification; exemplar and prototype theories. These two theories attempt to describe, with detail greater than the representative heuristic described above, the type of knowledge used and how knowledge is used to perform classification tasks.

In exemplar theories[6] a clinician performs DDX (disease classification) by recalling the specific previously experienced disease exemplar which best matches the presenting case. The diagnosis associated with the best matching, previously experienced exemplar, provides the clinician with the diagnosis for the presenting case.

In prototype theories[7, 8] the clinician performs DDX by comparing the presenting case to an abstracted representation of each of the possible disease classes likely to account for the case presentation. The disease class prototype which best matches the case presentation is the diagnosis that will be made by the clinician.

The types of knowledge (exemplars and prototypes) used in classification is different in the two theories. However, it is important to note that both of these classification theories clearly express (while the Representative Heuristic implicitly suggests) that classification is accomplished via the use of a pattern recognition mechanism. The importance of pattern recognition in KBIT's DDX paradigm will be discussed later.

ASSESSMENT ISSUES

The medical education literature contains research sufficient to question the psychometric properties (reliability and validity) of DDX assessment instruments. The realization of truly efficient and effective DDX-related ICAI tools will not occur unless their developers can first resolve these psychometric concerns, for which there are at least three prerequisites. First, there is a need to create an explicitly defined and cognitively sound DDX paradigm for modeling a DDX assessment instrument. Second, because expertise in general, and DDX skills in particular, are problem and disease-specific, medical educators will need to create an assessment format which is capable of measuring competency at the problem and disease-specific level. Third, these assessment instruments must provide reliable and valid disease- and problem-specific measures for DDX skills. We have already described a cognition-based DDX paradigm. Possible solutions to the second and third prerequisites are now described.

The reliability problem

The reliability problem stems from the following two notions. First, the lack of disease criteria for clinical diagnosis speaks to the variability with which a disease class will manifest itself in different individuals. Second, there are a number of common and important diseases that are likely to cause a given medical problem. Subsequently, students' skills for disease and problem-specific

DDX can be reliably assessed only by having them solve a number and variety of test cases (perhaps six or more) for each of the diseases relevant to the given problem.

For a medical problem such as "acute chest pain", for which there are nine common or important different causes, it appears that a student would need to be tested with approx. 54 test cases (six different cases for each of the nine diseases in the problem area). With conventional DDX assessment instruments, a test case takes approx. 5–15 min to work through. With these assessment instruments, a prohibitively large amount of time would be required to reliably test each student's DDX skills in this area.

Utilizing conventional assessment formats, medical educators almost universally utilize only 1 or 2 test cases per disease class, or worse, per problem area. By lumping a large number of different test cases and question formats together, a respectable reliability coefficient of 0.70–0.80 might be achieved. However, in reflecting upon the notion that competency is at very least, problem-specific, one must ask "What is it that their conventional assessment approaches are measuring?" The simple answer is that they are not reliable estimates of competency with problem-specific skills.

With little elaboration, the promise of KBIT as a reliable, problem- and disease-specific instrument for assessment, comes from three sources. First, expert systems are, by definition, problem-specific in application. Second, once a knowledge base (KB) has been input into an expert system, there is almost no limit to the number and variety of test cases that it could be given to solve. Third, the DDX performance levels achieved by the expert system would reflect the diagnostic utility and soundness of the KB from whom the KB was extracted. Problem- and disease-specific test reliability would be, theoretically, a relatively easy psychometric property to achieve.

The development of an instrument for expert system-based assessment of DDX skills would require the creation of an expert system shell capable of extracting a subject's KB in a time-efficient manner. The approach to KB extraction taken by the authors has been described elsewhere[9] but will be briefly reviewed later. However, in studies conducted in two separate problem areas ("Acute Chest Pain" and neurological "Weakness"[10]) KBIT produced KR-21 reliability coefficients >0.89 with only 100 cases per problem area.

The validity problem

When experts outperform novices in a test of DDX skills then the test is said to have "construct validity". Perhaps the most critical psychometric concern confronting medical educators has been that experts do not necessarily perform better than novices with conventional DDX testing instruments.

An inherent capability of an expert systems-based assessment instrument is the potential to achieve construct validity. Put simply, a knowledge base extracted from an expert should outperform the knowledge base of a novice. KBIT has provided valid assessments at the disease-specific level[11]. KBIT has also provided valid assessments at the problem-specific level in two distinct problems areas ("Acute Chest Pain" and neurological "Weakness" [10]).

KNOWLEDGE BASE EXTRACTION AND DDX SKILLS ASSESSMENT

The process to extract a knowledge base in KBIT utilizes a single, predefined, "bounded" problem–space matrix. The matrix columns represent a list of x common or important diseases known to cause the problem, while the rows represent a list of y common signs/symptoms associated with each of the diseases in the problem space. The KB extraction routine requires each subject to fill in the empty cells of the matrix. That is, the student's task is to declare their understanding of the percentage of patients with a given disease who exhibit a given finding. These feature frequency estimates define their knowledge of the relationship between each disease and sign/symptom (see Fig. 1).

Via a series of manipulations, KBIT transforms these relationships into a highly structured representation of the subject's KB, which contains four interrelated, yet distinct, cognitive constructs. The first construct is a one-to-one representation of the subject's simple declarative KB, i.e. the original feature frequency estimates. The second construct is a more complex declarative KB construct termed a disease prototype (one prototype is created for each disease in the problem

	Disease #1	Disease #2	Disease #...	Disease #...	Disease #x
Feature #1	65	50	20	35	40
Feature #2	75	20	90	20	50
Feature #3	30	40	35	15	80
...	90	20	20	10	40
...	90	95	30	05	20
...	85	95	80	10	20
Feature #y	10	50	75	90	20

Fig. 1. Subject's estimates of feature frequencies.

space). The third type of construct represents a form of procedural knowledge referred to as weighting rules. The declarative (prototype) and procedural (weighting rules) knowledge constructs are integrated into a fourth construct called a problem-specific DDX schema.

The purpose of these tranformations is to enable KBIT to use weighting rules and a fuzzy set theory-like inferencing mechanism based on pattern recognition to diagnose a collection of test cases. Diagnosis is conducted by having KBIT determine the degree to which each test case resembles or matches each of its internalized disease prototypes. Thus, KBIT's DDX information-processing paradigm emulates prototype-based classification theories. A test case is said to be correctly diagnosed when the disease class which has accumulated the greatest weight, i.e. highest degree of "prototype match", is the same disease class actually diagnosed for the test case. Three DDX skills measures are made for each subject. These are diagnostic accuracy, pattern matching and pattern discrimination. Diagnostic accuracy is defined as the number of test cases correctly diagnosed. Pattern matching is defined as the degree to which each of the subject's disease prototypes correctly matched the findings associated with all test cases representative of the same disease. Pattern discrimination is defined as the distance between a correctly diagnosed test case and the next most highly weighted disease class, i.e second leading hypothesis. Diagnostic accuracy, pattern-matching and pattern-discrimination values can be produced for disease-specific and overall problem areas.

CORRELATIONS BETWEEN SKILLS AND CONSTRUCTS

KBIT's assessment parameters represent measures of three different levels of DDX skills. Diagnostic accuracy represents a coarse DDX skills measure (both for a disease and for the general problem level) while pattern matching and pattern discrimination represent two finer, yet distinct, DDX skills measures. The authors have attempted to determine the degree to which refinement at one level of DDX skills might impact another DDX skill. Preliminary investigations suggest that diagnostic accuracy is more dependent upon pattern discrimination skills then pattern matching skills[8]. However, because of KBIT's design, each of the three DDX skills parameters represent estimates of the utility of each subject's four cognitive constructs. Given these inter-dependencies between skills and constructs, the finding that diagnostic accuracy is more dependent upon pattern discrimination than pattern matching suggests that it is the distinctiveness between an individual's prototype constructs which best accounts for diagnostic accuracy. This hypothesis represents the beginning of efforts to define more precisely the correlations between diagnostic skills and KB constructs.

ADVANTAGES OF AN EXPLICIT COGNITIVE AND INTEGRATED PARADIGM FOR ASSESSMENT AND INSTRUCTION IN DDX

There are several potential advantages to an assessment instrument based on pattern recognition. First, there appears to be the capability to provide reliable and valid measures of three different problem- and disease-specific DDX skills. Second, there is the potential to correlate these three DDX skills performance measures with each of the four distinct yet interrelated cognitive constructs which, within the KBIT DDX paradigm, are responsible for the DDX skills performance levels achieved. Third, there is the possibility of predicting (in background) how modifications not just at a given construct level (e.g. weighting rules), but more so, at a specific aspect of a particular construct (e.g. the weighting rule which relates the feature of "fever" and the disease class called pneumonia), would lead to $x\%$ improvement in, for example, the subject's diagnostic accuracy for pneumonia. Fourth, KBIT can use the prototypes and weighting rules derived from an individual expert or composite group of experts as the basis for modeling particular constructs or performance activities in novices.

CURRENT AND PROPOSED INSTRUCTIONAL FEATURES

The immediate challenge is to determine how to integrate KBIT's current assessment capabilities with an instructional module which optimizes learning. The approach taken thus far has been to base the construction of the instructional module on the work of Burton[12], who used a seven-stage strategy for the development of instructional aids. This approach is illustrated in Table 1.

Level 1 (Help—the lowest level), the student is provided with the tools and information necessary to navigate through the system via help through built in cues and instructions. The students are informed of the information they need to provide, and, how to perform specific tasks. In the KBIT program this option is fully implemented.

Level 2 (Assistance) and level 3 (Empowering tools), KBIT is rather weakly implemented. There is no context sensitive help nor is there an historical summary of the student's performance. However, there currently is an tool which allows the student to modify feature frequency estimates, transforms them into new weight rules and offers the student an opportunity to view the new levels of diagnostic accuracy resulting from these changes.

Level 4 (Reactive learning), permits the student to propose diagnostic strategies [i.e. determine the specific feature(s) to be used, the number of features to be used and their order] and test their strategy against the test case data bank. KBIT provides feedback concerning the accuracy of the strategy against a specific test case or all test cases in the data bank. Level 4 will support reiterative interactions with the subjects via a repetitive process of strategy changes and skills re-assessments.

Level 5 (Modeling), allows the student to observe an expert perform diagnosis on a given case and indicates why the expert selected a particular feature in solving the case. Eventually, as additional experts are entered, it is possible that a student could choose a specific expert to watch or KBIT could match a student with an expert based on similarities between expert and student over a number of cognitive constructs or DDX skill performance levels.

Level 6 (Coaching), is the process of assisting the student with suggestions as to which learning options would provide the most valuable information. This is currently planned as being done in two ways. First, as the student faces a learning decision (e.g. which construct changes to make), he/she can ask for help from the coach. Second, if the student makes an inappropriate selection the coach can interrupt and offer an explanation as to why that choice is not the best and even provide the student with a better learning option. Coaching will interact with the subjects at the construct levels of prototype and weighting rules modifications. An iterative process of KB modification and skills re-assessments is envisioned.

Table 1. Burton's categories of software aids

	Burton's examples	KBIT's tutoring possibilities
1 Help	On-line documentation	Glossary of terms Program navigation
2 Assistance	On-line Calculator	On-line calculator Context sensitive help
3 Empowering tools	Decison tree history for self review	Structured log of %/accuracy of results
4 Reactive learning	Challenge system with hypothesis Get feedback on consistency of choices	Current "simulation" plus possible tutoring excerpts
5 Modeling	System trouble-shoots fault while student watches	Student "watches" expert diagnose case
6 Coaching	System recognizes suboptimal behavior and breaks in	System recognizes lack of progress and suggests alternative activities
7 Tutoring	Teaches and test mastery	Teaches fundamental concepts

Level 7 (Tutorial), has not been implemented. However, the intention is to provide the student with free form access to all prior levels so that the individual style of the student can be taken into consideration.

CONCLUSION

The authors have made significant progress towards the development of an expert system-based ICAI tool whose single purpose is to support the development and refinement of the DDX knowledge and skills of medical students. The majority of the work to date has involved: (1) the development of an explicitly defined and sound DDX paradigm which serves as the cognitive foundation of the ICAI tool, and (2) the development of a psychometrically reliable and valid instrument for problem-specific assessment which measures DDX skills levels in a manner consistent with an explicitly defined DDX-skills paradigm. The authors are in the early phases of modeling the instructional phases of the ICAI tool.

The most exciting findings involve those which suggest that the assessment tool has provided a robust research environment for exploring the correlations between the DDX skills performance levels achieved and the constructs responsible for the DDX skills performance levels. These findings suggest that ICAI projects have great potential utility not as ends in themselves but also as research tools to be used to actively model and test information-processing hypotheses.

Acknowledgements—This research was funded in part by the Fund for the Improvement of Post Secondary Education (FIPSE) and SmithKline Beecham Foundation.

REFERENCES

1. Parsaye D. and Chignell M., *Expert Systems for Experts*. Wiley, New York (1988).
2. Cohen L. J., Can human irrationality be experimentally demonstrated? *Behav. Brain Sci.* **4**, 317–370 (1981).
3. Jungerman H., Two camps of rationality. In *Decision Making Under Uncertainty* (Edited by Scholz R. W.). Elsevier, Amsterdam (1983).
4. Shortliffe E. H. and Buchanan B. G., A model of inexact reasoning in medicine. *Math. Biosci.* **23**, 251–279 (1975).
5. Kahneman D. and Tversky A., On the psychology of prediction. *Psychol. Rev.* **80**, 237–251 (1973).
6. Norman G. R., Rosenthal D., Brooks L. R. and Allen S. W., The development of expertise in dermatology. *Archs Dermat.* **125**, 1063–1068 (1989).
7. Bordage G. and Zacks D., The structure of medical knowledge in the memories of medical students and general practitioners: categories and prototypes. *J. med. Educ.* **21**, 92–98 (1985).
8. Papa F. J., Shores J. H. and Meyer S., Effects of pattern matching, pattern discrimination and experience in the development of diagnostic expertise. *Acad. Med.* **65**, S21–S22 (1990).
9. Papa F. J. and Meyer S., An expert program shell designed for extracting "Disease prototypes" and their use as models for exploring the "Strong problem solving methods" employed in clinical reasoning. In *Further Developments in Assessing Clinical Competence* (Edited by Hart I. R.), pp. 354–364. Heal, Quebec, Canada (1987).
10. Papa F. J., Test of the generalizability of KBIT (an artificial intelligence-derived assessment instrument) across medical problems. Unpublished Ph.D. dissertation, University of North Texas (1991).
11. Papa F. J., Shores J. H. and Meyer S., The use of a pattern recognition-based, prototype-driven research tool to study cognitive constructs in medical decision making. *Proceeding of the 4th International Conference on Assessing Clinical Competence*, Ottawa, Canada. In press.
12. Burton R. R., The environment module of intelligent tutoring systems. In *Foundations of Intelligent Tutoring Systems* (Edited by Polson M. C. and Richardson J. J.). Erlbaum, Hillsdale, N.J. (1988).

Computers Educ. Vol. 18, No. 1–3, pp. 51–61, 1992
Printed in Great Britain. All rights reserved

EDUCATIONAL AND RESEARCH UTILIZATION OF A DYNAMIC KNOWLEDGE BASE

ALFREDO FERNANDEZ-VALMAYOR[1,*] and CARMEN FERNANDEZ CHAMIZO[2]

[1]Departamento de Informática, Universidad de Castilla-La Mancha and
[2]Departamento de Informática y Automática, Facultad de Ciencias Físicas, Universidad Complutense de Madrid, 28040 Madrid, Spain

Abstract—Student modelling is one of the most difficult areas in the field of educational computing. A promising approach to student modelling is based on trying to simulate the learning process. The system described in this paper can be regarded as a testbed to study issues in generalizing and understanding complex episodes, such as those that a student, or an expert, confronts when reading and solving problems. This paper introduces some of the issues raised during the development of our prototype: the relationship between knowledge representation and knowledge acquisition, and between natural language processing and memory structures. This is followed by an overview of the system and a more detailed discussion of the implementation of the prototype in the final sections.

1. INTRODUCTION

Student modelling is one of the most difficult areas in intelligent tutoring systems (ITS) research. Ideally, the student model should include an explicit representation of all aspects of students' behaviour and students' knowledge that relate to student achievement in learning. To derive the student model the ITS has to follow a student's interaction with the computer's program. From this monitoring the ITS tries to derive what the student knows, and where he is situated with respect to the domain knowledge represented in the computer. Therefore, a student model is not easily contructed, and student models implemented in real ITSs are only capable of monitoring the most simple aspects of students' behaviour.

In most computer-based systems, the emphasis has been on modelling the students' problem solving behaviour as a subset of the knowledge of the expert (overlay modelling). Other somewhat different techniques consider the student model as a subset of the expert model plus some appropriate components, such as "buggy" procedures or "mal-rules", which take into account the incorrect versions of the target knowledge that the student may have. In this way, a computer tutoring system can provide an explicit representation of students' misconceptions and errors so that pedagogical decisions, regarding remedial procedures, can be taken on a sound basis.

A promising approach to student modelling is based on trying to simulate the learning process (the actual mechanism of cognitive change). However, many difficulties arise from this approach. The processes of human learning are not completely understood, and different theories of learning exist that attempts to explain human learning experiences. To use this approach we would need to provide an explicit representation of the knowledge of the expert and the student, and a set of operators, or processes, capable of maintaining these knowledge bases.

With our system, we are trying to model some aspects of how humans, students or experts, acquire declarative knowledge when reading or studying. Therefore, the emphasis is not only on how students learn, but also on how experts learn about their domain of expertise. We are testing different algorithms, trying to model how persons incorporate textual information into their memories, and how they remember and reorganize their knowledge when reading more about a subject (or when trying to understand a textual explanation of a problem).

In the remainder of this paper we will introduce some of the issues which have been raised during the development of our prototype: the relationship between knowledge representation and knowledge acquisition, between natural language processing and memory structures, and between

---

*To whom all correspondence should be addressed at: Departamento de Informática y Automática, Facultad de Ciencias Físicas, Universidad Complutense de Madrid, 28040 Madrid, Spain.

high level schemata generation and understanding of a text. This will be followed by an overview of the system and, in the subsequent sections, a more detailed description of the implementation of our prototype.

2. KNOWLEDGE REPRESENTATION AND KNOWLEDGE ACQUISITION

Knowledge representation is a central topic in intelligent tutoring research. Most ITSs have four distinct components, or modules: the student model, the model of the expert (the explicit representation of the knowledge about the domain), the pedagogical module (explicit representation of a collection of teaching strategies) and finally the interface with the student.

In real ITS implementations, not all these modules have been fully developed, and researchers often concentrate on some of them at the expense of others; however most authors essentially agree with this module division.

Three of these four components (the expert, the student and the pedagogical modules) are basically explicit representations of the knowledge that humans have in some subject area. Therefore, it would be reasonable to assume that they share the underlying representation scheme and the processes which make that knowledge operational. Nevertheless, several problems arise out of the traditional ITS module division. First of all, it seems that this knowledge division does not reflect the idea that the basic mechanisms used by both, experts and students, to acquire knowledge must be essentially the same. It also refers, primarily, to a one-to-one situation involving a tutor and a student that only works in one way. However, in intelligent knowledge communication, we can see that both parties are involved in the acquisition of knowledge. Not only does the student learn but also the teacher improves his knowledge of pedagogical stategies and refines his ideas about the subject matter. Finally, it seems that this module division has contributed in some way to a model of learning that is mainly a static model. In general, traditional ITSs do not have an intrinsic way of acquiring knowledge and consequently they cannot modify themselves as a result of their teaching experience.

All the above considerations have led us to believe that the problem of knowledge acquisition must be considered along with the problem of knowledge representation, and that both must form an integrated system in which the basic representation scheme and knowledge acquisition process would be the same for both experts and students. In other words, we think that a system able to teach must be able to learn. This conclusion has an important corollary: the design and construction of ITSs to improve teaching effectiveness ought to proceed in collaboration with research in learning and learning simulation.

From the above discussion we can conclude that in an ideal ITS, the expert and the student knowledge bases would have different contents, but they must share the same learning procedures. Student's errors or misconceptions are not because experts and students have different learning mechanisms (or operators), but are due to the critical role that previous knowledge has in the learning process.

Many complex problems need to be solved, before a practical computer tutoring system can be developed following the principles we have been discussing. This is the reason behind constructing our prototype of a dynamic knowledge base (DKB): to test the knowledge representation mechanisms and the knowledge acquisition processes needed to build an ITS of this kind.

As we will see in the next section, knowledge acquisition has two different aspects in a computer-based tutoring system. On the one hand is the problem of acquiring domain knowledge, and on the other is the problem of learning about what the student knows. Our aim would be to build a system that would be able to generate its domain knowledge base (by means of its interaction with teachers) and its student model (by means of its interaction with students).

3. MEMORY STRUCTURES AND TEXTUAL INFORMATION PROCESSING

In the previous section we claimed that a teaching system must be designed on top of a learning system. However, the communication channel between humans and the kind of computer-based system considered here is usually restricted to a keyboard (and perhaps a pointing device). Therefore, the only way for this kind of system to learn is through sentences typed on the keyboard.

Thus, we need to focus our attention on the language we are going to use to communicate with the computer. This language does not need to be the same for teacher–computer interaction (to construct the expert knowledge base) as that needed for student–computer interaction. The first can be a formalized representation language, but for the second we need to consider the problem of processing some subset of natural language (NL). In our system we have tried to unify both problems.

We have chosen to base our approach to natural language processing on the ideas repeatedly expressed by Schank and his colleagues who consider language as a memory-based process[1,2]. From their point of view, language is the vehicle used to communicate knowledge between two memories.

We consider, as other researchers do[3,4], that there are two main problems in using natural language in a computer-based system. First, there is the problem of parsing natural language inputs into semantic structures and second, there is the problem of organizing and maintaining a dynamic knowledge base (a memory) into which we can incorporate the semantic structures generated by the parser. The problems are interrelated[5]. On the one hand parsing is based on the memory structures to which the system has access at the moment it starts to process the NL input and, on the other hand, understanding NL must play an important role in the construction of the memory structures or schemata.

The focus of this work is the second problem. That is, the problem of creating and organizing a long-term memory of semantic structures (or schemata), that will represent, at any given moment, the knowledge that the system has about the world. There is some logic in building the prototype of the long-term memory first. Semantic structures exist in the memory of the computer, not only for parsing but also as the result of the learning process. Research in learning simulation also gives some priority to the contruction of a memory model. Learning can be thought as the process of creating (and incorporating) new schemata into the memory[6].

4. EDUCATIONAL BASIS OF OUR APPROACH

The research work of M. Chi and her colleagues has played an important role in the design of our prototype[7]. We are trying to implement a model able to explain some of the outcomes of their work. A key idea in this work is that high level schemata come into the minds of both expert and naive problem solvers, when they are reading (and attempting to solve) a physics problem. More recently they have expounded a theory on the role of students' self-explanations in building these schemata, and the relationship between self-explanations and the quantity of the schemata that the students build[8].

She and her colleagues focus on the encoding of instruction, i.e. how the learner builds a declarative knowledge structure. They stress the relationship between the quality of the representation of knowledge and the strategies that they use in solving a problem. In recent work, Chi and VanLehn[9] also hypothesize that the construction of knowledge structures seems to embody several subprocesses, such as natural language inferencing and the generalization of self-explanations made by the learner.

To summarize, we assume in our work that people build complex schemata into their minds when they learn, and that they use these knowledge structures when trying to classify a problem or to understand a situation. Consequently, we have focused our attention on the process of creating complex patterns, or general schemata, from the input of the system.

5. AN OVERVIEW OF THE SYSTEM

We have implemented our DKB as a dynamic frame system. The inputs to the system are frames or networks of frames. To process a new input has a double effect. First of all the system creates specialization-links to relate the new information with the formerly acquired knowledge (a hierarchy of frame-patterns created previously). Secondly, the system reorganizes the structure of the knowledge base, changing the weights of the links of the previously integrated structures, making new frame-patterns and integrating them into the DKB.

At the present time we still have not implemented a general control function, so we have to test each of the main functions that process the input individually. At this stage of the research this is useful because we are still testing different strategies for learning and for reorganizing the memory. There are some other requirements we are also testing. For example, we consider short term processes, those which take place immediately after we add new information to the system, and long-term processes, those which re-structure the memory when we inquire about the knowledge the system already has.

In the following three sections, we will describe the representation formalism used for input, the structure of the DKB itself, and the operators, or processes, that create and maintain these knowledge structures.

6. DYNAMIC KNOWLEDGE BASE (DKB) IMPLEMENTATION

6.1. *Input representation*

In our prototype, and for testing purposes, we have been using descriptions of events, actions, persons or objects, (related to simple experiments about free fall) as input information. (We took this scenario from a traditional CAL program, named Galileo, that we developed to teach some basic concepts in kinematics.)

Conceptual Dependency Theory (CD) is the basis we use to formalize the input[10]. The key idea behind this theory is that meaning can be represented in a canonical, language-free manner[5,11,12]. CD is based on a representation of events by means of frames. Frames that, among others, include the following features:

> an actor,
> an action,
> an object on which the action is performed,
> a source of the action and
> a destination for the action.

We implement these frames, or CD structures, as a head concept (in capital letters, in the example below) and a list of slot-filler pairs in which, fillers are again CD structures. CD also provides a small set of primitive actions (such as MTRANS—meaning the transfer of information; PTRANS—meaning the transfer of physical location). Nevertheless, CD does not depend on a particular set of primitives; it is the methodology behind selecting primitives which is stressed. For example, we can represent the sentence: "Galileo tells Andrea to drop a small stone", as:

```
ACTION Type MTRANS
   Vf TELLS
   Actor GALILEO
   Object ACTION Type GRASP
      Vf DROP
      Mode NEGATIVE
      Actor ANDREA
      Object PP Is-a STONE
         Size SMALL
   From GALILEO
   To ANDREA
```

With this methodology we can also represent complex events. A complex event is represented by a network of CD structures, connected by means of different types of links (causal, temporal or intentional)[6]. We can think of this formalism in terms of a partitioned semantic network of concepts and words. The CD structures represent objects or actions, and the links between them express how these actions or concepts are related to one another. For example, we can use the network in Fig. 1 to represent the following event: "Galileo climbs to the top of a tower and from there he drops a small stone. The stone falls to the ground with increasing velocity because of the pull of gravitational force".

On a fully implemented system, natural language input will be converted by means of an expectation-based parser into a CD structure or a network of CD structures[3,4]. At present, in

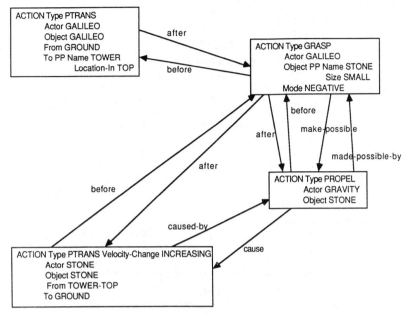

Fig. 1. CD-network that represent a complex event.

our prototype, we make this translation by hand, using the appropriate Lisp functions. As we have mentioned before, this methodology will permit us to work with an almost language-free representation of the meaning of the input. As we will see, this is important because in a learning system the representation language must be made easy to express the common patterns between different structures.

Other important questions are the different types of links we have within the input structures. In a semantic network we can distinguish two different kinds of links. Structural links, those setting up parts of a proposition or description, and relational links, those that establish causal, intentional or temporal relationships between structures and what Woods[13] has called "assertional links" because they make an assertion about the world by their presence.

In our model, structural links connect the CD's head concept with the list of its attributes, and they are implemented as one way relationships. That is, they impose a hierarchy in the structure. In our case these structural links can be created by the user when translating a text to the CD representation but they can also be created by the system when it makes new abstractions to represent the concepts, or frame-patterns, that make up the internal structure of the memory.

Relational links are those that relate CD structures within the input-network, and they are implemented as two-way relationships. These two-way relationships represent the fact that the input-information is not a hierarchical structure and therefore, it is possible for the system to look at it from different perspectives. (In our prototype that means the system can make different CDs out of the network, taking any of the nodes of the network as the head concept.) Relational links, as structural links, are created by the user when translating textual information to a network of CDs, but they can also be created for the system when it makes a network of concepts out of a CD structure. These processes of transforming a hierarchy in a network, give the system the possibility to change its "focus of attention". This has a strong influence on the organization of the system's knowledge base, as we will see in the following paragraph and when describing the system's processes.

To illustrate what it means to change the focus of attention, we can compare the two frame-patterns that can be obtained by changing the focus of attention within the network of Fig. 1 (in these patterns, variable fillers start with a "?" character). In the first case (Fig. 2), the head concept (the focus of attention) is the action of the gravitational force, and in the second (Fig. 3) the head concept is the action of the falling stone. These CD structures are the initial frame-patterns that the system creates after the first process of generalization. Eventually, after processing more

```
ACTION Type PROPEL
     Actor GRAVITY
     Object ?OBJECT
     <-After ACTION Type GRASP
               Actor GALILEO
               Object ?OBJECT
               Mode NEGATIVE
               After ?CAUSE
               Make-Possible ?CAUSE
               <-After ACTION Type PTRANS
                              Actor GALILEO
                              Object GALILEO
                              From GROUND
                              To PP Name TOWER
                                        Location-In TOP
     Cause ?CAUSE
```

Fig. 2. The object of Galileo's and gravity's actions must be the same. What the action of gravity causes is made possible by the action of Galileo and happens after the action of Galileo.

information related to free fall events, the system might be able to obtain the frame-patterns underlying the description of free fall experiments.

6.2. Structure of the DKB

In the first place, we have based the design of our system's knowledge base[14] on the work done by Schank and his colleagues on reminding and its uses in memory organization[2,15–17]. In his work, Schank revised the notion of "script" and introduced the idea of "memory organization packet" (MOP) as a type of dynamic high-level schema in memory that organizes and represents abstract knowledge shared by different "scripts". Various computer programs have been developed using this kind of memory organization[6,16–18]. Furthermore, case-based reasoning systems, that have been proposed recently as a more psychologically plausible model than rule-based expert systems, are also based on the same kind of memory organization[19]. Our system shares some basic mechanisms, and the notion of dynamic system able to create new schemata, or MOPs, with all these programs.

From a conceptual point of view the structure of our DKB has three main components (Fig. 4):

The root. The root of the DKB is a list of MOPs that can grow when the system gets new information. The system creates new MOPs (for us a frame-pattern), and adds them to the root when it does not find compatible structures in the nodes of the trees (the nodes of the trees are also frame-patterns, but are generated for other processes). The growing of the root represents the time factor of the system. Time factor is related to the newness of the information that the system gets. The system considers that an input is new (unusual) if is not compatible with any of the items it already has in memory. Initially, we have put in the root of our prototype three empty MOPs (they have a head concept, but the list of slot-filler pairs is empty): action (to describe actions), state (to describe the state of a system or object) and PP (picture producer following Schank's nomenclature). When we add new information, the system can add new MOPs at the root. We will discuss this process of adding new MOPs at the root later, but for now we want to state the

```
ACTION Type PTRANS Velocity-Change INCREASING
          Actor ?ACTOR
          Object ?ACTOR
          From TOWER-TOP
          To GROUND
            <-Make-Possible ?<-MAKE-POSSIBLE
            <-After ?<-MAKE-POSSIBLE
            <-Cause ACTION Type PROPEL
                         Actor GRAVITY
                         Object ?ACTOR
```

Fig. 3. In a free fall action the actor and the object are the same, the action happens after the event that makes the falling possible, and the cause is the action of gravity on the falling object.

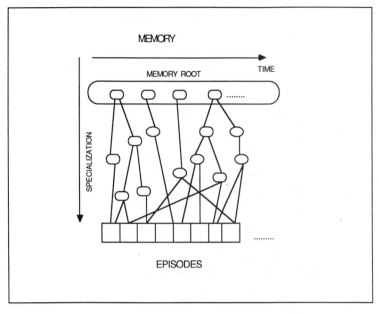

Fig. 4. Structure of the dynamic knowledge base.

importance of starting with a memory root with some basic MOPs (such action, state and PP). Figure 5 is an example of what kind of MOPs we can have in the root of the DKB if after starting the program we were to give it the information

```
ACTION type PROPEL
    actor PP type HUMAN
        name GALILEO
        profession SCIENTIST
    object PROJECTILE
```

In the example, the information we give to the system is indexed under the empty MOP ACTION, because this MOP is compatible with the input. But the system also tries to use as head concepts: PROPEL, PP, HUMAN, GALILEO, etc. and, as there are no MOPs in the memory which are compatible with them, the system creates new MOPs and adds them at the root. Working in this way, the system creates a kind of circular semantic for the symbols in the input frames. In the example, the symbol ACTION is something whose actor is a PP whose name is GALILEO, and GALILEO is the symbol that is the name of a PP, that is the actor of an ACTION. This idea of giving a meaning to the symbols (including slot symbols such as "name" or "actor") by means of the network which is connected to them is, at present, one of the aspects on which we are working in connexion with the design of the expectation-based parser.

The sequence of trees. Looking at the structure of the memory from the root, its middle part is made up of a sequence of trees. The roots of these trees form the root of the system and its branches make a specialization hierarchy of frame-patterns that may be thought of as a discrimination network that index input-information in an abstract way. The nodes of the trees are the MOPs, or frame-patterns, that represent the abstractions the system is able to create from the input episodes. The frame-patterns of Figs 2 and 3 are two examples of the content of these nodes.

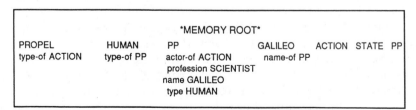

Fig. 5. Example of content of the memory root.

When the system receives a new input it searches its memory to find the most specific nodes compatible with the input information, and then it indexes the new input into each of these compatible nodes using "specialization links". In this manner, each tree grows by adding new branches and nodes (new specializations) to pre-existing ones. Specialization links are the structures that keep the differences between the slot-filler pairs of the input structure and the slot-fillers of the father-node. They are the third kind of relationship we use in our representation scheme. There are two types of specialization links: those that discriminate among MOPs, and those that discriminate between a MOP and the input structure.

The specialization links that connect trees' nodes have a weight. This weight is augmented each time the node is successfully accessed in a search operation, and vice versa. Using this weight as a threshold, the system can control the extension of the search it does in memory, and in this way control the situation-identification problem, focusing its attention on a narrow set of frames. It would also be possible to eliminate a specialization link, and as a consequence, the path of specializations that starts from it, if its weight is less than a certain value. But, at present, it is not clear how this value can be dynamically determined by the system.

Sequence of cases. These are the lowest level of the DKB structure and they form a sequence with all the inputs (CDs and networks of CDs representing events or cases) that the system receives. Because each case is indexed under multiple descriptions, more than one node of the trees above will have access to each of these episodes.

6.3. Processes that maintain the DKB

Our system uses the information it receives to build up the data structure that makes its "memory". This knowledge structure is shaped, as we have seen, by an increasing number of growing trees that index, in multiple ways, all the information the system receives. There are two types of processes responsible for creating and maintaining this structure. First, there are the processes that search the memory, finding previous abstractions compatible with the present input. The places where abstractions are found are also the places where to index the new information. Second, there are processes which create new schemata, or MOPs, that represent the abstract concepts implicit in the input. There are several options available in this second type:

- create a new MOP out of particular cases or instances
- create a MOP from other MOPs previously created
- create a new MOP and add it to the root of the memory.

All these processes have a number of implications for the memory model that we have implemented, some of them have already been mentioned, others we shall consider below.

6.3.1. Compatibility: searching and indexing new information into memory. Choosing a particular implementation of the compatibility function plays an important role in the overall performance of the system. The most commonly used general principle is that two CD structures are compatible if they do not have contradictory information. That means that to be compatible, two CD structures must have an equal head concept, and also the slots that have equal names must have compatible fillers.

Memory search starts at the root of the system, looking for the most recent MOP in the root list that is compatible with the input. If the system finds one MOP compatible with it, it starts to look deeper in the tree of that MOP, and it will return a list with the lowest (or more specific) MOPs in the tree, compatible with the input information. If the system does not find a MOP compatible with the input in the root, it creates a new MOP which will retain the main characteristics of the input. In our prototype that means that the system will retain the head concept and the relational links of the input CD structure. We can look, in more detail, at the kind of MOPs the system created in the example of the Section 6.2 (Fig. 5). To obtain the MOPs in Fig. 5, first the system changed the input, a CD structure, into a network, replacing its structural links by two-way relational links. Next, the system tried to index the network, using each of the potentially admissible head concepts in it. As the system did not find compatible MOPs in the root for these head concepts, it created new MOPs. These MOPs index the CD structures that the system created, changing the focus of the network. When the system, in continuing its operation, gets new information, some MOPs, as "PROPEL: type-of-ACTION", or as "HUMAN: type-of PP", will probably still be useful for indexing new information (and its confidence will be increased). But MOPs as "PP: actor-of ACTION, profession SCIENTIST . . . " etc. are too specific, and there will probably not be much information to index under them, so their confidence will be decreased, and eventually they will be removed from the root.

We shall now discuss another three questions that must be taken into account in the definition of the compatibility function.

The first of these questions deals with the problem of determining whether or not two CD-structures are compatible when the symbol, in the head of one of them, is the name of the concept, described in the other. For example, the symbol GALILEO can be the head concept of a CD structure with an empty list of slot-filler pairs. But this structure means the same thing as the structure whose head symbol is PP, and whose list of slot-filler pairs is "type HUMAN, profession SCIENTIST, name GALILEO, etc.". There is the same situation with the CD "STONE" and the CD "PP: size SMALL, is-a STONE, etc.". If these pairs of structures are tested for compatibility with the definition that we gave above, they will return "incompatible" because they have different symbols as head concepts. So the compatibility function must look at the content of the slot "name" (or at the slot "is-a") when testing for compatibility.

The other two questions are related to testing the compatibility of structures with variable fillers. As will be seen in the next section, we can have two types of variable fillers in the frame-patterns of our knowledge base. The first type of variable fillers are pc-var (for predicate calculus variables) and we have already seen some examples of these fillers in Section 6.1 (Figs 2 and 3) where we distinguished these variables with the initial char "?". In a variable filler of this type, the values it is bound to must unify. This type of variable can match any other filler of a slot with the same name in another structure, but the next matching between a pc-var, of the same name, and a second filler, will only be possible if the second filler is compatible with the filler to which the variable was bound to the first time. For example, if the variable filler ?ACTOR of the slot "actor" (in Fig. 3) is bound to the value STONE, it must unify with values of the other slots, where this variable is the filler again. In the example a value that would unify with STONE would be "PP: size SMALL, is-a STONE".

The second type of variables are sbl-var (for similarity-based learning variables). These variables are created by the system in the generalization process that will be discussed in the next section. We distinguish these variables with the initial char "¿", and the difference between them and pc-var is that sbl-var with the same name do not unify across the structure where they appear. Instead, they have restrictions. In our system, variables are implemented as head concepts of CD structures. In the case of pc-var, they have an empty list of slot-filler pairs, but in the case of sbl-vars, the list of slot-filler pairs it is not usually empty, it contains the attributive values that are necessary for a CD structure to be the filler of that slot. We can see below the generalized pattern of the two CDs shown in Fig. 6:

```
ACTION Type MTRANS
    Vf SAYS
    Actor ¿ACTOR Type HUMAN
        Profession SCIENTIST
    Object ACTION Type GRASP
        Vf LET-GO
        Mode NEGATIVE
        Actor ¿ACTOR
        Object PP Name STONE
            Size ¿SIZE
    From ¿FROM
    To ¿TO
```

This pattern-frame is compatible with a CD structure in which the filler of the slot "actor" could be any head concept on condition that it is from type HUMAN and profession SCIENTIST. The filler bound to the sbl-var ¿ACTOR, of the slot actor of the "object action", does not have to be compatible with the value bound to the first occurrence of the variable.

6.3.2. Creation of MOPs. Inductive learning is the basic process the system uses to create the MOPs, or frame-patterns, that make the nodes of the memory structure. In general, the empiricist algorithm consists in making a pattern more general or more specific, in response to feedback about

```
        ACTION Type MTRANS                        ACTION Type MTRANS
            Vf SAYS                                    Vf SAYS
            Actor GALILEO Type HUMAN                   Actor MARY Type HUMAN
                          Profession SCIENTIST                    Profession SCIENTIST
            Object ACTION Type GRASP                   Object ACTION Type GRASP
                        Vf LET-GO                                Vf LET-GO
                        Mode NEGATIVE                            Mode NEGATIVE
                        Actor ANDREA                             Actor JOHN
                        Object PP Name STONE                     Object PP Name STONE
                                     Size SMALL                              Size BIG
        From GALILEO                             From MARY
        To ANDREA                                To JOHN
```

Fig. 6. Two CDs that represent the same action, but done by different actors.

how well that pattern explains or classifies an instance. To make a pattern more specific, our system indexes specialized versions of the root-MOP below it. The indexing process we have described in the previous section groups together, under the same MOP-father, all the instances or events that are compatible with this MOP-father. A new MOP is created from these events if some of them share one or more features that are not present in the MOP-father. The new MOP is indexed as a specialization of the MOP-father, and the events used to create it are indexed under it[16,18]. New MOPs are not only created from instances, new MOPs can also be created from other MOPs.

To generalize its input, our program, as many other learning programs do, starts by replacing constants by variables. We use sbl-variables to generalize input instances, as we have seen in the example of the previous section. With sbl-vars we create patterns that can index a broad class of instances. But also the system can change the focus in the frame-pattern and create new root-MOPs. Using again the example of the previous section, the system would create, among others, the root MOP:

```
    ¿ACTOR Type HUMAN
           Profession SCIENTIST
```

Under this root MOP the system can specify all the information in which the actors are humans and scientists.

The other variabilization process that our system performs consists in replacing constants with pc-var. In this case the process that has most interest is the unification of the contents of all the slots that have compatible fillers, under the same variable filler. The MOPs that we create, by means of this process, are not merely a conjuctive generalization of several individual instances (this process might only need one instance). The focus of the process is now on the relationships between the components of the input structure. The individual characteristics of the fillers are summarized in the variable filler. The important feature that remains in the resulting pattern is that the same filler must play the same role in the same places. For example, in the CD below,

```
    ACTION Type PTRANS Velocity-Change INCREASING
        Actor ?ACTOR
        Object ?ACTOR
        From TOWER-TOP
        To GROUND
```

what is important is that the actor and the object of the action must be the same.

Or, in this second example,

```
    ACTION Type MTRANS
        Vf SAYS
        Actor ?ACTOR
        Object ACTION Type GRASP
          Vf LET-GO
          Mode NEGATIVE
          Actor ?TO
          Object PP Name STONE
            Size SMALL
        From ?ACTOR
        To ?TO
```

the "actor", and the "from" of an action, must be the same; and that the "to" of an action, and the "actor" of the "object action" must also be the same.

There are other learning processes in our system that we have not yet explored sufficiently. Among these, perhaps the most important are the different possibilities of how to use the weight factor of the specialization links, in connexion with the processes described above.

7. CONCLUSIONS

In this paper we have described a system intended to test the knowledge representation mechanisms and the knowledge acquisition processes needed to create a model of the student by modelling the learning process.

The current prototype of our dynamic knowledge base has been implemented in Allegro Common Lisp and it runs on a Mac SE, or a Mac II. At present, we have not introduced large amounts of information into the system. We have done all our experiments with only a small number of episodes. These experiments are essentially very simple, but they clarify some issues in the creation of the patterns that generalize the input, and the organization of the memory structure.

Future plans for the system include developing an agenda control structure to manage the overall behaviour of the system, and an expectation-based parser. By integrating an expectation-based parser we will be able to test the system in an interactive way with students and teachers.

REFERENCES

1. Schank R. C. and Rieger C. J., Inference and the computer understanding of natural language. In *Readings in Knowledge Representation* (Edited by Brachman R. J. and Levesque H. J.). Kaufmann, Calif. (1974).
2. Schank R. C., Language and memory. *Cogn. Sci.* **4**, 243–284 (1980).
3. Birnhaum L. and Selfridge M., Conceptual analysis of natural language. In *Inside Computer Understanding* (Edited by Schank R. C. and Riesbeck C. K.). Erlbaum, Hillsdale, N.J. (1981).
4. Martin C. E., Case-based parsing. In *Inside Case-Based Reasoning* (Edited by Riesbeck C. K. and Schank R. C.). Erlbaum, Hillsdale, N.J. (1989).
5. Schank R. C. and Riesbeck C. K. (Eds), *Inside Computer Understanding*. Erlbaum, Hillsdale, N.J. (1981).
6. Pazzani M., Learning causal relationships: an integration of empirical and explanation-based learning methods. Ph.D. dissertation, Technical Report UCLA-AI-88-10. (1988).
7. Chi M. T. H., Feltovich P. J. and Glaser R., Categorization and representation of physics problems by experts and novices. *Cogn. Sci.* **5**, 121–152 (1981).
8. Chi M. T. H., Bassok M., Lewis M. W., Reimann P. and Glaser R., Self-explanations: how students study and use examples in learning to solve problems. *Cogn. Sci.* **13**, 145–182 (1989).
9. Chi M. T. H. and VanLehn K. A., The content of physics self-explanations. Technical Report No. 12. Learning Research and Development Center, University of Pittsburg (1989).
10. Fernández-Valmayor A. and Fernández Chamizo C., Representacion del Conocimiento en los Sistemas de Enseñanza Basados en Computadora. *Rev. R. Acad. Cienc. exact. fis. nat. Madr.* **82**, 319–321 (1988).
11. Schank R. C., Conceptual dependency: a theory of natural language understanding. *Cogn. Psychol.* **1972**, 552–631 (1972).
12. Schank R. C. and Abelson R. P., *Scripts, Plans, Goals, and Understanding*. Erlbaum, Hillsdale, N.J. (1977).
13. Woods W. A., What's in a link: foundations for semantic networks. In *Readings in Knowledge Representation* (Edited by Brachman R. J. and Levesque H. J.). Kaufmann, Calif. (1975).
14. Fernández-Valmayor A., Diseño de una Base de Conocimientos y su Aplicación en un Entorno Educativo. Doctoral thesis, Universidad Complutense de Madrid (1990).
15. Schank R. C., *Dynamic Memory: A Theory of Reminding and Learning in Computers and People*. Cambridge University Press (1982).
16. Kolodner J. L., Maintaining organization in a dynamic long-term memory. *Cogn. Sci.* **7**, 243–280 (1983).
17. Lebowitz M., The use of memory in text processing. *Commun. ACM* **31**, 1483–1502 (1988).
18. Lebowitz M., Generalization from natural language text. *Cogn. Sci.* **7**, 1–40 (1983).
19. Riesbeck C. K. and Schank R. C. (Eds). *Inside Case-Based Reasoning*. Erlbaum, Hillsdale, N.J. (1989).
20. Fernández-Valmayor A. and Fernández Chamizo C., An educational application of memory organization models. *Proceedings of the ARCE International Conference on Advanced Research on Computers in Education*. IFIP & IPSJ, Japan (1990).
21. Langley P. and Carbonell J. G., Machine learning: techniques and foundations. Technical Report 87-09. ICS-University of California Irvine (1987).

Computers Educ. Vol. 18, No. 1–3, pp. 63–70, 1992
Printed in Great Britain. All rights reserved

INTELLIGENT TUTORING SYSTEMS ON SCIENTIFIC SUBJECTS: ARE PROTOTYPES READY FOR BROAD EXPERIMENTATION?

Monique Grandbastien

CRIN, University of Nancy 1, Campus Scientifique, B.P. 239, F-54506 Vandoeuvre Cedex, France

Abstract—Several prototypes of intelligent tutoring systems for scientific subjects have been developed within a national French research program. To progress either in identifying still unsolved problems or in transferring those prototypes to a wider community of users, it is necessary to make existing results available. This paper aims to describe the questions that this research program as a whole is addressing, as well as some existing prototypes and on-going work. General research results on this topic are presented, then by way of illustration the main features of some systems are briefly described.

INTRODUCTION

Artificial intelligence methods and techniques can be used in many ways to improve education software and to build teaching tools and learning environments that have never been available before. In this paper we focus our attention on systems including knowledge about the learning area (which enables them to solve problems by themselves and hopefully to provide accurate explanations), knowledge about tutoring guidance and strategies, using a more or less developed learner model and providing interface facilities. Such systems are often described under the paradigm of "intelligent tutoring systems" (ITS). In terms of learning activities these systems are mainly intended to support reasoning processes of the user.

Among many potential learning areas, there is a growing need for scientific education in all countries, either for schools and universities or for continuing education programs and in-service training for companies. Past and present research programs in the field of ITS have shown the need for numerous teams working for long periods to achieve significant prototypes; for further progress international cooperation is required. Such cooperation seems easier for scientific subjects which are less dependant on national cultures and curricula than others.

This paper aims at presenting some outcomes of a national French research program in artificial intelligence in the field of applications of knowledge-based systems to education. First, the general framework is presented, as well as the main questions that are addressed in the different teams taking part in the program. In the second part, some existing prototypes or on-going research are described which provide examples of possible outcomes from these research programs and an introduction to further reading. Finally, conclusions from participants in the seminar during the CAL91 conference are presented.

PART ONE

(1) The Research Context

Since 1985, a national research program in artificial intelligence has been initiated by the French National Scientific Research Center (CNRS) and the Ministry for Research and Technology (MRT). The program aims at structuring the scientific domain, coordinating and promoting the research produced within the program and finally bringing main research outcomes to a broad diffusion, especially in industry.

The research topics that are addressed in this program are structured around five main themes: (1) generic models for knowledge representation and inference; (2) specific inference systems such as plan generation, geometrical reasoning, multi-agent universes and qualitative reasoning; (3) machine learning, either by symbolic or by numerical approaches, including connectionism; (4) promoting work on meta-inference, heuristic search, meta-knowledge representation, variable depth reasoning and hypothetical reasoning; and (5) developing the design of knowledge-based systems by providing concepts, methods and techniques about knowledge acquisition, rule compilation, incoherence detection, explanation capabilities, knowledge-based systems architectures, including multi-expertise, inference systems typology, evaluation and validation techniques.

All these topics are either developed as fundamental research areas or in close relation with an application domain. In this paper we describe results of research applied to intelligent learning environments that were mainly conducted by teams involved in this national program or working in relation with it. Two national workshops were organized, the proceedings of those meetings are available[1,2]. The first workshop addressed the different functionalities that can be found in such systems. The main topics are learner model, adaptation to the learner, domain knowledge, pedagogical knowledge and their interrelations. Other sessions were devoted to authoring environments and technical training.

The last workshop dealt with intelligent learning environments for scientific subjects. The aim was to provide in-depth exchanges between people working on very close subjects, such as geometry or chemical problems. Before describing some prototypes, we try to underline what seems now to represent a consensus among this research community and what main questions are to be solved in the coming years. In the text, references to systems dealing with the discussed topics are made. For these references, systems are numbered according to the presentation order of the second part of the present paper.

(2) Main Outcomes and Questions

Interface facilities

Intelligent tutoring systems are often described as being composed of four main modules: knowledge on the domain to be taught; tutoring and pedagogical knowledge; learner model; and the interface module. Many authors would stress the growing importance of the interface module. Mainly from the new facilities available to build user friendly interfaces, using buttons, menus, multiwindowing, pictures or graphical displays sounds and colours. Drawbacks noted in previous educational software can be solved using these techniques.

New control and navigation techniques, such as hypertexts and hypermedia, can provide an alternative to the immediate resolution of difficult problems. For instance, learner models are often not powerful enough to provide the learner with the accurate information he requires; it may be interesting to provide hypertext where he will easily find the data he needs. Systems such as APLUSIX (1) and SOCRATE (5) include such facilities.

Knowledge representation

Several kinds of knowledge have to be represented. In terms of domain knowledge, main consensual characteristics are the necessity of a pedagogical oriented structuring of the domain, the need for additional knowledge used in explanation processes and the need for various presentations of this knowledge to the learner, particularly graphical. Systems described in (3) and (4) are good examples of what can be developed with advanced software tools.

In terms of reasoning processes, the concepts of plans and solving strategies are crucial. Many systems implement these concepts in terms of declarative rules and use them explicitly for learner guidance. Good examples are APLUSIX (1), CAMELEON (2), QUIZ (7), SOCRATE (5) and SIAM (6).

Finally, another problem is that of knowledge acquisition, especially for schools subjects. Domain knowledge has been formalized for years in school books and it would be interesting to extract the domain knowledge from those books in an automatic or semi-assisted way. Other perspectives may include the exchange of knowledge bases and the definition of formalisms facilitating the representation of knowledge for well identified target domains.

Learner models

Complex learner models will not be available for many years because of the lack of knowledge on deep cognitive processes. It seems more useful to develop simple models and to rely on the learner or the teacher for difficult decisions. As for interface facilities, the best solution may be to provide the learner with choices and to let him decide the best way. In other cases, the author may think it is not suitable for the learner to make this choice; in these cases, besides complex decision processes based on a weak learner model, a good solution may be to include an intervention by the teacher or by the monitor of the session.

This does not mean that we should not develop applications trying to model the learner, but lots of intermediate research are needed such as, for example, the automatic analysis of learner activities in order to be aware of their behaviour. The computer is an essential aid for the psychologist and for the educational scientist to observe the behaviour of large populations of students.

Learning situations and learning environment

The first ITS has too often worked as if the learner were alone, with nobody to help him and no other device available. This approach may be necessary for some specific needs, but it is probably not a general one. Intelligent systems must have knowledge about the potential environment of the learner, because this environment will often be of help during the learning activities. Further work has to be done to identify learning situations in which use of an ITS is adequate, and to identify what is the learning context and how this learning context can be partly described within the ITS, in order that the tutoring process takes account of it. This would certainly lead to more "realistic" products.

Authoring environment

No authoring environment is currently available to design and produce an ITS. This topic has been considered as crucial and it is addressed by several projects of the DELTA program initiated by the Commission of the European Communities. Parts of such environments have been specified, some prototypes are running, but there remains much ground to cover before authoring environments are available to produce intelligent learning software. Nevertheless partial results are available and should be used.

PART TWO

(1) Progressive Evaluation of Knowledge and Planification in the APLUSIX Learning Environment for Algebra (M. Saidi LRI, Bât. 490, F-91405 Orsay Cedex, France)

Scope of the work and intended users

APLUSIX is an ITS developed in the domain of algebra (factorization of polynomials and polynomial equation solving). APLUSIX runs on a Macintosh with a user-friendly interface. It provides two different learning modes: learning-by-example and a learning-by-doing. It aims to allow the user to acquire strategic knowledge in this domain of algebra, such criteria as to determine whether to go applying other transformations to a given expression or to abandon this current expression for a backtrack, also general problem solving skills such as exploring a search space by applying a set of heuristics. It can be used by pupils aged from 13 to 17 and for training adults in this field. It has been tested with high school students. Preliminary experimental results suggest that the system is an appropriate environment for studying skill acquisition in algebra. The individual protocols obtained from a more controlled experiment are currently being analysed in order to identify the heuristics the students may have discovered and the underlying learning mechanisms. Some results are presented in [3].

Main features in terms of learners activities and provided facilities

The learner can choose among three levels of expertise that which is closest to his own. Hence, the gap is not too wide between the learner's current knowledge and the state of knowledge he must reach in the near future. In the learning-by-example mode, the system displays the best search tree it can generate, given the level of expertise chosen by the student. In this mode, the learner can also query the system about its action in order to get explanations at factual or strategic level. In the learning-by-doing mode, the learner develops his own search tree by choosing at each step an expression and a transformation rule to apply. In this mode the learner can ask for help and get information about what the system would do in such a situation.

Domain knowledge and solving processes representation

The domain knowledge can be described as a couple (G,O), G being the general domain knowledge and O being the operative knowledge[4]. O is divided into five categories:

—R is the set of transformation rules,
—M is a set of plans,
—A is knowledge for matching,
—H is knowledge of heuristics,
—C is knowledge in calculus.

The sets M and H represent the reference know-how; they correspond to solving problem strategies. The set M is expressed in the form of plans defining goals to reach from the current situation. The implemented heuristics were formulated with the help of three mathematics teachers. These heuristics are not context-free as those defined by Bundy for the PRESS system[5] but are more powerful. The set components of O can be modified according to several levels of expertise.

Solving plans are implemented as production rules. For instance, to factorize the following expression $\langle (x^2-4)(x+2) + (x^2-9(x+4) - 9(x-2) \rangle$, following plan will be used:

plan/other-factor
if *it exists a transformation rule t which results in factorization of the sub-expression f **and** at least one of the products factors fac exists in the neighbourhood of expression f **then*** (*factorize f with t*)
(*factor-out fac*)
(*arrange*)

Implementation

APLUSIX is written in Le Lisp using SIM, a knowledge representation and inference system built for fulfilling the needs of this application.

(2) CAMELEON, a Solver that Identifies Obvious Situations in Elementary Analysis Problems (E. Bruillard, E.N.I. Bonneuil, route de Brévannes, F-94380 Bonneuil Cedex and LIUM, University of Le Mans, France)

Scope of the project and intended users

CAMELEON aims at being an environment to solve problems related to numerical functions for students at the end of secondary education. It starts with initial ideas written in CAMELIA where algebraic calculus and reasoning processes are cooperating. It aims at being self-explanatory and at visualizing its own research process by relying on declarative mathematical knowledge.

Main features

Several problem solvers have been developed in the field of algebra (see for instance APLUSIX in this paper). They have a common architecture which can be summarized as follows:

—determine the set of applicable transformations to the current problem,
—select the most interesting transformation,
—apply this transformation.

This cycle has been proved successful in many problems, but some limits have to be underlined. Such a cycle is well-suited for problems where deep mathematical knowledge is not used. The reasoning control is often limited, for instance CAMELIA is using a depth-first strategy and only comes back when a failure occurs. Further, the description language used is not powerful and declarative enough, for instance, in those systems it is impossible to be explicit in terms of explaining capabilities, e.g. the cognitive processes linked to the solving process cannot be described. CAMELEON aims at overcoming these drawbacks.

CAMELEON takes into account metacognitive behaviours in problem solving processes and aims at favouring them. It distinguishes between two kinds of heuristics, control heuristics and selection heuristics. The first ones are mandatory and make the difference between a beginner and an expert. The latter are determinant in terms of quality, they can be too particular and hide a lack of deep understanding of the domain, and can prevent the emergence of higher level of abstraction skills; the learning of heuristics of this kind is nevertheless useful to technically master a domain.

(3) Use of Graphics in ITS: an Example in Quantitative Chemistry (M. Bennani and J. Morinet-Lambert, CRIN, B.P. 239, F-54506 Vandoeuvre Cedex, France)

Scope of the work and intended users

An intelligent learning environment for quantitative chemistry is developed to help beginners in solving problems in this field (from 15 year old high school students to continuing education). This environment includes several components, a set of chemical knowledge (data bases, knowledge base and solving process), a module devoted to the analysis of the pupil's activities and the error diagnostic and help/advice functions using pedagogical knowledge. A first version of the environment has been developed in SCHEME for an IBM-PC and is currently being tested in several classrooms. In this version the provided interface is only based on text and menus.

Improvements to the man–machine interface are needed during the problem solving activity by using graphical symbolisms. Aiding graphics to support the learner's activities is of utmost importance to increase man–machine interaction flexible for ITS.

Main features of the provided graphic helps

Graphic aids are structured graphics represented as collections of objects defined by their geometrical shape, their size and their position. According to a decreasing degree on an abstraction axis, aiding graphics can belong to three main classes:

— communication graphics (charts, histograms, curves), the same shapes are used in many application fields as it is now currently available in spreadsheets and other related software,
— symbolic or remembrance graphics (trademark symbols, icons), they are more or less application domain dependent and often linked to one's cultural background,
— figurative graphics (outlines or skeletal drawings) which are simplified representations exhibiting main features of a complex reality.

If well chosen, these various graphics may support concepts and induce reasoning processes.

School chemistry books are full of graphic representations. Teachers that acted as pedagogical experts for this work identified three main reasoning levels during the problem solving process. The question was then: what graphic can be successful in supporting a part of the reasoning process at a given level? Two kinds of graphics were selected and developed.

One category consists of conceptual graphics; they belong to the second class mentioned before. The aim is to represent the different components that occur in a chemical reaction, with an emphasis on their internal structure. Hence, elementary entities are atoms and size differences, as well, links between them that have to be visualized using the usual 2D representations. In order to underline the dynamical aspect of chemical equations, an animated graphics has been created in which elements disappear from reagents to re-appear in resulting products.

A second category of graphics aims at visualizing existing relations between different values such as volume, quantity of product, and mass. For instance a figure has been elaborated by the teacher to show measure systems with indication of units and their organization, where boxes always contain variable data and balloons constants. The graphics are called relational graphics. Here again a dynamic management of the figure symbolizes transfers.

Knowledge representation and implementation

A first version of the system was developed on a Sun 3/60 workstation, using the expert system generator ART. Elementary graphical components were graphical objects, they were then composed and animated by the firing of selected production rules. Another version has been implemented on a PC using a Smalltalk and Prolog environment. Further work includes identifying the appropriate reasoning steps and learners' situations for which these graphics should be displayed.

(4) Development of Visualization Courseware Using Object Oriented Authoring Tools (R. Bonnaire and H. Perrin, Université Pierre et Marie Curie, boîte interne 235, 4 place Jussieu, F-75252 Paris Cedex, France)

Scope of the work and intended users

Computer simulations have been used for many years and have been found invaluable in the teaching of science. The COLOS project (COnceptual Learning Of Science) brings together eleven university teams for developing pedagogical simulations for science teaching at the university level. It has been initiated by Hewlett–Packard which provided a development platform consisting of an HP 9000/360 workstation and of RMG, an object oriented tool kit for authoring visualization software.

Main features and products

The role of a simulation is to induce intellectual work leading to a better understanding of the model of a phenomenon, and hence of the phenomenon itself. The interaction of the student with the computer is mostly controlled by "what if . . . " questions, and as vision is a powerful way to convey information, it takes advantage of the graphic capabilities of both new hardware and software.

Two applications were developed. The first is a simulation of fundamental electronic circuits based on an operational amplifier. Its goal is to show how given electronic defects of the Op. Amp. component operate on the properties of the circuit, and, if it is possible, how to correct these defects. The second one shows the trajectories of particles in various potential fields. It is intended to demonstrate the relations between absolute and relative referentials. These simulations are intended as a help for the student to get a better understanding of phenomena that are known to raise difficulties. They are a complement to traditional lectures and practical training.

As a conclusion of this production experience, the authors underline the advantages of using a development platform such as RMG, for easy building of microworlds for the teacher or for the learner and easy realization of user-friendly interfaces. The main drawback is that of any object-oriented environment, since it is necessary to know in depth a large class library to become really productive. Another drawback comes from the lack of portability of the developed software due to the necessity of efficient graphical display.

(5) Teaching Strategies for Improving Technical Diagnostic Skills (J. Moustafiadès, EDF, DER, 1 avenue du Général de Gaulle, F-92141 Clamart Cedex, France)

Scope of the work and intended users

A survey in current ITS research reveals convincing results with the expert module and the communication module in the teaching of either factual or strategic knowledge. More limited are the results of the tutoring component and the student model; that remark has to be related with the inherent complexity of pedagogical knowledge. Thus an important area of ITS's research deals presently with the art of tutoring itself. The work that is described here focuses on the representation of teaching strategies, with the purpose of teaching a rigorous technical diagnostic method rather than facts. This research was initiated in an industrial environment with the collaboration of experts in diagnostics and pedagogy; it produced the prototype SOCRATE for teaching diagnostic skills on numerical control equipment[6]. The first version was written in Common-Lisp and is running on a Texas Instruments EXPLORER-I workstation using G-Windows for graphical and multiwindowing purposes. The application has now been translated for a Macintosh universe.

Main features

First the question of how to identify pedagogical principles is addressed; by doing this, the author separates those which are relevant to the teaching topic from those which are domain independant. Several teaching strategies are presented. Some of them are directive and apply preferably to beginners; the learner has to follow the reasoning of the expert module step-by-step and to clarify each step. More flexible strategies apply in the advanced stages; the student is allowed to employ other diagnostic strategies. Then the tutoring module is able to measure acquired skills and insufficiencies of the student.

Second, different teaching strategies have to be orchestrated in computer tutoring sessions. A good strategy has to be sensitive to the student's knowledge state and to the difficulty of the task given to the student. In order to achieve this aim, a learner model is built up and maintained.

Finally, a model of the teaching activity is dressed up. The learning process is structured in a set of tutoring situations. These situations are related to the student's level according to the objectives of the topic to be taught. This leads to an ITS architecture based upon multiple tutoring modules, activated by a global tutor supervising the student's progression. The student's model consists of several submodels kept up-to-date and used by each tutoring module.

(6) Practical Application of Artificial Intelligence to Technical Diagnosis Training: SIAM (J. Courtois, Institut Supérieur d'Electronique de Paris, Paris Cedex and LAFORIA, Université Paris VI, 4 place Jussieu, F-75252 Paris Cedex, France)

Scope of the work and intended users

SIAM is a model-based expert system designed for diagnosis and meant for students in higher education (Polytechnic or University level) confronted with technical problems during practical work in physics. The aim of this system is, on the one hand, to help the student on the spot, and, on the other hand, to make him quickly autonomous when incidents occur by teaching him a diagnosis method. The system is adaptable to various kinds of equipment in different application fields such as electronics, optics, and mechanics.

Main features

In this context, designing an ITS implies providing advanced technical and pedagogical facilities. Several levels of metaknowledge are required, which enable it to be as independant as possible of its application fields and to describe, in a pedagogical and relevant way, the key steps of the cognitive process.

Most of the knowledge is represented by using models and descriptives. They allow easier acquisition of knowledge, reusability of the models and construction of relevant explanations about the diagnosis methodology.

SIAM has been used in experiments with students. Observations help to measure its impact and to evaluate design choices.

(7) A Multi-Agents Architecture to Improve the Pedagogical Capacities of ITS: QUIZ (M. R. Futtersack and J. M. Labat, LAFORIA, Université Pierre et Marie Curie, 4 place Jussieu, F-75252 Paris Cedex, France)

Scope of the work and intended users

QUIZ is a distributed ITS for learning bridge bidding. A set of generic tasks (to plan a lesson, to generate an exercise, to solve a problem, to explain a solution) is distributed among several specialists, which can perform their tasks in parallel. These agents are heterogeneous, each one uses kinds of knowledge and control strategies that are its own characteristics. Each agent owns a private working memory and communicates with the others by asynchronous message passing. QUIZ has four main agents, a tutor, which includes the dynamic instructional planner named KEPLER-ELFE, a problem solver and an explainer (which are expert systems written in SNARK) and a problem generator.

Main features

Increasing the flexibility is a key factor in improving the pedagogical capacities of ITS, because, in fact, the student's knowledge is built up only by himself. In developing this system the authors highlighted two levels of flexibility.

At the first level, the flexibility results from the determination of the curriculum, the choice of the pedagogical strategy and the degree of expertise used in the problem solver. This level is called "strategic" as the decisions taken have long term effects and are based mainly upon the student model. In the QUIZ system, the curriculum is determined by using an expert system represented by production rules. Four pedagogical strategies can be found, "expository", "guided learning", "free learning" and "gaming". Moreover the expert module solves bridge bidding problems at a beginner level and at an expert level.

At the second "tactical" level, the flexibility results mainly from the choices of exercise types, the advising, the corrections and the explanations. In QUIZ, the pedagogical actions are gathered and sequenced by means of plans, which are dynamically assembled from pieces that are memorized in libraries. If more than one plan is candidate to achieve one's aim, the planner chooses the better plan by using pedagogical metarules.

QUIZ is a running system, the knowledge of which is coded in SNARK, and implemented on an IBM 4381 machine.

CONCLUSION

It is time now to give an answer to the question included in the title of this paper. Not many prototypes are ready for broad experimentations but concepts and techniques are available that allow authors to build useful products. So what should be the objectives of future work in ITS?

A first requirement underlined the necessary multidisciplinary approach for such projects. It remains difficult but crucial to bring people from Artificial Intelligence, Cognitive Psychology and Education to work in teams from the beginning of a project to its achievement.

A second commonly agreed comment stressed the importance of early experimentation. The whole design team may learn a lot by looking at the way the students are using their system and decide fruitful changes after observations. Only an incremental design and implementation process allows for such early feedbacks, but it is certainly a realistic way of building such systems if we want them to be practically used before they become completely mature.

Another requirement deals with the necessity of planning the use of a prototype within a global learning strategy and experience shows that such a requirement should be taken into account at the very beginning of the design process.

Finally, the expression ITS itself was found inadequate to describe the target applications. Participants favoured the concept of powerful guided learning environments in which Artificial Intelligence provides techniques for building systems that really support students in learning.

Acknowledgements—Many of the ideas presented in this paper were discussed in working groups to which the author belongs especially "les journées de Cachan", "les journées FIAO de Genève"[7] and the group of authors [8]. I want to thank all my colleagues for the fruitful discussions they provided.

REFERENCES

1. Cachan, Journées EIAO du PRC-GDR intelligence artificielle (Pôle E). ENS de Cachan, Rapport 31/90 du LAFORIA, 4 place jussieu, F-75252 Paris Cedex 05 (1990).
2. Cachan Actes des 2° journées EIAO de Cachan, environnements informatiques d'apprentissage dans les disciplines scientifiques. ENS de Cachan, 61 avenue du Pt Wilson, F-94235 Cachan Cedex (1991).
3. Nicaud J. F., Aubertin C., Nguyen-Xuan A., Saïdi M. and Wach P., APLUSIX; a learning environment for acquiring problem solving abilities. *Proceedings of COGNITIVA '90*, Madrid (1990).
4. Nicaud J. F. and Saïdi M., Explications en résolution d'exercices d'algèbre. *Rev. Intell. Artific.* **4,** No. 2 (1990).
5. Bundy A., *The Computer Modelling of Mathematical Reasoning.* Academic Press, New York (1983).
6. Moustafiadès J., *Formation au Diagnostic Technique: l'Apport de l'Intelligence Artificielle* Masson, Paris (1990).
7. FIAO, Actes des journées francophones d'Informatique. La formation assistée par Ordinateur, Genève (1991).
8. Quéré M. *et al.* Systèmes experts et EAO. Editions OPHRYS, Paris (1991).
9. Blondel F. M., Schwob M. and Tarizzo M. A problem solving environment for quantitative chemistry. *Proceedings of the International Conference on Computers and Education,* Tokyo (1990).
10. Courtois J., Teaching diagnostic skills using AI: an architecture suitable for students and teachers. AAAI-91, Anaheim, Calif. (1991).
11. Labat J. M. and Futtersack M. R., *QUIZ, a Distributed Intelligent Tutoring System.* ICLS, Evanston (1991).

Computers Educ. Vol. 18, No. 1–3, pp. 71–76, 1992
Printed in Great Britain. All rights reserved

CASCADE: INTRODUCING AI INTO CBT

R. J. Hendley and N. Jurascheck

School of Computer Science, University of Birmingham, P.O. Box 363, Birmingham, England

Abstract—This paper describes a 3-year project to investigate and implement the introduction of AI techniques into tertiary education. The project involved a substantial training component as well as the production of a number of pilot projects. The paper gives the rationale for the initiative, reports on the structure of the training, gives an overview of the pilot projects and summarises some of the lessons learned.

1. RATIONALE

The training requirements of commerce and industry in the U.K. are changing rapidly, and will continue to do so over the next decade. The existing level of training is already a cause for concern: 70% of the current work force has received no training beyond the minimum school leaving age—a skill level which compares very unfavourably with that of other European countries, and with that which exists in many other parts of the world. Furthermore, demographic changes and the accelerating rate of technological change combine to cause a continuing increase in the amount of training required.

The annual number of school leavers has declined since its peak in the middle years of the previous decade, and will continue to decline throughout the rest of this century. This demographic change will lead to an increase in the average age of the work force, and will mean that the traditional route for introducing new skills into the workplace will be restricted, just as it is most required.

The rate of technological change is accelerating; it has been estimated that some two-thirds of the technology that will be in use in the year 2000 has yet to be invented. If industry and businesses are to compete effectively in a single European market, and internationally, they will need to take advantage of this technology. In order to do this they will need a labour force that is able to use and understand modern technology.

It is clear from the above that the amount of training which takes place in the U.K. will need to increase dramatically in the course of the next decade. The target population is changing and will continue to change; currently most training is aimed at school leavers. In future more training will be directed towards the existing work force and towards other groups which need to be brought (back) into the workforce, e.g. the long term unemployed, or women returners. Thus there will be a need for radical changes to the structure and delivery of training, and in the training methods employed, rather than simply an expansion of existing training, following existing patterns.

Changes in training requirements will bring about a need for changes in the methods of delivering training to trainees. Delivery of training by conventional methods will become more difficult because:

- A large proportion of training will be in new technologies. In these areas there will, by definition, be a shortage of skilled personnel and a concomitant shortage of people able to deliver training. Where such people are available, labour costs (and therefore training costs) will be high.
- Employers will want to minimise training costs. The direct costs of training will always be a concern, but the greater proportion of re-training (rather than initial training, e.g. of new employees) increases the potential costs incurred by loss of staff time. Thus there will be a greater requirement for training that is suited to the employer's needs and which is delivered when and where it is convenient for the employer.

These pressures on conventional training delivery methods will lead to movement away from large group, course-based training towards more individualised training.

1.1. Training requirements

Putting these requirements together gives us a picture of the future of training in the U.K. Looking at this picture in more detail, training will need to be:

- Cost effective: the training must work well, and yet be affordable, to encourage an increase in training.
- Appropriate to the trainee: the trainee should receive only that training which meets his/her needs. This will reduce training costs by reducing training time.
- Efficiently delivered: the appropriate training should be delivered by training methods which are matched to trainees on an individual basis. Again training costs will be reduced by reducing training time.
- Available when required: training courses should be available at any time (of year).
- Available when convenient: the units or modules which make up courses should be available at any time (of day). Employees may have short periods of time free for training, during the day or at evenings and weekends.
- Available where convenient: training should be available wherever it is convenient to the trainee (or his/her employer). This may be in the work place, at home or elsewhere.

1.2. Open learning and CBT

Given these requirements, a significant expansion in the quantity of training is only likely to be satisfied by a substantial acceleration of the movement towards open learning, whereby trainees are given relatively free access to training on a self-paced basis, and the role of the trainer moves closer to that of a manager of training. In addition, training will need to become more mobile, so that the training can go to the trainees, rather than vice versa. It is of course likely that such changes will only be achievable in practice by increased investment in training, whether from central funds or through an industrial tax as, for instance, applied in France.

Both the movement towards open learning, and the requirement for greater mobility imply that training methods themselves will be required to utilise new technologies to a much greater extent than has previously been the case. It is this factor that the CASCADE project has sought to address, by increasing the level of new technology (especially computer technology) skills and awareness among local trainers.

The most significant of the new technologies is the computer. Computers have been used in training for many years[1,2], particularly in large commercial organisations such as British Telecom and British Airways, where they can provide cost-effective training, especially for widely required basic skills. The computer can be used to present material, interact with the trainee, direct him to other materials and manage the learning process. The problems associated with conventional Computer-Based Training (CBT) are well known; they are principally the high cost of producing material, and the inflexibility of the teaching provided. The latter is due to the fixed structure of much of the material, requiring the instructional designer to have anticipated every possible student response in advance.

The use of AI (Artificial Intelligence) techniques (see, for instance[3–5]) and especially expert systems provides an opportunity to deliver more effective training and to broaden the range of situations in which CBT is appropriate. The use of a wide variety of presentational media and implementation techniques can also enlarge the scope and increase the effectiveness of CBT.

2. OVERVIEW OF THE CASCADE PROJECT

The project described here involves training trainers in computer based learning generally and, more specifically, in the application of AI and expert system techniques to CBT. The trainers receiving the training are lecturers from the tertiary education (Further and Higher) sector in the West Midlands area, with a range of subject specialisms and also a wide range of computer literacy (most were initially familiar with computers only as word processors). The project is a collaboration between the School of Computer Science (University of Birmingham), Birmingham City Council and Birmingham Expert Systems Unit.

As we have seen, one of the constraints on training growth will be the shortage of trainers skilled in the new technologies. A parallel problem exists in implementing the techniques mentioned above to increase the scope and effectiveness of CBT; i.e. there is a shortage of people with the appropriate skills. The first objective of the project is therefore to build up a pool of expertise within the FE sector, by the dissemination (*cascading*) of these skills throughout the college system over time. The other main objective is to build, use and evaluate a variety of individual training packages in a range of subject areas, all of which have an AI/expert system component.

The project was implemented in three phases, each of 1 year:

First phase—high level training: five full-time project staff were trained in CBL/CBT and AI techniques, with emphasis on the potential applications of those techniques to training problems. This phase provided a group of five highly skilled trainers to provide advice and to assist with development work in the second and third phases of the project.

Second phase—lower level training and development: twelve lecturers from Birmingham colleges were seconded part-time to the project. These were deliberately selected to provide a group with a wide range of educational (subject) knowledge, and a broad geographical coverage among the colleges in the area. These twelve received some training in CBT and AI, and then worked in collaboration with the five full time trainers from phase one to develop individual teaching packages in their specialist areas. All of the packages developed have an AI component; in most cases this is an expert system.

Third phase—implementation and evaluation: this is the current phase (1990/91), which involves the implementation of pilot projects in colleges, the evaluation of the techniques used and of the teaching material created with those techniques. Part time secondment to the project continues for the twelve trainees from phase two. This allows relief from regular teaching duties to:

- Apply the techniques learned and use the teaching packages developed.
- Assist in the evaluation of the application of AI techniques to CBT and of the packages created in phase two.
- Participate in the training of colleagues in these new techniques.

After the completion of this project it is expected that the five highly trained knowledge engineers and the twelve college lecturers will provide a pool of expertise within the Birmingham tertiary education sector which will lead to the development of further teaching packages for use in colleges and in industry. It is also hoped that the project will have provided the momentum for a sustainable increase in both the quantity and effectiveness of training, delivered as open learning with the assistance of new computer technologies.

3. OVERVIEW OF THE PILOT PROJECTS

Whilst training and the introduction of new technology in education was one of the aims of this project, an equally important aim was to be able to make recommendations regarding the successful implementation of these techniques into educational practices, in the short to medium term. To this end, each of the trainees was involved in producing at least one pilot project which will be followed through from specification to implementation in the classroom and beyond.

Rather than try to undertake this as a tightly controlled experiment (which in any case would not have been possible) these projects were selected to vary over a large number of factors. These include:

- The role of the system produced. There are a large number of ways in which AI techniques can be used in education. These include:
  —support for the administration of educational systems, for instance resource planning,
  —student advisory systems, both pastoral and educational. Two projects fall within this area. One provides an electronic prospectus with guidance from an expert system, the other is a training needs analysis system which also generates recommendations for schemes of study,
  —teaching systems. This area will be expanded upon below,

—educational advisory systems. These might, for instance, advise on course design or
  assessment,
—AI as a subject in its own right.
- The technology used. For instance, rule-based or frame based knowledge representations and
  the tools used.
- The subject area of the teaching material. All of the projects deal with vocational training,
  but they cover a range of subject areas from catering and nursing through to electronic
  engineering.
- The difficulty of the material and the abilities of the target students. The target students range
  from those with no formal qualifications to people with A-level or higher qualifications.

For teaching systems it is possible to use AI techniques in a number of ways. One way to classify
the approach is by the role played by the AI component. For instance:

- To model educational expertise. Here examples include: generating teaching strategies or
  tactics and the diagnosis of student errors.
- To model domain expertise or knowledge. There are a very wide range of possible modes in
  which this domain knowledge might be used. Some examples include:

  (i) to demonstrate behaviour. The student learns through a form of apprenticeship,
  (ii) to provide an explanation of behaviour. This would normally be regarded as an extension
       of (i),
  (iii) the student might be allowed to directly interact with the knowledge base. For instance,
        reading, debugging, extending or indeed constructing the knowledge base,
  (iv) to provide problem solving functions, either for a CBT program or directly for the
       student. Examples would include knowledge based simulations.
- To provide tools for user interaction—speech generation or input, for example.

Many examples do not, of course, fit neatly into just one of these categories. A help system, for
instance, would be likely to have both domain and educational expertise.

For teaching systems again, there are a number of possible roles that the system might
play—teaching, exercising, assessment etc.

It is important to stress that the individual projects which were developed as part of CASCADE
were not intended to function as stand-alone expert systems. In all cases the AI component was
an integrated part of a larger CBT package, which in turn was part of a larger structure.

3.1. Some examples of the pilot projects

As already stated there was a wide range of applications built. Some flavour of these can be
gained from brief descriptions of three of the projects.

- Electronics trouble shooting. This system is an exerciser for BTEC Electronic students. There
  is a library of exercises written in the BASE authoring support environment[6] and an expert
  system that selects the most appropriate exercise to present to the student. The decision is
  based upon a simple student model.
- Food hygiene. In this case there is a tutorial on food hygiene which is followed by a kitchen
  planner. The kitchen planner allows the student to build up a plan of a kitchen and then uses
  a simple expert system to validate the plan against hygiene rules and regulations, providing
  comments to the student as appropriate.
- Training needs analysis and course advisor. This system conducts a dialogue with a potential
  (commercial) trainee, identifies training needs and then generates a set of recommendations
  for courses and training material to be used. There are two expert systems used:
  —the first drives the dialogue with the trainee, selecting only questions which are believed
    to be relevant to the trainee,
  —the second builds a set of recommendations for courses on the basis of training needs and
    other background information such as experience, educational background, time con-
    straints etc.

3.2. Development environment

The project standardised on a 640 K PC as a delivery environment and on a set of software tools for development. These were:

- BASE (The Birmingham Authoring Support Environment)[6] which provides for the development of conventional CBT and the integration of expert systems and multimedia.
- IBM Linkway[7] for hypertext systems.
- RuleBase[8] for simple expert system applications.
- SD Prolog for more complex AI systems.
- Turbo Pascal for any special purpose software.

4. CONCLUSIONS

The programme is nearing the end of its third phase, with training material complete and being used, although the results of the evaluation are not yet complete.

It is clear that the *bootstrapping* process was largely successful and has led to an increasing awareness within the Birmingham FE sector of the value of computers in training and of the technology of AI and of its limitations.

It has become clear that, with access to suitable software tools, lecturers (mostly with very little computer experience) can produce high quality CBT materials fairly easily. However, for these people to succeed they do need a sound supporting infrastructure. In particular they need:

- Substantial help and advice in identifying the areas where the computer is appropriate and the techniques required to implement their training.
- Technical support to overcome, often minor, implementation problems. This support may take the form of advice or may involve implementation by an expert programmer.
- Access to reliable, easily used and quickly learned software tools.
- Critical assessment of their CBT materials—essentially editorial control.

Equally important to the success of the project was that all the people involved worked together for half a day per week which maintained enthusiasm and provided a forum for the exchange of ideas etc. and that the project also provided some relief from normal teaching duties.

The use of AI techniques in the CBT material raised a number of important issues. Whilst these are not new results, it is valuable to have them confirmed. In particular:

- The AI component needs to be integrated within the system, which is usually far from trivial to implement.
- Modelling domain knowledge, particularly that relating to procedural skills, and making it accessible to the student in an appropriate way, can be very difficult. If, for instance, an expert system is used to provide domain level problem solving, then it should be viewed as a problem solving resource, the results of which are used by a teaching component.
- The use of AI techniques to provide pedagogical expertise is relatively straight-forward and can be very effective. If, for instance, students are expected to undertake a modular computer-based course, this will normally represent a compromise across the needs of all students. Even if there is adaptability hard-wired into the course, this will be limited and error prone. A much better approach is to allow the course author to build an explicit strategy for navigating the student through the course. The experience within this project has been that this can be relatively easily achieved and that the results are very effective.
- Making knowledge explicit and easily modified leads to systems which are more consistent and more rational in their behaviour. Furthermore, the lecturers often end up with a much better understanding of their tasks. This is partly through having a mechanism in which to formally express their knowledge but also because the process of formally expressing this knowledge requires that they (possibly for the first time) need to give considerable thought to what they are doing.

It has also become clear that for CBT to be successfully used in the classroom there needs to be considerable enthusiasm from lecturers and that the college environment needs to support its use through making equipment available, and by providing the author with time for development and maintenance.

Overall, this project has shown that it is possible to produce CBT which incorporates AI techniques and that the results are suitable for use on the type of equipment presently available in tertiary colleges. The training which is produced is better than might otherwise be the case, particularly if an expert system is used to model teaching skills. In many cases, a simple system, with clearly stated knowledge can lead to much more appropriate use of a student's time. However, there does need to be a comprehensive infrastructure to support both the development and continuing use of CBT materials.

Acknowledgements—This work has been partially funded by the European Social Fund and Birmingham City Council.

REFERENCES

1. Barker P. G. (Ed.), *Multi-media Computer Assited Learning*. Kogan Page, London (1989).
2. Keller A., *When Machines Teach: Designing Computer Courseware*. Harper & Row, New York (1987).
3. Williams N. (Ed.), *AI Applications to Learning*. Training Agency, Sheffield (1989).
4. Sleeman D. H. and Brown J. S. (Eds), *Intelligent Tutoring Systems*. Academic Press, New York (1982).
5. Wenger E., *Artificial Intelligence and Tutoring Systems*. Kaufmann, Los Altos (1987).
6. Jurascheck N. and Hendley R. J., A multi-media authoring environment. *Proceedings of the 12th ECOO and 8th ICTE Conference*, Toronto, Canada (1991).
7. Linkway V1.0 Manual, IBM UK Ltd.
8. Rulebase expert system manual V1.0, Expert Systems Unit, Birmingham.

Computers Educ. Vol. 18, No. 1–3, pp. 77–83, 1992
Printed in Great Britain

0360-1315/92 $5.00 + 0.00
Pergamon Press plc

WRITING AND THE COMPUTER: AN INTELLIGENT TUTORING SYSTEMS SOLUTION

Chris Bowerman*

CCL UMIST, P.O. Box 88, Manchester M60 1QD, England

Abstract—The open-ended nature of writing at university level constitutes a problem for traditional frame-based CALL. Traditional CALL cannot cope well with open ended language use since it relies on being able to recognise fixed expressions. The types of such systems are mentioned, and the fact that writing cannot be satisfactorily handled in such a way is illustrated by examining an eclectic model of writing. This examination provides us with a set of objectives to meet. Having highlighted the nature of the writing problem and exposed the problems inherent for CALL systems developers, we present a solution based on intelligent tutoring systems technology. LICE is an intelligent tutoring system to aid students writing in German. It acts as a backend to a wordprocessor and is able to detect errors and provide tutoring as required. The system's architecture is described and the operation of the system is illustrated by examples in which LICE's key features are emphasised. We conclude by examining the success of the LICE project and gauging the extent to which it has met objectives. This discussion is then used to motivate further research.

1. INTRODUCTION

In this paper the application of Intelligent Computer Aided Language Learning (ICALL) to writing is examined. First we outline the nature of the writing problem and secondly sketch out a solution based on ICALL technology: LICE, a "Language Independent Composition Environment" for University students of German.

2. WRITING

Typical university-level modern languages tasks are to "Write something about German Society" or to "Write a letter of complaint". Such tasks are very open-ended in nature. The freeness of the input poses a problem for traditional frame-based CALL systems. Such frame-based systems rely on pattern matching, i.e. they have a fixed collection of predetermined acceptable expressions which they recognise. If the student enters expressions outside this set they will be treated as incorrect. Such a limited, closed response strategy is clearly unable to tackle open-ended writing tasks.

In order to build a CALL system to assist during writing we need a deeper understanding of the process of writing itself. This understanding will enable us to establish the requirements for our system. A number of models of the writing process have been proposed. None are totally satisfactory. Here we present an eclectic view based on [1–5]. In essence writing can be seen as a three-stage process consisting of planning, generating and revising[1].

Planning involves locating the information needed for the writing task and then organising this information. Planning takes place in two stages. Firstly, the concepts to be discussed are located and their interrelationships are established[3]. In other words a web or semantic net of ideas and interrelationships is produced at a cognitive level. A semantic net is not a suitable representation from which to produce a piece of writing since, being non-linear it does not make clear the ordering of the items in the final document. The ordering of the concepts in the semantic net is made explicit in the linear plan. The transformation of the semantic net into a linear plan is carried out by means of rules[3]. The production of the linear plan completes the first stage of the writing process.

The second stage, generating, involves expanding the plan into a full text. This involves generating objects (words, sentences, paragraphs) that fit into the plan, obey the grammar of the language and take into account such factors as audience, reader feedback and medium[4,5].

Planning and generating can therefore be seen to constitute goal based constraint satisfaction at several levels[3]. In other words the main goal of writing a given text is broken down into smaller,

---

*Present address: Sunderland Polytechnic, Langham Tower, Ryhope Road, Sunderland SR2 7EE, England.

more manageable goals. The goals achievable are not unlimited but are constrained. The writing activity is constrained by the semantic net, the linear plan and the grammar of the language. The interrelatedness of these levels means that modifying an entity at one of these levels has repercussions at others. Proficient writers are able to juggle this constraint hierarchy at ease: less proficient writers need support. The final stage, revising, consists of modifying the test according to mismatches with or modifications of the plan.

To summarise: our eclectic view of the writing activity constants of a three-stage, process-based model in which constraint-based text production is modified for a given audience. This model clearly amounts to more than just pattern matching hence traditional frame-based CALL architectures will not suffice.

A more effective writing system will need a greater understanding of text and writing and will need to support the student during the entire writing process. These more intelligent systems are based on the Intelligent CALL systems architecture (ICALL). LICE is such an intelligent system to help first year undergraduate students of German when writing. It is a cross between a support tool (which offers assistance during writing) and a training system (which offers writing instruction). LICE acts as an intelligent backend to a wordprocessor and is able both to critique and tutor.

3. INTELLIGENT SYSTEMS

There are three main components of an ICALL system[6] (the expertise, tutorial and student modules) (Fig. 1). We will first examine the nature of these modules in LICE before indicating how LICE supports the student writer.

3.1. The expertise module

The expertise module acts as a repository for knowledge. It is also used to check student input for validity. There are two types of knowledge stored in the expertise module: communicable

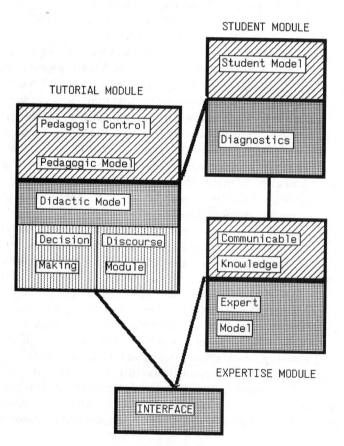

Fig. 1. LICE architecture.

```
FPSG RULE
[cat:s] -> [cat:np] [cat:vp]
[subj=np + vp]

FPSG LEXICAL ENTRIES
[cat:np] -> john
[pred=john]


[cat:vp] -> lauft
[pred=lauft<subj>]

FPSG PARSES
c-structure: [cat:s,[cat:np,john],[cat:vp,lauft]]
f-structure: [subj=[pred=john],pred=lauft<subj>]
```

Fig. 2. FPSG, e.g. John Läuft.

knowledge (the information which the system intends to convey to the student) and the expert model (the mechanisms which operate on this knowledge)[7].

Communicable knowledge on LICE is encoded in two grammars: FPSG and RST. The FPSG (functional phrase-structure grammar) grammar formalism employed in LICE is eclectic in nature, consisting of a blend of LFG f-structures[8], GPSG constituent structures (c-structures)[9] and a rule-to-rule, first order, semantics (s-structure)[10]. Since s-structure is not fully implemented in LICE it shall not be further discussed. Both c- and f-structures are discussed in more detail in Fig. 2.

c-Structures describe the syntax or word order of a sentence. FPSG c-structure is based on the LFG notion of c-structure but unlike traditional LFG makes use of feature-based rules. Analysing German poses a particular set of problems for the linguist; specifically word order and separable verbs.

In German the ordering of sentence components is much freer than in English, e.g. in the translation of "The doctor gave the patient the pill" the following translations are all valid: "Der Doktor gab dem Patienten die Pille", "Die Pille gab der Doktor dem Patienten" and "Dem Patienten gab der Doktor die Pille". The treatment of word order follows Uszkoreit[11] in generating different structures for these sentences. Also, the finite verb in German can appear in three main positions. Separate phrase structure rules for the three different verb positions are used and marked by an order feature: 1st position: y/n, e.g. questions, imperatives (e.g. Ist Les groß? Is Les tall?), 2nd position, e.g. direct statements, constituent questions (e.g. Les ist groß. "Les is tall"), verb final, e.g. subordinate clauses introduced by a complementiser, interrogative or relative pronoun (Der Junge, der groß ist "The boy who tall is"). Separable prefixes (e.g. aus-gehen, "to go out") are treated as independent lexical units known as *sepref* and are associated with the verb by means of features. c-Structure is thus a fairly standard feature-based phrase structure grammar. We will now examine f-structure.

In LICE f-structure is used to provide additional grammatical information to c-structure, e.g. the subject and object of a sentence. It is largely traditional in annotating c-structure rules with functions such as objects and predicates. The f-structure formalism is extended to allow filler restrictions to be placed on functions, e.g. subjects of particular verbs may be restricted to accept only animate entities. Not only does this enable the number of possible parses (interpretations) of a sentence to be reduced but it provides additional information which may be conveyed to the student. Four possible fillers have been used: +/- animacy, +/- abstractness, +/- temporal, +/- action. Close attention has been paid to subcategorisation (particularly of verbs) and this has been based on Helbig and Schenkel[12]. f-Structure is thus fairly traditional in approach but is extended to allow filler restrictions to be placed on functions. The second aspect of communicable knowledge is that of test organisation. Rhetorical structure theory (RST) has been adopted to this end. RST proposes a set of relationships which link sentences together to form larger units which are themselves interlinked to produce the overall text structure. Thompson and Mann[13] say little about how to compute text structure using RST. The approach adopted in LICE is to formalise RST relations as phrase-structure rules. Analysis at RST level then becomes a parsing problem. This can be seen in the following simplified sentences.

(1) Die Fließbandarbeit ist populär (Production line work is popular).
(2) Die Fließbandarbeit wurde vor dem Krieg entwickelt (Production line work was developed before the war).
(3) Nach dem Krieg wurde die Fließbandarbeit überall benutzt (After the war production line work was used everywhere).

The following (simplified) RST rules are required.

TEXT → BACKGROUND
BACKGROUND → NUCLEUS[subject = X], SEQUENCE[subject = X]
SEQUENCE → SATELLITE[subject = X,nach NP]
               NUCLEUS[subject = X,vor NP]

The categories of the RST rules match sentences by checking the constraints in the square brackets against the FPSG parse for that sentence. With a bottom-up chart parser such rules produce the following parse:

[BACKGROUND:1-3,NUCLEUS:1,[SEQUENCE:2-3,NUCLEUS:2, SATELLITE:3]]

What this parse indicates is that (2) and (3) form a sequence of events, i.e. they both have the same subject (Fließbandarbeit or production line work) and they both relate this subject to a particular point in time (der Krieg, i.e. the war) by means of "vor" (before) and "nach" (after). The sequence of events described in (2) and (3) provides background information to (1) which has the same subject. In other words in (1–3) the text is structured so that (2–3) provides additional background information about (1). Since we are able to work out the structure of the text we will consider it to be valid. If text structure cannot be established then the system will use the same ill-parsing techniques on the RST as the FPSG grammar to remedy the problem (see diagnostics below).

We have now covered the communicable knowledge used in LICE and can turn our attention to the second aspect of the expertise module: the expert model. In LICE this is based on a parser (a program able to understand text). The chart parser work bottom-up, breadth-first and is non deterministic. Representations are produced at each of the three levels of PFSG (for sentences) and RST (for text). If parsing proceeds without hitch further text may be entered but if errors are detected then the diagnostics of the student module will determine their nature. This module will now be examined.

3.2. The student module

The student module performs two main tasks: diagnosing errors in student input and recording them for use by the tutorial module[14]. There are two main types of error with which LICE deals: missing constituents (words) and constraint violations (e.g. subject-verb agreement failing to match). Below we look at an example of constraint violation.

Diagnostics are performed by ill-parsing strategies. When the expertise module fails to produce a complete parse for a sentence bottom-up, it is because constraints at one of the levels of FPSG have blocked the application of a rule (e.g. person and number features do not agree). Diagnostics then take control and examine the chart left by the bottom-up parser. Modified or relaxed rules are proposed by a top down parser to produce an "S" node (i.e. a correct sentence). The modifications required (e.g. forcing agreement) are noted in the student model.

The top-down parser is not a pure one. It must spot constituents that have been found bottom-up and use them, must propose missing constituents and must relax existing constraints to allow the parse to continue. This produces a large search space—particularly since some edges will be unanchored (i.e. when omitted constituents are detected their size may well be unknown). In order to manage the search space heuristics are used (e.g. prefer edges generated bottom-up, prefer edges covering the greatest amount of the input string).

For example in "The children drinks the milk", the parser would not be able to match "the children" with "drinks the milk" because these two parts of the sentence do not agree. In order to work out what is wrong the parser focuses on the second component of the sentence and determines the precise nature of the agreement problem by means of a (simplified) rule such as:

IF noun__phrase(third person, plural)
   AND verb__phrase(third person, plural)
→ make verb__phrase(third person, singular)
   AND add__student__model(agreement)
   AND reason("Subject was plural and verb was singular") (.2,1)

This rule states that if the subject and verb do not agree they should be made to agree by modifying the verb. The system then notes a slight problem with agreement in the student model so that if the student makes the same mistake repeatedly then the tutorial module can conduct a remedial session.

The type of student model used in LICE is teacher centred. The information held consists of a set of beliefs about the student's learning, e.g. "Sally finds agreement difficult", "Sally finds the genitive very difficult". Errors are divided into categories. Each category has an associated number or belief measure. This measure expresses the degee of belief that a particular category is problematic for the student. When a belief measure exceeds a threshold the tutorial module takes action. Below this threshold no action will be taken. The belief measures are updated as a result of errors detected by the diagnostic rules.

Error categories are not recorded as separate entities but are linked together in a tree. The belief measures of sub-categories are propagated up the tree to super-categories by taking the average of the values of their sub-categories.

Using a tree representation for the student model has a number of advantages (Fig. 3). High belief measures indicate the topics most in need of attention and enable tutoring to focus on the student's needs. An overall measure for a class of errors or specific measures for given errors can be obtained, offering a viable granularity of representation. The occurrence of a number of different but related errors will increase the belief measure for their supercategory thus increasing the probability that tutoring will be offered before too many mistakes have been made. At the end of a session a clear overall picture of the student's weaknesses and strengths is available for summary. Thus, the student module diagnoses student mistakes by using a top-down parser to detect the error and a production system to relax the constraints so that a parse can be completed. A belief-based student model is held. Having determined the nature of and recorded the mistakes the student is making, the system then hands control over to the tutorial component to determine what teaching needs to be performed.

3.3. The tutorial module

The tutorial module selects from its repertoire of teaching operations to suit the circumstances [7]. There are two factors to consider: pedagogics and didactics. Pedagogics incorporates both pedagogic control and the pedagogic model where the former concerns the overall teaching

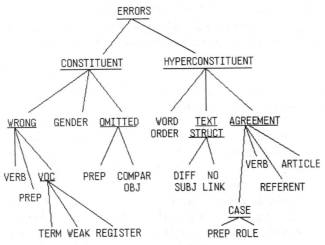

Fig. 3. Tree-based student model.

philosophy; namely the degree of student/system control, the nature of lesson planning (opportunistic or not) and the language teaching approach (meaning or grammar based).

The degree of student/system control is fixed to "student". LICE is a coaching environment, hence the main emphasis is on supporting students whilst writing and giving them a fair degree of freedom. For similar reasons planning is fixed to opportunistic, i.e. when coaching advanced learners there is little hope of planning the errors they make when freely generating text, hence it is better to react to problems as they arise.

LICE employs two teaching approaches[15]: communicative (meaning based) and grammar translation. The system starts up in communicative mode switching to grammar translation if the average number of errors per sentence over the first five sentences is low. Communicative teaching is reselected when the average number of errors per sentence is high. The switching mechanisms are relatively crude, but the aim of employing different approaches is intended to demonstrate the viability of such a scheme rather than to produce a complete computational model of the approaches. Once selected, the current degree of control, approach, threshold and degree of planning are all maintained in the pedagogic model for later reference by the system.

The second aspect of the tutorial module is didactics: didactics is involved with making decisions as to what and when to teach. Three factors come into play: diagnostic, pedagogic and didactic (domain and pragmatic) constraints. Diagnostic constraints relate to the areas in which the student is under-achieving and needs help as detected by diagnostics in the student model. Pedagogic constraints relate to the three factors (approach, control and planning) mentioned above. Didactic constraints come in two types: domain constraints which indicate which subjects must be taught before others and pragmatic constraints which involve issues such as not re-teaching the same point without having given the student a chance to absorb the new material and not repeating the same topic by mistake.

In LICE, as in MENO[7], a distinction is made between the high level didactic decisions (teaching strategies) and lower level dialog operations (teaching tactics and techniques). LICE's tutoring decisions module operates down to the level of teaching strategies at which point it hands over control to a discourse module which produces the lower-level system output. It is not intended to produce the discourse module. The output produced by LICE will consist of the calls that would be made to the discourse module. The calls made to the discourse module are based on a MENO-like discourse net. Six calls are possible: PROPOSE(X) (suggest that a problem exists with X), VERIFY(X) (check that there is a problem with X), REASON(X) (give the reason for the mistake X), REPAIR(X) (alleviate the problem with X) and IGNORE(X) (disregard the problem with X). These calls are made within certain ranges of the student module's belief measures.

On its first occurrence the problem will be PROPOSED (e.g. "A preposition has been omitted"), on the second occurrence the system will additionally explain the REASON for the error and on the third occasion the system will TUTOR. Thereafter the system will either give the REASON for the mistake or TUTOR. These decisions are passed to the interface for presentation to the user.

The tutorial module is thus made up of pedagogic control which establishes the overall teaching approach for the didactic system. The didactic system then chooses the topic to teach and when to teach it based on domain, diagnostic and pedagogic constraints. These choices are recorded in the didactic model for later reference (e.g. to ensure that topics are not over laboured).

3.4. LICE in operation

We have examined the mechanisms underlying LICE in theory. Now we shall look at the way in which LICE supports users in practice during writing.

In the prewriting stage, before essay writing commences, the system agrees an essay plan with the user. This could either consist of establishing both a task, topic and a text-type from scratch, e.g. a persuasive letter on disarmament, or informing the system of a predefined task, text-type and topic. This constitutes the prewriting section of the system which is not yet fully developed and users are currently restricted to a predefined topic, text-type and task.

After prewriting, the student moves to generating sentences and where necessary revising them. The sentences are input via the user-interface (snIF). snIF passes a user's sentence to the expertise module which checks the sentence for grammatically. If the sentence is well-formed no action is taken and the next sentence is examined. If, however, the expertise module cannot understand the sentence it is sent to the student module which diagnoses and notes errors. The tutorial module takes over after the student module. It looks at the type of error being made by the student (these are held in the student model). If there are no serious errors the tutorial module will allow the text sentence to be input. If, however, there are serious errors then the tutorial module takes remedial action before allowing the next sentence to be entered. This is the main way in which LICE supports users when writing: by detecting errors and reporting them to students at opportune moments so that they are able to revise their text on the spot.

The cycle of entering the sentence, checking for grammaticality, recording any errors and tutoring any serious problems constitutes the basic sequence of operations in LICE. This sequence of operations is repeated until all the text has been entered. At this point the text structure is checked against the plan agreed during prewriting. Any tutoring necessary on the text structure than takes place (offering further scope for revising text) before an overall appreciation of the student's performance is given and the session terminates.

4. CONCLUSION

It can be seen that LICE is an almost complete ICALL system (except for the prewriting and discourse components). As such the viability of ICALL has been proven. The system only handles one domain, text-type and language at present but the mechanisms employed are independent of these and more are planned to prove generality. The endeavour has been held back by imperfect knowledge of linguistics, teaching and learning and has had to rely on introspection. More extended research is required both formally and into extending the present prototype system in order for its full potential to be realised.

Acknowledgements—This work was completed under the supervision of Dr C. Zähner (CCL UMIST). The author is currently supported by an SERC studentship.

REFERENCES

1. Flower L. and Hayes J., Writing research and the writer. *Am. Psychol.* **41,** 1098–1105 (1986).
2. Kintsch W., Towards a model of text comprehension and production. *Psychol. Rev.* **85,** 363–394 (1978).
3. Sharples M. and O'Malley C., A framework for the design of a writer's assistant. In *AI and Human Learning* (Edited by Self J.). Chapman & Hall, London (1988).
4. Randquist M., The TT schema as a necessary prerequisite of skilled writing. *Text* **5,** 371–385 (1985).
5. Miller L., Computers for composition: a stage model approach to helping. *Visible Lang.* **20,** 188–218 (1986).
6. Elsom-Cook M., AI and CAI at the OU. *CITE Report 4.* Open University, Milton Keynes (1986).
7. Wenger E., *AI and Tutoring: a Computational Approach to the Communication of Knowledge.* Kaufmann, Los Altos (1987).
8. Sells P., *Lectures on Contemporary Syntactic Theories* CSLI, Stanford (1985).
9. Gazdar G., Klein E., Pullum K. and Sag I., *Generalised Phase-structure Grammar.* Blackwell, Oxford (1985).
10. Dowty D., Wall R. and Peters S., *Introduction to Montague Semantics* Reidel, Dordrecht (1981).
11. Uszkoreit H., Word order and constituent structure in German. *CSLI Lecture Notes No. 8.* Stanford (1987).
12. Helbig G. and Schenkel W., *Wortebuch zur Valenz und Distribution deutscher Verben* VEB Bibliographisches Institut, Leipzig (1982).
13. Thompson S. and Mann W., Rhetorical structure theory: a framework for the analysis of texts. *IPRA Papers in Pragmatics* 1 (1987).
14. Polson M. and Richardson G., *Foundations of Intelligent Tutoring Systems.* Erlbaum, Hillsdale, N.J. (1988).
15. Richards J. and Rogers T., *Approaches and Methods in Language Teaching, A Description and Analysis.* Cambridge University Press (1986).

Computers Educ. Vol. 18, No. 1–3, pp. 85–88, 1992
Printed in Great Britain. All rights reserved

AN ENVIRONMENT FOR PHYSICAL GEOGRAPHY TEACHING

P. L. Brusilovsky[1] and T. B. Gorskaya-Belova[2]

[1]ICSTI, Kuusinen Strasse 21b, Moscow-125252 and [2]School 243, Oktyabrsky pereulok 11, Moscow, U.S.S.R.

Abstract—Using computers in teaching will have the best effect only when we seriously revise our approach to education itself. In this paper we suggest a possible computer approach to learning geography, based on modelling. To verify this approach we have developed a computer-based unit for the physical geography course which included an intelligent learning environment and which is described in this paper. We tried to use the capabilities of modern hardware (graphics, colour, sound), a modern user interface (windows, menus, icons) and experience of artificial intelligence (AI) applied to education.

INTRODUCTION

Geography was one of the first domains where AI methods were applied for educational purposes [1–3]. The idea of modelling as a universal approach to studying the complex interrelations within the subject became popular long ago in such knowledge domains as maths, physics, and economics. Following Davydov[4], four main characteristics of models are important from a pedagogical point of view.

Models are a means of cognition
Models are representative of the original object which are more appropriate for learning about that object in some way
Models retain the main characteristics of the original
Models are specific to each original object

Taking these characteristics of models into account, the process of modelling can be regarded as a movement from complex, byzantine reality to a model in which reality is deliberately simplified, but with the most significant relations and processes emphasized. The process of dismodelling (from model to reality) allows new insight, enabling the learner to penetrate deeper into the nature of reality.

We consider modelling to be the main method for acquiring knowledge. Dealing with a model, the student learns about it element by element. Gradually, the model becomes constrictive as its limits are appreciated, leading to demands for a more sophisticated model, and so on. Moving from model to model, students absorb the "architecture" of science. The goal is to organize this movement intellectually. Thus the entire course must be assembled as an expanding system of interacting models. Within a modelling approach the computer plays the role of an educational laboratory for investigating the world. This approach is quite well developed now in geography education, where it is regarded as one of the four main approaches to using the computer[5].

Traditionally, the notion of modelling or simulation is related to building mathematical or quantitative models of any process or situation. This tradition originates from the field of physics, and quantitative models are used successfully in all the subdomains of physics. Unfortunately, geography seems to be not quite as appropriate a field for quantitative modelling. As David Unwin writes[5, p. 29]:

> "Surprisingly, since a very large amount of courseware making use of simulation techniques has been developed for use in primary and secondary school geography, it seems to be received wisdom that real world systems of interest to geographers in higher education are too complex to be modelled in any useful way for CAL".

As a result, the use of modelling techniques in CAL has concentrated on the obviously "quantitative" areas such as climatology or population demography. One of the possible solutions

System: Choose the geographic position of your island

Student: <puts the point on the computer map>

System: Decide the structure of the ocean bed in the island location

Student: Continental rise (platform)

System: Decide the type of the Earth's crust

Student: Oceanic

System: Decide the origin of the island

Student: Continental

System: Decide the tectonic structure of the island

Student: Platform

System: Decide the relief of the island

Student: Low mountains

System: Decide the climate of the island

Student: Check <top level menu item>

System: <verifies the student's options> The type of the Earth's crust is oceanic - an error!

If the structure of the ocean bed in the island location is a continental rise (platform), then

the type of the Earth's crust is continental. The relief of the island is low mountains - an

error! If the tectonic structure of the island is a platform, then the relief of the island is a

plain.

Fig. 1. The simplest dialogue within the test-kind script. All comment are in ⟨ ⟩ brackets.

to this problem is the use of qualitative (vs quantitative) models in education[6]. This approach is quite well developed now in the field of medical education. Two examples of the use of qualitative models in the field of geography are the well-known systems Meteorology Tutor[2] and Why[3]. Instead of mathematical formulas, knowledge about simulated processes or situations is represented in qualitative models in the form of transition networks[2], scripts[3] or rules[6]. Thus qualitative modelling approach leads us into the field of artificial intelligence and expert systems.

The structure of the learning environment

The learning environment ISLAND* is for 13–14 yr old students taking a course in the physical geography of oceans and continents. It is the practical result of our studying the problem of modelling with the aid of computers. The pedagogical goal of the environment is to make a transference from the isolated and simple notions of physical geography to the computer modelling of their essential relations in a natural geographical complex.

The computer environment presents several related systems (scripts) realized on an IBM-compatible PC. Working with one of these systems, students find themselves on an island, the position of which can be chosen (depending on the script) either by the student, the system, or the teacher on the map displayed on the screen. Then, knowing the position, the student must decide the natural characteristics of the island: its origin, tectonic structure, climate, the type of crust, soil, flora and fauna. The system enables the student to choose the island in the north part of the Atlantic ocean, and to determine all its natural components, which depend on the position, and to verify the answers. The main abilities of the system can be demonstrated on the example of simplest "test" script (Fig. 1). At the start, the system gives to the student a computer map, where the island's position is marked. With each subsequent question the system offers a menu of possible answers, from which the student makes a selection. The actions of the system are not predetermined, as in traditional CAI systems. For any island position and any of the natural components chosen, the system can verify and comment on all the student's answers. Such capabilities are provided by expert knowledge of the natural complex regularities in it. The knowledge base consists of the rules representing the different natural complex relations. These rules are offered in the IF-THEN form

*The first research script of an ISLAND environment was designed and tested during the summer International Computer School in 1989 in 1989 in Dubna. The authors were joined by psychologist Dr Vadim Khoziev (Moscow University) and Slovakian, German, Bulgarian and Russian schoolboys. All the languages of the test subjects, and English, were supported by the system. The "test" script was written by Moscow University student M. Zyryanov in 1990. It is being used in practice during geography lessons at Moscow School 243.

IF the structure of the ocean bed is a continental rise,

THEN the type of the Earth's crust is continental,

AND the tectonic structure of the island is a platform.

IF the type of the Earth's crust is continental,

THEN the origin of the island is continental.

IF the tectonic structure of the island is a platform,

THEN the relief of the island is a plain.

Fig. 2. The rules from the ISLAND knowledge base that are relevant to the dialogue in Fig. 1.

(Fig. 2). There are about 60 rules, obtained from several experts in the field of physical geography. In addition, the system has a simple inference machine which can apply the rules to the chosen options, put them into logic chains, and make inferences from the data. The knowledge base and inference machine form a simple expert system, which is the heart of the ISLAND environment. The knowledge in the ISLAND environment can be used in two main regimes: demonstrative and control. In the demonstrative regime, the system can give examples of both forward and backward inference: a student or teaching inputs the climate and the system shows the relevant animals (consequence); and vice versa if the relief is known to be flat, information about its origin may be requested (the reason). In the control regime the system can verify whether or not students are right in their choice of the natural components, the characteristics of the given island. To obtain it, the system solves the same problem comparing its own answers with the student's step by step. With such a verification technique, the system can not only evaluate the student's answer as right or wrong, but also check whether the logical inference was right and even determine what lack of knowledge caused the student's current mistake. It is the student's knowledge of the determinancy principle in the island natural complex structure which is tested as well as the ability to think logically using this knowledge. In spite of having all the rules stored in the knowledge base in a special internal format suitable for processing, the system can generate inferences, information about errors and explanations in natural language (Fig. 1). All the natural language messages may be generated in any of the several languages (Russian, English etc.) provided by the system. For introducing a new language we only have to form vocabulary information files for this language.

Student interface to the ISLAND environment

Many of the facilities of a graphical user interface are used, including colour and sound. The choice of geographic position of the island can be made by students themselves with the aid of a screen computer map of the northern part of the Atlantic ocean. The current location is marked on the map with a graphic marker which can be moved over the map using the arrow keys to any desired position. To select the proper value of each of the island components, iconic and text menus are used. Each possible value of the natural complex components is provided with a different icon. Movement along the list is by means of the arrow keys. Icons can be used to form a so-called report screen, which is the "instant look-up" feature of the system. A smaller map shows the island's position and one icon for each component. If the value of a component has already been selected by the student, then the corresponding icon appears, and for the remaining components question marks are displayed. The report screen provides the student with visual information on progress. It shows visually the mistakes made by crossing out the icons of incorrect selections. In demonstration mode, the icon is supplied with a text string underneath giving the name of the corresponding parameter value, e.g. "Low mountains", "High mountains". In test mode all icons are textless—and the selection of the name of the icon is one of the student's tasks (this is a requirement of the teachers who use the system).

Dialogue scripts

The environment also enables us to build various teaching scripts as separate systems for various educational targets. At the present time two scripts have been built—"research" and "test". In the research script the student leads. Having noted the position of the island, other components may be fixed in any order, or the report screen may be requested to verify the choice, or a choice may be changed and checked again. The research script gives a student an environment for independent work and experiment, which is becoming more and more popular for the educational systems. This script can also be used by a tutor when explaining or revising the material. The test script is aimed to control and estimate the students knowledge. Here the system leads. It first asks the student to choose the position of an island and then select from the menus the values of all the remaining eight components. Finally the system checks up the choice, displays the errors on the report screen, and generates statements about the errors together with explanations and gives a mark.

Classroom test of ISLAND

Experiments with the ISLAND test script were made in two ways: in a paper-based exercise and with the computer in control. The aims of this experiment were: first, to determine the level of the students' accomplishment concerning the idea of the unity of nature; second, to evaluate the effectiveness of computer control; third, to compare the results of the paper exercise and computer control.

In the first stage, the students were given questions of various kinds and of increasing complexity.

(1) Explain the peculiarities of a given natural environment, e.g. explain what the value of a component means "in reality"

(2) Determine the geographic position of the given natural environment, i.e. where on the map could an island have this climate, flora etc.

(3) Determine and describe an absent component in a natural environment, i.e. all but one of the components are known—try to derive the missing value from the other components

(4) Find the mistakes in a description of a natural environment, e.g. tigers in an arctic climate

Four of the eight students tested coped with all tasks, two of them failed the third and fourth types, and two of them only managed the first type. Such a result confirms our supposition that students lack of a full conception of a natural environment, because only those who managed the third and fourth types established the relations between the components in ten deep structure levels.

The same students were given a test script of ISLAND. The students had already had experience with computers, so we can compare their answers with the real knowledge level because the novelty element is excluded. We expected that the results would be poorer compared with the paper control, because of the lack of modelling program experience. But the results with computer control turned out to be higher. Five of those tested, after establishing the component interrelations, created the natural environmental model (which corresponds to solving all the paper tasks). Two of the students failed to determine one component (it corresponded to solving three types of tasks), and one student failed to make a model of a natural environment.

The extended help system raised the chance of weak students to solve the problem, and the three-level help structure enables the failing student to solve the problem in the end, which is impossible with the paper control, where a weak student simply gives up. The advanced students after further experience with the program were able to create a mental model of a natural environment. Thus, the number of students with the complete concept of a natural environment after having worked with the computer program increased from four to seven.

Acknowledgement—The author is grateful for the assistance of Dr David Unwin, Department of Geography, University of Leicester, during the preparation of this paper for publication.

REFERENCES

1. Carbonell J. R., AI in CAI: an artificial intelligence approach to computer aided instruction. *IEEE Trans. Man–Mach. Syst.* **11**, 190–202 (1970).
2. Brown J. S., Burton R. R. and Zdybel F., A model-driven question–answering system for mixed-initiative computer-assisted instruction. *IEEE Trans. Syst. Man Cybernet.* **3**, 248–257 (1973).
3. Stevens A. L. and Collins A., The goal structure of a socratic tutor. In *Proc. of the 1977 Annual ACM Conference*, pp. 256–263, Seattle (1977).
4. Davydov V. V., *Problems of Developing Education*. Pedagogika, Moscow (in Russian) (1986).
5. Unwin D. J., Using computers to help students learn: computer assisted learning in geography. *Area* **23.1**, 25–34 (1991).
6. Clancey W. J., The role of qualitative models in instruction. In *Artificial Intelligence and Human Learning* (Edited by Self J.), pp. 49–68. Chapman & Hall, London (1988).

Computers Educ. Vol. 18, No. 1–3, pp. 89–100, 1992
Printed in Great Britain. All rights reserved

LEARNING BY BUILDING RULE-BASED MODELS

Mary Webb

The Advisory Unit for Microtechnology in Education, Hatfield AL10 8AU, England

Abstract—Computer based modelling offers opportunities for the enhancement of the learning environment. A study of teachers' perceptions of the types of modelling activities which they felt could be usefully undertaken by children suggested that many of the tasks fall in the category of qualitative models of logical reasoning. The Modus Project, a collaboration between the Advisory Unit for Microtechnology in Education, Hatfield and King's College, London has implemented a rule based expert system shell, Expert Builder, which makes the knowledge structure and inference mechanism clearly visible to, and manipulable by, the user through a graphical user interface. The shell has been widely tested by the educational institutions which have joined the Modus Club. Results of these investigations have led to an outline of a methodology for expert system modelling as a learning activity. It is hoped that this can be further developed and documented so that teachers can use it with their students and gradually enable the students to undertake more of the modelling process by themselves. The shell, with some minor modifications can be used for a variety of simple modelling activities and the project intends to extend these facilities by combining the environment provided in Expert Builder with that of another modelling environment, Model Builder which provides facilities for quantitative and dynamic modelling.

INTRODUCTION

Developments in the curriculum which emphasize child centred, constructivist and problem-solving approaches, together with opportunities provided by more powerful and friendly software have led to a new interest in computer-based modelling. There is a growing body of evidence, e.g. Osbourne and Gilbert[1], Riley[2] and Cumming and Abbott[3] that computer-based modelling offers opportunities for the enhancement of the learning environment. Modelling activities may help the learner to develop higher level thinking and problem solving skills as well as leading to increased understanding of the subject matter as a result of selecting, restructuring and reexamining knowledge. In addition, the increasing importance of modelling in business, industry and research suggests that students should understand the processes and develop skills in modelling. The National Curriculum in England and Wales has recognized this opportunity by including modelling in the attainment target for information capability[4]. This expertise is expected to be gained through activities which arise out of study in various curriculum areas.

A study of teachers' perceptions of the types of modelling activities which they felt could be usefully undertaken by children suggested that many of the tasks fall in the category of qualitative models of logical reasoning[5]. These models are based on heuristics rather than precise mathematical relationships and are concerned with relationships between concepts such as causality and dependence. Models of this type can be constructed to guide decision making, diagnose a problem, make predictions and classify objects. Many teachers felt that it would be desirable to provide tools to aid pupils in structuring and ordering ideas and relationships.

The software tools which were available for constructing this type of model included logic programming languages such as Prolog and expert system shells. Both of these environments are declarative in approach so that modellers can focus on specifying their knowledge rather than on creating procedural structures. Some studies have been done with children using Prolog[6] and with Mitsi, a simpler front end to Prolog[3] but a significant drawback of this approach was the lack of graphical facilities. Some studies had been carried out using a commercial expert system shell, Xi, in schools and these concluded that the process of building an expert system as an aid to learning merits research but the requirements in such a shell for education were not the same as for business and industry and commercial shells such as Xi were not suitable[7–9]. Another study by Wideman and Owston[10] suggested that "the externalization of reasoning demanded by the knowledge base development task forced students to employ rigorous and systematic thinking in order to succeed". Further studies in secondary schools[11,12], found that it was useful for students to draw diagrams on paper to clarify ideas and an important conclusion was that a diagrammatic view of the rule structure was desirable. Studies in primary schools[13] also suggested that a diagrammatic approach is desirable and that "expert system shells can provide a useful tool by which young children can be made aware of the underlying structure of their knowledge".

These studies had all made use of a rule-based approach probably because these shells were more readily available to schools. Another study[14] suggested the use of frames as the basis of a knowledge representation language for school children. Frames are particularly useful for representing objects and therefore facilitate the construction of classification systems but in order to build a greater variety of models it is necessary to integrate production rules and frames[15,16]. The language then becomes much more complex and it is considerably more difficult to provide the model builders with a clear view of how the modelling metaphor works.

As a result of these studies conducted by members of the project team and others, the Modus Project, a collaboration between the Advisory Unit for Microtechnology in Education, Hatfield and King's College, London implemented a rule-based expert system shell, which made the knowledge structure and interference mechanism clearly visible to and manipulable by the user through a graphic user interface. The shell, which is called Expert Builder works in a similar way to commercially available rule-based expert system shells, the major difference being the graphical interface and the lack of some of the more complex facilities.

In order to obtain the views of a larger section of the education community, the Modus Club was set up and membership was open to any educational institution. As well as a regular newsletter, members received a copy of Expert Builder and were invited to make comments and suggestions and send examples of models they or their students had created. The membership includes approx. 230 educational institutions ranging from primary schools to higher education and including some advisory centres and schools of education. The largest group are secondary schools. Some members returned questionnaires, others commented verbally. Secondary school members, who did not provide feedback were contacted by telephone. A number of workshops were held where teachers were able to work with, and assess, the possibilities of the software. In addition, more detailed investigations have been carried out in two primary schools and two secondary schools. There are also a number of overseas members and centres in Finland and Moscow are undertaking classroom-based research with the software. A Finnish version has been produced and a Russian version is under development.

In this paper the results of these wide ranging investigations to date are described and the kinds of models which teachers and students have constructed or attempted to construct are classified. Issues arising from classroom experiences are discussed and an attempt is made to outline a methodology for modelling activities using rule based expert system shells. The methodology may have wider applications. The strengths and limitations of this type of environment are also identified and some pointers for future software development in this field are provided. Some of the issues raised and conclusions reached from the CAL91 workshop which focused on these questions are also outlined.

NATURE OF EXPERT BUILDER

Expert Builder is a rule-based expert system shell with a graphical user interface. It runs under Microsoft Windows (versions 2 and above). Using Expert Builder a qualitative model is constructed by building a logical diagrammatic structure on the screen using mouse-controlled tools (see Fig. 1). The diagram consists of boxes with textual clauses connected together into a logical construction using the logical operators AND, OR and NOT. The boxes are linked by threads using the cotton reel tool. When the lower part of box a is linked to the upper part of box b, a depends on b. In rule form this can be read in two ways:

   a if b
   if b THEN a

The diagrammatic representation obviates the need to choose between these methods of representing rules. The user can interpret the diagram in either of these ways or view it as a causal dependency structure. It is helpful to avoid the necessity of using one of these textual representation of rules because each is more suitable in certain circumstances and they are used in other programming languages to have different meanings. The IF THEN construction is used as a procedural representation in many programming languages whereas in this system it is a declarative structure representing a piece of knowledge. Rules of the "conclusion if premise" structure are appropriate if the users are constructing a system using a top-down approach where they are deciding what the possible conclusions are first and secondly specifying the conditions under which they would apply. Where the user is working forwards from the conditions towards the conclusions, it may be more intuitive to think of the rules as IF THEN rules. The diagrammatic structure also emphasizes the logical nature of the construction therefore minimizing the tendency to confuse it with natural language which was noted in investigations with text-based shells[11].

Many qualitative models require a number of levels of rules to be specified leading to a diagram where rules are chained together as shown in Fig. 2.

In addition to the clause boxes there are special boxes containing the word "advice". An advice box can be joined to the top of any clause box thereby designating that clause as advice to be proved by the system. This provides the goals and starting point for the search strategy of the inference engine.

The inference mechanism uses a backward-chaining depth-first search. When it reaches a statement for which there is no condition, it asks the question of the user.

The user can ask questions of an Expert Builder model in two ways. Firstly, the user can click on any statement box with the question mark tool to ask "is this statement true or false?" The system tries to prove that statement to be true using its inference mechanism. The result is shown on the screen by means of the boxes becoming coloured or shaded as shown in Fig. 2. The second method is to click on an "advice" box in which case the system will try to prove a piece of advice to the user starting from the left of the screen. A person building a system can designate any number of statements to be "advice" statements by linking them to an advice box and the system will try to prove each in turn. When an advice clause is proved it is presented to the user in a dialogue box. The user can also volunteer answers by using the "tick" or "cross" tool to click on the statements. This provides a fast method of testing the model with different sets of data and simulates a forward-chaining process.

There are two views of the model: the normal view and a long distance view. The latter is used to move around on a large model and to view the execution trace and hence detect inconsistencies in the logic.

Most expert system shells have an "explanation" facility. This is generally a trace of the reasoning used. This has been criticised[17] for being of little help to the end user who is solving

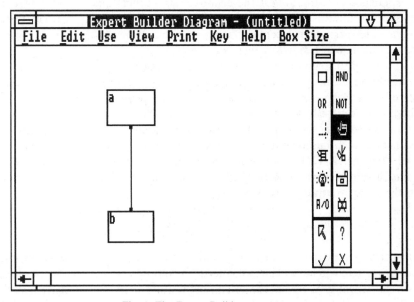

Fig. 1. The Expert Builder program.

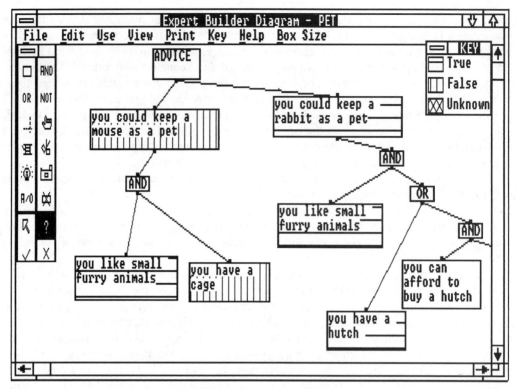

Fig. 2. The diagrammatic trace of the inference process.

a problem. However, it can be helpful as a debugging aid. Expert Builder provides the facility as a dynamic diagram as already described. In addition, Expert Builder has a facility for the model builder to provide a page of explanation, which may be an illustration, for each clause. There is, therefore, opportunity and encouragement for the learner, who is building a model, to explain the terms being used.

Teachers views on the potential of a graphical expert system shell

Of the 30 members who returned questionnaires, all but 2 saw potential for students to learn by building models in this environment in a wide range of subject areas. All but 5 of these had substantial experience of using IT. Of the approx. 120 teachers and advisory teachers who took part in workshops using this software, approx. 70% thought that this type of software could be useful across a wide range of subjects but some science and maths teachers thought that a more quantitative treatment was needed in their subjects.

They found the logical structure diagram for constructing rules generally easy to work with once they had understood its nature. Clearly any diagrammatic representation will use conventions which must be learnt. A few teachers commented that they would like the diagram to be the other way up. These were generally approaching a task from the conditions and working towards the conclusions and in some cases they revised their view when they tackled further tasks. A small group of teachers who had used systems with textual rules of the "conclusion if premise" form had previously felt that the IF THEN construction was more natural for children. They now felt that the diagrammatic representation circumvented this issue and provided a better alternative by focusing on the logical nature of the structure.

TYPES OF MODELS

When constructing an expert system model the builder needs to have a purpose in mind to envisage how the system will be used. Modellers are encouraged, in the documentation, to construct the model so that it will give advice to the end user rather than simply being a set of knowledge which the user can question, because this makes it easier to design and structure the model.

Table 1. Types of models
developed by users

Advisory	35
Diagnostic	7
Classification	6
Planning	4

In the documentation, models were described in four categories, advisory, diagnostic, planning and classification. These categories were based on the kinds of systems which had been developed for business applications and the cababilities of Expert Builder. They were intended to convey the range of uses of Expert Builder and also to reflect the approach which might be used in constructing the system. The models sent in by users have been grouped into these categories (see Table 1).

Advisory systems give one or more pieces of advice about what decision to make in a particular situation. Such systems are generally built using a top-down approach starting from the possible decisions and then determining under what conditions they would apply. When these systems are used a backward chaining inference mechanism is appropriate. The majority of systems created by users came in this category.

Diagnostic systems attempt to analyse the cause of observations, e.g. diagnosing a fault in a machine. It is often suggested that a forwarding-chaining inference mechanism is needed because the user should be able to input relevant facts and the system work from those towards a conclusion rather than working through a whole range of possibilities which may be irrelevant. Expert Builder has no true forward-chaining inference mechanism but does have a volunteer facility so that users can input the information available and the system then does a search, using backward chaining but based only on the given information to prove whatever is possible given those facts. From the users viewpoint this is equivalent to forward-chaining. It is also suggested that the modeller may want to work in a forward direction starting from the conditions and working towards a diagnosis. In practice the modellers in this study, teachers and students did not always work in this systematic way. They usually started with a mixture of faults and possible causes and worked partly top-down and partly bottom-up.

Planning systems intended to help in planning or designing an artifact are generally constructed by starting from the constraints and needs and working towards the solutions. They normally result in a large number of pieces of advice. Again a forward chaining or pseudo-forward chaining approach is required when the system is uses.

Classification systems may be regarded as a special case of a diagnostic system where the purpose is to classify an object as belonging to a particular group.

Outlining these four types of system helped to inform of the range of types of system but does not give much indication as to how to go about building a system or how difficult the task is likely to be. As a result of analysing the systems built by users and some of the difficulties they reported it has been possible to identify 5 qualities of a problem or process which is to be modelled which affect the construction task. These are:

The number of advice clauses
The complexity of the conditions
Whether some pieces of advice are mutually exclusive
Whether the order is significant
Whether some questions are mutually exclusive

Generally, as might be expected, the simplest modelling tasks are those with a small number of advice clauses where order is not important and the advice and questions are not mutually exclusive.

The number of advice clauses

The number of advice clauses could vary widely from one to a large number limited only by the memory of the machine. The range can be grouped into three main types:

Models with only one possible outcome, which is either true or false, e.g. the king is a good ruler/the king is not a good ruler

Models with a small number of clearly identifiable possible outcomes
Models with a large number of possible conclusions

Models with only one possible outcome are relatively simple to construct. The task involves deciding which factors will affect the conclusion and in what combinations. The task can be well structured and the approach is top-down. Many of the models developed successfully by club members were of this type. Secondary school teachers were able to use this type of modelling for short exercises which could be completed by a group of children within about 30 min. The children focused on the conditions which were necessary to produce the conclusion, e.g. second year geography students built models which decided whether or not a site was suitable for an Indian village (see Fig. 3). The modelling environment provides a more interesting medium than pencil and paper for structuring these ideas and it enables testing of the model. Having built their model which decides whether a site is suitable, the students can test it by inputting the characteristics of particular sites. Groups of children can also test models built by other groups.

Models with a small number of clearly identifiable possible outcomes can be constructed in a similar way to those described above. The conclusions are specified and then the main factors which determine those conclusions are identified. It is possible to consider each conclusion individually and to build up a rule tree for each. An example of this was a project undertaken by sixth form students in which they built a model which advised on which case should be used for a word in German where there are four possible cases (Fig. 4). Again such modelling tasks can be successfully undertaken by students but the task can become more complex if the clauses are mutaually exclusive or if the order is significant.

In models with a large number of possible conclusions it is generally difficult to identify all the conclusions at the outset of the modelling task. It is still possible for fairly young children to attempt such tasks provided that the model does not require other complex qualities, e.g. groups of 10–11 yr olds built models of what method of communication to use in different circumstances. They started by identifying some of the forms of communication which they knew about and then thinking about when it would be appropriate to use them. They gradually added further communication systems and further conditions as they found out more information and clarified their ideas. A possible pitfall is to try to solve too many problems within one system and it is worth

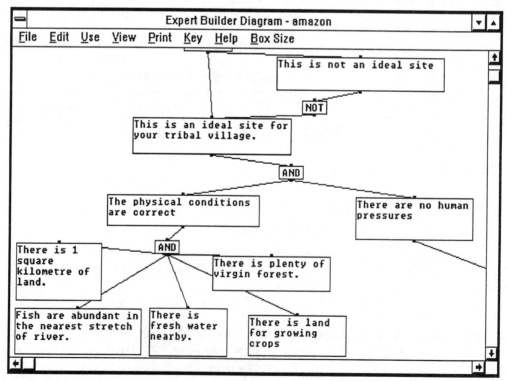

Fig. 3. A model which determines whether a site is suitable for a tribal village.

considering whether the problem can be subdivided. Some club members have suggested they would like a facility to enable one expert system to load another when a particular conclusion is reached. This is probably undesirable because it introduces a further procedural element into the system. However, a number of modellers have made use of the explanation facility to guide users to go on to other models.

The complexity of the conditions

Models with only one conclusion can become more complicated if the combinations of conditions are more complex, e.g. in a model of the battle of Hastings built by a class of primary school children, they decided that a premise should depend on two out of three of the conditions being met. They therefore had to identify all possible combinations of conditions (Fig. 5).

When there are only a small number of advice clauses the elucidation of which combination of conditions lead to particular conclusions can be an interesting and manageable exercise in which the modeller first lists the factors and then decides how they should be combined. The teacher whose class built the Battle of Hastings model felt that the exercise to identify the combinations was useful to undertake once with a class but that a helpful addition to the software would be to be able to define operators which would return true if, for example, any two clauses out of a set were true. This suggestion was also made independently by a group of history teachers.

Are the advice statements mutually exclusive?

This question was one which caused significant problems for both teachers and students. It concerns the nature of the way most expert system shells work. The system attempts to prove the first piece of advice. When it has proved one piece of advice it presents it to the user and gives the option for more advice. The assumption is that there may be more than one possible solution to a problem. This is helpful in many situations, e.g. in some circumstances it is possible that more than one method of communication would be appropriate. However, there were a number of models where students or teachers wanted the system to come to only one conclusion out of a number of possible ones. In such models, if the rules are semantically correct and the user gives answers which are correct and consistent the system would only give one conclusion. However,

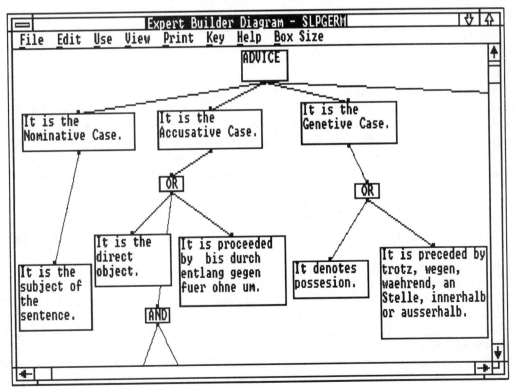

Fig. 4. A model to decide which case to use for a German word.

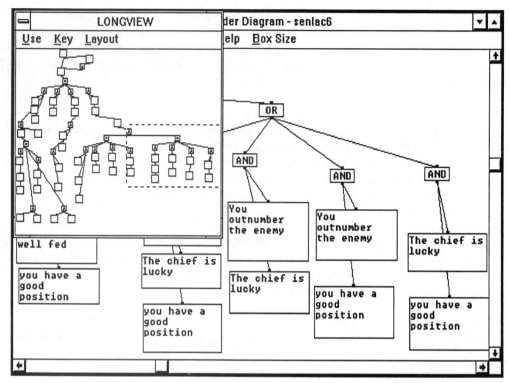

Fig. 5. A model with only one outcome but more complex conditions.

some modellers wanted to prevent users from giving inconsistent information. They therefore spent considerable time making sure that the user could not input contradictory information. They were therefore focusing on the procedural aspects of the system rather than the declarative. This tends to detract from the learning associated with organising the subject matter which is expected to be a benefit of the modelling activity. This problem would be partially overcome if the system included variables and if questions could be presented with a selection of possible answers. However, this would tend to increase the complexity of the modelling environment.

The order of conclusions

A number of modellers wanted to give a series of pieces of advice in order, e.g. a group of sixth formers built a model which advised on choosing a site to build a house, and then building it selecting appropriate materials etc. They therefore made use of the order of search used by the inference engine of left to right. They were able to construct a system which successfully gave advice in order for some sets of conditions but not others. They found the need to describe a series of events which were dependent on previous events as well as current conditions quite difficult to achieve. The students would have been more successful if they had broken the problem down and built several different systems, e.g. one to choose a site, another to select building materials and another to choose a fuel and heating system. For a first modelling activity it is better to analyse these tasks separately and build them as separate models. It would be feasible to build the models on the same page and the results from one model could feed into another as it is possible to make an advice statement a condition for another rule diagram. However, linking the separate diagrams does add another level of complexity to the modelling task.

Expert system shells are not well suited to time-based sequences. They are intended to draw conclusions based on conditions at a particular point in time. As mentioned previously, a major advantage of using an expert system shell for modelling is considered to be that the task is declarative rather than procedural. The dilemma arises because all expert system shells must have a search strategy and a starting point. If this is hidden from users, they may not be able to fully control it but must have ways of influencing it, e.g. by assigning priorities to rules. In Expert Builder the simple left-to-right search strategy is not a feature which is emphasized in the documentation or in demonstrations but it is clearly apparent from the diagrammatic trace. A number of students, including primary school pupils, discovered it. They made use of this feature to provide a series of pieces of advice. Expert Builder is well suited to this purpose since it is a simple matter of arranging boxes from left to right on the screen but it is a different type of modelling task from one concerned with analysing the conditions which affect a particular decision and it may distract from the task which the teacher intended. Some teachers made use of the feature whereas others felt that it should be removed or hidden. The aim of the Modus project is to make the environment as transparent as possible to modellers and to enable them to make their own decisions about which features are appropriate to the modelling task. However, modellers should be aware that making use of the sequential nature of the search strategy introduces a different metaphor into the modelling environment and combining this with the rule metaphor adds a higher level of complexity to the modelling task. Novice modellers are advised to focus on one or the other and the rule metaphor provides more scope for the future.

Some work has been done constructing time-based simulations using a rule based PROLOG shell called Linx[18]. This type of environment is more suitable where a sequence of events is required but Linx tended to emphasize the sequential nature of a situation rather than the rules which govern the links between stages, and there was no diagrammatic representation of the structure. Ideally modellers should be able to select an appropriate tool when they have analysed the nature of the model intended to build, but developing a clear conceptual view of the capabilities of even one simple software environment for modelling represents a considerable achievement for most students.

Are some questions mutually exclusive?

This issue arose when certain questions became irrelevant as a result of previous answers and the model builder wanted the system to skip certain ones. Some sixth formers who were attempting to build a system to diagnose faults in a model car abandoned their idea and instead constructed a system as a checklist to guide someone through giving the car a complete overhaul because they could not overcome this problem. There are two ways to deal with the problem using the facilities provided by Expert Builder. The first is to suggest to users that they volunteer their answers rather than allowing the system to present all questions. This will at least reduce, if not eliminate the number of irrelevant questions which the user is asked. The second technique is to use the logical structure of the roles and the left-to-right search strategy to structure the model in such a way that irrelevant questions are not asked. This is possible but is more difficult and depends on the procedural nature of the inference engine. The ability to enable the user to select from a choice of answers would make this process easier.

The modelling process

Stages in the modelling process were outlined in the original documentation of Expert Builder as:

1. Identify the area of interest
2. Decide on the scope and purpose of the model
3. Identify the important factors affecting the problem
4. Construct the model
5. Test the model with a number of different sets of data
6. Repeat steps 3–5 as necessary

As might be expected, in the primary schools and in the subject-based lessons in secondary schools stages 1 and 2 of the process were done by the teacher. The students went on to attempt stages 3–6. Students studying computing or information technology at GCSE or A level did attempt all stages. Stage 2 is particularly important for ensuring a successful model and more guidance is needed. At stage 5 observations showed that it is better to break the task down and tackle a piece at a time, testing regularly to ensure that the logic is correct. Some children adopted this strategy without being told and those who did were most successful. Their reason for doing so appeared to be that they were not quite sure how the system operated and whether their model would behave as they expected, so they tested it step by step and in so doing gained a better understanding of the modelling metaphor. Other groups of students may have had a clearer initial view of what they wanted to include. They created a large number of boxes containing the relevant knowledge but then had much more difficulty deciding on the logical relationships.

Towards a methodology for expert system modelling

The actual process of model building through the tree-structure diagram varies depending on the qualities of the model as outlined above. However, some general principles can be outlined in the light of comments from users and observations of both teachers and students attempting to construct models. It has been possible to define the modelling process in more detail as it might apply to a group of learners and to move towards defining a methodology:

(1) Identify the area of interest. This stage is likely to arise out of the study of a particular topic and should take a broad view and build up a rich picture as suggested by Checkland in his methodology for systems design[19]. This is important to avoid false assumptions and to ensure that the modelling exercise is placed in a context. Activities arising from study in other curriculum areas tend to go through this stage more naturally but those which start in information technology lessons are less likely to fufill this stage unless the teacher pays particular attention to it.

(2) Decide on the scope and purpose of the model. Here it is necessary to consider who will be the end users of the model and how they will use it. It is also important to decide on the boundaries of the problem and the level at which it will be tackled. The modeller needs functional mental models of the software environments available and what they do. A decision must be made as to whether the modelling task should be approached in a qualitative or quantitative way and whether rule based modelling is appropriate.

(3) Consider the qualities, as outlined earlier in this paper, of the problem and hence the degree of difficulty of the model building task. Students should be encouraged to focus on the declarative nature of the knowledge. At this stage the modeller will have decided to use an expert system shell as a modelling tool but after further consideration it may be necessary to return to stage 2 and revise the aims or to change the approach to the modelling task and perhaps use different software. If a different approach to the modelling task is taken, e.g. if it is decided to construct a dynamic quantitative model of the process then it will probably be necessary to consider a different set of qualities of the problem or process.

(4) Consider whether the problem should be separated into component tasks. Generally it is desirable to do this as much as possible even if the separate models are later combined.

(5) Decide whether the approach is generally top-down or bottom-up and identify the important factors affecting the problem probably using a rough list on paper. If students start by putting a large number of factors on the screen in boxes the screen tends to become cluttered.

(6) Build the model in stages and test at each stage to see whether the model is behaving as expected.

(7) Evaluate the model with data from the real world.

(8) Repeat steps 5–7 as necessary.

Stages 2 and 3 are crucial for determining whether the focus of the modelling activity will be on selecting, structuring and clarifying relationships within the subject matter of the model or on overcoming problems of fitting the model to the software environment. The latter may help to develop general problem-solving skills and may be considered worthwhile in an information technology course but are merely frustrating for teachers (although not necessarily students) in other areas of the curriculum. When the modelling activity is seen as an integral part of the curriculum work, the teacher has generally performed stages 1–5 of the modelling process perhaps with some discussion with the students before going on to allow the students to carry out stages 6–8. Teachers generally selected their topic and modelling approach by basing them on examples provided. The elucidation of the qualities of the problem or process to be modelled, described in this paper, may help to give teachers more confidence in identifying suitable topics for modelling and hence enable them to allow students more flexibility in negotiating their tasks.

The methodology outlined here can be applied more generally although at stages 3, 4 and 5 the modeller's mental models of the problem and the software environment need to be matched. It would be advantageous to provide a more integrated environment as envisaged by the Modus project[20] so that modellers who approach the task from one angle but then decide that the model requires other features can find suitable facilities within the same software environment.

THE CAL91 WORKSHOP

This workshop brought together educationalists and colleagues from industry. The participants explored the Expert Builder and examined models developed by students and teachers. Part of the workshop involved using Model Builder, another modelling environment which has been developed recently by the Modus project, so that the two approaches could be compared. Model Builder[20] is an object-oriented environment for constructing dynamic systems models. The discussion focused on the nature of modelling tasks and their value as learning activities and how people learn how to model. An important additional perspective was obtained from contributions from colleagues in industry who used modelling software in order to train adults about industrial processes. They had found that even where the resources are available to build sophisticated and realistic simulations, it is necessary to work with simplified models where learners can understand how the models function to come to an understanding of the nature of the processes and problems. The group agreed that constructing and interacting with simple models is a valuable learning activity and that the lack of accuracy of a model is in no way a disadvantage in a learning situation. Evaluation of the model and recognition of its limitations is very important. The interactive nature of the learning situation promoted by the use of both Expert Builder and Model Builder were felt to be of prime importance. Learners were encouraged to interact both with the software and with each other. It was felt that this type of simple modelling environment was useful for adult learners as well as children.

The modelling metaphor of Expert Builder was agreed to be particularly appropriate for organising ideas and many topics could be modelled using simple sets of rules. In working with learners in industrial organisations it had been found that rule-based systems were much easier for learners to use than frame-based systems. Expert Builder was felt to be more suitable for learners to build their own models rather than working with models supplied by the teacher. Model Builder could be used for both types of exercise. The group found difficulty in defining how people learn how to build models. Most were experienced modellers themselves and felt that their success in building models derived from knowing what was possible and how to achieve it having built similar models before. The suggestion of looking for features of problems and processes which show similarity to others already tackled corresponds to the approach adopted by teachers who generally looked at the examples provided and followed a similar but often slightly modified pattern when they constructed their model. It was reported that some people seem naturally to be better modellers than others and this does not appear to be linked with intelligence. This may be because they are better at identifying similarities between problems which would be consistent with observations of children modelling where some children seem better at detecting resemblance between logical representations than others.

CONCLUSIONS

Modelling activities in education

The shell in its present form with some minor improvements can be used for a variety of modelling activities which not only introduce children to the process and techniques of modelling but help them to clarify and organise their ideas about the subject matter of the task. It is important that these tasks are selected with care and the methodology outlined in this paper needs to be developed and documented further and introduced to teachers so that they can use it together with their students and gradually enable the students to undertake more of the whole modelling process themselves.

Issues for future software development

A number of features, which users have requested, have already been mentioned in this paper including variables, ability to specify that a conclusion will be true if 2 out of 3 of the conditions are true. Other common requests were the ability to do some arithmetic and to include weighting factors. The latter was particularly requested by history teachers who felt that it should be possible to assign numerical values as weightings to variables. This type of model is the basis of a number of existing historical simulations. The great majority of users liked the graphical interface and ease of use. This included those who asked for the more advanced features outlined here. This implies that these additional facilities must not interfere with ease of use. The Modus project intends to provide these facilities by combining the environment provided in Expert Builder with that of another modelling environment, also developed by the project, Model Builder. The aim will be to retain the simplicity of the current user interface while providing more sophisticated facilities for more advanced users. This will be achieved by allowing further features to be added as required by the teacher or student.

REFERENCES

1. Osbourne R. and Gilbert J., The use of models in science teaching. *School Sci. Rev.* No. 62 (1982).
2. Riley D., Learning about systems by making models. *Computers Educ.* **15**, 255–262 (1990).
3. Cumming G. and Abbott E., Prolog and expert systems for children's learning. In *Artificial Intelligence Tools in Education* (Edited by Ercoli P. and Lewis R.), pp. 163–175. North Holland, Amsterdam (1988).
4. DES/WO, Technology in the National Curriculum, HMSO (1990).
5. Webb M. E. and Hassell D., Opportunities for computer based modelling and simulation in secondary education. In *Computers in Education* (Edited by Lovis F. and Tagg E. D.), Elsevier/North Holland, Amsterdam (1988).
6. Ennals J. R., *Beginning Micro-Prolog.* Horwood, Chichester (1983).
7. Bignold P., Expertech Xi in comprehensive school maths and computer studies. Paper presented at PEG conference, Exeter, July (1986).
8. McCarthy S., Xi in the primary curriculum. Paper presented at PEG conference, Exeter (July 1986).
9. Davies S., Xi in the comprehensive curriculum. Paper presented at PEG conference, Exeter (July 1986).
10. Wideman H. H. and Owston R. D., Student development of an expert system: a case study. *J. Computer Based Instruct.* (1988).
11. Webb M. E., An investigation of the opportunities for computer based modelling and the possible contributions to children's learning in secondary schools science, focusing on biology. Dissertation for Associateship in education, King's College, London (1987).
12. Hassell D., The role of modelling activities in the humanities curriculum, with special reference to geography: and investigative study. Dissertation for Associateship in education, King's College, London (1987).
13. Galpin B., Expert systems in primary schools. British Library Research paper 73; British Library Research and Development Department (1989).
14. Valley K., Designing an expert system shell for use in education. Paper presented at PEG '88 conference, Copenhagen (July 1986).
15. Aiken J. S., Prototypical knowledge for expert systems. *Artificial Intell.* **20**, 163–210 (1983).
16. Stefik M., An examination of a frame structured representation system. *Proceedings of the 6th International Conference in Artificial Intelligence*, pp. 845–885.
17. Gilbert N., Explanation as process. *Proceedings of the Fourth Workshop of the Alvey Explanation Special Interest Group*, IEE (1989).
18. Briggs J., Brough B., Nichol J. and Watson L., *Linx88.* PEG, Exeter (1988).
19. Checkland P. B., *Systems Thinking, Systems Practice.* Wiley, Chichester (1981).
20. Hassell D. J. and Webb M. E., Modus the integrated modelling system. *Computers Educ.* **15**, 265–270 (1990).

Computers Educ. Vol. 18, No. 1–3, pp. 101–107, 1992
Printed in Great Britain

0360-1315/92 $5.00 + 0.00
Pergamon Press plc

THE ARTIFICIAL INTELLIGENCE APPLICATIONS TO LEARNING PROGRAMME

NOEL WILLIAMS

Communication and Information Research Group, Sheffield City Polytechnic, 36 Collegiate Crescent,
Sheffield S10 2BP, England

Abstract—The Artificial Intelligence Applications to Learning Programme has been funded since 1987 by what is now known as the Training, Enterprise and Education Directorate (TEED). The Programme aimed to explore and accelerate the use of AI technologies in learning, in both the educational and industrial sectors. The ten demonstrator projects were evaluated for their impact on industry and on further and higher education, while the project was in progress and later during its dissemination phase. The most useful outcomes of evaluation emerged during the latter phase, when the innovations had had an opportunity to become established and brought to market. There were issues related to technology-drive and the need to find problems for which the solution existed through group collaboration. One profitable line of development was to use AI to enrich training systems. An ideal training system must feel "good" to the client, should go beyond existing adaptive training systems, offer a high rate of training, be cost effective, have visual appeal, give sophisticated feedback, should fit closely with the user's current practice, and should have a shelf life of more than 3 years.

BACKGROUND TO THE SEMINAR

The Artificial Intelligence Applications to Learning Programme has been funded since 1987 by the Training, Enterprise and Education Directorate (TEED, previously the Manpower Services Commission, the Training Commission and the Training Agency). It was run by the Learning Technology Unit (LTU) of TEED and funded in three separate phases over 3 years. The Programme aimed to explore and accelerate the use of AI technologies in learning and involved projects in both the education and industrial sectors. Finance was curtailed by Treasury towards the end of the Programme, so not all planned activities have taken place. In particular the dissemination phase of the Programme has been substantially delayed.

The Programme was conceived as a number of related projects. Ten demonstrator projects were commissioned to illustrate different applications of artificial intelligence to training. Two further projects ran in parallel, evaluating the impact of the Programme on industry and on further and higher education. A number of smaller activities were also funded to disseminate information about AI in training. The outcomes of the Progamme will be integrated into the future work of the LTU. Outlines of all these projects and the evaluations can be found in Refs [1,2].

EVALUATION OF THE PROGRAMME

The Programme evaluations ended in March 1990. However, few dissemination activities had taken place by this date so necessarily little evidence of awareness was found. Subsequently several activities have taken place which have raised awareness, but these could not be formally taken account of in the evaluation.

Impact on further and higher education: the findings

Evaluation of the impact of the Programme on further education (FE) and higher education (HE) had been carried out by census covering all FE institutions and HE departments; interviews with project teams at the beginning, end, and 6 months after completion of projects; and follow-up surveys for three categories of institution, namely those using AI at the start of the Programme, those planning to use AI and those without AI. The evaluation showed that there was more AI in HE (47%) than FE (28%) but these figures were probably inflated due to the difficulties of defining AI. It suggested that most AI in HE was in research, but in FE most was in teaching, that the main area of interest was in expert systems and that projects were usually funded internally. Follow-up surveys showed continued positive attitudes to AI even though there was a *decreasing* use of AI over the period of evaluation. Responses showed less use, fewer projects and that many institutions who has said they planned to use AI, did not. The most common reasons given for this decline were lack of funds, lack of expertise and turnover of staff.

In terms of the impact of the Programme on individual projects, the evaluators found increased knowledge and awareness of AI, as well as exploration of new and unique techniques and improvements in learning and teaching. They found that projects provided a stimulus to technological development and increased the marketability of staff. However, against these strengths the evaluators identified several problems. For example, there was little use of project expertise outside the project. Applications tended to stay with the project team. There were also problems of marketing and dissemination. Colleges and HE institutions had little expertise in marketing, so did not know what to do once they had a product. Evaluation also suggested that few new links with industry had been developed and that evaluation of the effectiveness of individual projects was not as complete as it might have been.

Thus the FE and HE evaluation team had identified several issues to be considered in future similar activities. In the first place, reactions to the Programme had been disappointing and there was little evidence of raised awareness or perceived impact, largely because dissemination activities had not taken place. Much of the demonstrable awareness had, in fact, come through the evaluation activities themselves. As a related problem, the evaluators believed that defining AI itself was problematic. They had found that AI always needs further definition. Hence there was a problem for marketing AI applications, tools, techniques and expertise.

The evaluators also believed the Programme had experienced severe problems with continuity, due to difficulties with Treasury funding which had complicated the planning and execution of individual projects. Consequently the time scale appeared too optimistic for all the activities the projects were supposed to carry out.

Finally evaluation suggested that there were problems determining the balance of development and dissemination within the available time and with the balance of development and evaluation.

The evaluators derived three general issues for education from these observations. First were the problems of focusing an initiative, as it was not clear where the best place would be to concentrate a new initiative in AI and Learning. Second were the problems of developing expertise. Generally, academic staff acquired AI (and IT) expertise in *ad hoc* and haphazard ways, which led to a lack of strategy and coherence in the building of AI learning applications. Third were the problems of infrastructure. It appeared that FE and HE did not have the right structures to pick up new technology in staff development and support, in marketing, in dissemination or in links with industry.

Impact on industry and commerce: the findings

The National Council for Educational Technology (NCET) evaluated the impact of the Programme on the industrial sector. It had, as with the educational evaluation, ended in March 1990, though the final report had been able to take some account of the *potential* impact of subsequent activities. Initially a baseline of awareness was established, using a variety of sources. The evaluation concentrated on key sectors and conducted random surveys through lead bodies within those sectors, supplemented by media surveys, analysis of exhibitions and informal interviews. All these sources conveyed similar messages.

As a result of the Programme many technologies had been explored, and much material had been produced which could be valuable to industrial developers. There appeared to be a need to adapt the AI technologies for them and present appropriate development advice. However, there was also a need for more trials of the demonstrator projects to establish robustness in the workplace.

The Programme also aimed to accelerate appropriate application of AI technologies to learning, but, due to lack of dissemination, the evaluators believed two more years would have to elapse before signs of such acceleration might be seen. Nor was the evaluation able to find evidence from the demonstrators of cost effectiveness in training. In any case, evidence suggested that industry would not make training decisions based on comparative costs of learning outcomes. Industry's decision-making appeared much more pragmatic.

The evaluators also assessed advances in the application of AI technologies in training in industry. High awareness was found in training supply firms but not in demand firms. As might be expected, the highest demand awareness was in large firms. The two major factors determining this awareness of AI in training were the experience of a firm in AI applications to business and its prior use of computer-based training.

NCET also estimated the growth of the applications of AI technologies in industry and commerce after the Programme. They believed such growth would depend on applications that can show hard evidence of business benefits, such as cost saving, flexibility, new training and improved business performance.

The evaluation raised a number of issues for further discussion, as possible future development from the Programme. These included the need to cross the boundary between system trials and true industry applications trials, the need to identify the criteria industry used in taking on and using new technology, the need to develop practical guides for industry and the need to investigate business and commercial applications of AI systems that could also be used for training.

Both evaluations showed that the Programme had been significantly affected by the way it was funded. Both also identified a strong relationship between computer assisted learning (CAL) or CBT and AI. Typically trainers and educators would not consider AI if they had not already CAL or CBT expertise.

Discussion of the evaluations

The industrial evaluation had shown a considerable lack of awareness on the demand side, with many firms believing AI actually was CBT. Rediffusion, for example, had disseminated information extensively through its sales force and after 2 years, still found a general ignorance of CBT.

Part of the difficulty seems to be with marketing training innovation generally. For example, System Applied Technology does not use the terms "AI" or "ITS" to sell training systems to clients. Instead they market by demonstrating the reduction in training time, the consequent staff savings and the comparative costings for conventional CBT. So, in presenting AI to trainers, it has to be explained in the context of existing CBT, not as something separate, and in most contexts there is no value in making a distinction between them.

Expecting positive outcomes from evaluations conducted concurrently with the Programme itself seemed unrealistic. In particular, dissemination, marketing and further development only took place *after* the Programme had ended. The most useful evaluation could therefore not take place until between 6 and 18 months *after* the Programme. Meaningful evaluation depends on a realistic sense of what is possible, but expecting useful results from evaluations concurrent with a Programme is not realistic.

As a model for evaluating future initiatives in learning technologies, concurrent evaluation may only be worthwhile as a formative influence on individual projects. However, because different objectives can be served by evaluation, a clearer definition of the intended evaluation and its outcomes in each particular project will give everyone concerned a clearer sense of how the evaluation is to work in each case. The relationship between overall *Programme* evaluation and individual *project* evaluations also needs clearer specification, and project evaluations can be more effective if they address specific characteristics and techniques of the work on which developers need feedback, rather than projects as a whole.

Exploration of dual use systems

NCET's industrial evaluation had seen a growth in the use of business AI applications, especially expert systems. In some cases the business expert diagnostic system is also now used for training (e.g. by using fictional case study material), backed by paper-based training. Expert system marketeers are moving in on training applications, using expert systems for training because they can be shown to reduce training time.

Meeting industry adoption criteria for training

Some of the problems addressed by training can be solved by AI, by removing the need for training. Solutions should be sought for *performance* problems generally, not just training problems, addressing real business objectives; e.g. by hiding AI within otherwise conventional training or performance support. Dissemination by promoting the surface effects of AI not the underlying causes addresses general issues of performance so is more likely to open up budgets.

Dissemination activities

Since the end of the evaluations, dissemination had continued. Recent and continuing dissemination activities have included the Intelligent Learning Technology Initiative, which has established five user clubs to develop training applications using AI; the Adaptive Training open learning awareness package, developed by System Applied Technology; AI in Training Awareness Seminars, held jointly by System Applied Technology and Rediffusion and the production of an AI in Training video. Dissemination proved to be important. The topic encompasses how the ideas, outcomes and techniques developed by the Programme might become more widely available, and how specific products could be marketed. The LTU intends to include the outcomes of the Artificial Intelligence Applications to Learning Programme in any future seminars and general dissemination activities and will integrate any future AI work into its other activities. Separate dissemination of the outcomes of AI projects is not intended, however. Nor does the LTU have a marketing role, for it brings projects to prototype stage but leaves marketing to project institutions and other interested organisations. The LTU is not able to support total market-place dissemination but rather dissemination at conferences, workshops and other public events.

There is some concern about the lack of specific dissemination. Project teams indicated a lack of awareness of the activities and outcomes of other projects. Representatives of other interests wished to know what had taken place and how they could find out about it. There is also some concern that the many positive outcomes of the Programme will be lost if not targetted for specific audiences.

In some cases, the Programme has resulted in products, such as the DUBS small business advisor, which are now being sold. The LTU supported any such dissemination activity by project teams, whether as publication or product. Whilst TEED has to sanction any such activity, which exploits or employs the results of the Programme, such agreement is not normally withheld.

In this context several people have proposed independent publication of edited versions of the project reports, e.g. as a book documenting successes of Technology Based Training, focusing perhaps on the tools, techniques, educational principles and the nature of the teams needed. However, LTU as yet have no plan for a synthesis of individual project reports.

Marketing

Although the LTU can influence marketing it cannot implement general marketing strategies itself. Currently the key concepts to market are neither AI nor CBT on their own, but open and flexible learning (OFL) which includes the use of technology-based training (TBT). Small institutions may not be able to market without external funding, as they lack the skills, management and facilities to do so. For example, at Castle College, despite highly successful trialling of the CUSTOM package (a package for teaching customer care skills to catering students), it cannot be taken into the market-place without external support. The LTU sees consortia as the best way to achieve this, with TEED owning little of each consortium. Others suggest that if there is value in the Programme then entrepreneurs will exploit it, but it cannot be left to the market-place. For example, System Applied Technology would create a market by raising awareness of clients, which means taking technological solutions to industry looking for appropriate problems to solve. Consequently the best activity for the LTU might be to create a climate in which individual entrepreneurs and project teams can promote the products, skills and knowledge which they now have as a result of the Programme, through awareness-raising activities.

The LTU might indeed be able to create a climate conducive to successful marketing on the project firms' behalf, especially for applications in the electronics and finance areas. However, this climate might not particularly serve the interests of educational institutions.

Ownership of information

Educationalists are also interested in access to the information which came out of the Programme. The ownership of information from projects which were joint-funded by public and private interests is a barrier to the possibility of dissemination through shareware because of the private element. Public investment means the information is freely available, but source code remains proprietary. However, educationalists interested in obtaining the ideas developed by LTU funding should have no difficulty as the prototypes are Crown Copyright, even where intellectual property rights belong to the creator. Many collaborating firms (such as Rediffusion), in any case, operate an open door policy and are keen to provide information generally. With further development, prototypes can be sold, providing the Crown agreed (e.g. by arranging to recover its costs) so it is likely that some additional products might appear.

Consortia

Although consortia might not work for education, such an approach would produce cost benefit in industry, which is the LTU's primary measure of success. Perhaps industrial consortia would not release information created by such projects, causing other projects to go over already explored ground. Against this, such explorations would usually be needed in any case, producing significant variations in each particular context. Educational institutions *could* benefit from consortia if they were willing to back marketable products (e.g. Bradford University's ELF system).

Perhaps there should be different consortia with different ranges of expertise with a view to exploitation. For example, by building in explicit exploitation points of different kinds into projects, different ends could be served. Academics, for example, might be more interested in the generic features of interface design or in the techniques, which are the benefits meaningful to them, but not a directly marketable product. However, academic institutions typically could not join in consortia as heavily investing clients. So consortia would not generally feed academic needs.

Whilst the project developers believe that AI technology did produce worthwhile results, there are still only a few applications around. This is probably because companies take a high risk, for training is seen as an absorber not a producer of resources, and trainers knew nothing of AI and distrust it. Those barriers must be overcome before applications could become widespread.

The problem is perhaps even wider than this, as trainers generally do not use CBT. LTU research suggest that OFL is used only in about 9% of U.K. firms, CBT in 10 % of those, and AI in only a small percentage of *those*. In contrast, however, 33% of large firms are exploring OFL, because they have training professionals and can provide cost-effective training. Small and medium firms cannot do so without specialist help. Furthermore the advisors, such as small business counsellors, are not recommending technology-based training solutions to small and medium firms because of their own lack of knowledge. So a priority is to convince such intermediaries of the value of OFL and TBT. Convincing intermediaries is difficult because they typically rely on their early training, belonging to an era before OFL and TBT. Nor can small firms command the budgets needed for solutions of the sophistication of the Iccarus type. They need simpler and cheaper tools.

LESSONS LEARNED

Technology led development

In principle, development should be led by finding solutions to problems, but there is a wide belief that a substantial line of innovative development has to be technology led. Otherwise new techniques would not be tried, discoveries could not be made, and no "visionary" or exploratory work was likely to take place.

There is a need for "collective envisaging", allowing projects to pool expertise and skills in a collective view of what might be possible. The LTU could perhaps fund a forward-looking group to promote the results of the Programme for precisely this purpose. A development route which identifies a solution, then looks for a problem, sometimes works. Once it *has* worked, and a match between solution and problem can be shown, then others are able to find similar problems.

Richer training systems

One profitable line for development is to build on the U.S. systems approach to training (the conventional sequence of tutorial, practice and test) by enhancing such systems with some simulation and logical decision making to give richer training systems. Some new developments, such as hypertext, have also caused trainers to reflect on the nature and quality of training in new ways and discover both inadequacies of conventional provision and new forms of training provision. Such developments do pay for themselves because they are reusable. For example, different learner needs and experience can be satisfied by such a "rich" system in ways which are beyond the scope of conventional CBT.

The ideal use of AI in a training system

An ideal training system which uses AI must feel "good" to the client, should go beyond existing adaptive training systems, should offer a high rate of training, should address an application area where it is cost effective, should possess only some state of the art technology, should have visual appeal, should give sophisticated feedback, should fit closely with the user's current practice, should be able to reason a little more competently than a user and should have a shelf life of more than 3 years.

AI can also be useful in restricting the problem space in complex models of machines for fault diagnosis. Rather than representing human expertise AI can be used to prune the search space in, for example, a model of a faulty machine.

Tools

There is a need for high level authoring tools which experienced teachers can use to develop teaching materials which include an AI component and enable people to work with a familiar educational vocabulary and with educational objectives and prerequisities. Educational software development may only expand when more tools, such as HyperCard, are available. However, even HyperCard uses a language of "cards" and "buttons", not a vocabulary familiar to educationalists.

AI tools should perhaps be given to trainers and domain experts, rather than software specialists, but suitable tools are not likely to appear for some time. AI might also be used to provide a set of tools for developing instructional materials, e.g. by using existing expert system shells. However, existing expert systems are either inadequate or require additional programming to create appropriate interfaces.

Most tools are far too difficult for the average trainer. Creating such tools is a genuine AI research problem, particularly tools that will enable people to express their expertise comfortably. The complexity of mapping high level educational concepts onto robust AI routines suggests that such tools will not be available for several years. There is also a need for constant underpinning of research, or the whole development of AI in training will decline. Academics are not generally motivated to take material into the marketplace, but are intellectually fired by such research, and so need that support. If this passion is not capitalised upon to create many "vignettes" of what might be done with the technologies, U.S. and European AI project consortia will simply fill the need, as they are already beginning to do.

Cost benefits

It is now realistic to expect cost benefits of AI technology. Robust examples demonstrating those benefits are available both from the Programme and elsewhere. One such benefit is that AI allows the building of better training, and is no more expensive than conventional CBT and demonstrably more cost effective than other means. Most AI training activities cost the same as conventional CBT. AI is also able to show benefit in specific areas, notably in simulation and fault diagnosis. For example, in the Rediffusion Tate & Lyle training system, expert assistance during the training event proved to have many fewer bugs compared with conventional authored CBT. Building and updating declarative components in training software (as in the IKBS component) is also much easier than the equivalent procedural tasks (e.g. in building the user interface).

One area for improvement is in building good quality text for the interface. This can be more expensive than building the knowledge base, as the correct, most appropriate wording for the audience is expensive to achieve. Knowledge for IKBS is relatively easy to get but the communication is much harder. Thus, implementing AI is faster than conventional programming, but sophisticated dialogue takes longer. Cost savings can be clearly demonstrated, as is shown in the data in Table 1.

Table 1. Projects run by System Aplied Technology (all data in pounds sterling)

Application	Costs	Application savings in year 1	Cost of comparable training	Saving on training
Running boilers	160,000	450,000	196,000	36,000
Disk training	94,500	430,000	105,750	56,250
Assurance	116,000	85,000	147,000	31,000
Building society	150,000	250,000	155,000	5000

A further identified benefit of AI in training is an increase in *effectiveness*. In the SAT boiler system, Waterfront, training is given when trainees needed it, i.e. when they have a problem. With an expert system by the elbow of the operator it can act as an adviser and diagnostic tool in normal use, until its output is not understood by the operator. At that point training can bring the operator's understanding to the necessary level. So in the Waterfront expert system there is a resident tutor which at any time in consultation with the expert can give definitions and can offer tutorials on the terms used (including 25 h of embedded CBT). This has the function of training at the moment of greatest need. The same system can be used differently for induction of people who began with no knowledge. Training Needs Analysis (TNA) identifies the start point (in the Waterfront system, by using another expert system which knows about training in the areas of boiler technology), giving the learner a profile scored on different components of the training. With that knowledge the tutoring system can then select the training needed, and refine the model by monitoring the learner during the course of training, giving an individualised training route. System Applied Technology believe there are savings of 35% on training time because all the redundant information is omitted from the training. Effectively this saves three staff per year and it could not have been done as cost effectively without AI.

OUTCOMES

There is some worry that the positive outcomes of the Programme, of which many have been identified, will be lost. Perhaps the LTU could disseminate existing information more widely, improving access to project and Programme outcome information and creating a climate of awareness in which existing successes could be developed and marketed, especially by disseminating the training and cost benefits of AI.

Funding strategies for any future Programmes might also be reviewed, along with projected timescales, and the role of project evaluations could be clarified at the start of projects, whilst summative Programme evaluations might be delayed until after the Programme. The LTU will investigate ways of incorporating AI training in other applications, of building AI into future projects, in different contexts, and of developing AI training tools for the non-specialists. Whilst AI still proves an exciting area for many involved in learning technology, it will only succeed by appropriate integration within other technologies, such as in intelligent simulation.

REFERENCES

1. Williams N., *The Training Agency Conference for Contractors on the Artificial Intelligence Applications to Learning Programme*. Learning Technology Unit, TEED, Moorfoot, Sheffield (1989).
2. Goodman L. M., Evaluation of the Further and Higher Education (FHE) Section of the Training Agency's "AI Applications to Learning Programme". *Educ. Train. Technol. Int.* **26**, 322–334 (1989).

Computers Educ. Vol. 18, No. 1–3, pp. 109–118, 1992
Printed in Great Britain. All rights reserved

IMPLEMENTING CAL AT A UNIVERSITY

M. D. Leiblum

University of Nijmegen, IOWO/CAL Group, Montessorilaan 3, Postbus 9104,
6500 HE Nijmegen, The Netherlands

Abstract—This article reports on a major review of the status of CAL at the University of Nijmegen, and includes planning and policy recommendations made to the governing board of the university. The list of major recommendations are included. It describes some current factors influencing CAL development in The Netherlands and at the university. A complete content description of the final report is presented which may aid others needing to perform similar studies. Additionally a model presenting 12 phases related to CAL development, implementation, and evaluation is briefly described, as well as several implementation strategies. The article concludes with a review of some effects that a change in policy may produce.

1. INTRODUCTION

The University of Nijmegen (KUN), is a medium-size (staff: about 2800; enrollment about 12,000; established 1923), public, Dutch higher education institution. The Centre for R&D into Higher Education (IOWO), is a centralised service agency providing general didactical, research and training support to the university. It does not fall under any faculty, but rather is part of "general services", similar to the computing centre, and library.

The CAL group, one section within the IOWO, is struggling with the realities and problems of keeping CAL alive at this university. For close to 20 years, this group, perhaps the oldest continuously operating CAL agency in The Netherlands, has involved itself, on a modest scale, in introducing and stimulating the usage of modern teaching technologies among internal staff and students. An earlier article, "A Decade of CAL at a Dutch University"[1] gave a detailed review of these early stages. This article reports on the current situation but primarily reviews a major project, undertaken at the request of the university's governing board, to produce a CAL planning and management strategy review for the 1990s.

2. SOME FACTORS AFFECTING THE DUTCH UNIVERSITY CAL CLIMATE

Those familiar with Dutch higher education are aware of the immense problems and adjustments the universities have faced during the past 5 years: (i) revamping and shortening of curricula and maximum study periods, (ii) creation of a "second phase" of university study, similar to the American, "Masters Degree", (iii) major cutbacks in internal funding accompanying cost consciousness plus greater dependance on external finance, (iv) complaints that universities are not providing graduates attuned to the needs of industry, competition from vocational schools and more dramatically (for staff), (v) loss of tenure, forced earlier retirement and indeed dismissals due to reorganisation, predicted lower enrollment, and the higher cost of education. In addition, the "publish or perish" syndrome is now affecting most academic departments, and continuous reviews of the quality of personnel and educational programs are being made. All these elements have contributed to the discomfort, frustration, and indeed overwork on the part of many university staff. University personnel, some pampered for many years, had to come to grips with a new harsh economic reality. Of course many changes were truly needed and perhaps over a longer term, the results may be positive. In the shorter term there is instability.

All the previous factors inevitably affect the ability to implement and manage CAL. When teaching staff lose their desire to raise instructional standards because the research (read publish) activity becomes over stressed, CAL will suffer. When no "credit" is given (equivalent to a publication) for CAL courseware development activities, CAL will suffer. When administrators do not allocate time or compensate academic staff for CAL activities, CAL will suffer. When hard cash has to be paid for CAL assistance where it was previously freely granted the same is true. When staff fear the possibility that automated teaching techniques and new media technologies may replace some of their hallowed, traditional or familiar teaching styles, CAL will suffer. When staff fear job loss, when curriculum contents undergo rapid changes, when new facilities or funds for updating aging hardware, courseware, and systems are not available, CAL will suffer. When faculty educational committees, or high level administrators see no need to set policies or standards, or assume a "laissez faire" attitude regading CAL, it will suffer. Unfortunately, many staff and faculties see CAL merely as a luxury, an add-on cost, more for the student than benefiting themselves.

3. BACKGROUND AND DESCRIPTION OF THE PROJECT

In late 1989, and early 1990, the IOWO's CAL section, at the behest of the governing board, worked on an assignment to prepare a planning and policy guideline review and inventory of computer-based-instructional activities for the university. The real impulse for the project, arose from a desire of the director of the IOWO, to clarify the situation regarding CAL usage. It was linked to his feeling that CAL might better be stimulated and coordinated by top-down, faculty-level (educational committees) policies or mandates about CAL, rather than by the bottom-up (e.g. individual teaching staff who felt the "urge") approach to selecting the medium for instructional support.

The situation actually arose from re-organisational and policy changes within the IOWO itself. The CAL group had, for the major part of its existence, initiated or responded to requests from individual instructors across all academic curriculums, for CAL development and advisorial support. If these instructors saw, or could be convinced of the benefits of CAL to resolve one of their instructional problems or could aid students, then, via a specific in-take and selection procedure carried out by the CAL group itself, service hours from this group would be provided without charge and with little bureaucratic or administrative interference. The results were a large production of (mostly) successful, but smaller CAL initiatives spread across the various academic disciplines[1].

These earlier stages can in many cases by characterised as the "start-up" phase. We felt that the time had come for us and the university to enter the so-called, "productive", phase. The characteristics of these phases are given in Table 1 (taken from Mirande[2]).

Forced by financial cutbacks in university support, which within a short time, will only amount to about 50% of actual operating costs, the IOWO underwent a re-organisation (1988–1990) and became semi-independent. It became more commercially oriented and adapted a policy of direct charges for all services. A much larger portion of its clients came from outside the university. A restricted and carefully controlled number of service hours could be requested from the university itself (divided across all faculties, largely based on enrollment figures), and these are paid for through central funding. It should be noted that the current IOWO (about 35 part-time and permanent staff) is divided into several sections, each performing certain types of educational R&D and training activities, of which the CAL group is only one section. Thus, in essence, each section within the IOWO may be granted a part of the maximum number of hours "freely" provided to each faculty.

There is an unevenness in service distribution; thus some faculties may make minimal or no use of CAL but instead other IOWO services (teacher training, evaluation, curriculum assessment studies or research) while for others, the reverse is true. In a sense, there is some (friendly)

Table 1. Some differences between "start-up" and "productive" usage of CAL

Characteristic	Start-up	Productive
Initiative	Individual teacher	Faculty or department
Unit of analysis	Course segment	Course(s)/curriculum
Function	Mostly remedial	Substitutive, innovative, complementary
Selection-criteria	Teacher-driven	Didactic and economic analysis
Developed by	Initiator	Professional team
Implementation	As "add-on"/extra	Integrated carefully into curriculum
Maintenance and management	Not specified	Standard procedures

competition, even between internal IOWO sections in providing services but a great deal of cooperation also. Some problems have resulted however, caused by faculties requesting more hours than can officially be granted. In these instances, the faculty would have to come up with hard cash. These cases are few and far between, since most faculties are already. financially strapped and usually choose to devote limited funds to research related, rather than didactical (teaching) expenses. The result then, in some cases, is that individual instructors requesting CAL assistance, cannot be supported, not because of lack of willingness of available IOWO personnel, but rather because time has not been authorised by their faculty's coordinating officials.

By adapting the "productive" criteria (of Table 1) for selecting or initiating projects (which must largely come about by careful analysis, concurrence, and support by faculty head or educational committee) and following well-established procedures and guidelines, we hoped to (i) limit the choice to very well-deserving projects, (ii) make productive and cost effective use of available service hours, and (iii) set a stronger case for extra-budgetary support occasionally available from special funds.

One of this project's goals then was to determine whether the stimulation of CAL via a more coordinated and "top-down" approach could be successful and to recommend strategies for implementation. That is, to provide some recommendations about how faculty dean's or educational committees should look at CAL, what policies were needed, and what were the manpower and facility needs of each faculty.

4. ANALYSIS AND METHODS

A broad outline of the study was constructed. It was decided that first a general inventory of the current situation, per faculty (total of nine), need be made. This was to determine: (i) the actual use of CAL within the faculty (ii) the attitude, opinions, and wishes of teaching staff regarding the medium and the existing situation, and (iii), same as for (ii) but with the target group of faculty deans or other high-level administrators.

Inventories were designed to collect, among other items, information and data about: specific courseware packages used per faculty; the physical (facilities, computer and software configurations), strategical (policies if any), and attitudinal CAL environment; identification of problems related to CAL use (or non-use); "wish-lists" on the part of staff; and suggestions for revised management strategies or policies.

The primary tools used to collect needed information were questionnaires (several) and structured interviews (numerous). Recipients were selected based on knowledge of earlier CAL activities, and a preselection questionnaire was sent to educational committees or department heads. Since not all university teaching staff were approached we cannot assume that the inventory is complete. We estimate a 10–20% "miss" rate, but are sure, however, that the most "CAL active" staff were reached.

Based on the inventories a set of guidelines and recommendations was proposed, per faculty and for the general governing board. This final report (rather lengthy and detailed) was reviewed by that body, and an additional request was made to produce a more compact "brochure", containing summative data and the most significant specific recommendations. The latter would then be distributed to a wider university audience.

5. THE REPORT AND BROCHURE

The final report[3] and brochure are written in the Dutch language but a partial, first version was writen in English and may be requested by those seriously interested in the contents. The intention here is to present an idea of the structure and content outline, which may be useful to other researchers requested to perform similar studies. A condensed summary of actual findings and recommendations is given in the next section.

112 M. D. Leiblum

The final report, produced by this author and Dr Marcel Mirande, is structured as following:

Part 1: Recommendations for management

Subdivided into 5 major sections and subsections, entitled; "Recommendations related to ... (i) the stimulation of CAL, (ii) the choice or selection process of CAL, (iii) the development of CAL, (iv) the usage of CAL, and (v) introduction or implementation strategies. The preceding sections were produced by the authors, from the information and data collected previously.

Part 2: Current status of CAL at KUN

Divided into 3 sections with subsections. The first section outlined the procedures used in collecting information. The second, for each faculty, gave a brief description of actual status (usage statistics), constituted problems, desired modes of CAL or applications, and suggested management or policy changes (all as specified by those interviewed or responding to questionnaires).

There are nine faculties: Letters, Law, Social Sciences, Physical Sciences, Medicine and Dentistry, Mathematics and Informatica, Philosophy, Theology, and Management Science. The final section presented summative statistics; charts, graphs, tables and short discussions based on the individual (per faculty) data. Several are shown in this report. The subsections (10) related to: Number of CAL programs (on hand) per faculty (see Fig. 1); The type of courseware (Fig. 2); The number of self-produced versus acquired Computer Workpackage (CW) packages (Fig. 3); The production tools used for CW development (Fig. 4); The usage "life" of CW; Distribution of usage per study year; Total number of student users; Average CW completion time; Appreciation by students; Usage problems; and final discussion.

Part 3: Background information about CAL

It was assumed that most readers had only superficial knowledge about CAL, thus a fair portion (1/3) of this report provided background or orientation information about the medium itself. These seven sections (with sub-sections) were titled: forms or modes of CAL; forms of CMI; the CAL development process; the components of CAL; the quality or advantages of CAL; the complaints or disadvantages of CAL; the general use of CAL in The Netherlands and abroad. Finally, appendices were included which contained (not filled-in) actual questionnaires and structured interview forms.

It was hoped that this background information might stimulate further interest among KUN staff. It was not our intention however to distribute this 100+ page report to all teaching personnel

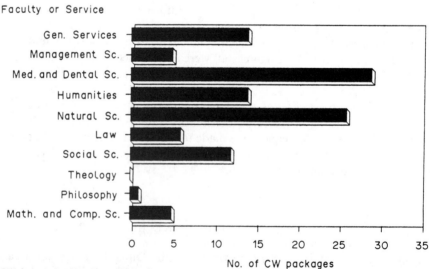

1. Not all CW is currently operational.
2. IOWO (Gen. Serv.) has more CW than indicated. Shown on request.

Fig. 1. CAL courseware per faculty (No. of CW packages).

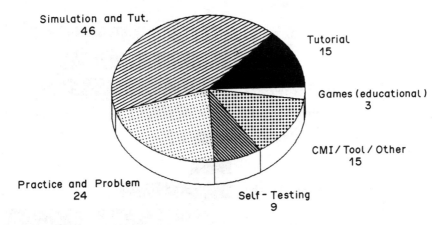

Simulation and Tut.
46

Tutorial
15

Games (educational)
3

CMI / Tool / Other
15

Self - Testing
9

Practice and Problem
24

Most packages are combinations of more
than one type, e.g. tutorial and simulation.
Classifications are "loose".

Fig. 2. CW packages vs type of CAL (No. of type packages at KUN).

(too costly). It was sent to all faculty or department heads plus members of the governing board, plus members of the university's CAL special interest group. It also received a wider distribution among other Dutch universities and R&D agencies. The report was welcomed and generally favorably reviewed by the governing board (and others). The chancellor of the university suggested that a very compressed and differently directed (target group) brochure be prepared, that could better serve a CAL "marketing" or strategical purpose, e.g. include specific suggestions for getting started with CAL.

The prepared brochure was titled; "Supplementary, Substitutive, and Innovative: Use of CAL at KUN and proposals for managing development"[4] (translated). In about 10 pages this brochure summarises the major findings of the report and further suggests some strategies for implementation, e.g. pilot projects, in-depth vertical feasibility studies per study discipline, horizontal (cross-discipline) studies. Also presented was a plan suggesting 12 phases for the previous studies.

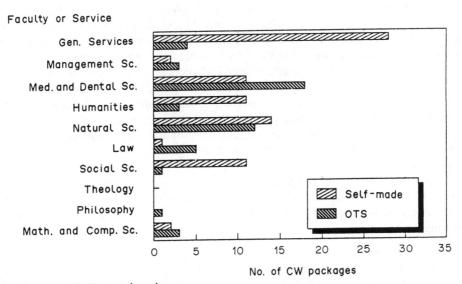

Faculty or Service

Gen. Services
Management Sc.
Med. and Dental Sc.
Humanities
Natural Sc.
Law
Social Sc.
Theology
Philosophy
Math. and Comp. Sc.

Self-made
OTS

No. of CW packages

Many packages are jointly produced
between faculties and service agencies.
Total no. exceeds no. of CW packages.

Fig. 3. CW in-house; self-made vs OTS (OTS, off-the-shelf).

Authoring vehicle

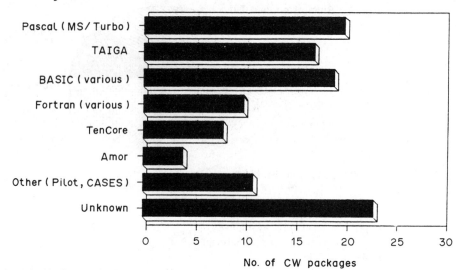

1. Ready-made CW seldom mention language
"Unknown" is therefore high.

Fig. 4. Authoring/programming languages (to produce courseware).

6. DISCUSSION AND RECOMMENDATIONS

From the figures included herein, the reader can get an idea about the general status of CAL within our university, e.g. use per faculty, number of programs, types of CW, etc. There is thus no need to discuss the data further except to state that our university was one of the top Dutch university CoA (centres of activity). This data reflects the earlier environment, when activities were rather *ad hoc* (grass-root level) determined, where CAL services were "unlimited" and less costly, and where basically no top-down policy making or CAL guidelines existed.

Via questionnaires and interviews it became readily apparent that most university staff who had some CAL experiences, were dissatisfied with the current situation (see Section 2). There was little standardisation, some personnel conflicts, little support from administrators or educational committees (in the form of funding for personnel or acquisitions) or compensation for CAL development. Most activities were initiated in a "piggy-back" fashion (making use of existing facilities used for other purposes; no budgets for CAL). CAL was seen by most not as a substitutive, but rather a minimal supplement or remedial tool for students. In general, faculty deans felt that if an individual instructor wanted to use CAL in some form, it was his own "business". The teacher was primarily responsible for the contents and didactical strategies of courses without much external interference. Several active CAL instructors had campaigned for further support, but were generally rebuffed, e.g. "if you need assistance, shift funds from "research" budgets to your "teaching" budget". It is remarkable that progress was made in this environment. It was largely due to the responsibility and dedication of a handful of innovative teachers, some external support from computer manufacturers (i.e. IBM), and early policies of the IOWO and skills of the CAL group itself.

The question now is how will CAL prosper under the rather newly established service policies of the IOWO (detailed in Section 3) and via the recommendations made in our reports.

The general recommendations made to the university's governing board are summarised in the following list.

(A) There is a need for a coordinated CAL management policy which should be established by and for each content discipline, e.g. physics, biology, mathematics, languages. Subject matter educational committees may determine needs and facilities and selection criteria.

(B) These policies should support teaching staff within a study discipline who wish to initiate CAL. An infra-structure should be created that helps in implementation, usage and evaluation, and can eventually assist in funding.

(C) Each subject matter discipline should appoint a CAL coordinator (part-time, among existing personnel) whose tasks may include: publicising policies and facilities; searching for OTS courseware; evaluating materials, finding external funding opportunities.

(D) Continue support of the existing, university wide, CAL special interest group (about 30 members on paper, much fewer are active). Each CAL coordinator should join. This group may be asked to keep abreast of state-of-the-art activities and developments, and hold workshops or seminars.

(E) Before applying CAL, develop detailed guidelines establishing (project) selection or "go-ahead" criteria, e.g. needs analysis, searchers for ready-mades, standards, minimum number of users, stability of CW, and cost-effectivity.

(F) It is preferable to "acquire" CW rather than to develop it yourself. Exhaust all other possibilities before undertaking self-development. Purchase "campus-licenses" to reduce costs, explore cooperative, networked, or other sharing arrangements.

(G) In line with (F), produce a yearly CW catalogue, indexed by subject matter, containing lists and descriptions of OTS CW. Local faculty coordinators to assist in collection and dissemination, but produced by the IOWO.

(H) The university should create a separate, central, "innovation and stimulation" fund for the development of needed CW. Each subfaculty to submit projects; an evaluation committee to select.

(I) Stress and support inter and intra university cooperation, cooperation with vocational training schools, international and CEC agencies.

(J) Given the need for "teamwork" in CAL development, the university should continue supporting the central agency supplying existing CAL services.

(K) Investigate and support the expanded use of student assistants for CAL development; provide compensation in a tangible form, to teaching staff involved in development.

(L) Create a separate extra fund for CAL R&D which should fall under the administrative umbrella of the IOWO.

(M) Try to standardise on use of the most popular microcomputers for CAL, e.g. industrial standards. These currently are the IBM PC (or compatibles) and Macintosh.

(N) Current (computer) facilities for CAL need expansion, e.g. more color monitors and graphics. Stress should be on expanding facilities for CD-ROM and videodisk configurations.

(O) Encourage a priority arrangement, in current large group microcomputer facilities, for CAL users. If sufficient need exists, create smaller, dedicated, CAL locales within a faculty.

(P) To advance the "CW life" of each product in use, appoint someone within each study-discipline to maintain and monitor CAL usage. This may be the coordinator.

(Q) Each courseware product in use should receive proper evaluation; not just an informal review by the instructor, but a more vigorous analysis of data and control on proper integration.

7. CAL PHASES AND IMPLEMENTATION STRATEGIES

Although presented in the report, a concise outline of the typical phasing of CAL development was included in the brochure, as well as several possible ways for administrators within a faculty to get the CAL ball rolling within their study disciplines. These suggestions are certainly not new to educational technologists, but were expressed as guidelines to be followed in place of the earlier less structured approach, and because the new CAL environment, vis-à-vis limited services by the CAL group, forced the specification of well-planned (time and manpower) projects. It was also outlined to demonstrate the "professional" approach which now had to be followed, the seriousness of the situation, e.g. no mere experimental try-outs or unbound agreements between individual instructors and the CAL agency. In the past, instructors often approached cooperative projects with a, "I'll see if I have the time", attitude.

(A) Phases

The 12 phases outlined were divided into 3 categories, namely: management of development; management of implementation; and management of evaluation.

Falling under development were:

Phase 1: Analysis of current instructional difficulties or educational problems. Inventory and analysis, possible solutions.

Phase 2: Collecting and disseminating knowledge about the possibilities of CAL, e.g. educational, technical, organisational and financial.

Phase 3: Inventory of the current status within the discipline. Carry out usage or feasibility studies, specify priorities and set operating conditions.

Phase 4: Formulate a clear CAL management policy. Relate to the entering situation, formulate goals, set "go/no-go" selection criteria, gain support and plan for technical, financial, and cooperative assistance.

Falling under implementation were the following phases:

Phase 5: Study where and how CAL can best be used. Differentiate between the various types of CAL, determine correct integration into curriculum or course, formulate the requirements that CAL must fulfil.

Phase 6: Select and budget for a CAL application. Establish the costs (time and facilities) and provide detailed specifications of planning.

Phase 7: Acquire the desired CAL, either via searches for ready-mades or self development. Manage its completion.

Phase 8: Implement as planned. Prepare for installation and training, the infra-structure needed, monitoring and control, the test–retest cycles for improvement.

The evaluation phases include:

Phase 9: Evaluate the implementation by determining whether goals were reached, strategies were followed. Consolidate and determine follow-up strategies.

Phase 10: Consolidate the use of CAL, e.g. try to strengthen its acceptance by staff and students, the use, management, maintenance and evaluation.

Phase 11: Disseminate knowledge, experience, and approaches with an eye to future cooperation, financing and support.

Phase 12: Reformulate management policies and choose follow-up procedures.

(B) Strategies

(1) The pilot project. The simplest strategy recommended was, for beginning users (the starting phase), the pilot project. A study discipline having absolutely no previous CAL experience, would do best to implement one or more initial CAL packages, preferably a ready-made package or quickly prepared package having high relatedness to the curriculum and a known instructional problem, e.g. students need self-testing facilities in preparation for examinations.

(2) The "in-depth" strategy. Following the beginning user phase, an "explorative use" strategy is recommended. This strategy consists of a systematic study (needs analysis or feasibility) of a complete study discipline (curriculum) to determine wherein CAL can best be applied. The goals are to determine where: (i) CAL can best be applied from an educational and economical viewpoint, (ii) to determine the actual form, e.g. types of CAL needed and expected results, and (iii) the development of a set of systems and procedures that can be carried over to other subject matter ares. On the basis of this in-depth strategy, experience is gained which makes it possible to follow up with an, "in-breadth", strategy.

(3) The "in-breadth" strategy. Basically following the procedures previously identified and developed during the in-depth strategy, but now applied across a greater number of study disciplines. For example, if the in-depth strategy was applied to one foreign language study, it might now be applied to all, or the entire Faculty of Letters and Humanities.

8. EFFECTS OF NEW POLICY CHANGES AND REPORT

The long term effect of the IOWO/CAL group service philosophy changes and repercussions of the study, can only be guessed at. Hopefully it will lead to improved service, and cost and educationally effective applications.

A direct effect of the report has been the granting of a major (spread over 4 years) "innovation" project by the Medical Faculty. This involves a full-scale study of the medical and dental curriculums to determine if, where, and how, CAL can best be used, as well to develop courseware. Thus, the "in-depth" or actually "in-breadth" strategies previously mentioned, will be put into effect. This same approach has been requested by an outside educational institution, and is likely to be requested by other university departments (when budgets become available). Tools and experience developed and gained during these studies will be very beneficial to the IOWO and clients.

Another effect is that all new potential CAL intakes must be carefully discussed, presented to faculty committees or heads for approval and ranking. Choices must be made based on the project being "educationally responsible" (instructionally effective, possibly less expensive), being financially responsible (the ability to regain initial investment expenses spread over a long period, e.g. 5 years), and it (the materials) being fully integrated into the course or curriculum as well as having the full cooperation of the instructor as a development partner.

Based on the previous point, there has been a reduction in the amount of new project intakes, as individual staff members who may have some interests or wishes, struggle with the need to convince their department heads or educational committees, that their project is worthwhile. Since an entire faculty only receives a limited number of IOWO (the central service agency) hours, and other non-CAL services are available, the faculty decision makers themselves must establish priorities. Thus a number of potentially interesting and useful smaller projects may have to be delayed or permanently shelved. We are hopeful that larger, more encompassing projects will receive approval in the initial stages, which can later be followed up by more restrictive applications.

A secondary effect is that, without easier (administratively) and less costly centralised support, a faculty or study-discipline will initiate projects on their own. That is, call upon internal staff, usually less experienced, to perform some CAL functions. There are two sides to the coin. Developing internal expertise is desirable but given the atmosphere previously described (Section 2), few volunteers will be found, and there is an increased likelihood that the wheel will be rediscovered. Also likely is less standardisation of facilities and tools, as individuals go their own way.

Another effect has been on the types of services and tools made available by the CAL group itself. Rather than offering a full range of support in all cases, which can be very time-consuming and beyond the range of faculty/IOWO budgets, shorter and more specific tasks can be performed. Thus, for example, rather than fully developing a CAL self-testing system and performing all programming tasks using its "own" sophisticated authoring tools, a simpler or more user friendly authoring vehicle may be delivered to a requestor allowing him to produce independently. In this case, the CAL group service would be limited to evaluation, or suggestions for improvements. Similarly, wherein earlier the group occasionally offered teaching assistance to faculties or gave internal courses, this has been sharply reduced due to the costs involved. Thus the service provided shifted to providing resource information and materials which could be used by the requesting agency. While this may appear to be in conflict with some earlier mentioned effects, these shorter tasks are important to our general "advisorial" university function, help others to gain "starting-up" experiences, and just as important, provide some needed service hours to keep our group functioning.

A direct effect has also been the dire need to seek and obtain outside commercial contracts. Without this added income, the group may be forced to cut back personnel or indeed disappear. This situation has resulted in more attention to "marketing", and equally likely, choosing more profitable external contracts than internal (university) applications. Needless to say, the time available or that which could be spent for research or self-development activities, has been sharply reduced. We are guardedly optimistic about the future, given some early commercial successes. The general feeling is that, "big is beautiful", i.e. the larger our agency becomes, the more likely that we can compete in the marketplace and concurrently provide better services to the university.

REFERENCES

1. Leiblum M., Derks K. and Hermans D., A decade of CAL at a Dutch University. *Computers Educ.* **10**, 229–243 (1986).

2. Mirande M., Computerondersteund Onderwijs: van particulier initiatief naar onderwijsbeleid (CAL: from individual initiative to educational management). In *Onderzoek van Onderwijs*. In press.
3. Leiblum M. and Mirande M., Computerondersteund onderwijs aan de KUN: aanbevelingen, stand van zaken, achtergronden (CAL at KUN: recommendations, status and background). IOWO, KU Nijmegen (1990).
4. Mirande M. and Leiblum M., Aanvullend, vervangend en vernieuwend: gebruik van computerondersteund onderwijs aan de KUN en een voorstel voor beleidsontwikkeling (Complementary, substitutive, and innovative: use of CAL at KUN and a proposal for educational management). IOWO, KU Nijmegen (1990).

Computers Educ. Vol. 18, No. 1–3, pp. 119–125, 1992
Printed in Great Britain. All rights reserved

SOME PROBLEMS OF MATHEMATICAL CAL

C. E. Beevers, M. G. Foster, G. R. McGuire and J. H. Renshaw

Department of Mathematics, Heriot-Watt University, Riccarton, Edinburgh EH14 4AS, Scotland

Abstract—This paper describes briefly some problems of mathematical CAL and suggests ways to combat them. Within the context of the CALM Project for Computer Aided Learning in Mathematics we highlight three main areas of difficulty—mathematical display, input and evaluation. These problems are illustrated using examples from software developed at the Heriot-Watt University in Edinburgh and at Southampton University; the examples are taken from both calculus and algebra.

1. BACKGROUND TO THE CALM PROJECT

The CALM Project for Computer Aided Learning in Mathematics was established at the Heriot-Watt University in Edinburgh in October 1985. CALM was one of the 149 projects funded by the Computer Board as part of the Computers in Teaching Initiative. Throughout the initial phase of CALM, pilot groups were monitored and both formative and summative evaluations were made. CALM produced software in the form of a computerised tutorial system to enhance the teaching of calculus to large groups of engineers and scientists. One unit of software, covering roughly 2 h of conventional teaching, was prepared for every week of a 25-week course. The teaching strategy in the units followed the structure below for each topic in each unit:

Theory sections—to consolidate the lecture
Worked examples sections—to illustrate methods
Motivating examples—to stimulate interest
Test sections—to enable students to check on their own strengths and weaknesses and provide feedback of progress to the teacher

The CALM Project produced software on the Research Machines Nimbus for a course on differentiation, integration and an introduction to numerical methods and differential equations. The CALM software has been used regularly by over 800 undergraduates on the Riccarton campus of the Heriot-Watt University alone. We have published details of the early formative and summative evaluations of CALM and the interested reader is directed to references [1–3] for further information.

At Southampton University one of us (JHR) has ported the CALM software onto the IBM and the whole package has been sold to over a dozen institutes of higher education throughout the U.K. In the last 12 months further work at Southampton has produced software in the CALM style in the area of basic algebra including vectors and complex numbers.

Throughout the CALM Project we have become increasingly aware of the special problems mathematics poses for the designer of CAL materials. In the following sections we illustrate some of these problems and where possible suggest some remedies.

2. DISPLAYING MATHEMATICS

Mathematics has a language of its own and therein lie the problems for CAL in mathematics. Equations that require fractions, powers, subscripts or special symbols all present problems for authors of mathematical software.

It is useful to have tools for displaying the common requirements in mathematical text. Placing a fraction on the screen with numerator, denominator and horizontal divide line is often needed. This can be easily accomplished with a routine to put a variety of fraction styles onto the screen in any given colour and pixel position.

The basic symbols like $+$, $-$ etc., are available in the standard character set. Other symbols like $\sqrt{}$ and $\int$ can be found in the extended character set. However, not all the characters required are available. For example, there are characters, such as the partial derivative symbol ∂, which are not available even in the extended character set. In this case we have used the facility of a User Defined Font within Prospero Pascal to set up the new characters. Our routine copies the standard IBM character set table into the CALM font table and then it redefines those codes we need.

3. INPUT OF MATHEMATICAL EXPRESSIONS

The difficulty of entering mathematical symbols is relatively easy to overcome. However, the problem of inputting mathematical expressions without demanding the full rigour of Pascal grammer is more complex and is also related to the interpretation or evaluation routine which will be used (see Section 4 below).

The standard microcomputer keyboard does not include many mathematical symbols. The symbols in the extended character set may be entered by holding down the ⟨Alt⟩ key and entering the appropriate code on the numeric keypad. It is unreasonable to expect a student to learn these key codes so we have set up the first four function keys to generate the most commonly required symbols, i.e. $\sqrt{}$, π, ^{2} (as in x^2) and Θ.

We reduced some of the rigours of Pascal grammar in a number of ways. For example, the $*$ for multiplication became optional and a power mode enabled students to input expressions like x^7. Indeed, we even allowed the common mathematical shorthand for expressions like $\cos(x)*\cos(x)$ to be entered as $\cos^2(x)$. However, we retained the use of brackets around the arguments of functions believing this to be a meaningful point of both mathematical and Pascal grammar.

However, input difficulties remain. The problem is best illustrated by example:

for the input of $\dfrac{1}{x-1}$ type $1/(x-1)$ and not $1/x-1$ which is interpreted as $\dfrac{1}{x}-1$; and

for the input of $\dfrac{2x}{3\pi}$ type $2x/(3\pi)$ and not $2x/3\pi$ which is interpreted as $\dfrac{2x\pi}{3}$.

The one-line input for the multi-line language of mathematics can be overcome with the correct use of brackets but this does cause difficulties for the weaker students. A more radical solution is planned in which we provide an interpret key utility to display in mathematical format how the one-line input is understood by the computer. This development is being built into the next phase of the CALM Project in which we are developing software units on the mathematics needed for university entrance.

4. COMPARING AND EVALUATING EXPRESSIONS

When an algebraic expression is evaluated, the numerical value of the expression is calculated for fixed values of the variables (if any) in the expression. We require this tool for at least two reasons. Firstly for direct calculation of the values of a function which is to be plotted as a graph. Secondly it is used as a step in the process of checking student answers and as such it underpins our testing facilities. Multiple choice testing, though it has its place in mathematics, cannot be the main way of assessing student understanding. More conventional forms of testing require facilities to evaluate and compare mathematical answers.

Some programming languages, like BBC BASIC for example, provide an evaluation function, but Pascal does not. Ours[4] is a recursive procedure based upon established routines.

In the test the main step is to decide whether an answer, input by a student as a string of characters, is right or wrong. This decision is made by another function called *Compare*. The student answer has to be compared with the true answer which is a string supplied by the setter of the question.

The normal process for comparing two strings would be to check that corresponding characters in the two strings are the same. In mathematics, however, there may be many different correct formats for the same answer. Consider an example in which the answer is a numeric constant.

With true answer 8/9, acceptable student answers would be

$$8/9, \quad 16/18, \quad 1 - 1/9, \quad +8/9, \quad 0.889 \text{ etc.}$$

Another example involving a function of one variable:

With true answer $x^2 - 1$, acceptable student answers would be

$$x * x - 1, \quad (x - 1)(x + 1), \quad (x + 1) * (x - 1) \text{ etc.}$$

These two simple examples illustrate that standard string comparison of mathematical answers is untenable. It would be extremely demanding on memory requiring the storage of all possible formats for acceptable answers. This could be infinite.

The approach adopted in our procedure *Compare* is to look only at values of the expressions represented by the student answer and the true answer and compare them over a suitable range of values of any variables used in the expressions. Answers are restricted to real constants or real, single-valued functions of one or more (up to five) variables. In practice this presents no real restriction. The expression is then evaluated by our procedure.

As well as the student answer and the true answer, the information required by *Compare* is the set of variables used in the true answer, the range $[a, b]$ and, the number of points c in this range at which the answers are to be evaluated. The algorithm also requires a tolerance t and a failure rate f.

To compare answers representing constants only one value for the student answer and one value for the true answer need be computed. If the two computed values agree exactly, the two constants are then taken to be the same. If the two constants are expressed in different forms, however, round-off error accumulated during evaluation will lead to different values for the two equivalent constants. Although in some circumstances this discrepancy can be large, in general the values are close.

For example:

With true answer $1 + \sqrt{2}/2$, some correct student answers are

$$1 + 1/\sqrt{2}, \quad 1/(2 - \sqrt{2}), \quad (\sqrt{2} + 1)/\sqrt{2} \text{ etc.}$$

Therefore when comparing two constants it is desirable in practice to consider them equal even if their values do not agree exactly but are almost the same. In *Compare* a student answer is considered "equal" to the true answer if the relative error is less than or equal to some prescribed tolerance t.

The relative error is calculated as the ratio of *abs* (value of true answer minus value of student answer) to *abs* (value of true answer). If the value of the true answer is zero then the absolute error is used instead of the relative error.

The necessity for this is even more apparent in the following example. With true answer π, acceptable student answers would be close numerical approximations such as 3.142 or 22/7. Taking $t = 0.01$ (allowing 1% relative error), student answers given by expressions with values lying in the range $[0.99\pi, 1.01\pi]$ are accepted by *Compare*. In this case 3.14 is accepted but 3.1 is not.

For answers representing functions of one or more variables the situation is more complicated. Mathematically, two functions are equal if their domains are the same and if their values agree at all points of the domain. However, it is impractical to evaluate both functions at all points of the domain. Therefore in *Compare*, functions are compared by evaluating them only at a finite set of points in their domain.

Consider functions of one variable, x say. The student answer and the true answer are now functions of x defined on all or part of the real line. The finite set of evaluation points is chosen by defining an interval $[a, b]$ of the real line ($a \leqslant b$) and a number of points c ($c \geqslant 1$). These evaluation points are chosen randomly from a large number of equally spaced points in $[a, b]$ including the end-points. The values of the two functions are considered to be "equal" at a point in the same way as for constants where the relative or absolute difference is compared with t, the supplied tolerance. If the values of the true answer and the student answer are "equal" at all of the c points then the two functions themselves are considered to be "equal".

The failure rate f can be set to allow a certain number of disagreements between values of the two answers. Examples of its use can be found in [4]. For most situations involving functions of one variable, f should be set to 0.

The values of a, b, c and t should all be chosen to fit in with the definition of the true answer. Care must be exercised in choosing values for these parameters.
For example:

> With a true answer of $1/(x^2 - 1)$:
> suppose we take $a = -0.1$, $b = 0.1$, $c = 7$, $t = 0.01$ (1% relative error). The values of the true answer and student answer will then be compared at seven randomly-chosen points in the interval $[-0.1, 0.1]$ of x.
> Consider two possible student answers:
> 0 and -1.
> Both the true and the student answers are well formulated strings and give proper functions of x (both student answers are constant functions of x). For the first student answer the relative error at any point in the interval is 1 which is greater than t. This leads to this student answer being rejected by *Compare*. However, for the second student answer the relative error at any value of x is
>
> $$\text{abs}((1/(x^2 - 1) + 1)/(1/(x^2 - 1))) = x^2$$
>
> which is $\leqslant t$ for all x in the range $[-0.1, 0.1]$. Thus, this student answer will be accepted by *Compare* and consequently this second answer is regarded as correct though it is not.

This last answer illustrates the need for care in choosing values for the parameters a, b, c and t. Here the true answer is defined for almost all x values yet $[a, b]$ has been restricted to a small interval $[-0.1, 0.1]$. It would be more appropriate if a range like $[1.5, 10]$ is chosen. This interval covers a wider range of values of the true answer from 0.8 down to about 0.01.

Another example of a true answer where a, b, c and t have to be chosen with care is the answer $e^{100x} + x$. For, in this case, the true answer is in two parts with the values of e^{100x} dominating the answer for $x > 0$ and the values of x dominating the answer for $x < 0$. Hence, a range of values for the evaluation points must straddle zero so that both parts of the answer are checked. In this case $a = -1$, $b = 0.1$, $c = 7$ and $t = 0.01$ would serve the desired purpose.

It is almost impossible to construct an acceptable answer close to the true one without prior knowledge of the evaluation points and of the true answer itself. However, if the student answer adds a very small quantity to the true answer then this would provide a student answer which is strictly wrong but it would be accepted by *Compare*.

> For instance, with the true answer $\cos(\pi x)$, to be checked over the range $[-0.45, 0.45]$ with $c = 7$ and $t = 0.01$, the student answer, $\cos(\pi x) + 0.005 \sin(2\pi x)$, has relative error
>
> $$\text{abs}(0.005 \sin(2\pi x)/\cos(\pi x)) = \text{abs}(0.01 \sin(\pi x)) \leqslant 0.01$$
>
> This is within the value of the tolerance t. Thus, this student answer would be accepted by *Compare*.

In general, the construction of such a solution requires knowledge of the value of t and the true answer. Such small errors must also be allowed to permit the use of rounded approximations to constants such as π, $\sqrt{3}$, $1/7$ etc.

From the above it is clear that the true answer must be known before a reasonable attempt can be made to produce a student answer to beat *Compare*. Furthermore, other devices, such as restricting the length of the student answer, make the construction of such incorrect answers more difficult. Hence, it is evident that only inappropriate choice of values for the parameters a, b, c and t can lead to *Compare* accepting *bona fide* incorrect answers.

Usually, relative error is more restrictive for smaller values of the answers than for the larger values. Thus, an interval $[a, b]$ should be chosen to cover as wide a range of the values of the true answer as possible and it should include those values of x at which the true answer takes its smallest value. The parameter c should be an integer between 6 and 11. The tolerance t should be chosen to allow some flexibility in approximations for the smallest value of the true answer (apart from 0 of course). This flexibility allows approximate values for constants in the answer such as 22/7 for π etc.

The failure rate parameter f was set up to allow "sloppy" student answers. For example:

> With true answer $x + 1$ take $a = -2, b = 2, c = 11$ and $t = 0.001$ (0.1%) and consider a student answer $(x^2 - 1)/(x - 1)$.
> These two functions are strictly not the same since the student answer gives a function not defined at $x = 1$.
> If the failure rate $f = 0$ and $x = 1$ happens not to be chosen randomly as an evaluation point then Compare would accept the student answer.
> However, if $f = 0$ and $x = 1$ is chosen as an evaluation point then the student answer would be undefined at this point and Compare would reject the student answer. This might be considered rather harsh, especially if the common factor was not an obvious one.
> Setting f non-zero, say at 0.1, which allows 10% of evaluation points to lead to failure, would allow Compare to accept the student answer even with $x = 1$ as one of the evaluation points.

An even more difficult situation concerns functions which are defined on a restricted range of the x-axis. For example:

> With true answer $\ln(\mathrm{abs}(x - 1))$ (note the abs) a student answer might be given as $\ln(x - 1)$.
> Strictly speaking this should lead to Compare rejecting it unless only values of $x > 1$ are specified.
> Similarly a student answer $\ln(1 - x)$ should also be rejected unless only values of $x < 1$ are specified.
> However, both of these answers might be acceptable even though they apply only for two different restricted ranges of x.

A large value of the failure rate f combined with an interval covering both restricted ranges could be used in Compare to allow "sloppy" answers as in the example above. However the failure rate f was designed to deal mainly with occasional values where the answers might be undefined or do not match. Therefore, in general, f is given a low value.

Sloppy answers like those in the last example can be dealt with by considering ranges for the evaluation points other than $[a, b]$. In function Compare the student's answer and the true answer are considered at points in $[a, b]$ and then if required at points in $[-b, -a]$. If they are found "equal" over either range then Compare accepts the student answer. For example:

> From the last example, with true answer $\ln(\mathrm{abs}(x - 1))$ student answers $\ln(x - 1)$ and $\ln(1 - x)$ would both be accepted by Compare with an appropriate choice of $[a, b]$ and a small value of f.
> With $[a, b] = [2, 9]$ and $f = 0$ then $\ln(x - 1)$ is accepted by Compare over the range $[2, 9]$ while $\ln(1 - x)$ is accepted over the interval $[-9, -2]$.

Further illustrations, including examples of functions of two variables, can be found in [4] and the interested reader is directed there for more discussion on issues raised above.

5. CALM IN THE 1990s

The decision to use Pascal to program the original CALM software was made in 1985 when authoring systems were limited. In mathematical applications the disadvantages of using such systems outweighed the advantages. At the start of a new project it was important to look at products which have become available since then.

In reviewing the current authoring systems on the software market, we were looking for three attributes:

Portability—the software should run on a variety of hardware in particular PC, Macintosh and possibly SUN workstations;

Flexibility—a tutor who uses the courseware should be able to adapt a lesson to her/his own needs; and

Extendibility—it should be possible to augment the authoring system with commands and functions which overcome the problems specific to Mathematics as described in previous sections.

One system which has all the necessary qualities is Authorware. In Authorware icons are placed on a flow line to build up a diagram of the lesson. There are icons for display, animation, erase, wait or pause, decision, interaction, calculation and a map icon. The interactions include text input, clicking on buttons, hotspots or pull-down menus and moving objects. The calculation icon gives access to a wide range of functions and variables. The map icon "wraps up" a complex structure into one icon still allowing the overall structure to be viewed.

Authorware answers the portability requirement since it is currently available on the Macintosh and a PC version running under Windows is soon to be released. There is also a commitment from the creators of Authorware to port it to the X windows environment.

Authorware is flexible as it uses graphic logic to set out the structure of a lesson. This "structure" is then run and the content of the displays and the responses to interactions are added as they are encountered by the author. A completed lesson can also be edited in the same way so that text can be changed or whole sections can be rearranged with ease. A tutor can therefore add his or her own "stamp" to the courseware. Templates can also be set up using the model feature of authorware. Many of the display difficulties described in Section 2 disappear since the author can arrange a screen of expressions with fractions, powers etc. directly.

On the Macintosh additional functions can be incorporated into Authorware by the means of XFNCs and XCMDs. These are code resources whose specification was set up to allow for extensions to HyperCard. The same effect can be achieved under Windows on the PC by the use of Dynamic Link Libraries (DLL). There are also commands within Authorware which enable execution of external applications.

The problems we have identified in the area of mathematical CAL can be summarised under three headings: display, input and evaluation and checking answers. The windowing environments on both Macintosh and PC provide tools which alleviate some of the problems. The use of mathematical fonts provides all the symbols that may be required in display and input. The cut and paste feature allows complex mathematical expressions to be set up in dedicated mathematics type-setting programs such as MathType, Formulator or Expressionist and copied into the Authorware presentation window. Drawing packages or user-written programs can be employed to display accurately graphs of functions etc. These graphs can then be passed as graphic objects to Authorware.

Code resources (XCMD/XFNCs or DLL) can be designed to provide the additional features required such as evaluation of mathematical expressions and the comparison of student's mathematical answers with the true answer.

Finally, the option to launch other applications from within Authorware opens up the possibility of using dedicated mathematical software such as computer algebra packages, graph plotters etc.

It seems that many of the mundane problems have been resolved and resources can now be concentrated on the more exciting challenges to developing CAL in Mathematics.

Acknowledgement—The authors are grateful to the Department of Trade and Industry for their financial support of the CALM Project.

REFERENCES

1. Beevers C. E., Clark D. E. R., Cherry B. S., Foster M. G., McGuire G. R. and Renshaw J. H., The CALM before the storm! *Computers Educ.* **12**, 43–47 (1988).
2. Beevers C. E., Clark D. E. R., Cherry B. S., Foster M. G., McGuire G. R. and Renshaw J. H., The CALM Project—an evaluation. *Conference on Mathematics Curriculum*, pp. 285–298. Napier College, Edinburgh, (1988).
3. Beevers C. E., Foster M. G. and McGuire G. R., Integrating formative evaluation into a learner centred revision course. *Br. J. Educ. Technol.* **20**, 115–119 (1989).
4. Beevers C. E., Cherry B. S., Foster M. G. and McGuire G. R., *Software Tools for Computer-aided Learning in Mathematics.* Gower, Aldershot (1991).

Computers Educ. Vol. 18, No. 1–3, pp. 127–133, 1992
Printed in Great Britain. All rights reserved

THE CORE GUIDED DISCOVERY APPROACH TO ACQUIRING PROGRAMMING SKILLS

Tom Boyle and Sue Margetts*

Department of Computing, Manchester Polytechnic, John Dalton Building,
Manchester M1 5GD, England

Abstract—The CORE approach is a design method for constructing learning environments based on principles derived from studies of language and cognitive development. The method has been applied so far to the design of learning environments for acquiring programming skills. This approach is in direct contrast to traditional didactic, rule based approaches where instructions are first given, and practice to implement these instructions follows. The CORE approach, by contrast, engages the student as an active problem solver from the very beginning. The central principle is to present the user not with abstract rules to be learned but with concrete examples to be understood. These key examples are followed by a series of questions and feedback answers which allow the learner to clarify and extend their understanding. The other two major features of the method are to set a clear context for each learning session, and to get the learners to express and reflect on their knowledge at the end of each session. A computer aided learning environment for Pascal has been developed for IBM PC compatible machines. This was used with groups of students for an extended period of time. The students' assessment of the CORE Pascal learning system as an effective and enjoyable learning environment was very positive.

INTRODUCTION

The aim of the CORE approach is to develop effective environments for acquiring information technology skills. The development of the method so far has focused on the acquisition of programming skills. The traditional method to teach programming is to use lectures, textbooks and practicals. Broadly speaking lectures and textbooks are used to convey information and practicals give the opportunity to put that information into use. This approach is essentially didactic. The students are first told about the language and then expected to put into practice what they have been told. There are, however, a number of problems with this approach which can create very real obstacles to the learning process.

A central problem is the splitting off of the relatively passive assimilation of knowledge of the language from the active involvement in applying this knowledge. The manner in which the teaching situation is approached can further complicate this problem. Teaching tends to be focused, to too great an extent, on a concern for the target language, and how this may be represented, rather than with a deep concern for the learning process itself. This approach is concerned with the presentation of the formal rules of the language which have to be explicitly learned. However, this didactic, abstract, rule oriented approach can produce substantial learning problems. The problem was summarized by one programming lecturer commenting on the textbooks for a major programming language who said, "you can understand the textbooks if you already understand the language".

The CORE approach is in direct contrast to this rule based approach. It aims to foster and support a more natural form of learning. It seeks to involve the learner from the very beginning in making sense of and carrying out meaningful actions in the language he/she is learning. A range of research in psychology, especially developmental psychology, indicates that people are active and constructive in making sense of their world (e.g.[1–4]). Furthermore, structuring the context in which problems are presented can have a crucial effect on the learners ability to make sense of a problem and thus to activate these natural problem solving skills. In particular, studies have dramatically demonstrated the influence of presenting a problem in an abstract vs a more familiar setting[2]. A problem which can be solved easily when presented in the context of a framework of familiar objects can become extremely difficult when presented in an abstract disembedded form.

---

*Now at Bury College.

Certain formats of presentation thus seem to enable people's problem solving skills; other contexts seem to disable these skills. The aim of the CORE method is to develop learning environments, embodying design principles derived largely from studies of language and cognitive development, which will activate and encourage the use of dynamic natural learning skills.

THE LEARNING PRINCIPLES UNDERLYING THE CORE APPROACH

The name CORE summarizes the four main elements of this approach: Context, Objects, Refinements and Expression. These principles have been implemented in a booklet which gives an introduction to a small sub-set of Lisp[5], and in a full CAL tutor for Pascal which is described in this paper.

Context

Each learning block in the CORE approach starts by providing the learner with an overall view of the skills he/she will have acquired by the end of the block. This is achieved by presenting the learner with an example of the type of skills that will be acquired. These new skills are presented in the context of a complete program or procedure. The context section for the first learning block of the Pascal Tutor is presented in Fig. 1(a).

The intention is that the user should get a view of the new skill without being overburdened by technicalities. This relates to the findings of Donaldson[2] about the importance of presenting problems in a meaningful context. The context section helps the learner to make holistic sense of what is happening. A similar function applies to the "advance organizer" proposed by Ausubel[6]

This is a simple Pascal program:

```
program TheFirst;
begin
   write ('This is the first of many, many programs');
end.
```

It displays on the screen

This is the first of many, many programs

By the end of this section you will be able to write a simple Pascal program for yourself.

(Note: students worked with a Turbo Pascal system)

Fig. 1. (a) Context screen for first learning block.

This is a valid program heading

```
program DrawSquare;
```

These are also valid program headings:

```
program count;
program X;
```

Fig. 1. (b) Examples screen for first learning block.

Is this a valid program heading?

```
program simple;
```

- -

Yes it is—compare it with the examples on the previous screen.

Is this a valid program heading?

```
Program SIMPLE;
```

- -

Yes. Program headings can be written in upper or lower case letters.

Fig. 1. (c) Extract from refinement section in first learning book.

and evaluated by Mayer[3] who found that the provision of an orientation section was particularly useful for students studying unfamiliar or technical material.

When developing the Lisp CORE materials Boyle and Drazkowski[5] left out this section with individual students. In this situation the students involved commented on the lack of a framework which would give them an overall view of where they were going.

Objects

A central concern of the CORE method is to replace abstract didactic teaching of rules with a more natural form of learning. In this approach abstract rules are replaced with concrete objects from the domain to be explored. These "objects" take the form of clear central examples of the construct or skill to be learned [see Fig. 1(b)]. This approach was influenced by studies of early language learning. Children seem to form word meanings based on early exemplars of the use of the words, and then gradually refine the meaning through feedback obtained from parents and others[7,8]. The extensive work by Rosch and her colleagues has shown the importance of central exemplars in concept representation in adults[9,10].

The examples demonstrate the new constructs to be learned as separate entities. Having seen how the constructs operate in context the learner may now concentrate on studying them as distinct structures. These examples provide the basis for the learner to form an initial idea or hypothesis about the construct. Thus the student is actively involved from the start in trying to understand and make sense of the target structure or operation. The initial conception formed by the student provides the entry to the next stage—the refinement phase.

Refinement

The student is presented with a series of carefully selected and graded questions. He/she tries to answer each one before moving on to the next. The student is then given an answer with feedback on why this answer is correct [see Fig. 1(c)]. This is vital so that the student can learn from his/her mistakes and progressively refine the underlying representation of the new structure or operation.

In this approach mistakes are not regarded as bad but as opportunities to learn. If the student is actively involved in making sense of the evidence presented to him/her and testing out their ideas then they will naturally make mistakes. If appropriate feedback is made available they will also learn more effectively than if they were passive recipients of someone else's rules. This method also allows complexities to be revealed gradually. This helps to avoid the information overload which textbooks often inflict on students by trying to cover all conceivable variations and possibilities in one abstract rule right from the start.

Inferring their own ideas allows students to formulate these representations in a way which makes sense to them rather than having ideas imposed from without. This brings up the question of how adequate are these representations. It is the function of the next section to get the students to explicitly use the knowledge and skills gained. This provides a clear test of the adequacy of the knowledge and skills gained by the students.

Expression

There is an interesting question over what should count as an adequate expression of the students' knowledge and skills. In the Lisp study the students were asked to express in their own words the underlying rules they had inferred. This allowed an explicit check on the completeness of the underlying representations the students had formed. Boyle and Drazkowski[5] questioned whether it was necessary to get the students to express their knowledge in this "metacognitive" form as an explicit rule. They suggested that an alternative form of expression is to solve appropriate problems which require an application of the knowledge and skills gained. This is the approach adopted in the Pascal Tutor program. In the Tutor program the Expression stage is implemented by getting the students to write computer programs which require knowledge of the skills and concepts covered in the learning block.

DESCRIPTION OF THE PASCAL TUTOR

The first implementation of the CORE method was in a booklet form, and the target implementation was a small sub-set of Lisp[5]. The choice of a booklet form of implementation at this stage was deliberate. It allowed an assessment of the CORE method separate from the extra attractions which could be added with a CAL implementation. The first year Polytechnic students who used the booklet assessed it very positively. The CORE approach, however, lends itself naturally to a CAL implementation. For the present study a fairly full CAL tutor for Pascal was developed and used with A level and Open Learning students. This program runs on IBM PC compatible machines.

The CORE Pascal Tutor consists of a "shell" which loads, displays and allows appropriate manipulation of text files. The material in the text files is structured according to the CORE method. The user is presented with a series of learning blocks. Each block begins with a title page and then a Context page. The Context page presents the new construct or skill as part of a complete program or procedure. As the tutor progresses the new constructs and skills are presented within program settings which are familiar to the learner on the basis of what they have learned before. Figure 1(a) reproduces the text from the Context page for the first learning block in the Tutor.

The Context page is followed by one or more screens where key examples of the new item are presented in isolation. This fulfills the second function in the CORE approach—presenting "objects" from the domain to be understood rather than giving abstract rules. The question/answer Refinement phase follows immediately. The questions are presented normally on the top half of the screen; when the learner requests an answer it is displayed on the bottom half of the screen. The question/answer sequences are carefully structured. The questions (and feedback) usually first deal with possible variations in the target construct. As the sequence progresses they tend to integrate the construct with others already learned so that the learner can see how the construct works in context. Finally, in the Expression phase the learner is asked to write a program which requires the application of the skills acquired. One program is extended over several blocks. This permits the learner to get the feel of building up and using a moderately large program. Feedback, in terms of a model answer to the programming task, is supplied to the students, though access to this can be restricted until the student has completed the program.

The learning blocks are selected from the main menu. Choice of a learning block is made by moving a highlighted bar to the option to be selected and pressing the return key. The screen layout and colour scheme, where appropriate, were chosen to imitate Turbo Pascal convention (there is also a monochrome version of the program). The screen is boxed in light blue with a dark blue strip across the bottom of the screen. This strip contains the names of keys used to navigate through the files. The keys are contextually appropriate to the type of screen being displayed at the time. Text is yellow with highlight in white (reverse video on Hercules mono screens).

The screens are envisaged as pages. Once a user has selected a learning block he/she can move forward and backward at will through the "pages". In order to make use of peoples' expectations these movements through the screens are achieved by pressing the "PgUp" or "PgDn" keys. Text can also be scrolled on a screen when necessary by using the arrow cursor keys. The "Esc" key returns the user to the main menu.

The method of implementation as a shell which loads and manipulates text files permitted great flexibility in the development of the system. The study was strongly learner centred. If the students requested changes which affected the text files these could be made very simply on a word processor. The new of amended file could then be loaded by the shell when required. It also means that the shell is available for developing learning packages for different languages. The new "tutor" would be developed as a series of CORE structured text files which could be loaded and presented by the software shell.

ASSESSMENT OF THE CORE PASCAL TUTOR

Learner groups and their use of the Pascal Tutor

The Pascal Tutor was used for an extended period with an A-level group. To provide further feedback the Tutor was also used on a more informal basis with an open learning group and some evening class students.

The A-Level group consisted of 16 first year Computer Studies students. These were all male. Learning a computer language is a compulsory part of the syllabus. This group had already been studying Pascal for 3 months when they started to use the Pascal Tutor. A similar style of teaching, however, had been used for many of their class sessions. This group had been using the Pascal Tutor for 2.5 months when the main assessment questionnaire was given out.

The second group was a mixed bunch of seventeen open learning students aged between 19 and mid 60s. These students worked in an Open Learning Workshop on an individual basis. They relied on self teaching packs with guidance from a tutor for most of their learning. Most of them had enrolled on a computer literacy course but agreed to try to learn Pascal with the Tutor program for extra interest. As they worked on an individual basis their exposure to the program varied from a few to about 20 h.

There was also a group of about five evening class students (male and female aged between 30 and mid 50s). These students had enrolled for a spreadsheet course and they intended to re-enroll in the following term for a Pascal module. They finished the spreadsheet course very quickly and were happy to have the opportunity to move directly on to learning Pascal using the Tutor program. These students spent five 2-h sessions on the package.

The groups thus used the Pascal Tutor for different periods of time. They also started at different points. The open learning and evening class groups started from the beginning. The A-level group, who had already studied Pascal for 3 months, started several blocks in with "While . . . Do" loops. This point has to be kept in mind when the results are considered.

METHOD OF ASSESSMENT

The students were asked to fill in a questionnaire when they had used the Tutor package for the periods mentioned above. The aim of the questionnaire was to assess the students' reactions to using this method of learning. The questionnaire asked the students how effective they thought the method had been, how much they enjoyed using this approach and how effective they thought this method would be for learning another computer language. The students were also asked to rate their degree of understanding for each learning block in the Tutor that they had used. All ratings were on scales from 1 to 5 where 5 normally indicates a very high rating and 1 indicates a very low rating.

In addition to the formal data obtained from the questionnaires informal interviews were used to gather further information about the reactions of the students. This information helps to give a richer background to any trends revealed in the questionnaires.

RESULTS

The results for the open learning and evening class students are combined in the tables as the groups were similar in composition and there were comparatively few evening class students. The results are based on the students who returned the questionnaire in time.

The students were asked how much they enjoyed using the package. The data are given in Table 1. Judging from these results and the comments of the students in the informal discussions they certainly seemed to enjoy using the package. The A-level students voted unanimously not to return to a conventionally based system when given the chance after 6 weeks with the Tutor. Five of the open learning students came in to the college for extra periods in their lunchtime for several weeks to use the package.

The students were also asked to rate how effective they found the package in helping them to learn Pascal, and whether they would be confident if they had to learn another programming language using the CORE Tutor approach. The results are given in Tables 2 and 3. As can be seen the ratings are positive especially for the open learning/evening class group. The difference in

Table 1. Enjoyment level

Rating	5	4	3	2	1	Mode
Open learning and evening class	10	4	2	0	0	5
A-level students	0	9	7	0	0	4
Overall	10	13	9	0	0	4

5 = very enjoyable; 1 = not very enjoyable.

Table 2. Effectiveness for learning Pascal

Rating	5	4	3	2	1	Mode
Open learning and evening class	8	5	3	0	0	5·
A-level students	4	8	4	0	0	4
Overall	12	13	7	0	0	4

5 = very effective for them; 1 = not very effective for them.

Table 3. Confidence in the method for learning programming languages

Rating	5	4	3	2	1	Mode
Open learning and evening class	8	5	3	0	0	5
A-level students	0	7	9	0	0	3
Overall	8	12	12	0	0	4

5 = very confident; 1 = not very confident.

ratings between the groups in Table 3 may reflect to some degree the relative confidence of this mature group and the mainly 17 year old A-level group.

The students were also asked to rate their understanding of the material covered in individual learning blocks. The numbers of students who studied specific blocks varied widely because of the different entry points and rates of progress. For the mature group, however, the mode and median for the first six learning blocks were, in all cases but one, ratings of five. The ratings for the A-level students were, in all cases but one, ratings of four and five. The one exception was a rating of 3 for a block on receiving and using values in procedures. The students thus generally thought that they understood the material well, though unsurprisingly with a slight tendency to less understanding as the difficulty of the module increased.

DISCUSSION AND OVERVIEW

The information gained from the informal interviews generally supports the questionnaire results. The section which was most visible to the students was the Refinement section; more comments were made about this than any other section. With the exception of one individual all the students liked the question and answer approach very much. As one said, "it enabled us to understand what was required and what could be done".

The students did not directly refer to the Context and Examples sections unless prompted. When asked a direct question they all said they thought it was useful to have these two sections; it had seemed so obvious they had not commented on it. In the Boyle and Drazkowski study the Context section was omitted in tests with some individual students. In this situation the students commented on the need for orienting information.

In the Expression phase the students had to write their own programs based on material in the learning blocks. As one might expect this was viewed as a very positive feature. The students were particularly pleased that they were able to write a "real" program right from the first learning block. This acted as a powerful incentive to move on to the next section. Over several blocks (blocks 3–14), the program the students were asked to write was treated as a project, i.e. the same program was gradually extended and refined. This feature, which enabled the students to build up a quite large program, was universally popular.

The students commented positively on a number of other features. They liked very much working at their own pace; they also liked the facility to print out key pages using one simple keystroke, and they seemed to find the general presentation attractive.

The biggest problem was in moving between the Tutor and the Turbo Pascal editor. There are several ways this can be handled on a computer; these were tried but none was completely successful. One option was to run the Tutor program from DOS and quit the Tutor when ready to write a program. They could then load Turbo Pascal, write their program and then run it. They would then have to quit Pascal before re-entering the Tutor. This is rather cumbersome. An alternative which was quicker but caused even more problems was to load Turbo Pascal, and then temporarily leave it using the Operating System Shell option which retains Pascal in the memory of the computer. The Tutor was then loaded, run and exited as normal. To return to Pascal the student need only type "exit". Neither of these, however, seemed to work well with students who were having trouble switching between the packages. The optimal solution is to have a simple one key command for switching between the packages. This facility was not available for the package before the assessment was carried out but a facility of this type has been included in a later version of the Tutor.

The overall assessment of the CORE Tutor Package is thus very positive. There are difficulties in teasing out the contributions of the various elements. How much is due to the CAL presentation, for example, and how much to the CORE pedagogical approach used? The study by Boyle and Drazkowski had kept the elements separate. This study indicated that the CORE approach without a CAL implementation was positively rated. However, in the end a practical task is accomplished by combining the strengths of different elements, and the assessment must reflect the combined effect of the elements rather than their individual contributions. At present a second CORE package for Modula-2 is being developed and assessed with first year Software engineering students.

REFERENCES

1. Piaget J., Piaget's theory. In *Carmichael's Manual of Child Psychology* (Edited by Mussen P. H.), 3rd edn. Wiley, New York (1970).
2. Donaldson M., *Children's Minds*. Fontana, London (1978).
3. Mayer R. E., The psychology of how novices learn computer programming. *Comput. Surv.* **13**, 121–141 (1981).
4. Groeger J. A., Computation—the final metaphor? An interview with Philip Johnston-Laird. *New Ideas Psychol.* **5**, 295–298 (1987).
5. Boyle T. and Drazkowski W., Exploiting natural intelligence: towards the development of effective environments for learning to program. In *People and Computers 5: Proceedings of the 5th Conference of the British Computer Society Human–Computer Interaction Specialist Group* (Edited by Sutcliffe A. and Macaulay L.). Cambridge University Press (1989).
6. Ausubel D. P., *Educational Psychology: A Cognitive View*. Holt, Rhinehart & Winston, New York (1968).
7. De Villiers J. G. and De Villiers P. A., *Language Acquisition*. Fontana, London (1978).
8. Kuczaj S. A., Thoughts on the intensional basis of early object word extensions in comprehension and/or production: support for a prototype theory of early object word meanings. *First Lang.* 93–105 (1986).
9. Rosch E., Categories and coherences: a historical view. In *The Development of Language and Language Researchers: Essays in Honour of Roger Brown* (Edited by Kessel F. S.). Erlbaum, Hillsdale, N. J. (1988).
10. Neisser U. (Ed.), *Concepts and Conceptual Development: Ecological and Intellectual Factors in Categorization*. Cambridge University Press (1989).

Computers Educ. Vol. 18, No. 1–3, pp. 135–141, 1992
Printed in Great Britain. All rights reserved

A COMPUTER-BASED LABORATORY COURSE IN MATHEMATICAL SCIENCES

Neil Pitcher

Department of Mathematics and Statistics, Paisley College, High Street, Paisley, PA1 2BE, Scotland

Abstract—Our computer-based laboratory course in mathematical sciences has evolved over a number of years. Details are given of the three main elements of the course as it currently stands. The first is the use of graphics-based software to illustrate important mathematical concepts; the second is a series of case study problems in which the use of the computer is emphasised as a part of the overall solution process; the third is a short course in the use of DERIVE, which is a relatively new computer algebra product. The philosophy which underlies the course as a whole is discussed, and there is an account of how the course has developed and is developing in response to constructive comment from lecturing staff and students. In the B.Sc. degree within which the course is located, this innovative approach has been found to be highly beneficial to students in promoting a sound and well balanced grounding in the whole range of skills which are of importance to the mathematical scientist. It is contended that the approach and philosophy described point the way ahead for mathematically-based courses generally, and should be widely adopted.

1. BASIC DETAILS

In the first year students take three Science subjects, of which one is Mathematical Sciences. The Mathematical Sciences laboratory course is a compulsory part of a first year unit in Mathematical Sciences leading ultimately to a B.Sc. or B.Sc. (Honours) in Mathematical Sciences, or other Science-based degree titles. The number of students involved is about 150. The Mathematical Sciences course unit takes up about one-third of the student's contact time at first year level, and the Laboratory takes up one-third of their time (i.e. 2 h per week) in Mathematical Sciences. The Department of Mathematics and Statistics has three Computer Laboratory rooms devoted to the activities described, each equipped with ten microcomputers: these are IBM PS/2 386 machines, and some Acorn BBC computers which run on an Econet network. Printers are on hand. A full-time software technician is employed and a heavy demand is made on lecturing staff, in contact time and for assessment. Most of the software used has been written within the Department, and versions are available to run on IBM PC or BBC machines. A list of these programs with brief details is given in Appendix 1, and copies may be obtained on request for educational use.

2. DESCRIPTION OF THE LABORATORY PROGRAMME

A laboratory component was initially introduced into the first year Mathematical Sciences unit in 1982, with a view to enabling students to acquire those important skills for which traditional style lectures and examinations were not appropriate, namely for problem-solving and visualisation and communication skills. It was felt that the effective use of well-written software would help in achieving these objectives. In the initial period, however, a number of problems were experienced[1].

First it was difficult to manage a session in such a way that students were led into genuine mathematical activity. By this we mean being presented with a problem, puzzling over it and then coming up with suggested solutions, which are evaluated until the stage is reached where a final report can be presented describing the work carried out. Sessions tended to fall into one of two traps. The first was providing too much information and giving too many operating instructions, with the result that the student became a passive spectator, merely pressing keys as instructed. The second trap was quite the opposite, in which too little information was given and the student was left unclear as to what the objectives of the session were, and of how the problem related to other areas of the course. The solution was to ensure that well structured worksheets were available, with clear objectives, clear but concise operating instructions and appropriately stated open-ended problems for students to discuss and investigate in groups, prior to the production of a brief laboratory report for assessment. It has become the practice of the Department to collate all of the laboratory worksheets into a single booklet, which all students are required to purchase.

The exercises contained in these worksheets are related to lecture courses in algebra and calculus which run in parallel with the laboratory sessions. Some exercises illustrate important concepts and emphasise the visualisation of mathematical ideas. Others extend the subject matter of lectures into wider areas. A list of the worksheets used is given in Appendix 2, and a specific example of a worksheet is given in Appendix 3. Students work in groups and submit for assessment laboratory reports and courseworks. In some classes a computerised assessment package, Questionmark, is used. Their marks are stored on file, and they subsequently have access to the answers to review their work. The advent of these laboratory sessions has had a significant impact on lecture classes, with substantial revision of their content, reflecting a more practical overall approach.

A second problem arose in the area of communication skills, particularly in writing. The laboratory reports were a useful mechanism for ensuring that the main points from a session were appreciated by the student, but they tended to be hastily written, with the result that the quality of presentation achieved by students remained constant through the year, instead of improving. This impression was confirmed by the results of student questionnaires, which indicated that only 17% of students felt that the laboratories had helped them develop good skills in report writing. For this reason it was decided to introduce a form of assessment whereby students would be required to produce good quality reports on particular problems. This has taken the form of a series of three case studies, in which students work typically in groups of three on a specific problem which is stated in non-mathematical terms. Over a period of 2 weeks per case study, the groups receive relevant mathematical background information, then use mathematical methods and the computer to obtain a solution to the problem, and then produce a single group report, which describes the mathematical content and concludes with an account of the group's solution, stated in non-mathematical terms. Marks are awarded both for mathematical content and for quality of presentation. In particular it is made clear to students that the following specific faults will be penalised: lack of a sensible report outline; unclear explanation, errors in spelling and grammar, untidiness; misuse of mathematical symbols and arguments. Since the inception of case studies in 1989, 52% of students have indicated in the questionnaire that their skills in report writing have been helped, a marked improvement on the previous figure.

Students are not required to write their own programs within the case studies, as programming is taught elsewhere in the degree course. Instead, students use packages to generate results, and are required to give descriptions of the computational methods (such as the Bisection Method) used within the software. Examples of particular case studies are: Mathematical Ecology, Pollution Control, and the application of Engineering Mathematics to the design of a yacht mast. (See Appendix 4 for an example of one of these case studies.) A member of staff supervises groups of 18 or so students. Each group is responsible for the organisation of its own work, in terms of discussing solution strategies, assigning to each other the carrying out of investigations and experiments using computer packages, and the production of a group report, for which the use of word-processing software is encouraged. All students take a basic course in the use of the computer which includes an introduction to Wordperfect.

Activity of this kind is demanding for first year students, both intellectually and socially. For this reason the laboratory sessions operate in two phases. In Phase One, students work on small problems and produce brief laboratory reports, as described previously. This prepares the students for the more substantial pieces of work undertaken in Phase Two, the Case Study stage. This approach provides a step-by-step introduction to problem solving, giving students the opportunity to develop a good communication and problem-solving skills steadily over a period of time.

More recently a third phase has also been introduced into the laboratory programme: a short course in the use of DERIVE[2,3]. This software has become available recently, and its use in educational institutions is increasing. In marketing publicity it is stated that DERIVE amounts to "2000 years of mathematical knowledge on a disk". This seems to be a fair description. Briefly, DERIVE does algebra, calculus and statistics calculations, and produces graphs and surface plots. The driving force behind its development has been to make mathematics more exciting and enjoyable by eliminating the drudgery of performing long calculations[2]. As such its use fits in well with the philosophy of the laboratory course described in this article. Moreover, given that software of this nature is likely to have as strong an impact on algebra and calculus as the scientific calculator did on arithmetic, it seems indefensible for any mathematically-based degree course to exclude its use. For these reasons a short course in DERIVE has been given for the past 2 years, towards the end of the laboratory course. The initial impression has been highly favourable and a brief account of its main benefits is now given.

An important benefit of DERIVE is that it offers the possibility of students tackling problems involving much manipulation, without the calculation totally dominating the exercise. For instance in a recently quoted classroom example[4], the calculation of the maximum brightness of Venus involved the differentiation of the expression

$$\frac{r - \cos\theta + \sqrt{1 + r^2 - 2r\cos\theta}}{(1 + r^2 - 2r\cos\theta)^{3/2}}.$$

With software like DERIVE, the whole problem can be solved at a single sitting, so that the exercise can realistically be presented as a case study, with the focus of assessment being on a report of the whole problem-solving process, rather than on the single issue of calculation.

A second point to be made is that, contrary to what might be thought, it is quite possible to use DERIVE to improve students' manipulation skills in algebra. They can be given calculations to carry out by hand, and then use DERIVE to check their work. An important observation is that the answer to a problem can take a variety of equivalent forms, and this needs to be understood when interpreting computer output. An example is the differentiation of the function $(\cos x)/x$. Using the Quotient Rule by hand, a student may well obtain the answer $(-x\sin x - \cos x)/x^2$. DERIVE gives it as $-\cos x/x^2 - \sin x/x$, which at first glance looks different. It is instructive for students to explain why the two forms are equivalent.

Another issue is the importance of entering data and using mathematical symbols correctly. An example of this occurred when a student, required to enter the expression $1/(x + 2)$, omitted the parentheses and obtained the wrong answer to the problem stated. This enabled the student to realise the relevance of the correct use of parentheses.

3. CONCLUSIONS

The initial goal at the inception of the Mathematical Sciences Laboratory in 1982 was to enable students to acquire the important skills of problem-solving, visualisation and communication in a technologically-based learning environment.

Achieving this goal has been a progressive learning experience for the teaching staff involved. When the laboratory component was introduced, no special training was available for staff, and we have simply learned from the experience from year to year, through evaluation meetings and in response to student questionnaires. In addition we have been guided by the general approach of other projects with a similar orientation[5,6], particularly in the area of exploiting the potential of the computer as an interactive learning medium in calculus. More recently we have applied a similar approach to linear algebra[7], and have produced material in collaboration with staff from other institutions at international workshops at the Microelectronics Educational Development Centre, Paisley College, in 1988 and 1990. In these efforts the main priority has not been to produce highly sophisticated software, but rather to address the important issues in learning raised by wide availability of computers, in expectation of an evolution of software in time. Thus many of our laboratory worksheets are not specifically limited to the Department's own software, but could readily be adapted to form the basis of activities using other products, including graphics calculators.

The whole exercise has been highly beneficial for our students. Naturally, not all their comments have been full of praise: indeed it has been largely through analysing student questionnaires that the course has evolved to its current state. Most of their comments, however, have been definitely favourable. The laboratories have helped to clarify material covered in lectures, according to 57% of students; they have given students working knowledge and experience of mathematical modelling (64%), they have helped students to integrate different areas of Mathematics (58%). The bulk of students (67%) have stated that the first year Mathematical Sciences course is better with the laboratories than without. Also, quite importantly, most of them (59%) have enjoyed it. The laboratories provide a positive and enjoyable working environment, in which interaction and discussion are the order of the day. This creates a good general atmosphere in the class, leading to greater confidence and maturity among students than was achievable when using traditional teaching methods alone. This is an ideal preparation for employment.

A particularly encouraging aspect of the laboratory classes is the benefit they bring to many students who were previously perceived as "weak" in mathematics. In many cases they are weak in analytical skills, but not necessarily in problem-solving or graphical skills. Such students often flourish in laboratory classes. This facilitates gaining a degree for those students who enter higher education with less than the usual formal qualifications.

The principal piece of evidence for the encouraging statements made above has been the success rate for our students in recent years. Over the past 3 years an increasing number of students have entered the course with less than the minimum entry requirements. Some 87% of those in this category sitting examinations have passed. The overall pass rate in the same period has been 90%.

The whole experience indicates that the effective use of the computer within the Mathematics curriculum does far more than just facilitate the delivery of information: it actually changes for the better the way in which the subject is perceived and approached. It makes possible a more balanced treatment of mathematics, whereby problem solving, visualisation and communication, and practical skills receive their due prominence alongside analytical skills. In traditional courses most attention was given to these latter skills with the result that many students were denied the opportunity to develop the former equally important skills. This tended to result in graduates with an unbalanced view of mathematics, who then had difficulty in adjusting to the industrial environment.

It is also worth mentioning that the experience has been useful for some staff, enabling them to see the potential of using computers in mathematics, and the benefits of a more open system of learning. This has had a good consequential effect in other courses.

In a wider context a number of issues are raised for those concerned with mathematics education. First there is the question of the place of technological tools within the curriculum, and the possibilities these afford of a radical reform of mathematics education at all levels, including schools. An issue related to this is the question of how to make the best use of the new computer algebra products, such as DERIVE, within the curriculum. There is a need for discussion of the fundamental pedagogical issues raised: do we still need to teach differentiation methods, integration methods, factorisation and so on? Can we simply leave it all to the computer to do? Recently, a working group on DERIVE teaching material has been set up under the auspices of the Computers in Teaching Initiative. This provides a forum in which such issues can be discussed.

A further issue is the monitoring of mathematical laboratories. Activities of the kind described in this article are being adopted by many departments, sometimes in an *ad hoc* way. There do exist excellent schemes for the exchange of software and worksheets through the Computers in Teaching Initiative, but there is also a need for the quality of such courses to be monitored nationally, and criteria of excellence to be agreed upon and made available, so that departments embarking on such an approach can benefit from the experiences of others.

The experience of the author's Department indicates that the incorporation into the curriculum of computer-based activities of the kind described provides a timely opportunity to achieve a thorough reform of the learning of mathematics at all levels.

REFERENCES

1. Burnside R. R., MacDivitt A. R. G., Pitcher N. and West E. T. Mathematics teaching for the next millenium. *Proceedings, The Fifth International Conference of Technology and Education*, Vol. 1, pp. 444–447 (1988).
2. DERIVE, a mathematical assistant program. *Software plus User Manual*. Soft Warehouse, Honolulu (1989).
3. Herman E. A., Review of Derive. *Am. Math. Mthly* **96**, 951 (1989).
4. Andrew A. D., Morley T. D. and Neff J. D., How bright is Venus: a calculus example. *Proceedings, The Third Annual International Conference on Technology in Collegiate Mathematics* (1989).
5. Tall D., *Graphics Calculus*. Glentop, Barnet (1986).
6. Schwartz J. L., The representation of function in the algebraic proposer. *Proceedings, The Eleventh International Conference, Psychology of Mathematical Education* (1987).
7. Pitcher N., Visualisation in linear algebra. *Int. J. Math. Educ. Sci. Technol.* In press.

APPENDIX 1

Software Details

Program title	Description
GRAPHPLOTTER	Graphs user specified functions within desired window. Up to nine graphs can be overlaid
SANDWICH SQUEEZE	Draws upper and lower rectangles corresponding to Riemann sums for a monotonic function specified by the user. Sums are calculated for up to 2000 vertical strips
TRAP/SIM	Implements Trapezium and Simpson's Rule for integration
BISECT	Implements Bisection Method, displaying all intermediate values
COMPO	Illustrates the Chain Rule for composite functions
MATMUL	Computes successive values for two or three component linear vector recursive equations
ELIMINATOR	Carries out row operations for up to 6 × 6 matrices
MATRIX	Illustrates the concepts of eigenvalue and eigenvector
WORDS	Forms permutations of sub-strings of words of up to 7 letters
GRASSHOPPER, RANDOM WALK	These programs illustrate specific random walk scenarios and display summaries of simulation results
COIN	Simulates coin tossing and displays summaries of results
PASCAL	Illustrates Pascal's Triangle and various networking problems

APPENDIX 2

List of Laboratory Worksheets

1. Introduction to keyboard and use of programs within a menu structure
2. Random Numbers. Software: COIN, GRASSHOPPER, RANDOM WALK
3. Networks and Pascal's Triangle. Software: PASCAL
4. Counting and Pascal's Triangle. Software: WORDS
5. Quadratic functions
6. Cubic functions
7. Trigonometric functions
8. Rational functions
9. Taylor polynomials
10. Beams, bending and polynomials.

Software: worksheets 5–10 all use GRAPHPLOTTER.

11. Estimating integrals. Software: SANDWICH SQUEEZE, TRAP/SIM
12. Composite functions and the chain rule. Software: COMPO
13. Solution of linear equations. Software: ELIMINATOR
14. Leslie matrices. Software: MATMUL

APPENDIX 3

Laboratory Worksheet on Rational Functions

Objectives

To provide experience in the graphing of rational functions, with particular reference to the importance of asymptotes.
To provide experience in the use of calculus in sketching the graphs of rational functions.

Definition

A RATIONAL FUNCTION is the result of one polynomial function being divided by another:

$$f(x) = \frac{p(x)}{q(x)}.$$

EXPERIMENT 1. THE FORM OF THE CURVE $y = \dfrac{c}{x-a}$

Task 1. Sketch carefully on graph paper the graph of

$$y = \frac{1}{x}$$

on the domain $-5 < x < 5$.
The curve which results is called a HYPERBOLA. What two lines are the asymptotes to this curve?
In what follows, you will be using the program GRAPHPLOTTER.

Task 2. Investigate the form of the curve

$$y = \frac{c}{x},$$

where c is a constant. (Try a few c values: -1, 2, 3 etc.) Present a clear conclusion in your report.

Task 3. Investigate the form of the curve

$$y = \frac{1}{x - a}$$

where a is a constant.

What two lines are the asymptotes to this curve?
What is the general form of the curve

$$y = \frac{c}{x - a}$$

(a and c are constants)?

EXPERIMENT 2. ADDING OR SUBTRACTING TWO RATIONAL FUNCTIONS
OF THE FORM $y = \dfrac{c}{x - a}$

Task 4

    (i) Add together the functions $1/(x - 2)$ and $1/x$ by bringing them to a common denominator.

    (ii) Use the computer to obtain a sketch of the function which results.

    (iii) Discuss with your tutor the way in which the curve approaches each of its vertical asymptotes. In particular pay detailed attention to the **sign** and **magnitude** of the function just to the left and just to the right of each vertical asymptote. Relate this to the position of the graph near to each asymptote.
    Describe clearly in your report exactly how the algebraic form of the function is related to the form of the curve near each asymptote.

Task 5. Repeat Task 4, considering instead the subtraction of one rational function from the other:

$$\frac{1}{x - 2} - \frac{1}{x}.$$

Differentiate the resulting function with respect to x and hence obtain the coordinates of its turning point.
Use the graph which was drawn by the computer to check your answer.

CALCULUS TASKS

Task 6. Without using the computer, make a sketch on paper of the graph of

$$y = \frac{1}{x - 1} + \frac{1}{x + 1}$$

Consider carefully the positions of asymptotes and turning points.
Use the computer only to check the graph you draw.

Task 7. Do the same for

$$y = \frac{1}{x - 1} - \frac{1}{x + 1}.$$

If you have time, you might also evaluate second derivatives, in order to investigate points of inflexion in Tasks 6 and 7.

APPENDIX 4

Case Study on Pollution Control

    Polluted water from a factory is being discharged into the sea. There is a legal requirement that the company discharge this polluted water at a rate of no more than 3000 m³ h⁻¹, otherwise a large fine is risked. The Technical Department has come up with the solution of inserting a probe vertically through the top of the discharge pipe, to detect the height of polluted water pouring through the pipe at any given time. This probe is to be connected to a warning light in the Control Centre, to give warning when the liquid level in the pipe is too high. The warning light will go on as soon as the liquid rises to a level high enough to touch the top of the probe. The problem is to calculate, to the nearest millimetre, the exact length of the probe which is required.

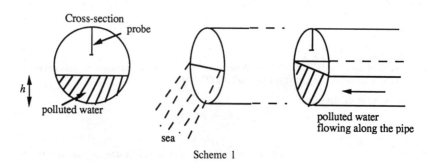

Scheme 1

Data and assumptions

The discharge pipe is assumed to be horizontal, and of circular cross-section. Its diameter is 1 m. The polluted water is pumped along the pipe in such a way that the surface of the liquid is perfectly horizontal at all points and the water is always in motion at a constant speed of 2 m s^{-1}. The volume of a cylinder is equal to the product of its cross-sectional area and its length. The probe is inserted absolutely vertically, through the highest point in the pipe's cross-section.

Suggested work

(1) If the depth of polluted water is h, then obtain an expression involving h for the area of a vertical cross-section of the polluted water.
(2) Use the Method of Bisection, or some other method if you wish, to calculate the maximum height h which satisfies the legal requirement of 3000 m^3 h^{-1} as the rate of discharge.

Suggested Outline for Group Report

Problem statement

This should be a short description of the problem and what you are trying to accomplish. Use your own words; do not merely copy out the description given at the head of this sheet. Provide diagrams to illustrate your account.

Assumptions and data

List clearly all the fundamental assumptions you make in formulating your equations, and the data given.

Mathematical solution

This is the main part of the report where you should clearly show all the steps in your calculations, and all relevant results. Any computer programs used should be fully described, and a summary of computed results given.

Conclusions

Based on your results, state your solution of the problem as originally stated.

Quality of presentation

Badly presented work, even if mathematically correct, will be penalised. In particular marks will be deducted for each of the following faults:—

(a) Lack of sensible report outline
(b) Not enough clarity in explanations and presentation of results
(c) Too many errors of spelling, punctuation, grammar and syntax
(d) Too untidy
(e) Too careless with the use of mathematical symbols (brackets, => sign, = sign, etc.).

Computers Educ. Vol. 18, No. 1–3, pp. 143–148, 1992
Printed in Great Britain. All rights reserved

DEVELOPING THE USE OF IT WITHIN MATHEMATICS THROUGH ACTION RESEARCH

Howard Tanner

University College of Swansea, Department of Education, Hendrefoilan,
Swansea SA2 7NB, Wales

Abstract—Information Technology (IT) is a cross curricular competence within the British National Curriculum which should be developed *through a range of curriculum activities*. This paper reports the extent to which IT skills are used or developed within mathematics at present and examines factors which are limiting development. The results of an action research project which investigated the extent to which IT skills could be taught within the mathematics curriculum are described. Recommendations are made about training needs and the management of IT within the school curriculum.

INTRODUCTION

The IT in Mathematics Project was funded by The University of Wales, Faculty of Education, and ran from April 1989 to April 1991. The project surveyed the extent to which IT was used in the teaching of mathematics and examined the extent to which IT skills could or should be taught within mathematics.

Information technology is concerned with the handling of information, whether numbers, words, pictures, sounds or other forms. Contemporary usage emphasises the *electronic* means of information handling and in particular the use of computers. This paper concentrates on those aspects of information technology.

BACKGROUND

Computer Studies was first introduced into the curriculum of British schools in the 1960s and *was developed and taught largely by teachers of mathematics*. Computer studies extended beyond the boundaries of mathematics, however, and in 1982 Cockcroft[1] recommended that it "should not be regarded as part of mathematics but should ideally exist within a separate department". Mathematicians were criticised for emphasising programming and numerical operations rather than the wider aspects of data processing and social implications! The implication was clear, using computers to teach mathematics was interfering with the task of learning **about** computers.

During the 1980s, by far the largest usage of computers in secondary schools was in Computer Studies or Computer Literacy courses where, rather than learning with computers, students learned about computers. Students on Computer Literacy courses were often to be found mastering keyboard skills or studying decontextualised examples of applications packages. The cognitive and imaginative demands made were frequently slight and the "basic skills" learned were often not transferable. Certainly there is evidence to suggest that IT was rarely used as a tool in other subjects[2,3].

The HMI report "Information Technology from 5 to 16"[4] offered a "shift of emphasis towards the integration of IT into the curriculum as a whole" and suggested that: "pupils should not regard IT and information related activities as a distinct area of study".

The non-statutory guidance for technology in the National Curriculum was similarly clear[5]:

> It is not intended that IT should be regarded as another subject. On the contrary, the development of IT capability is best achieved through a range of curriculum activities.

The advice is sound, but the change may not be easy to effect.

CURRENT USAGE OF IT IN MATHEMATICS TEACHING IN ENGLAND AND WALES

During the summer term of 1989, schools known to use IT to support mathematics teaching were visited and lessons observed. Informal interviews took place with a selection of teachers from these and other schools and a questionnaire was devised and trialled.

During the Autumn term of 1989, the questionnaires were sent to a random sample of 142 secondary/middle/higher schools in 12 local educational authorities in England and Wales. Replies were received from 266 mathematics teachers in 86 schools (a response rate of 61%). Results reveal that the majority of mathematics teachers (65%) use computers but not usually in the manner required by the National Curriculum. (Figures are valid percentages of teachers' responses.)

The software used tended to be subject specific rather than generic. Programming languages were not often used, although many teachers claimed to know how to program (49% Logo, 68% BASIC).

Very little use was made of spreadsheets or databases (7 and 8% of teachers respectively) although some teachers claimed to have knowledge of them (53 and 61% respectively).

52% of teachers listed other software which they used. More than 60 different packages were listed but by far the greatest usage was made of the SMILE programs. The only IT skill required to use such software is the ability to load programs, and it is possible to use them with minimal teacher input which may go some way to explaining their popularity.

Just over half the teachers claimed to have had some sort of training, although not many could be described as being well trained.

12% had attended long courses or courses leading to a qualification.

42% had experienced short courses or occasional days of school based INSET.

39% claimed to have had no training.

Training needs features strongly amongst the inhibiting factors mentioned by non-users of both spreadsheets and databases, approx. 70% welcoming training on the use of these packages.

The statistics also reveal, however, that a large part of the problem is not how to use the technology. More teachers have taught themselves that part. The main difficulty is in seeing how the technology fits into the established mathematics curriculum. The more open ended the package, the less obvious is its application. Unfortunately, much of the INSET provided during the 1980s concentrated on the technology rather than its educational use[6]. Perhaps more disturbing is the high percentage (55%) claiming that they do not have sufficient access to computers.

Learning about computers and their uses in special lessons whilst being unable to use them in a genuine problem solving situations is likley to lead students to a distorted view of technology. The skills and attitudes which might be said to constitute computer literacy are more likely to be developed if technology is met in context so that applications can be discovered naturally.

Computer literacy, like any literacy, requires regular use if it is not to decay. Efforts should be concentrated on software which is generic rather than subject specific and so that it can be used in several subject areas simultaneously.

THE ACTION RESEARCH PROJECT

In the summer term of 1990 an action research group of four schools was established to research and develop the use of IT in mathematics teaching. The schools concerned were not chosen for the extent of their IT usage, but rather for their willingness to participate in a development project which would demand an investment of time and a willingness to share experiences and experiment with new techniques. The schools drew pupils from a variety of backgrounds.

THE TEACHERS

The computer experience of teachers varied greatly within the schools. Each school had at least one member of the department who was comfortable about using computers; each school also had staff who did not use computers in their teaching.

One member of each mathematics department was designated "research coordinator" for the project. His/her function was to provide support for teachers and ensure effective monitoring of developments. Each school had a room containing a network of 15 BBC master computers, managed by a teacher who was also "network manager" for the school.

THE DIRECTION OF THE ACTION RESEARCH

All the mathematics departments felt under pressure for curriculum time and a commonly expressed opinion was that there was no room in a crowded curriculum to add on lessons in IT skills.

Concern was expressed that, although it might be possible to do good mathematics with generic software such as spreadsheets once pupils were familiar with them, mathematics teachers could not afford to lose curriculum time to teaching the software.

The agreed aim was to teach good mathematics using computers in such a way that pupils would develop IT skills as a natural by-product of the lessons almost without noticing it. The extent to which this might be possible was one of the major questions to be addressed by the project.

The perceived need was the development of suitable mathematical applications of computers which would enable pupils to cultivate the required IT knowledge and skills, but keep mathematics rather than technology to the fore.

The group agreed to concentrate initially on the use of spreadsheets in mathematics teaching. All the research coordinators were familiar with the spreadsheet Grasshopper.

THE TEAM TEACHING DAY

The project began with a team teaching day in each school to familiarise all the teachers in the department with the use of the network, the basic functions of the spreadsheet and the aims of the project. In line with the philosophy that mathematics education rather than technology should be to the fore this was not done by direct teaching but by participation in team taught lessons led by the project director.

The activities utilised a set of "starter" worksheets based on pre-prepared spreadsheets templates. Initial activities required pupils to load files and change data to achieve an optimal result. The task for the pupils is to alter the positions of the numbers 1–9 (in a 3 × 3 array) to maximise the total where row and column entries were multiplied to provide row/column totals.

The efforts of the pupils and their teachers were soon concentrated on strategies which might achieve a solution. The fact that a spreadsheet was being used quickly faded into the background. Most pupils began by using trial and error, but more logically based strategies soon began to appear.

The activity was a useful one in mathematical terms and was best experienced using a spreadsheet rather than paper and pencil, as the technology removed the arithmetic, allowing the pupils to concentrate on strategy and generalisation. The pupils and their teachers also learned important IT skills. They learned about the distinction between data and formulae, how to change data and how to load files. A few learned how to write formulae. More importantly, because the learning took place in context, they also learned that a spreadsheet is a valuable tool when instantaneous recalculation is useful. Similar "starter" type activities were used to develop other IT skills.

THE IMPACT OF THE TEAM TEACHING DAY

By the end of the team teaching day, those teachers who had been unfamiliar with Grasshopper were familiar with the basic functions such as copy, formula, graph and random. The teachers who had been unfamiliar with the use of spreadsheets in teaching mathematics also learned that is was sometimes possible to contrive learning situations in which IT skills were learned but in which the focus remained primarily on mathematics. Perhaps the most important effect, however, was on the teachers who felt unsure of themselves in the computer room, and this was that most of the skills required were those of mathematics teachers rather that IT specialists.

A set of class sets of starter worksheets was left in each school for trialling and development during the succeeding months. All the teachers concerned agreed to attempt some of the activities and develop others for reporting back at the first network meeting. Reaction to the team teaching day was very positive and all the teachers claimed to have found it valuable.

SUPPORT IN SCHOOL

The research coordinator in each school was allocated two half days supply cover for each of the months, June, July, September and October to enable him/her to assist teachers who lacked confidence in the computer room and monitor progress of the project. The supply cover must be regarded as a token amount of time offered as the research coordinators gave support far over and above this allocation.

Research coordinators (and also computer managers) gave support in a variety of ways, but the two most common were: pre-lesson support and in-lesson support. Several teachers felt the need to "walk through" the lesson on a computer in advance with the assistance of a colleague to remind themselves of commands and identify potential pitfalls. This technique seemed to work well and built confidence. Many teachers preferred to have immediate technical support in their first few lessons using computers and asked the research coordinator to remain in the lesson with them and teach alongside them. The need for in-lesson support diminished as the project progressed and confidence grew.

At the end of each lesson involving the use of spreadsheets to teach mathematics the teachers were asked to complete a lesson evaluation report which was collected by the research coordinator. The observations of the research coordinator, the project team and the evaluation reports were discussed at the network meetings. This ensured that progress was evaluated on a continuous basis and that new ideas and approaches were shared between the schools.

EXPERIENCES WITH SPREADSHEETS

The initial activities attempted after the team teaching day were very successful. All the lesson evaluation forms recorded a positive response to the activities, although some modifications to the worksheets were requested. All agreed that the activities were mathematically valid and with one exception considered that the activities were best experienced using a computer. All the teachers claimed that they would use the activities again although sometimes in a slightly modified form.

In all cases it was reported that the pupils enjoyed the lessons. "They were interested and enthusiastic and worked hard all lesson" was a typical comment. This must be balanced against the observation that many pupils treated activities on the computer as a game. Some teachers reported that pupils were satisfied with trial and error techniques and were unwilling to develop other strategies. This confirmed our own observations. Many pupils seemed to consider that as the lesson was computer based it was unnecessary to record results or strategies. This aspect of pupil attitudes to technology proved difficult to overcome, but clear teacher expectations did seem to have a positive effect.

As the project progressed it became apparent that IT knowledge and skills were being learned by both teachers and pupils. New spreadsheet functions were added gradually, and pupils became familiar with: cell referencing, labels, data, formulae, copy, graph, random, and standard functions such as sum. Lessons were taught to pupils with a range of abilities, from years one to four. Due to the nature of the activities, it was the mathematical content rather than the IT skills involved which limited access. Pupils from all the ages and abilities proved capable of dealing with the technology at the template level.

There are three levels of spreadsheet use which should be considered (see also Arganbright[7] and Straker[8]):

    (i) Pupils modify or adapt a template prepared by the teacher.
    (ii) Pupils prepare a spreadsheet to a teacher's design.
    (iii) Pupils create spreadsheets to their own design to model problems.

The majority of lessons taught during the project were at level one due to pressure of curriculum time within the limited duration of the project but a range of activities was developed and trialled which remained primarily focused on mathematics but which extended pupils to level three. Pupils with a range of ages and abilities attempted the activities, and it proved possible for even low ability children to operate at level three.

Most teachers began database work by asking pupils to manipulate pre-prepared data. One teacher had collected data about each child in her class; e.g. house number, hair colour, and had entered the data herself. The pupils then had to search the database and draw graphs to answer questions. Others teachers used imaginary data which had been prepared by West Glamorgan Computer Center about space creatures and pirates. Activities included providing a list of suspects for "crimes" which had been committed.

The main aims of these lessons were mathematical and centred on the interpretation of graphs. Precision of language was also encouraged; e.g. the distinction between "and" and "or". The computer plotted the graphs quickly and sometimes provided meaningless graphs thus forcing attention onto interpretation rather than drawing. The teachers all agreed that the activity was good mathematics and was best attempted with a computer. The pupils learned the IT skills involved easily and unobtrusively. Several teachers described these activities as ones which they particularly enjoyed teaching.

EXPERIENCES WITH LOGO

Logo was approached in different ways in the four schools. In two institutions its use was already established in the lower school curriculum. All the schools concentrated on the graphical capabilities of the language and taught the pupils a basic set of commands including repeat: and To: to enable them to construct procedures to draw repeating patterns.

An element of discovery learning was included in the teaching of the language in most cases, but the degree of guidance varied according to the teaching style which predominated in the school concerned. Teachers reported success in teaching the essential commands to their pupils with both investigative and heavily guided approaches.

In one school, a simplified street plan of Swansea had been created in Logo and pupils were asked to guide the turtle between landmarks. This work was linked to the SMP booklet "Maps plans and grids". Others linked Logo to the drawing of polygons and the rule for external angles. Some simply wished the pupils to work procedurally to draw patterns.

Teachers' aims for Logo teaching varied and were sometimes uncertain. Some regarded the purpose of such lessons to be the teaching of a programming language. Others considered the purpose to be the teaching of geometrical concepts. For some its importance was due simply to its presence in National Curriculum examples. Most agreed that Logo had a mathematical content, mentioning angle, length or "a feel for geometry". Some agreed with Papert's contention that working with procedures helped children to think systematically but others were more sceptical.

Reactions to Logo were more varied than to spreadsheets or databases. Some teachers listed Logo as a topic they particularly enjoyed teaching but others specifically mentioned it as a topic they disliked, describing the activities as "boring" and the language as "primitive". Some considered BASIC a more suitable language to use in mathematics. The value of Logo to mainstream secondary mathematics teaching was considered less obvious than with spreadsheets or databases which were described as "more realistic" and "more useful".

Confidence and knowledge about teaching with spreadsheets was consistent over all four schools. Confidence and knowledge about the use of Logo, however, was concentrated in the two schools who had developed packages of work and activities using Logo. In discussion at the network meeting teachers reported lack of time to develop activities as a major constraint. The existence of a structured programme of activities and worksheets using spreadsheets and Logo enabled teachers with a weak knowledge base to use technology which they would otherwise have rejected. Open ended software requires both technical knowledge and teaching ideas before it can be used effectively.

FACTORS INHIBITING COMPUTER USE

Sufficient access is judged on personal criteria. The three teachers who used computers only on "special occasions" claimed that they had sufficient access, while two (of the eight) teachers who used computers every week claimed to have insufficient access. Frequency of use varied considerably between schools. The greater use of computers was made in the school where the computer manager was in the mathematics department—he facilitated access for his department. This school had integrated IT work into the curriculum and classes were timetabled into the IT room on a formal basis. Another school in which usage was high had distributed responsibility for IT across subject departments and had allocated Logo to mathematics. This was built into the department's scheme of work, and time in the IT room was formally allocated to mathematics. Building IT into the scheme of work in a structured way enabled departments to plan needs well in advance and facilitated access. Departments which relied on *ad hoc* arrangements encountered greater difficulties with access.

SUMMARY OF MAIN FINDINGS

(i) Generic computer software can be used to enhance the teaching of mathematics.

(ii) IT skills relating to the use of generic computer software can be taught effectively in the context of lessons whose aims are primarily mathematical. Separate IT lessons are not required.

(iii) The majority of mathematics teachers need training in the use of generic packages.

(iv) The training required is not simply technical. In fact the greater need is for training in how to use computers to support subject learning.

(v) Beginners with computer software often need support in the classroom in the early stages.

(vi) Lack of access to computers is a problem for many mathematics teachers. The domination of computer resources by Computer Studies or IT lessons often prevents access by subject departments.

(vii) The integration of computer based lessons into schemes of work facilitates forward planning and thus access to hardware. *Ad hoc* arrangements are less likely to succeed.

(viii) With moderate support, teachers are able to develop and apply both the technical and educational skills and knowledge which are required through school based action research.

CONCLUSION

The shift of emphasis away from IT as a separate subject and towards integration into the curriculum as a whole is educationally sound. To be achievable, however, a large scale programme of in-service training is required. This training should concentrate on the contribution which IT can make to subject teaching rather than on the technology itself. Emphasis should be placed on the application of generic software across the curriculum. Much of the training could take place in school.

Computers are a relatively scarce resource in schools. Access for subject teaching with computers will remain difficult while lessons about the computer continue to make first call on resources. The best way to learn IT skills is in context. Courses on Computer Studies or Computer Appreciation are not required and should end. Computer Studies teachers should change their role to that of computer adviser to the many teachers who will continue to require support.

Activities which develop IT skills through subject teaching should be built into the schemes of work of all subject areas. Generic software which can be practised across the curriculum should be emphasised. Advisory teachers and teacher trainers should concentrate efforts on the development of such activities.

REFERENCES

1. Cockcroft W. H., *Mathematics Counts*. HMSO, London (1982).
2. D.E.S., *Report by H.M. Inspectors on Aspects of the Work of the Microelectronics in Education Programme*. HMSO, London (1987).
3. Mallatratt J., A review of the effectiveness of national policies in the U.K. aimed at providing in-service training support to teachers to enable them to use computers in non-computing subjects (i.e. computing across the curriculum), *Proceedings of EURIT 90*, Herning, Denmark (1990).
4. D.E.S., *Information Technology from 5 to 16: Curriculum Matters 15*. HMSO, London (1989).
5. D.E.S./W.O., *Information Technology in the National Curriculum: Non-statutory Guidance for Teachers*. HMSO, Cardiff (1990).
6. Mallatratt J., *op. cit.*
7. Arganbright D., Mathematical applications of an electronic spreadsheet. In *N.C.T. Yearbook*, pp. 96–108. N.C.T., New York (1984).
8. Straker A., Mathematics with a spreadsheet. In *Micromath*, Vol. 15, pp. 33–35. A.T.M., Derby (1989).

Computers Educ. Vol. 18, No. 1–3, pp. 149–154, 1992
Printed in Great Britain. All rights reserved

0360-1315/92 $5.00 + 0.00

WHO'S IN THE DRIVER'S SEAT?
TECHNOLOGY, THE ARTS AND EDUCATION

J. Dale Burnett

Faculty of Education, University of Lethbridge, 4401 University Drive, Lethbridge, Alberta,
Canada T1K 3M4

Abstract—A review of four major computer based software developments and their impact on education leads to the conclusion that we should be cautious about emphasizing technology. The metaphor suggests that while technology is the vehicle, and education the passenger, it is the arts, through a sensitive teacher that should be the driver.

INTRODUCTION

I would like to focus on four developments during the last decade that I believe have had, and will continue to have, a strong influence on how computer technology affects education and the arts. The first of these was the introduction of the computer programming language Logo. Logo was a computer-based environment that provided new ways of thinking about some topics as well as introducing new topics that could then be examined by traditional means. Analytic geometry was extended to Turtle geometry. Logo enriched ideas from the domain of language (i.e. triangle) by providing new forms of representation such as algorithms (REPEAT 3[FD 75 LT 120]) or dynamically constructed graphic images. An idea could be represented both algorithmically and graphically. However, Logo was more than just a computer language; its use in schools raised issues of pedagogy and philosophy. The second development that I would like to identify is that of Desk Top Publishing (DTP). DTP took word processing an important step forward: graphics were now part of the layout. Aesthetics and taste became important issues. Third, I would like to discuss HyperCard. HyperCard is much like an iconic form of Logo. They may both be viewed as software erector sets. The inclusion of sound to symbolic (words, numbers) and graphic environments makes HyperCard an interesting next step in the evolution of software. In addition to the possibilities of a "pure" HyperCard application, there are the new possibilities that have been opened up using HyperCard as a controller for laser discs, CD-ROM disks and video cassette recorders to create a multimedia presentation. Multimedia represents the fourth development, even though its use is just beginning in business and industry and widespread educational use is relegated to the future.

Most of the emphasis to date has been on how this emerging technology might facilitate traditional topics. Consideration of the arts, for example, leads to suggestions of how a multimedia presentation might provide the student with the equivalent of a tour through the Rijkmuseum in Amsterdam. Concomitant with multimedia software are graphics of software packages that are rapidly opening up a totally new medium for artistic expression. However, I would like to examine the other side of the mirror. The principle point that I wish to put forward is that the arts may have a more important role to play in directing how technology might be used in education than technology may have in directing the future of the arts. The primary focus in education should not be on technology, nor should it be on the arts. The primary focus should be education. But the arts may have something to say to education.

Logo and the visual arts

It is slightly more than a decade since Logo was introduced to schools. Logo, microcomputers and Seymour Papert's book, *Mindstorms* [1], combined to create a genuine impact. Papert entered the educational debate with his concerns about appropriate and inappropriate uses of the technology. His call that the child should program the computer rather than having the computer program the child struck a responsive chord in many hearts and minds. Yet much of Papert's message was missed. Many believed that the issue was programming, and that Logo should be the vehicle since it had certain advantages over other languages. These were people who usually believed that programming was an important component of computer literacy and a necessary prerequisite for a successful life in a technologically oriented society. Such views are now widely challenged.

However, a re-reading of *Mindstorms* is time well spent. In the Foreword, Papert recounts his early childhood and using a model of gears to facilitate his learning of equations. He then identifies "what I still consider the fundamental fact about learning: . . . The understanding of learning must be genetic. . . . What an individual can learn, *and how he learns it* (emphasis added), depends on what models he has available" (p. vii). He goes on to say, "Second, I remember that there was feeling, love, as well as understanding in my relationship with gears" (p. viii).

Numerous research studies on Logo have noted the importance of locus of control in student activities. This is still a point that is missed by many educators and curriculum developers. Education involves both processes and products. How does one go about learning how to learn? It is widely recognized that one must build one's own knowledge. For example, most educators would accept the statement that one must learn algebra before calculus, and arithmetic before algebra. Yet it is an oversimplification to make such an assertion. What does it mean to "know algebra"? And how does one arrive at this state; It is not a linear sequence as the original statement would seem to imply. Rather it is a life-long modification of insights and facts and their complex interrelationships, supplemented with emotions, feelings, memories and imagery.

To use a popular metaphor, learning is turbulent. It is full of eddies and cross-currents. The process is a rough ride. We do our students a disservice by always trying to find a calm ride. First, they fail to gain experience with difficult learning situations. Second, a curriculum that is smoothed out is boring. It is boring to the students and it is boring to the teachers. Educators that were involved with students, teachers and Logo in the early 1980's know how exciting it was. Today, much of the excitement is gone. Why? I would like to suggest that one of the main reasons is that we have succeeded in packaging Logo. Textbooks and courses abound that prescribe the next step to be taken. This is not to say that there is not a place for calm waters, only that we have overdone it. We need to let our students experience the white water as well.

Two books exemplify the role that Logo might play. One is a book about mathematics, the other a book about art. Abelson and diSessa'a *Turtle Geometry* [2] is a mathematics classic. They begin the book with a set of Preliminary Notes which begin, "This is a book about exploring mathematics, and the most important thing about exploring mathematics is for you to do it rather than just passively read what we've written" (p. xix). Thus, the verb 'explore' has two connotations: one is to be active, the second is to be self-directed. Finally, it is not about learning Logo. Logo is simply the vehicle for exploring.

The second book is Clayson's *Visual Modeling with Logo* [3]. In the first chapter Clayson writes, "This is not a book about Logo . . . the goal of the book is to get you to build visual models" (p. 6). Clayson also discusses the issue of copying another's programs. He advocates the copying of procedures early in one's apprenticeship in order to develop basic skills, but then goes on to recommend, "play rough with them . . . Get into the habit of tinkering" (pp. 4–5). There is pedagogy here, but also philosopy. Respect for the learner is paramount.

It is tempting at this point to advocate that the technology be used as a tool to facilitate the development of other skills, and in particular, following the theme of the title, artistic perspectives. The medium may be electronic, but this is simply the addition of another dimension to the art world. Such developments are to be commended. However, this is to miss the point as far as education is concerned. Is it the role of an art teacher to show an aspiring (and perspiring) student exactly what and how to draw? Of course not. It makes no difference whether the medium is electricity or charcoal. Thus, the main contribution that art education can make to education in general is that of pedagogy. Give the student some paint, some suggestions, some encouragement, some advice about a technical problem, and some freedom to learn. In this case, art education and Logo are in synchrony.

DTP and aesthetics

Desk Top Publishing has rapidly emerged as a natural sequel to word processing. Once again, it is the technolgy that makes it happen. As we moved from mechanical typewriters to electronic characters, it was not that big a leap to the idea of including graphics. The issues with this new technology are not spelling and grammar, but style, form and good taste. Given that one has more fonts that one ever imagined were possible, does that mean that they should all be used on the same page? The advertising industry and the field of typography have evolved a set of prinicples over the last 100 years to assist composers in the production of effective and pleasing layouts. Much of this knowledge has yet to reach education. In many word processing courses our emphasis has been on keyboarding. In English classes that are fortunate enough to have ready access to computers, the emphasis continues to be on the mechanics of language rather than on the nuances of effective communication. However, now effective communication must include the visual arts as well as language, and they must all be integrated into a cohesive and integrated whole.

There is a deja-vu aspect to the present situation. Art was an important means of expression in the middle ages and during the renaissance. Visual imagery is now making a comeback through the media, and will undoubtably soon be introduced into our schools. However, as has been recognized since the turn of the century, a photograph is not a painting. Neither is clip art. This is not to suggest that technologically produced images are inferior to those produced by an artist. Rather, it is to suggest that we have just begun to experience the effects of computer supported materials and have still to evolve a reaction to them. Some of the recent photographs of fractal images[4] are breathtaking, in part because the human eye has never seen such detailed complexity, and in part because the human mind has never thought about the conceptual ideas underlying these images[5]. A. Bartlett Giamatti, president of Yale University between 1978 and 1986, writes, "Our problem as a society (United States) is that we have fostered disconnectedness; we have created a false separateness between social research and policy-making, thinking and politics, ideas and power" ([6], p. 95). He goes on to lament the lack of a sense of history in the American culture—a disconnectedness with the past. There is much of this same sense of disconnectedness with many of the products of this new technology. The images often appear harsh because they lack of sense of relatedness with anything. The tacit message is often: we can do it with a computer, therefore we should do it. Where is the cultural tradition in the product?

When words and images are combined the effect may be quite different than either of them alone, and quite different than some simple additive function. I would like to illustrate this point with the following example. The first essay in John Berger's book "Ways of Seeing" [7] contains a reproduction of Van Gogh's painting, "Wheatfield with Crows". On the next page is the same painting with the following caption: "This is the last picture that Van Gogh painted before he killed himself". The result is dramatically different. I would have liked to scan that photograph and paste it into this paper (a simple technical task), But I am not yet sure of the what procedures should be followed to obtain the appropriate permission. Quoting a sentence from another source is one thing, mechanically reproducing an image is likely quite another.

It is recognized by typographers that, "The first step to thinking creatively about type has nothing to do with studio skills or techniques; it is a matter of mental attitude and the acquisition of a well stocked mind" ([8], p. 12). A similar statement might be applied to the reader (viewer?). It is the mind of the receiver that ultimately determines the received message, whether it was the intended message or not. There is an increasing role for education here. Books (e.g. [9,10]) are now being created for the novice desk top publisher. There are skills to be learned, but there is also a necessity for aesthetic factors to be incorporated into the final product. Art appreciation and interpretation, perhaps even actual art courses (using either conventional materials or technology), photography, video production should all form part of the background.

HyperCard

HyperCard is a more ubiquitous development. Classification of the software has proved difficult. Many people view it as a form of data base. Others view it as system software, as a set of tools for designing other applications. The latter view seems to be more popular, certainly it is more exciting. Data bases do not conjure up images of excitement. Yet there is one feature of data bases that I believe has relevance to an appropriate role for HyperCard in education. They begin empty. Just as an artist begins with a blank canvas. The idea is to think of HyperCard as an information storage and structuring environment[11] rather than and opportunity for curriculum presentation.

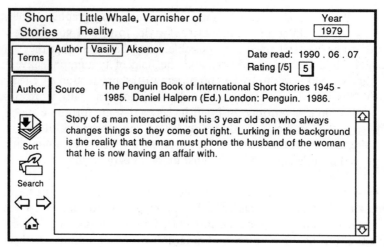

Fig. 1

The emphasis should be on the students as active organizers of their own knowledge rather than relatively passive observers of the knowledge structures of others.

As a quick personal example, it was relatively easy to construct a small set of HyperCard stacks to keep track of short stories that I am reading. Here is an example of the screen display from such a stack (Fig. 1).

By clicking on the "Author" button I am switched to another stack that contains information on the author (Fig. 2).

It is worth noting the beginning of the entry labeled "Grolier Electronic Encyclopedia". I have a CD-ROM player attached to my computer, and I can easily access information on the CD-ROM disk, copy it and then paste it into a document or file that I am currently working on. It is very fast and effective. This type of capability will soon be in the hands of our students.

Very clearly computer interfaces have entered a new era. This is best exemplified by the Macintosh computer and its visual desktop metaphor. Linguistic metaphors have been with us for a long time. So have visual metaphors: witness the large number of allegorical paintings for the 16th through 18th centuries. But the realization that such visual metaphors could serve a practical purpose is relatively recent. HyperCard has provided a second visual metaphor, the stack of cards. It is a particular rich metaphor since one can then extend the idea to include other visual metaphors when designing the cards themselves. Metaphors upon metaphors Visual and linguistic. Imagery is becoming a new form of literacy. People that thought that computer literacy would mean programming missed it by a mile.

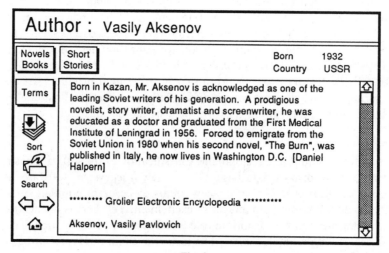

Fig. 2

Multimedia

The latest actor on the stage is multimedia. However, there is a relative lack of awareness of two previous technological ventures into education that had a similar emphasis. In the late 1960s and through most of the 1970s there were two large-scale computer-assisted instruction projects that had most of the capabilities of today's multimedia stations. One was the IBM 1500 System project that established 24 sites in North America, the other was the PLATO project originating out of the University of Illinois. Both systems provided sophisticated student stations using touch sensitive display devices with computer controlled audio and slide capabilities. The IBM Project lasted for just over 20 years, and derivations of the PLATO project are still operational. Yet the educational microcomputer movement seems relatively unaware of the existence of either project, nor of some of the lessons that could be learned from them. Now that the technical capabiltiy is in the hands of almost everyone, each person or center is in the process of inventing its own personal wheel.

If you are a program developer this technical capability is very exciting. Bells and whistles are great if you are the one who is ringing them. We are now in the first phase of using this capability. I would characterize this phase as that of the "quick impact". Multimedia presentations seem designed to stun the audience. The same sequence of development that seems evident with desk top publishing is also appearing with multimedia system and with those designing such materials, namely if the technology makes something possible then we should incorporate that feature into the product. In the case of DTP one ends up with a cluttered page, with multimedia one ends up with sensory overload. Carefully designed instructional materials, taking into account a deep understanding of the topic, and with lengthy consideration of what we know about learning and children, are still to appear.

Once again, I hope that we remember one of the consistent findings from the Logo literature, and from the Arts: is is more beneficial if you let the student have a sense of ownership in the result. Instead of having curriculum experts combine their wisdom to produce the materials of the 1990s, I would like to suggest that we treat multimedia like a new form of paint. Let's give it to the students and have them produce their own materials. These materials would not be intended for public or commercial distribution (neither are the millions of term papers that are written each year), but would form a sort of audit trail of the individual's own learning. They would constitute part of the student's learning portfolio, just as art students compose their art portfolios today. These portfolios would constitute an important evaluative component of the student's learning. Just as the arts do not appear to have succumbed to the sirens of objective testing, perhaps education could escape from their songs and begin to consider other evaluation alternatives as it continues its journey.

CONCLUSIONS

Education is in danger of becoming seriously hurt as it hurtles down the highway in its new technology. The vehicle is fast, shiny and dangerous. The back seat drivers are full of advice. Many teachers and teacher educators are championing the use of technology without a careful examination of the underlying assumptions and philosophies that buttress any approach. Perhaps we should listen to those from the arts.

I am not an artist, as anyone who knows me can attest. Yet I have an image of art education. I see students spending a substantive proportion of their time actually doing art. I see instructors moving about the class offering brief comments, suggestions, praise, exhortations and critical analyses of various features. Others have recognized the value of this model. It is a recurring theme in Papert's writing on Logo. Alfred North Whitehead also emphasized the point. Many of us who were fortunate enough to meet John Coleman in the Mathematics department at Queen's University, either as students or as colleagues, learned to refer to Whitehead's writings on education. Let me end with a sentence from his book, *The Aims of Education* [12]. "In estimating the importance of technical education we must rise above the exclusive association of learning with book-learning. First-hand knowledge is the ultimate basis of intellectual life" (p. 51).

Education may be the driver, but I would like to see it take more of its direction from the arts as it hurtles down the road to the future. I would also like to see it take Whitehead's admonition that occasionally it might be a good idea to get out and walk for a bit.

REFERENCES

1. Papert S., *Mindstorms*. Basic Books, New York (1980).
2. Abelson H. and diSessa A., *Turtle Geometry*. MIT Press, Cambridge, Mass. (1981).
3. Clayson J., *Visual Modeling with Logo*. MIT Press, Cambridge, Mass (1988).
4. Peitgen H.-O. and Richter P. H., *The Beauty of Fractals*. Springer, Berlin (1986).
5. Mandelbrot B., *The Fractal Geometry of Nature*. Freeman, New York (1977).
6. Giamatti A. B., *A Free and Ordered Space*. Norton, New York (1990).
7. Berger J., *Ways of Seeing*. Penguin, Harmondsworth (1972).
8. March M., *Creative Typography*. Mitchell, Rexdale, Ontario (1988).
9. Miles J., *Design for Desktop Publishing*. Chronicle Books, San Francisco (1987).
10. White J. V., *Graphic Design for the Electronic Age*. Xerox Press, New York (1988).
11. Apple Computer Inc., *HyperCard Stack Design Guidelines*. Addison–Wesley, Reading, Mass. (1989).
12. Whitehead A. N., *The Aims of Education*. Free Press, New York (1929).

Computers Educ. Vol. 18, No. 1–3, pp. 155–162, 1992
Printed in Great Britain

0360-1315/92 $5.00 + 0.00
Pergamon Press plc

BLOCKS TO THE EFFECTIVE USE OF INFORMATION TECHNOLOGY IN HIGHER EDUCATION

Nick Hammond,[1] Nigel Gardner,[2] Simon Heath,[3] Michael Kibby,[4]
Terry Mayes,[5] Ray McAleese,[5] Christine Mullings[6] and
Annie Trapp[1]

[1]CTI Centre for Psychology, University of York, Heslington, York YO1 5DD, [2]Programme on Information and Communication Technology, University of Oxford, Oxford, [3]CTI Centre for Land Use Studies, University of Aberdeen, Aberdeen AB9 1FX, [4]Centre for Academic Practice, Strathclyde University, Glasgow G1 1QE, [5]Institute for Computer-Based Learning, Heriot-Watt University, Edinburgh EH1 1HX and [6]CTI Centre for Textual Studies, University of Oxford, Oxford, U.K.

Abstract—This paper reports on the outcome of a seminar addressing issues in the exploitation of IT in teaching within Universities in the U.K. The seminar brought together experts with a range of experience in the use of educational technology, and focused on educational and organisational issues rather than on technical ones. Three surveys of the views of University lecturers on the use of computers in teaching, and the associated problems, are reported, followed by discussion of educational and organisational routes to lowering some of the existing barriers to more effective applications of educational technology.

INTRODUCTION

Why are computers so little used for teaching in the U.K. university sector? And why is what use there is almost entirely limited to tool-based applications? Why is it so rare for CAL to be integrated into the curriculum? Certainly microcomputers are starting to become widely available to teachers and students, and there is increasing information on available software and courseware within disciplines. For instance the Computers in Teaching Initiative (CTI) supports a vigorous programme informing lecturers of the availability of computer-based teaching materials and the opportunities they offer (see[1] for further information on the Initiative). Despite coordinated efforts such as these to promote the effective use of computers in teaching, the uptake is not as high as many have hoped.

The reasons for this are many: some no doubt reflect the quality and nature of the available materials, and others concern the educational context in which the technology is to be used. The instructional goals embedded within a piece of courseware all too often fail to match the goals of the course it purports to support. Yet other reasons may concern the organisational and political context: institutions and departments, whether by intent or default, may give little assistance to those wishing to exploit innovative approaches. Indeed, some argue that the key factors required to develop educational computing in universities are organisational, and advocate a strategic approach through centralised but cooperative management[2]. Certainly models of the adoption of computing into the university curriculum based solely on characteristics of individual lecturers tend to have little predictive value[3].

This paper results from a seminar convened to explore these educational and organisational barriers to the effective exploitation of computers in teaching, and to consider possible solutions. The seminar brought together two groups of experts, the first drawn from the staff of CTI Centres with particular knowledge of the problems of users—teachers and learners—and the second drawn from educationalists. The contributors were provided with a list of questions, intended to serve three roles: to define the scope of the seminar, to give a context within which the individual contributions could be viewed, and to help define issues for further research and clarification. The questions are shown in Fig. 1. The extent to which these questions were addressed was obviously limited, but they nevertheless provide a structure for this paper.

```
┌─────────────────────────────────────────────────────────────────────┐
│ 1.   DEFINING THE PROBLEM                                             │
│                                                                        │
│ 1.1  What is the current take-up and pattern of use of computers-based │
│      learning in higher education? Is take-up commensurate with the    │
│      available resources and quality of software/courseware, or is     │
│      there evidence for additional blocks?                             │
│                                                                        │
│ 1.2  What are the perceived barriers and incentives to the use of CBL  │
│      in HE? How are such findings to be interpreted?                   │
│                                                                        │
│ 1.3  How well or poorly is CBL integrated into educational practice in │
│      HE, and why?                                                      │
│                                                                        │
│ 1.4  What are the key features of the organisational (and political)   │
│      context which contribute to the problem?                         │
│                                                                        │
│ 2.   TOWARDS SOLUTIONS                                                │
│                                                                        │
│ 2.1  What suggestions for change (technical, educational,              │
│      organisational) result from surveys of usage and barriers to use? │
│                                                                        │
│ 2.2  What opportunities could new technology or approaches (whether in │
│      software development or in use) bring to help overcome blocks in  │
│      the use of CBL in HE.                                            │
│                                                                        │
│ 2.3  What changes in educational practice might help?                  │
│                                                                        │
│ 2.4  What changes in organisational policy or structure would be most  │
│      effective in overcoming barriers?                                │
│                                                                        │
│ 2.5  How should change best be instigated (at the technical,           │
│      educational and organisational levels)? What policy is adopted by │
│      existing groups?                                                  │
│                                                                        │
│ 2.6  What can be learned from the situation elsewhere (other sectors   │
│      of education and overseas)?                                       │
└─────────────────────────────────────────────────────────────────────┘
```

Fig. 1. Questions on the use of information technology in education provided to contributors to the seminar.

SURVEYS OF LECTURERS' VIEWS

A number of authors have identified characteristic barriers to the uptake of educational technology, for example[4]. Factors cited include the shortage of lecturers' time, poor rewards for teaching innovation or courseware development and the "not-invented-here" syndrome[5]. However, we have found no published reports of systematic surveys within this area to substantiate these claims, and so the work reported below is of particular interest despite the inevitable methodological problems with surveys of this sort.

The CTI Centres, from which the first group of experts in the seminar were drawn, are in a unique position to report on current practice and problems. The Centres are responsible for promoting computer-supported learning within their particular disciplines, and there is no other comparable body which combines subject expertise, educational and technical know-how and wide access to the views and activities of university teachers. Summary findings from surveys conducted by three CTI Centres are presented below. The surveys reflect on the state of current practice (questions 1.1 and 1.3 in Fig. 1) and the perceived incentives and barriers to computer use in teaching (questions 1.2 and 1.4).

Questionnaire surveys on blocks to computer use

Reasons for the slow adoption of CAL by university lecturers has been investigated in two surveys by the CTI Centre for Land Use Studies. The first survey addresses academic staff within the Centre's discipline area throughout the U.K. and the second focuses on one campus—the University of Aberdeen—but encompasses lecturers from all subject areas. Some key results are presented in Fig. 2 (national survey of discipline-specific staff) and Fig. 3 (survey of Aberdeen staff).

For the first survey, respondents were asked "what factors inhibit you in the use of computers in your teaching?" and to tick the three most important of nine factors described in the questionnaire (see Fig. 2 for details). Respondents were also invited to specify additional factors. In the second survey, respondents were asked to rate the importance of nine factors on a scale of 1 (very important) to 4 (very unimportant).

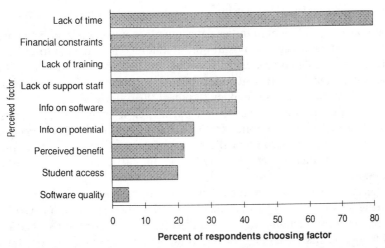

Fig. 2. Percentages of respondents indicating factors perceived to inhibit use of computers in teaching. The nine factors were: staff perceive benefits but have insufficient time to investigate or develop teaching software; financial constraints; lack of staff training; lack of support staff to assist lecturers in the use of computers; lack of information on suitable software for use in teaching; not enough information on the potential of computers as an aid to learning; staff do not perceive benefit from the use of computers in teaching; insufficient access for students to the computer hardware; poor quality of available software.

The predominant finding from both surveys is that staff perceive lack of time (whether for modifying courses, evaluating courseware or developing materials themselves) as a major barrier. Also high on the list of priorities are lack of support staff, lack of training and lack of information on suitable materials. It is interesting that factors such as lack of student access to hardware and quality of software are not considered to be such strong blocks to computer use. These findings accord with the view that significant improvements could be brought about by changes in organisational policy: for lecturers to find time implies in part a change in institutional priorities through policies, support structures and rewards, and in part a reduction in the size of perceived barriers. Perceived barriers to the adoption of CAL can be lowered through better information, staff training and the provision of appropriate development tools. Both institutional structures and national structures are likely to be necessary to achieve this.

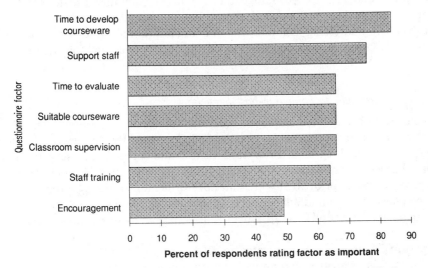

Fig. 3. Percentages of respondents rating each factor as important or very important. The factors were: lack of time to develop CBL courseware; lack of support staff for software development and maintenance; lack of time to evaluate the potential of computers in teaching and to remodel the course to incorporate existing CBL courseware; lack of suitable CBL courseware; lack of staff for supervision of students in the use of CBL courseware during formal or *ad hoc* class time and lack of suitably equipped classrooms; lack of staff training in the application of computers in teaching; lack of encouragement for integration of CBL in your courses and recognition in promotion assessment.

Questionnaire survey of problems and benefits in the use of computers for teaching humanities

In 1990, a national survey of all humanities departments in universities, polytechnics and colleges of higher education was conducted by postal questionnaire. The aim was to discover the current level and nature of the use of computers in teaching and research in the humanities community in the U.K. The questionnaires were sent to heads of department, and about half were completed by a person of this status, and thus were likely to reflect their viewpoint. Questions addressed such issues as availability of computing resources in departments; whether formal courses on computer use were offered (learning about computers); the use of computers to teach specific parts of the curriculum (learning with computers) and the reasons for introducing a computing element into courses. Effects on departments were explored, and in particular the perceived benefits and problems experienced.

More people perceived benefits from the introduction of computing than experienced problems with its use. Benefits related mainly to staff interests, and particularly to improved IT skills among staff, increased research productivity and saving time (all scoring over 70%). Use in teaching and perceived benefits to students were much further down the response scale. Since the questionnaire was addressed to staff this is perhaps hardly surprising.

The most prominent problems reported were associated with costs and staffing. Many respondents quoted "lack of money, lack of space and lack of time". Cost problems included both initial capital funding and the ability to upgrade and expand equipment. There was considerable feeling that low priority was given to humanities or arts computing needs. Staffing problems concentrated on lack of staff experience and skills in the field of IT; lack of time for picking up such skills, for setting up or maintaining equipment and for producing software or for teaching with computers. Inertia was seen as more of a problem than staff or student resistance as such. Lack of information relating to use of IT did not figure highly as a problem.

When problems and benefits were examined by discipline, there was a marked tendency for those experiencing the most benefits to also experience the most problems, and in reverse, those experiencing the fewest benefits also experienced the least problems. This trend seemed to be dependent on amount of resources available, amount of instruction (to both students and staff) and actual use in teaching. Although it might seem an obvious point, it appears that it is only through increased familiarity leading to increased use that both benefits and problems are recognised. It seems to be an evolving situation, where once resources are made available they are used firstly to enhance staff interests and then filter down to use with students. To encourage the spread of computer use to enhance teaching and learning in the humanities, a good place to start would be with a better overall IT strategy, particularly addressing the political and organisational issues of improved funding, especially for undergraduate facilities, and to enable staff to acquire the necessary skills and experience.

Interview survey of attitudes to computer-based teaching

The third survey to be reported employed a different methodological approach. When visiting psychology departments to give presentations, the CTI Centre for Psychology conducts semi-structured interviews with teaching staff. Prior to a visit, a number of both users and non-users of computer-based teaching are identified and appointments arranged. The interviews last about 30 min and generally occur prior to any presentations or demonstrations by the CTI Centre. The purpose of the interview is to find out how the lecturer currently uses computers, their knowledge of computer-based resources and their attitudes towards computer-based teaching. The key findings are summarised below.

The first part of the interview concentrates on actual usage of computers in teaching. Lecturers responsible for teaching statistics or running laboratory practicals are more likely to use software packages than other lecturers. This confirms the finding of a previous questionnaire that virtually all departments use computer facilities for teaching statistics and practical classes[6]. Few lecturers report using simulations, demonstrations, self-testing materials or structuring tools (such as concept mapping[7]) within their teaching. It is also rare for computers to be used to support innovative methods of presentation or teaching methods. For example, liquid crystal display units are not widely used and, with some notable exceptions, there is little use of electronic communication with students.

The interviews also suggest that lecturers tend to call on tools they already use for their research for teaching purposes. For example, word processing packages are used to prepare course notes, reading lists; data analysis packages are used to analyse class practical results; and in some cases a specific software package is used for both research and teaching. This has implications for the purchasing policy within departments. An *ad hoc* policy all too often results in a research culture based on workstations and Apple Macintosh hardware and a teaching culture based on PC hardware, to the detriment of teaching innovation.

The second part of the interview was concerned with attitudes to the use of computers in teaching. When asked what the main motivating factor would be to introduce computer-based teaching into their own course, the most frequently cited reason given by lecturers was the availability of good software. In some cases this reflected a lack of knowledge of existing software. Others claimed that their courses would not be improved by computer-based teaching methods. When asked to describe three ways in which computers might be potentially used on their course, the comments revealed a narrow view of how software could be used for different purposes and of the potential for introducing innovative teaching methods.

The majority of lecturers interviewed showed a positive attitude to computer-based teaching in general but were less enthusiastic about its relevance on their own course. They generally perceived their department's attitude as positive, even if not matched by resourcing, but were less clear about the attitude of their organisation. Indeed, no-one reported being under any pressure either from their peers, department or organisation to introduce CAL into their courses. Lecturers considered making radical changes to their course a low priority and expensive in terms of time and reward. In most departments, lecturers could receive some technical support but no training or guidance in preparing or utilising computer-based materials.

Discussion

The three surveys provide some insight into the questions listed under Defining the Problem in Fig. 1. They confirm previous reports that computer use in teaching is predominantly tool-based, with little use of tutorial, demonstration or other teaching-support software. Failure to develop these latter uses may result in part from lack of available products, but it stems also from ignorance of what is available and how software might be used in innovative ways. Advice on these matters within institutions seems virtually non-existent. However, the main perceived blocks are lack of time (and, by implication, a low priority on the part of individuals and organisations), lack of resources (particularly in non-science areas) and lack of support and training. In view of the suggestion that those with most experience were also aware of the most problems, it would be interesting to know how the perception of blocks to IT use in teaching changes with practical experience. It is likely that some of the respondents were hypothesising from a state of blissful ignorance.

Turning to the organisational context, it is clear that few institutions explicitly reward teaching innovation. It is of particular interest that, despite recent political rumblings on teaching quality, few lecturers perceived any pressures from their department or institution to introduce innovative approaches to their courses. The surveys help identify a number of routes for bringing about change, whether through the better provision of information, through the design of more suitable software tools or through organisational means. The next section explores some of the issues behind such changes.

EDUCATIONAL AND ORGANISATIONAL ISSUES

The second group of experts at the seminar on which this paper is based is drawn from those with experience of promoting educational and organisational change. We make no attempt to cover the full range of issues and possible strategies for solutions; rather the participants provided some snapshots of particular directions that might be taken. The following section suggests a direction for the development and use of courseware materials and tools, while the final section discusses background issues to institutional support for computer-based learning.

Towards educationally-effective courseware

One route to solving the problem lies in the provision of more appropriate courseware and software tools. Certainly some progress has been made in increasing available information through the provision of catalogues of computer-based teaching material by the subject-specific CTI Centres. However, the use of existing software is widely recognised to fall far short of what is thought to be desirable. It is difficult to make unqualified statements about the use of computers because, as Lewis[8] points out, very little evaluation of the use and usage of IT to support higher education has been performed.

Those who use such phrases as the "not-invented-here syndrome" are underestimating and undervaluing the conventional process by which lecturers prepare and update their materials. They refer to textbooks, monographs, the research literature, and their own research and experience for sources of factual material, ideas, representations, and organisation during the preparation of lecture notes, seminars and tutorials. What emerges is that lecturer's interpretation of the topic to be taught. Computer-based materials are quite justifiably approached in the same manner when being considered for inclusion in a lecturer's course materials. However, most courseware is not amenable to the same process of seamless incorporation into the body of a lecturer's course materials, but must be used as it stands or be rejected. Too often the latter option is taken.

Designing an environment in which existing courseware may be re-used in various applications has been addressed during the recently completed exploratory phase of the EC DELTA programme because of its fundamental importance to the economic and practical viability of much effort put into the creation of courseware. In the SAFE project (D1014), the concept of half-fabricates is developed, which recognises that various tools may operate at various stages during the construction of learning material, so that the output of one tool is the input to the next[9]. An alternative model for reusability, which emerged from consideration of the structure of hypermedia data elements in the same project, is that all items of a hypermedia database should have the same data structure, whatever the medium of the content or the modality by which they are presented to the learner. This allows a set of common database tools for structuring the database, although the multimedia content of each item in the database clearly requires medium-specific editors[10].

The latter representation of re-usability has significance not only at the stage of authoring hypermedia courseware, but also for all its other users, who may tailor the original, probably very large, database as a resource base of learning material in a particular subject area. Such users may be courseware developers, who may structure or restructure parts of the database for commercial reasons, teachers who may modify it for the pedagogical reasons indicated above, and learners who may edit or supplement the database as part of the learning process[11].

While hypermedia is being widely considered as a means of generating and delivering computer-based teaching because of its interactivity and exploratory mode of use[12], its potential for supporting re-usability on a large scale may in the final outcome be the prime factor in its wide adoption in learning.

Towards institutional support for computer-based learning

Conkin[13], in his 1987 review of hypertext, asks why it took over 20 years before the early pioneering demonstrations of the hypertext idea were taken out of the research and development laboratory and implemented in real working contexts. It is usually assumed that it took this long because the idea needed the available technology to become powerful enough to implement it in a usable and effective way. More importantly, Conklin argues, the idea itself took a long time to be fully appreciated. Thus, the very idea of the computer as a cognitive tool, as an augmenter of individual human intelligent performance, was a concept that required a long gestation period. It may be that this represents a necessary process, and we are seeing the same slowly-dawning realisation about CAL by the mainstream world of education. Perhaps the main blocks to implementation of CAL on a worthwhile scale lie in the fact that we have not yet put the idea across properly. On the other hand, we may be guilty of selling the wrong idea. To expect the educational system to go from a world almost totally without technology, except where teaching people how to use the technology is the point of the exercise, to a world where most learning occurs from a computer screen, is too big a jump. Just as with hypertext, the idea that the computer can be a tool to help students learn, not so much by acting as a multimedia delivery mechanism for knowledge, but by augmenting the learner's ability to ask questions, to explore, to form active strategies and so forth, is an idea that is so obvious that we (the converts) do not even bother to spell it out. Yet the full implementation of this idea would have the most radical consequences for higher education. It would mean that we would be accepting responsibility for shaping the learning process. This is not something that Universities have previously been anxious to do. In fact, to do so would require a reappraisal of priorities because what is being offered is not a technological "fix" to make higher education more cost effective, but a requirement to take seriously something that has previously only received lip-service, that is learning itself.

Universities are places that the outside world looks to for expertise, yet they are notoriously weak in applying advanced knowledge to their own organisation and procedures. To take a random example, there are occupational psychologists in most U.K. Universities who advise industry on selection procedures. Yet this expertise is almost totally ignored in the University's own selection procedures. It is much the same with teaching. University teachers, as we all know, are neither professionally trained, nor properly recognised, by their own institutions as teachers. The point is that Universities do not know how to implement new technology in their own service, even if it has been developed by its own researchers. Even if they did know how to do this, the innovative implementation of technology for teaching would not solve the problem that policy makers want to solve, which is how to teach ever-increasing numbers of students with almost no increase in resources. It might ultimately be possible to use CAL to achieve real gains in learning with less contact with teachers, but to get to this point will require a considerable investment of both resources and attention to the learning process.

Part of the problem lies in the confusion between research and development. We are equipped to pursue the former but not the latter. Yet most of the real problems in this area are not problems of research *per se*. Of course many research problems remain, but the most challenging aspects are those of creating large-scale change. We must build and demonstrate systems that are effective learning environments, but we must also test their effectiveness in the context of real implementation, that is in real pedagogical experiments on a large scale (with appropriate safeguards for individual students). As researchers, we must raise the profile of evaluation and make sure that the same ingenuity goes into evaluation as into the design of the instructional software.

Principal Alistair MacFarlane, who has been responsible for setting up Heriot-Watt University's Institute for CBL, has said that Universities should be involved in the large-scale development of this technology, but that they cannot do it alone. The intensely supportive learning environments on which Universities will concentrate a few years hence cannot be produced, at present, by the efforts of the staff from the institution itself. On the contrary, the development process will need to be a collaboration with equipment manufacturers, software producers, and possibly publishers. It is unlikely that we can succeed without such collaboration, while it is also the case that such development could not occur without us.

CONCLUSIONS

The seminar sought clarification of the issues raised by the question listed in Fig. 1. In this it proved partially successful. The first section of the paper, summarising findings from three surveys of lecturers' views and practices, revealed a pattern of IT use and perceived barriers to its use compatible with a general lack of institutional concern and support for computer-based learning. The surveys also pointed towards potential routes for change, but the overall low level of innovative use of IT for teaching means that what evidence does exist on the strengths and weaknesses of specific approaches is eclipsed by wider concern for the more general barriers to its use. So while some of the solutions proposed in this paper may well meet requirements of lecturers, the surveys provide no further insight into such solutions as they are currently so rare. The second section, concerned with educational and organisational issues, discussed some directions for courseware development and for institutional support.

There is a great danger that support for the use of technology focuses on the technology rather than on the use. Whilst it is clearly important to provide the infrastructure support, the technical backup and information on what is available, this is only the starting point, the enabling condition, for what follows. This point was made by contributors to the seminar particularly in relation to the development of CBL support in universities in the U.S.A. Educational technology, once we move away from computers as mere replacements of existing tools, inevitably raises questions about its optimal use for the learning within the particular educational and institutional context. As argued in the preceding section effective use of computer-based learning requires a reappraisal of how learning should take place within universities.

It is too often the sole responsibility of the lecturer not only to identify courseware or software, but to devise a sound educational strategy for its use, to negotiate suitable resourcing and to fight the organisational inertia in the practicalities of carrying through an innovative teaching project. On the whole, U.K. lecturers receive no formal training in educational theory and practice, though one hopes they have picked up the requisite skills for conventional teaching methods. To move beyond the familiar boundaries requires an uncomfortable questioning of one's presuppositions. Venturing into unknown territory also incurs risks of failure or institutional disapprobation. The finding that perception of benefits and of problems go hand in hand suggests that use of educational technology may well lead to a questioning of educational methods: espousing educational technology seems inevitably to lead us down a road of educational change. If this view is accepted, then the implementation of educational technology should be the responsibility of not just the technologist: psychologists concerned with cognitive change, educationalists concerned with educational change and policy-makers concerned with organisational change all have distinctive and important roles to play. Computer-based learning is about education, not computers.

REFERENCES

1. Darby J., The computers in teaching initiative. A progress report. *CTISS File* **10**, 3–5 (1990).
2. Bidin A. R. H. and Drabble G., An organizational approach towards the development of educational computing in a university environment. *Computers Educ.* **14**, 137–143 (1990).
3. Mudd S. and McGrath K., Correlates of the adoption of curriculum-integrated computing in higher education. *Computers Educ.* **12**, 457–463 (1988).
4. Darby J., Computer literacy or computers in teaching? *CTISS File* **11**, 48–49 (1991).
5. Gardner N. and Darby J., Using computers in university teaching: a perspective on key issues. *Computers Educ.* **15**, 27–32 (1990).
6. Hammond N. V. and Trapp A. L., Computers in psychology teaching in the U.K. *Behav. Res. Meth. Instrum. Computers* **23**, 118–120 (1991).
7. Trapp A. L. and Hammond N. V., Concept mapping tools: a different approach. *Psychol. Softw. News* **2**, 10–11 (1991).
8. Lewis R., Computers in higher education teaching and learning: some aspects of research and development. *CTISS File* **11**, 3–7 (1991).
9. Derks M., Bulthuis W., Monaghan P., Keane M., Easterbrook M., Nienhuis E. and Bloemberg W., Learning material development, tools, and environments. DELTA SAFE project (D1014) Report OS-ID/1. Philips, Eindhoven (1989).
10. Hatzopoulos M., Dimopoulou K., Gouscos D., Spiliopoulou M., Vassilakis C. and Vazirgiannis M., DELTA SAFE project (D1014) Report HYP/20 Final Report on hypermedia databases. Philips, Eindhoven (1991).
11. Kibby M. R., Tanner G., Mayes J. T., Knussen C. and Grant S., DELTA SAFE project (D1014) Report HYP/21 Final Report on user interfaces for hypermedia. Philips, Eindhoven (1991).
12. Jonassen D. H. and Grabinger R. S., Problems and issues in designing hypertext/hypermedia for learning. In *Designing Hypertext/Hypermedia for Learning* (Edited by Jonassen D. H. and Mandl H.), pp. 3–25. Springer, Heidelburg (1990).
13. Conklin J., A survey of hypertext. MCC Technical Report, No. STP-356–86, Rev. 2 (1987).

Computers Educ. Vol. 18, No. 1–3, pp. 163–170, 1992
Printed in Great Britain. All rights reserved

HYPERCOURSEWARE

DOUGLAS SIVITER and KEITH BROWN

Department of Computing and Mathematics, Polytechnic of the South Bank, Borough Road,
London SE1 0AA, England

Abstract—Hypercourseware is a conceptual framework for developing computer-based flexible-learning material. This paper summarizes the main principles on which hypercourseware is based and discusses software tools which have been developed for authors and end-users to manage and manipulate hypercourseware. The main motivation which underpins the work is a desire to see the educational potential of hyper systems further exploited by the widespread availability of powerful yet easy-to-use tools for hypercourseware management.

1. INTRODUCTION

Within any computer-based education system (CBES) there is embodied some educational subject matter. Crudely, this is some representation of concepts, knowledge, skills, to be explored, learned, taught, etc. This subject matter is referred to as courseware.

The term hyper systems is used to refer to the ever increasing list of software products which provide some combination of hypertext and software development capabilities. Examples include HyperCard™, SuperCard™, LinkWay™, Guide™, Toolbook™ and Plus™.

1.1. Hyper systems for computer-assisted education

The educational potential of hyper systems is increasingly being recognized by many developers of computer-based education systems. Hyper systems are used by educational authors as preferred development systems because they provide much higher level facilities than traditional programming languages, and provide much more flexibility than educational authoring tools, many of which are unbearably over-prescriptive. However, most hyper systems were not designed specifically for educational use and therefore need considerable enhancement if they are to function well as large-scale courseware authoring tools. The required enhancements include appropriate conceptual frameworks and the tools to support such frameworks.

Hypercourseware is an example of a conceptual framework which exploits hyper systems for developing large-scale, computer-based, flexible-learning courses. It is described in Section 3.

1.2. The need for hypercourseware management systems

Users encounter many difficulties while trying to exploit hyper systems[1–3]. Users can be baffled by fundamental issues like "where am I?" "where else is there to go?" "where have I already been?" "where should I go next?" "how can I get there?" and by more ambitious issues like "how can I modify this resource?" Hypercourseware is potentially subject to all the same difficulties. To combat them, authors and end-users need powerful yet easy-to-use tools for managing and manipulating hypercourseware. The distinction between author and end-user is frequently blurred. The terms manage and manipulate are used to refer to the interleaved activities which authors might perform such as constructing, structuring, editing, viewing and navigating courses, and building tours through those courses. End-users of hypercourseware need tools which facilitate viewing, navigation, touring and guided exploration. A hypercourseware management system (HMS) is an integrated collection of such tools. Section 4 describes an HMS developed at South Bank polytechnic. Ideally, systems like this should be as widely available as word-processors so that a real craft can emerge in hypercourseware development.

CONTENTS

Fig. 1. A contents page.

2. AN EDUCATIONAL CONTEXT FOR HYPERCOURSEWARE

A project at South Bank polytechnic was set up to develop a CBES which exploits hypercourseware to teach about distributed computer systems. The project's aims can be summarized as:

- To develop a general purpose hypercourseware management system which could be used to manage and manipulate hypercourseware for any subject.
- To develop hypercourseware specifically for people requiring knowledge of distributed computer systems.
- Within the hypercourseware, to incorporate interactive simulations of computer networks.

This paper is concerned with the first of these aims and describes some of the theoretical and practical issues involved in developing tools for the management and manipulation of hypercourseware. The paper is necessarily brief; a more detailed account is available in [4]. The distributed systems courseware is briefly discussed to illustrate an application of the system.

2.1. Examples of using hypercourseware

Several information technology courses within South Bank polytechnic include modules which teach about distributed systems. The distributed systems courseware is not explicitly bound to any of these course modules; it is a separate evolving resource which is already broader than any of them. Some of the course modules selectively exploit the currently developed courseware to supplement traditional teaching methods. Such uses provide formative information. Various open-learning courses could be formulated from different subsets of the overall courseware; example packages are currently being formulated for distribution outside of the polytechnic.

The distributed systems courseware is just one example of exploiting the general-purpose HMS. Other courseware currently being developed includes a multimedia course and a flexible-learning package for careers education and guidance. An interesting example, which accompanies the HMS, is a stand-alone course for teaching authors how to develop hypercourseware using the system.

2.2. A summary of educational requirements

Hypercourseware was defined to meet various educational requirements. This section summarizes just the higher level ones. Specific requirements for the HMS are outlined in Section 4.

2.2.1. Flexible learning. Hypercourseware is an attempt to provide a conceptual framework for developing large-scale, flexible-learning courses. Flexible-learning courses are, by definition, to be used in a variety of ways, e.g. as stand-alone open-learning packages or used by lecturers guiding groups of students.

2.2.2. Adaptability. This is regarded as a fundamental property of hypercourseware. Large flexible-learning courses are difficult to develop and always need updating. Even if a team of authors is convinced that they have specified and implemented a useful courseware resource, the next educationalist who tries to exploit the courseware will almost certainly want to change some aspects. There is also an obvious educational potential for systems which provide students with the means to adapt material.

2.2.3. Structure, modularity and access. There are clear benefits to be derived from appropriate structuring of any resource and it is essential that this structuring coincides with flexible access to any section of the resource, i.e. users should always have the means to access whichever section they choose without being obliged to follow pre-determined routes through the resource.

2.2.4. Guidance. It is not sufficient to supply well-structured courseware resources and then just hope that users will intuitively exploit the resource in some meaningful manner. Guidance at various levels is required to accompany the subject matter.

2.2.5. Integration with other resources. Hypercourseware can accommodate and integrate many computer-assisted learning packages which are produced using applications, programming languages, educational authoring systems and more recently hyper systems. Hypercourseware is also completely amenable to multimedia approaches.

2.2.6. Exploiting hyper systems. This can be regarded as an aim and/or a strategy. This requirement simply recognizes that the most viable route to satisfying all the previous ones is to exploit the many powerful qualities of hyper systems; especially the adaptability, the presentation facilities and the software development facilities.

3. HYPERCOURSEWARE PRINCIPLES

This section describes a workable definition of hypercourseware upon which a variety of hypercourseware management systems could be developed.

3.1. A viable definition of hypercourseware

In defining hypercourseware, an attempt has been made to define an adaptable generic structure for courses, so that authors can develop courseware using whatever specific structure they desire. A compromise is required; the definition needs to be sufficiently specific to enable the development and use of authoring tools, but not so specific that it restricts authors' styles or is incompatible with currently available hyper systems such as HyperCard.

A preliminary definiton of hypercourseware is:
   —hypercourse is a collection of topics;
   —a topic is a collection of educational activities;
   —an educational activity is a collection of primitive activities.

This is obviously a somewhat loose definition. The rest of this section will clarify the definition and show that it achieves the compromise mentioned above. An authors' responsibility is to use this loosely defined structure as a basis for developing coherent hypercourseware. Authors need to determine what constitutes a coherent collection of related topics for a particular piece of courseware, and what constitutes a coherent collection of related educational activities for each topic in a course. This definition is then extended to incorporate tours and guided exploration. They can sometimes be regarded as integral parts of the hypercourseware or can be regarded as ways of using it. Tours and guided exploration are familiar ideas found within many software packages (especially adventure games). They are also discussed in hypertext literature, e.g. [5].

3.2. Structural aspects of hypercourseware

There are real benefits to be derived from the appropriate structuring of any hyperspace. Well structured domains are easier to assimilate and navigate than chaotic domains. The definition of hypercourseware must remain flexible with respect to structure since different subjects will benefit from different approaches to structuring, and different authors will hold different opinions on how best to structure various subjects. Hypercourseware therefore needs to have a powerful, flexible approach to the structuring of the collection of topics and to the structuring of the collections of educational activities for any topic.

3.2.1. Topics as collections of educational activities. Consider first a single topic within a piece of hypercourseware; a topic is a collection of educational activities. As examples, the educational activities for one topic might include some traditional ideas such as stating the objectives of the topic and the prerequisite knowledge a user should have before embarking upon the topic; providing presentations, resources, assignments, sample solutions, assessments, etc. A "where next?" activity could be included which contributes to the idea of guided exploration through a collection of topics. An educational activity can be composed of any combination of primitive activities, e.g. read a piece of text, look at a picture, listen to a sound, look at an animation (computer-based or video-based), play with a computer-based interactive device (e.g. simulation), or even follow some instructions to perform an assignment away from the computer. This definition of an educational activity is therefore completely amenable to exploiting multimedia applications.

As a guideline only, within hypercourseware the number of educational activities devoted to any single topic should be small. The rationale being that too many activities for a topic is usually an indicator that the topic is too large, and would probably benefit from being decomposed into several smaller sub-topics. This makes it totally feasible to use a flat structure for the collection of educational activities for a single topic. The flat structure can then be presented to a user as a simple map view, i.e. an activities map (see Fig. 2).

Within any educational activity, e.g. a presentation, the structure is totally the responsibility of an author and can be as simple or as complex as desired. One approach is to keep the structure of an educational activity deliberately simple, typically a linear excursion through primitive activities with occasional sub-excursions, none of which depart significantly from the particular educational activity being pursued and none of which perform any radical navigational steps such as changing topic. Excursions are intended to feel like temporary journeys away from, and usually back to, the topic homeground. Orientation for the user is thus supported by always knowing which topic is currently being investigated.

3.2.2. Courses as hierarchical networks as topics. If a piece of courseware consists of just a few topics with no structuring then a simple navigational metaphor can be used, i.e. just provide a simple map of the collection of topics. This, however, does not readily scale up to courseware of any significant size, and it does not readily lend itself to displaying structured collections of topics. Imagine a course containing dozens of topics, each containing several sub-topics, which themselves contain several sub-topics; the inadequacies of a simple map view become immediately apparent.

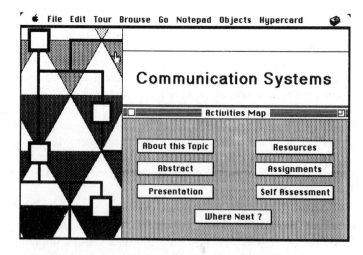

The Activities Map for a Topic named 'Communication Systems' currently visible over the Homeground for that Topic.

Fig. 2. A topic's homeground and activities map.

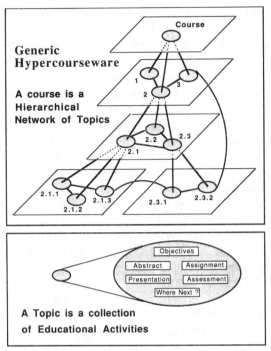

Fig. 3. Generic hypercourseware.

Figure 3 illustrates the way in which collections of topics can be structured in hypercourseware. Figure 3 shows only a very small example; most real courses would be too large to draw in this illustrative manner.

The example course structure in Fig. 3 has three main topics, i.e. 1, 2 and 3. Topics would ordinarily be named, but numbering is more useful for this illustration. Topic 2 is shown as having three sub-topics, i.e. 2.1, 2.2 and 2.3. Topics 2.1 and 2.3 are also shown as having sub-topics. This is a traditional structuring approach which hypercourseware must facilitate.

Also in Fig. 3 is an illustration of a network approach to structuring the collection of topics. There are many arcs connecting topics, e.g. 1–2, 2.1–2.3, 2.3.2–3, etc. Each of these arcs indicates that an explicit link has been made between two topics. It is not necessary to anticipate exactly why authors would want to explicitly link topics but it is obviously essential that this facility should be supported within hypercourseware.

Given the structuring and linking facilities which must be supported in hypercourseware, it is appropriate to employ a hierarchical network of topics as the underlying data structure. This gives hypercourseware the capability of structuring topics and linking topics but does not imply that authors must extensively exploit both these features simultaneously. In simple cases a course can still be a small, flat, unlinked collection of topics.

4. HYPERCOURSEWARE MANAGEMENT TOOLS

For any significant example of hypercourseware the underlying data structure is probably going to be very complex and will easily provide endless opportunities for becoming "lost in hyperspace". High level tools are therefore required which provide users with the means to view and manipulate useful abstractions of the structure. This section discusses some of the main functional requirements for these tools and outlines how the requirements have been addressed within South Bank's HMS. The discussion focuses on a main component of South Bank's HMS called the Course Browser.

4.1. Main facilities

4.1.1. Integration with Macintosh and HyperCard. The tools for managing and manipulating hypercourseware need to look and feel like typical Macintosh applications but must simultaneously run as though layered on top of HyperCard. This has been implemented using a toggling menu bar so that either HyperCard's menu bar is visible, or the Browser's menu bar is visible. While the Browser's menu bar is selected HyperCard is effectively in the background providing an operational platform upon which a new collection of facilities is layered. The new facilities offered to the user are oriented towards hypercourseware manipulation, e.g. Open Course, Open Tour, Show Contents, New Topic, Delete Activity, etc.

4.1.2. Selectable levels of user access. There are three categories of user ranging from *authors*, who have access to all facilities, to *readers* who have limited scope to refashion the courseware. All courses can be updated and customized in Author Mode. The following description of requirements and facilities focuses on Author Mode and in all cases the Reader Mode can be assumed to use exactly the same tools but with selectively restricted options.

4.1.3. Hypercourseware manipulation. An integrated set of tools is required for creating, manipulating, viewing and navigating the collections of topics within a course and the collections of educational activities within each topic. Viewing and navigating are fundamental activities for both authors and readers; they underpin the creation of, and interaction with, the courseware structure. The highest levels of viewing and navigating are essentially unrestricted browsing and unrestricted access to any sections of the courseware. In addition to this unrestricted browsing, facilities are required which support tours and guided exploration.

4.1.4. Creating and editing educational activities. The educational activities which comprise a topic are implemented as either HyperCard stacks or Macintosh applications (e.g. animations, simulations). Hence the tools for developing the activities are not necessarily part of the HMS; an activity can be developed externally from the HMS and imported into a topic. However, because HyperCard underpins the HMS it is permanently available within the HMS as a main option for developing activities.

4.1.5. Viewing and navigation facilities. There is no single tool or facility which will satisfy all authors' and readers' viewing and navigation requirements for all courses. Rather than try to define one major tool it is preferable to incorporate a variety of integrated tools which provide multiple views of the hypercourseware. Hence a tool which is conceptually similar to a contents page may be desirable for a particular course, or simply preferred by a particular user, whereas an alphabetical index of topics may be preferred in some other circumstances. Typically a suite of viewing tools provides the flexibility to switch approaches for whatever reason. A map-oriented view is a popular idea which provides a further alternative to a contents page or an index. A map tool is a device which generates explicit maps of the courseware. The maps can be used directly for navigation or can be customized to represent some other navigation metaphor. So, for example the nodes in a map, representing topics in a course, could be redrawn as rooms in a house if this was felt to be appropriate.

In South Bank's HMS, topic navigation is supported by tools such as the Contents View, Index View, Map Views, Links View, etc. The complete set of tools has its own internal management system which ensures that each of the currently visible views is updated whenever a user changes topic. The tools always reflect the user's current position within the course. The same tools are also used to construct and edit collections of topics. See Figs 4 and 5 for examples of navigation tools which provide multiple views of a course.

4.1.6. Orientation facilities. A particularly important requirement for the HMS is that it helps users to avoid becoming lost in hyperspace. In combination with the viewing and navigation facilities, orientation is additionally supported by the provision of landmarks, called Home-Grounds. Each topic possesses a unique HomeGround which is displayed (behind any currently visible tools) whenever the user changes topic. (See Fig. 5.)

4.1.7. Tours and guided exploration. In addition to tools for building the courseware, authors have facilities to build predetermined tours of courseware which users can then follow. A tour is a facility to be exploited by any user who does not yet have the confidence to explore the subject area in a self directed fashion. Authors can also use "linking" and "where next?" facilities to contribute to guided explorations of courseware. Guided exploration is for users with sufficient confidence to determine their own branching through the courseware. A particularly important requirement is that users have the facilities and the flexibility to either follow tours or conduct their own explorations of the courseware while being free to adopt or ignore the guidance offered by authors.

indicators of the open topic   sub-topics of the open topic

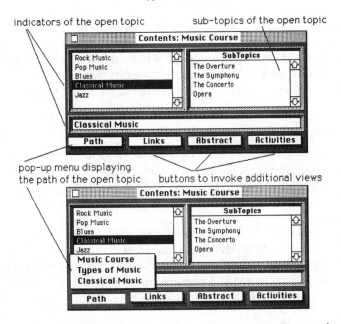

pop-up menu displaying
the path of the open topic   buttons to invoke additional views

A Contents View of a simple course. The open topic is currently Classical Music which has four neighbouring topics and four sub-topics. The Path button is a pop-up menu which in this case indicates that Classical Music is a sub-topic of Types of Music, which in turn is a sub-topic of the top level i.e., Music Course. A user can navigate through the topics hierarchy by selecting a neighbouring-topic, a sub-topic, or a parent-topic from the path.

Fig. 4. Content View.

4.2. User interface

An inevitable complexity in this project derived from the fact that there are many levels of interaction with hypercourseware, ranging from courseware management at the author level through to performing some educational assignment at the user level. For the styles of the user interface, in the context of this project it was better to exploit existing popular styles rather than invent obscure new approaches. A variety of existing styles were possible influences, for example the traditional Macintosh application interface, the various interfaces adopted by people developing material in HyperCard, and Smalltalk 80™[6]. The main challenges in user interface design

An Index View allows users to select from an alphabetical list of all the topics in the course. Selecting a topic immediately navigates to that topic's homeground

Fig. 5. Index View.

were how to be consistent across the whole range of facilities, how to adhere as closely as possible to the Macintosh interface guidelines[7], and how, when appropriate, to develop innovative interface ideas which extend the interface design within the spirt of such guidelines. A further constraint was that since HyperCard's existing functionality needed to be available to users from within the HMS, the HMS user interface needed to extend, but blend in with HyperCard's existing user interface.

4.3. Course Browser development

From the outset it was intended that Browser development would use prototyping and incremental development, and be object-oriented in nature. The development started with a speculative prototyping phase, which involved producing many series of diagrams of user walkthroughs. These helped to determine the basic functions and user interface which authors and readers would desire.

An object-oriented approach to Bowser design resulted in the creation of managers, each manager object being commited to certain functional areas in much the same way as the Macintosh toolbox is sub-divided into managers. The paradigm which influenced the design of the navigation tools is the model/view/controller (MVC) concept from Smalltalk 80™[6]. Every course has an underlying model which is accessed and manipulated by a set of view/controller devices, e.g. a Contents View.

5. CONCLUSIONS

The project, reported in this paper, set out to provide a workable definition of hypercourseware and to produce tools for the management and manipulation of hypercourseware; in creating Course Browser these aims have been essentially satisfied. It represents our first implementation of a hypercourseware management system; it is an extension to the educational potential of HyperCard and provides authors with the facilities to develop and repeatedly adapt large well structured courses.

Acknowledgement—The project reported in this paper has funding from the Learning Technologies Unit which is part of the Training, Enterprise and Education Directorate within the U.K. Government's Department of Employment.

REFERENCES

1. Nielsen J., Hypertext. *Commun. ACM* **33**, 3, 297–310 (March 1990).
2. McAleese R., Navigation and browsing in Hypertext. In *Hypertext Theory into Practice* (Edited by McAleese R.), pp. 6–44. Blackwell Scientific, Oxford (1989).
3. Canter D., Rivers R. and Storrs G., Characterising user navigation through complex data structures. *Behav. Informn Technol.* **4**, 93–102 (1985).
4. Siviter D. and Brown K., Hypercourseware management systems: Course Browser. Department of Computing and Mathematics, Polytechnic of the South Bank, London (1991).
5. Hammond N. and Allinson L., Travels around a learning support environment. In *CHI 1988 Conference Proceedings: Human Factors in Computer Systems* (Washington, D.C., May 1988) (Edited by Soloway E. *et al.*), ACM Press, New York (1988).
6. Goldberg A., *Smalltalk-80.* Addison–Wesley, Reading, Mass. (1983).
7. Apple Computer Inc., *Human Interface Guidelines; Hypercard Stack Design Guidelines.* Addison–Wesley, Reading, Mass. (1987; 1989).

Computers Educ. Vol. 18, No. 1–3, pp. 171–177, 1992
Printed in Great Britain

0360-1315/92 $5.00 + 0.00
Pergamon Press plc

AUTHORING AND EVALUATION OF HYPERMEDIA FOR EDUCATION

G. A. Hutchings,[1] W. Hall,[1] J. Briggs,[2] N. V. Hammond,[3] M. R. Kibby,[4]
C. McKnight[5] and D. Riley[6]

[1]Department of Electronics and Computer Science, University of Southampton, Southampton SO9 5NH,
[2]School of Information Systems, Kingston Polytechnic, Kingston upon Thames, Surrey KT1 2EE,
[3]Department of Psychology, University of York, Heslington, York YO1 5DD, [4]Centre for Academic
Practice, University of Strathclyde, Glasgow G1 1XW, [5]HUSAT Research Institute, Loughborough
University, Loughborough and [6]Department of Geography, Polytechnic of North London, Holloway,
London N7 8DB, U.K.

Abstract—Hypermedia encompasses the modes of learning and interaction associated with conventional
CAL, but it also allows greater learner control, access to multimedia learning materials and a variety of
modalities of interaction with the learning material which are only now becoming apparent. Nevertheless,
for a hypermedia document to be educationally effective, the author must consider the learning goals and
activities it must support, how the nature of the domain will relate to the learning activities, and how
learners will differ, and then provide appropriate support tools. Authoring large hypermedia documents
demands facilities to manage links, and to create them automatically. Methods considered included the
creation of generic links, applicable to more than one document, use of knowledge-based rules to generate
links, and the use of file interchange formats for reusability of information. Authors should avoid the
dominant browse and retrieve model and consider a range of activities—in any case simple hypertext has
been shown to be insufficient for effective learning. Evaluation of such systems and materials in use has
many facets, including usability, the effectiveness of guidance tools, the learning achieved. Evaluation of
hypermedia systems is different from CAL because of the new vocabulary and syntax of interaction which
is required.

INTRODUCTION

Hypermedia encompasses the modes of learning and interaction associated with conventional CAL,
but it also allows greater learner control, access to multimedia learning materials and a variety of
modalities of interaction with the learning material which are only now becoming apparent. The
work of Beeman[1] with Intermedia indicated that its most interesting aspect was not, as might
have been expected, its short-term novelty for the learner (the Hawthorne effect) but that most
learning seemed to occur with those who had prepared the course material rather than those who
received it. This observation is supported by those who advocate learning through the construction
of representations of a knowledge domain (e.g. with SemNet[2]). It is not usually possible to
support such activities with conventional CAL because of the separation of authoring from the
learning environment. However, the essentially simple structure of hypermedia makes it easy to edit
or insert additional material (both links and nodes) into an existing hypermedia database, and then
allow the database management system to handle the consequences[3]. Thus editing and similar
activities, which may be collectively named "tailoring" of hypermedia, may extend from publishers
to courseware designers, teachers and, especially, the learners themselves.

Such models of hypermedia for learning require methods for formative and summative
evaluation which encompass and extend far beyond those of conventional CAL. While evaluation
methods for any form of learning are ill-defined and subject to controversy[4,5], the ultimate
aims of evaluating hypermedia are clear: to enhance computer-based learning through improved
design of authoring and learning environments and of learning materials. These topics were
discussed at the CAL '91 seminar on Authoring and Evaluation which formed the basis of this
paper.

LEARNING FROM HYPERMEDIA

The first question to ask embarking on an evaluation is: "What makes for educationally effective
hypermedia?" Creating an amorphous network of nodes and links through which the learner is left

to sink or swim may be even less effective than a strait-jacket of programmed learning. As Nielsen[6] points out:

> Every extra link is an additional burden on the user who has to determine whether or not to follow it. And if there are too many links leading to uninteresting places (because "they might be relevant for some readers") then readers will quickly become disappointed and learn not to trust your judgement.

An associated problem is one of "going round in circles", whereby users do not identify and ignore links to nodes which have recently been viewed. Prudent link creation can reduce this phenomenon, but Briggs *et al.*[7] have implemented a short term memory utility in order to mitigate the problem. The user is able to indicate the desired number of intervening nodes before one is re-presented or revisited, thus suppressing links to those which have been offered too recently.

There is evidence of other problems associated with learning from the more basic forms of hypermedia: getting lost, "failing to see the wood for the trees", failing to find material, unmotivated rambling, and problems with the interface[8]. Nevertheless, Hammond maintains that hypermedia *can* provide a framework for highly effective learning: for a hypermedia document to be educationally effective, the author must take into account some of the characteristics of how people are likely to use and to learn from hypermedia.

Unfortunately the nature of human learning (and of computer use in general) is such that prescriptive design guidelines have limited utility. However, current psychological theory provides some helpful pointers for designers of educational materials:

- Learning is not unitary; there is room for a spectrum of approaches to CAL in general and learning from hypermedia in particular.
- Knowledge domains differ widely in their natural structures and in the requirements they demand of the learner.
- Learners differ, not only in terms of abilities, strategies and styles, but in their goals and contexts.

Learning is both *situated* and *distributed*. It is situated in the sense that the way people learn, and the cognitive abilities they use, depend on the nature of the learning situation. It is thus not surprising that a great range of activities is typically called upon in learning—some active, some passive; some creative, some reactive; some directed, some exploratory—and that the nature of learning, and of the tools and situations that support it, is task dependent.

Learning is also distributed in the sense that there is a strong coupling between the internal goals, representations and actions of the learner and the external form of the learning materials and their delivery. The cognitive activity is shared across learner and materials. Put more simply, in the dynamic world of hypermedia, learners' goals and actions are likely to be shaped by the moment-to-moment display of information in front of them.

These general qualities of learning mean that the author needs first to consider what learning goals and activities the hypermedia is likely to support, how the nature of the domain will relate to the learning activities and perhaps how learners will differ, and then to provide appropriate structures and tools to support these learning requirements. Learning requirements can be related to the tools typically provided by hypermedia systems using the dimensions shown in Fig. 1. The figure summarises three relevant dimensions along which hypertext-based learning systems, and computer-based learning in general, vary: *control, engagement* and *synthesis*. Control refers to the degree to which the learner rather than the system controls exposure to learning materials, the particular learning activity or strategy. Engagement refers to the extent that learners are required to process the materials actively rather than passively. Synthesis refers to the nature of the learning activity: does it require the learner to create materials or relationships rather than merely observe them? These last two dimensions are not independent since creative tasks generally require active engagement, although the converse is not true.

In the figure, these dimensions define a cube, crudely divided into eight regions by dichotomising each dimension. Basic hypertext systems can be located in the lower back left region since these typically allow learner control, provide only passive engagement and merely present materials to the learner. However, more advanced hypermedia facilities and variations in learner tasks allow

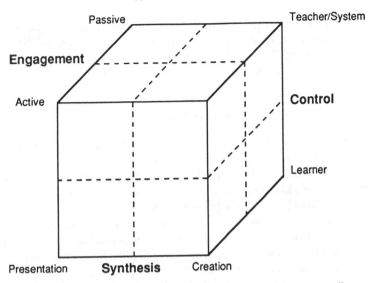

Fig. 1. Relationships between learning tasks and tools provided by hypermedia systems.

"movement" along the dimensions. The benefits of learners control afforded by hypertext and hypermedia systems are persuasively championed by hypertext advocates, but all too often this hides an assumption that the goal of learner understanding can be equated with the goal of information provision. If learning also needs thought, then it is often the case that more explicit direction and control, to restrict the learner to realistic goals and to a sensible part of the domain knowledge, needs to be judiciously mixed with freedom of action. System guidance may vary from the explicit step-by-step constraints of programmed learning, through optional fixed sequences, such as guided tours[9], to advice over learning activities and sequencing of materials. The provision of navigation tools (maps, indexes, overviews and so on) can also help learners define their goals and actions.

The second dimension, engagement, identifies a potential problem with hypermedia, as presentation can result in merely passive browsing. One strategy is to provide learners with external motivation for making the best of the information available, perhaps through imaginative learning assignments. Another strategy is for the system itself to provide the learning challenge and engage learners more actively as they move around the hypertext structure. This is the philosophy behind the StrathTutor system[10]. Alternatively, the system can provide a range of learning activities which move outside strict hypermedia: problems to solve, demonstrations, simulations, self-assessment and so on. The construction of hypermedia systems should move away as quickly as possible from the passive browse only mode which most systems incorporate, and authors should think in terms of a network of all kinds of activities, e.g. modelling and simulations.

In terms of the synthesis dimension, allowing the learner access to authoring facilities provides a creative capability, although letting the novice learner loose with the full complexity of an authoring system is not likely to be a productive enterprise. More limited and directed facilities for creativity may be more educationally effective. These could include self-generated tours, use of annotation facilities, the creation of concept maps[11], "knowledge jigsaws"[8] or multimedia essays "repurposed" from a variety of existing materials. Different learning requirements will benefit from each of these tools.

Browsing, retrieving, annotating, editing, reporting and co-working are all possible learning tasks in a hypermedia system[2]. It appears therefore that the message for the hypermedia designer is to think carefully about how learners will use his or her system. As McKnight et al.[12] point out:

> If hypertext is to achieve its potential, we must repeatedly remind ourselves that the
> user has a job to do, and design the technology to support the task.

Making the activities which are computer-based as interesting and attractive as possible is only part of the answer to the problem of how to design effective hypermedia material. Deep learning is more likely to take place away from the machine, during students' periods of reflection, discussion, writing and active attempts at explanation. Even though the hypermedia machine has impact, its effects are transient, easily forgotten and external. Authors of effective hypermedia should appreciate that they are designing learning activities and mental experiences rather than screen displays or hypertext networks: process is foremost over product.

AUTHORING

Much of the hypermedia that has been produced for education to date, though often very professionally produced and highly motivating to use, is relatively small in scale; typically HyperCard, or HyperCard-like, stacks with at most a few hundred cards and a corresponding number of links. We have very little experience of authoring large hypermedia systems, of the order of say 10,000 items and 100,000 links, which many believe will demonstrate the real potential for hypermedia. Given this scale of operation, it is clear that the process of linking pieces of information to other related or associated pieces of information cannot be undertaken as a purely manual task. Any authoring system must provide some facility for automatically creating at least a subset of all the links to be included.

There are a number of ways in which this has been approached. Fountain *et al.*[13] have described a system, Microcosm, in which the link information, instead of being embedded in the documents, is separated out. This separation allows links to be *generic*, i.e. they are not applicable to only one document, but may be used with a whole class of documents. This greatly reduces the authoring effort required, since a new document can be brought into the system and immediately contain links. The Microcosm philosophy is that hypermedia links in themselves are a valuable store of knowledge. If this knowledge is bound too tightly to the documents, then it cannot be applied to new data.

Alternatively, Briggs *et al.*[5] have described the use of knowledge-based rules for generating hypertext links entirely automatically, in a system developed to support community pharmacists. However, one of the problems of generating links automatically is to provide semantically meaningful "anchors" or link names. It may prove necessary to provide tools to allow the author to rename links that have been generated to give the reader a clearer notion of the link that is being followed and the expected destination. Readers also need visual cues to remind them of the types and purposes of the nodes they are reading, and there is a need to provide additional "knowledge" to prioritise the links. These priorities will change as the context of use changes.

A third method of reducing the burden of authoring is to use an interchange file format which allows hypermedia systems constructed in one environment to be imported into others, thus removing the need for information structures to be recreated. One such method that has received much attention is the use of mark-up languages such as SGML—Standard Generalised Mark-up Language—and LaTeX. At the start of any project to create a hypermedia database there will already be a large body of material in existence, much of it in the hands of publishers. Kibby *et al.*[3] considered existing practice where extensive use is made of mark-up languages as a means of coding their internal structure. It is significant that documents encoded in mark-up languages may be translated, with an appropriate document type definition (DTD), into hypertext form with relative ease[14,15]. Although under development, there exist no appropriate standards for multimedia within any of the mark-up languages to allow the language to be used to define hypermedia documents. Nevertheless, some means of representing the structure of hypermedia documents is essential if systems of the size indicated above are to be constructed which are flexible, easy to interpret, and usable by typesetters (for concurrent conventional publication).

EVALUATION

Usability

Usability is usually associated with five parameters[16]:

Easy to learn: The user can quickly get some work done with the system.
Efficient to use: Once the user has learned to use the system, a high level of productivity is possible.

Easy to remember: The casual user is able to return to the system after some period without having to learn everything again.

Few errors: Users do not make many errors during the use of the system, or if they do, they can easily recover from them.

Pleasant to use: Users are subjectively satisfied by using the system.

It is extremely important for the development of usable computer products to conduct empirical usability testing, since real users will always interpret some aspects of an interface design in ways other than those intended by the designer[6]. Nielsen[17] describes a method used during the iterative design process called *discount usability engineering*, whereby rapid feedback on various aspects of interface design allows more iterations of the design to be tested. When two users or so have been observed having problems with a particular aspect of the interface, then that aspect is altered and the new design is retested.

Hall *et al.*[18] used questionnaires and interviews to assess the interface to a hypermedia system for cell biology. The questionnaire presented a mixture of positive and negative statements about the system, relating to content, presentation/interface and student attitudes towards the technology, and prompted the student for responses on a 5-point scale (strongly agree, agree, disagree, strongly disagree and no comment). In addition, the interviews gave students the chance to voice opinions about things not mentioned in the questionnaire, or about more general themes or topics. Many students, especially in the early stages of the study, commented about the environment in which workstations should be set up. Originally Hall *et al.* presented their system to students in a practical laboratory, but soon moved it to the reference library as a result of the students' requests. Such factors should not be overlooked when planning the introduction of this sort of technology into the curriculum. However, despite these practical issues, the overwhelming response of students was positive, with the majority indicating that they would welcome material for a wider range of topics.

Directed guidance

Hammond and Allinson[9] suggest that hypertext can provide the basis for an exploratory learning system but that by itself it is insufficient, needing to be supplemented by more directed guidance and access mechanisms. In order to investigate this suggestion, they conducted an experiment in which all subjects used the same material held in a hypertext form, but with differing guidance and access facilities available. The baseline group had "raw" hypertext with no additional facilities, while other groups had either a map or index of guided tours available, and a final group had all three facilities (map, index, tours) available. Half of the subjects were given a series of questions to answer while accessing the material (a directed task) while the other half were instructed to make use of the material to prepare for a subsequent multiple-choice test (an explanatory task).

Perhaps surprisingly, Hammond and Allinson report no reliable differences between task conditions for the three groups which had a single additional facility, although in all three groups the facilities were used to a substantial extent. However, in the group having all three facilities available there was a significant task-by-facility interaction. Those subjects performing the exploratory task made little use of the index but significant use of the tours, while those performing the directed task made little use of the tours and far more use of the index. Thus, Hammond and Allinson argue that after only 20 min subjects were able to employ the facilities in a task-directed manner.

It has been suggested that hypertext is more suited to browsing than directed retrieval tasks. Following from this suggestion, Jones[19] hypothesised that more incidental learning would occur in a browsing task than in a task requiring the use of an index. The argument advanced by Jones was that the links in a hypertext node represent an embedded menu and that the context provided by the node should encourage the connection of the ideas at either end of the link. In other words, the learner's semantic net is more likely to be elaborated or more learning is likely to occur.

Two groups of subjects were used in Jones's experiment. Both groups used the same hypertext database, but one group was shown how to browse through the information using the links and were explicitly instructed not to use the index, while the other group were instructed in the use of the index and were not informed about the active nature of the highlighted words on screen (which were described to them as "clues to other index entries"). Subjects were given 5 questions to answer from the database, but afterwards were given 10 questions to measure incidental learning.

Unfortunately Jones's experiment failed to support her hypothesis. No significant differences were observed in terms of performance on the incidental learning questions. It is possible that the nature of the questions given to the subjects to answer from the database did not encourage incidental learning. This is certainly suggested by the low overall success level of subjects on the incidental learning test—the highest mean number correct for any group was 1.56. Even in the five target questions, taking all groups together, no question was answered correctly by more than half of the subjects. This suggests that the task was not particularly sensitive to the effect of the experimental manipulations and hence we can do little more than agree with Jones that "much more research is needed".

These and other results indicate that more has been claimed for hypertext than has been demonstrated. This should not be taken to imply that hypertext cannot have a role in education. However, as Hammond and Allinson[9] found, it means that we need a clear view of the tasks which any particular hypertext is intended to support. The design of any hypertext should proceed from a consideration of the users and the tasks they wish to perform. McKnight *et al.*[20] describe the development of a hypertext version of the journal *Behaviour and Information Technology* based on such design principles.

Furthermore, McKnight says it is possible that hypertext packages may be useful tools for students (and teachers) in the organisation and structuring of knowledge which usually precedes any coherent written output. Traditionally (and leaving aside output in the form of computer programs), we require this output in the form of essays which adopt a normal prose form, in which one sentence follows another, paragraphs follow paragraphs and so forth. Of course, the semantic structure of the essay may be far from linear and very few people write the final prose version with no preparation. This preparation usually takes the form of exploring, gathering facts, ideas, references and making generally unconnected notes. If the essay is to be of any size, these initial notes may well be kept on index cards. Slowly, though, the notes start to be organised, with some being rejected, others grouped together and some thread of argument being woven through them. It is in these stages before prose output that hypertext systems would seem to provide a useful tool. Perhaps if we could devise a method of grading a hypertext we might not need prose output at all!

Learning

To be able to evaluate learning in hypertext, we need to know that learning has occurred. The two important words here are *know* and *learning*. In order to know that learning has occurred in an educational establishment, it is usually required that we measure it in some way—course-work grades, exam marks and so forth. Now, any sensible system of measurement is based on a sound theory of the property to be measured and unfortunately, in the case of learning, we know very little about it in the educational sense. We can measure the number of nonsense syllables a person can retain, but when it comes to measuring the restructuring of knowledge which (we hope) goes on as a result of our teaching, it has to be admitted that marks and grades represent a rather weak level of measurement. This is the undercurrent to the problem of educational evaluation and is something that is no doubt familiar to us all in some shape or form. However, on a day-to-day basis we do attempt to educate and it is only right that we should similarly attempt to evaluate this education.

CONCLUSIONS

A number of conclusions can be drawn from this discussion. Firstly, with respect to authoring, if large systems are to be envisaged, the process must become semi-automated to relieve the strain on the author. With current technology this cannot be fully implemented, but any general purpose authoring environment must provide at least *some* automatic link creation facilities. Authors must consider very carefully the purpose of their hypermedia system: is it intended as a general source of reference or as directed tutorial material? The style of authoring will vary depending on the answer to this. Large hypermedia systems should be based on generic resource bases of information which can be tailored to suit individual needs, thus reducing the burden on authors to create their own material from scratch. Regardless of the purpose of the system, it must be interesting and enjoyable. Authors should try to get away from the *browse and retrieve* model of hypertext/media which has predominated so far, and think more in terms of a network of activities. Hypermedia systems will eventually need to become context-sensitive, with links offered and information presented which reflects the users' experience, interests and current usage. *Raw* hypermedia is not sufficient to support effective learning. Educational hypermedia must be able to support a variety of interaction/learning styles with graphical browsers, guided tours, etc.

Secondly, with respect to evaluation, it is essential to test thoroughly any system before it is used in an educational setting to ensure that it actually works properly. Studies of how students use hypermedia systems are important as they can give guidance as to the syntax/vocabulary of interaction involved. This means that testing methods used in the past, with naïve users, are no longer valid.

Creating and evaluating effective learning materials are not easy tasks, and the same is true when applied to the field of hypermedia. However, this should not serve to discourage or dissuade developers from doing so, as evaluation is an essential part of creating interesting, enjoyable and effective learning material.

Acknowledgements—The authors wish to thank all those who participated in the Authoring and Evaluation of Education Hypermedia session at CAL '91. Without their comments and discussion during and after the session, this paper would not have been possible.

REFERENCES

1. Beeman W. O., Anderson K. T., Bader G., Larkin J., McClard A. P., McQuilian P. and Shields M., Hypertext and pluralism: from lineal to non-lineal thinking. *Proceedings of Hypertext '87*, pp. 67–88. University of North Carolina, Chapel Hill (1987).
2. Fisher K. M., Semantic networking: the new kid on the block. Paper presented to the NATO Advanced Research Workshop on Mindtools, Twente University, The Netherlands (1990).
3. Kibby M. R., Tanner G., Mayes T. R., Knussen C. and Grant S., HYP/23 Final Report on Hypermedia (HYPERATE): the SAFE project, DELTA project P7061 (D1014) (1991).
4. Marchionini G., Evaluating hypermedia-based learning. In *Designing Hypermedia for Learning* (Edited by Jonassen D. H. and Mande H.), pp. 355–373. Springer, Heidelberg (1990).
5. Knussen C., Tanner G. and Kibby M., An approach to the evaluation of hypermedia. *Computers Educ.* **17**, 13–24 (1991).
6. Nielsen J., The art of navigating through Hypertext. *Commun. ACM* **33**, 297–310 (1990).
7. Briggs J. H., Tompsett C. P. and Oates N. S., Guiding learners through a medical Hypertext database using knowledge based rules. In *Knowledge Based Environments for Teaching and Learning: Proceedings of 6th International PEG Conference*, Genoa (1991).
8. Hammond N. V., Tailoring hypertext for the learner. In *Mindtools: Cognitive Technologies for Modelling Knowledge* (Edited by Kommers P. A. M., Jonassen D. H. and Mayes J. T.). Springer. Berlin. In press.
9. Hammond N. and Allinson L., Extending hypertext for learning: an investigation of access and guidance tools. In *People and Computers V* (Edited by Sutcliffe A. and Macaulay L.). Cambridge University Press, Cambridge (1989).
10. Mayes J. T., Kibby M. R. and Anderson T., Signposts for conceptual orientation: some requirements for learning from hypertext. In *Hypertext: State of the Art* (Edited by McAleese R. and Green C.), pp. 121–129. Intellect Books, Oxford (1990).
11. Trapp A. L. and Hammond N. V., Concept mapping tools: a different approach. *Psychol. Soft vare News* **2**, 10–11 (1991).
12. McKnight C., Dillon A. and Richardson J., Problems in Hyperland? a human factors perspective. *Hypermedia* **1**, 167–178 (1989).
13. Fountain A., Hall W., Heath I. and Davis H., Microcosm: an open model with dynamic linking. In *Hypertext: Concepts, Systems and Applications (Proceedings of the European Conference on Hypertext)* (Edited by Rizk A., Strietz N. and André J.), pp. 298–311. INRIA, France (1991).
14. Niblett T. and van Hoff A. (1989) Structured Hypertext documents via SGML. Poster presentation at Hypertext II, University of York (1989).
15. Rahtz S., Carr L. and Hall W., Creating multimedia documents: Hypertext processing. In *Hypertext: State of the Art* (Edited by McAleese R. and Green C.). Intellect Books, Oxford (1990).
16. Nielsen J., Evaluating Hypertext usability. In *Designing Hypermedia for Learning* (Edited by Jonassen D. H. and Mandl H.), pp. 147–168. Springer, Heidelberg (1990).
17. Nielsen J. Usability engineering at a discount. In *Proceedings of the Third International Conference on Human–Computer Interaction, HCI International '89*, Boston, Mass. (1989).
18. Hall W., Hutchings G., Carr L., Thorogood P. and Sprunt B., Interactive learning and biology: Hypermedia approach. In *Advanced Technologies in the Teaching of Mathematics and Science* (Edited by Ferguson D. L.). Springer, Heidelberg (1991).
19. Jones T., Incidental learning during information retrieval: a hypertext experiment. In *Computer Assisted Learning* (Edited by Maurer H.). Springer, Berlin (1989).
20. McKnight C., Dillon A. and Richardson J., *Hypertext in Context*. Cambridge University Press, Cambridge (1991).

Computers Educ. Vol. 18, No. 1–3, pp. 179–182, 1992
Printed in Great Britain. All rights reserved

A METHOD FOR EVALUATING THE EFFICIENCY OF PRESENTING INFORMATION IN A HYPERMEDIA ENVIRONMENT

MEGAN QUENTIN-BAXTER and DAVID DEWHURST

Division of Health and Science, Leeds Polytechnic, Calverley Street, Leeds LS1 3HE, England

Abstract—The recognised difficulties in evaluating computer assisted learning (CAL) material are increased when material is presented within a hypermedia environment. With the emphasis of hypermedia firmly placed on individual control of an extensive information-base it is difficult to compare learning *per se*, since it cannot be assumed that students have witnessed the same subject information. The knowledge and experience of each student will affect their ability to utilise the interactive media, and this may be reflected in the amount of information accessed and subsequent motivation to use the product. Here we describe a method which has been developed to investigate the efficiency of presenting information in a hypermedia environment, and determine what cues are favoured for navigation and possibly learning. Questionnaires elicit background information and student attitudes to the program. Automatic tracing of student actions provides a detailed account of the information accessed within the program and the interactive tools employed. Classifying interaction into discrete units and counting these relative to the time spent using the program may give a comparative measure of interactivity. Comparing the efficiency of different CAL programs is possible where interaction can be classified into the same broad categories for each.

INTRODUCTION

As a fundamentally new concept for presenting computer assisted learning (CAL) material hypermedia has stepped into a previously unoccupied niche. The remarkable speed with which it has passed from near-obscurity to reality may be accredited to relentless marketing, and perhaps a deficiency in questioning the ability of hypermedia to get the educational message across. Hyper-systems have been readily accepted by educational CAL developers largely because of the ease of program development and a general fascination with the possibilities offered by linking information in a non-sequential way. Some studies report improved pluralistic, cognitive style and increased student motivation through using hyper-systems[1] although a number of weaknesses have been identified[2,3]. However, the success of CAL depends on whether it achieves its learning objectives by efficiently delivering information across the range of students it is intended to reach and evaluating the effects of learning via hypermedia-based CAL may be more difficult than for other CAL material, since it cannot be assumed that students have covered the same subject information.

An evaluation of the advantages of presenting CAL via hypermedia may be roughly divided into two areas: (i) the efficiency of the program (aspects of the user interface and functional design); and (ii) the subject material learned from a particular CAL program. Here we describe a method for investigating some aspects of the efficiency of presenting information in a hypermedia environment with a view to establishing a comparative method for evaluating subject learning from a particular program.

METHODOLOGY

The evaluative technique described is implemented within a hypermedia-based CAL program developed to teach, by investigation, the functional anatomy of the rat and provide a possible alternative to a rat dissection[4].

This program takes advantage of HyperCard® (using the Apple Macintosh® microcomputer) to present scanned photographic images and diagrams of a rat dissection. Information is presented in response to student initiatives via a variety of interactive features. These include responding to requests for information, (both visually and textually), and providing testing facilities. Annotations appear as the pointer passes over a structure in the image and a hypertext database offers textual support. If requested, the program will visually highlight structures in an image, or present questions which may be answered by clicking the mouse on the structure specified. Three user modes (browsing, testing and a combination mode) influence the type of interaction available to an individual. Graphic images are linked allowing students to click the mouse to progress through the dissection or to see more detail, and a map is available to assist with navigation and spatial orientation.

Each graphic or chunk of text is a discrete piece of information representing a single concept or idea within the context of the package. Within the program there are thirty-one annotated graphic images each with an average of fourteen annotations, six outbound links and between one and four interactive tools depending on which user mode is selected. There are one hundred and twenty-five units of text available via hypertext with an average of forty-one words and two hypertext links each. This number was kept constant for this experiment although it is possible to alter the hypertext database through a pass-controlled "Input Text" user mode. Items of text appear in response to a keyword entry from the user. For each keyword defined in the hypertext database there are approximately thirteen associated words (including common mis-spellings and abbreviations) whose entry will result in the presentation of the same text. In total there are six hundred and twenty-five discrete units of information available to every user. The program was designed to be suitable for a variety of age groups and may also be used to prepare students prior to attempting an actual dissection, or used as revision material. The program potentially offers up to 5 h of use.

Evaluating the efficiency of the program

In order to obtain information about the efficiency of the environment, groups of students were asked to browse within the information and then to complete a questionnaire. These were prepared to obtain details of previous computer experience, the familiarity of an individual with the subject portrayed, to evaluate student attitudes to the hypermedia environment and to note individual perceptions of the quantity of information contained within the program. In order to examine individual performance and preference for interactive features, the program was adapted to include a tracing device. This records the type and duration of every interaction between the student and the computer for subsequent analysis. Where possible, adjustments were made to take machine processing times into account so that data for a particular task reflect true student interaction and not the processing speed of a particular computer. Students were advised that their use of the program would be traced and were asked to identify themselves to the program and to the questionnaire in the same way so that student traces and questionnaire responses could be matched. To investigate changing preferences and attitudes over time the experiment was repeated with students who had become familiar with the operation of the program. Student groups were targeted for inclusion in this study according to their previous knowledge of biology and their aptitude with Macintosh microcomputers.

Although attempts were made to eliminate the effects of the speed of the computer, tests indicated this was not always successful and that the timing data could not be relied upon to accurately reflect student-computer interaction. Where it was likely that trace analysis would be quantified and expressed as a proportion of time spent on isolated activities, it became necessary to devise alternative methods or quantifying the data.

Quantifying the trace data

In a hypermedia-based CAL program such as the one studied, the actions of a user initiate the presentation of information. There are a fixed number of units of information available in the program. The trace records the actions of a user and each unit of information accessed by them. Counting the number of units of information accessed and type of actions initiated by an individual may thus provide a basis for comparing actual progress with self-perceived progress, and with the progress of other students.

Units of information. In the program studied there are three sources of subject information and two sources of program information. A unit of subject information is a single graphic or textual node depicting the subject portrayed in the program. Examples of units of subject information include a graphic image, an annotation or an item of text presented via hypertext. Each graphic image has an associated (fixed) number of annotations. Program information is available either as a program help or as a map for navigation and spatial awareness. Accessing either of these may be counted as accessing a unit of program information.

Actions. Actions may be divided into implicit actions, modal actions and isolated actions. The first occurs whenever a unit of information is presented to the user and these are easily quantified by counting the number of units of information accessed. Modal actions occur when the user temporarily defers control of the environment to the computer. The computer may control or guide the user at these times, often offering a limited selection of response and usually including a "cancel" option. For example a modal action occurs when a student enters a question series. When questions are presented a limited selection of possible responses are supported (answer the question or cancel). If a question is answered incorrectly the program guides the user to satisfy some criteria (attempt the question again, ask to be shown the real answer, or cancel) before presenting another question from the series. Isolated actions are defined as those occurring when action taken by a student does not result in either the access of a unit of information or in deferring control to the computer. Examples of isolated actions include when a structure in an image is highlighted, shaded or animated. A special example of an isolated action occurs when an attempt to obtain information is unsuccessful, such as entering an unsupported keyword, or clicking the mouse on areas where there are no links availble.

DISCUSSION

Using the rules above, a profile of the types of actions taken and units of information accessed by a user may be created for each student using the program. From these user profiles it is possible to identify (i) precisely what, and how often, subject or program information was pursued by individuals; and (ii) the interactive tools they relied upon or preferred to use. The questionnaire responses yield information about attitudes to the environment, an individual's perception of the information available in the program, and provide a basis for comparing the activity of students or like groups according to previous experience of the computers used and knowledge of the subject portrayed. From the combination of these data it is possible to identify factors contributing to the efficiency of presenting information in a hypermedia environment.

The efficiency of a hypermedia environment may be regarded as the effectiveness of the user interface and functional design to provide a student with the best opportunity to obtain all the relevant subject information that the program is able to offer. Some examples of factors affecting the efficiency of a CAL program include:

the amount of time an individual has in which to use the program;
the size of a group sharing a computer or terminal;
the organisation of information and the way it is linked;
the effects of aesthetic design and the use of sound;
the interactive tools preferred both initially and after experience of the program;
the type of interactive method employed by a student (browsing or directed);
conveying the quantity of information available to the user (time investment required by them);
the ability to learn from the knowledge and experience of the user.

The method described considers many of these factors and may provide a means of assessing or recording an individual's ability to assimilate and reproduce information. However, it has not been successfully applied to evaluating conceptual learning via hypermedia.

Tracing activity behaviour within hypermedia courseware may become an integral part of hypermedia CAL packages. Apart from providing valuable insights for the purpose of evaluating aspects of a program, tracing may be critical for providing on-line activities where activities are tailored to the immediate experience of the user. If activity data is "remembered' for individuals it may be possible for a program to develop an understanding of the requirements of each user and tailor the presentation of information to match. (However, there are ethical considerations to be taken into account when storing data about an individual.)

Acknowledgement—The authors would like to thank the Lord Dowding Fund (NAVS, U.K.) for their financial support of this project.

REFERENCES

1. Landow G., Context32: Using Hypermedia to teach literature. *Proceedings of the 1987 IBM Academic Information Systems University AEP Conference*, Milford, Conn. IBM Academic Information Systems (1987).
2. Conklin J., Hypertext: an introduction and survey. *IEEE Comput.* **20**(9), 17–41 (1987).
3. Raskin J., The Hype in Hypertext: a critique. *Hypertext '87*, pp. 325–330. Department of Computer Science, University of North Carolina at Chapel Hill (1987).
4. Quentin-Baxter M. and Dewhurst D. G., An interactive computer-based alternative to performing a rat dissection in the classroom. *J. biol. Educ.* In press.

Computers Educ. Vol. 18, No. 1–3, pp. 183–193, 1992
Printed in Great Britain

0360-1315/92 $5.00 + 0.00
Pergamon Press plc

PROVIDING COMPUTING FOR DISTANCE LEARNERS: A STRATEGY FOR HOME USE

Ann Jones, Gill Kirkup, Adrian Kirkwood and Robin Mason

Institute of Educational Technology, The Open University, Walton Hall, Milton Keynes MK7 6AA,
England

Abstract—Major changes are occurring in British higher education which will continue over the next decade. These include widening access to higher education, e.g. among mature adults and people from other European countries; developing distance and open learning for use in parallel with face-to-face teaching and the expansion of CAL to support various forms of pedagogy. These trends may conflict. Expanding the pedagogic uses of information technology, e.g. unless designed very carefully, may create new barriers to access for some potential students. Educational policy makers, course designers and teachers must address such potential conflicts. This paper draws on recent experience at the Open University (OU) of expanding the use of home-based computers for distance education students. In 1988 the OU implemented a policy in which students on specified courses were required to provide extensive access to personal computers in order to study their course material. By 1990 over 13,500 students were doing this. The experience of these students has been monitored and evaluated and lessons from it indicate some of the major issues such a strategy would involve for any institution considering similar developments.

INTRODUCTION

There has been a steady growth in open and distance learning as an alternative and a complement to face-to-face teaching in post school education. The advantages of distance education include economies of scale, the possibility of students combining study with full-time paid work or domestic duties and flexibility in patterns of study. The Open University (OU) has successfully used distance education techniques for 21 years and currently has over 116,000 registered students, of whom 75,000 are studying undergraduate courses. To provide such distance teaching the OU has adopted a multi-media approach which includes self-study course texts, television and radio broadcasts, video and audio cassettes, audio visual material, home computing and computer assisted learning (CAL) and face-to-face tutoring. The degree structure is modular, with students having an almost free choice from over one hundred full- and half-credit courses that can be accumulated to make up an individual's degree profile; six credits for the B.A. degree, eight credits for the B.A. (Hons) degree.

Providing computing access to students who are distributed across the British Isles as well as offshore and in Europe has been both a logistical and a technical problem. To start with the OU adopted a "network" approach, initially to support computing for the Mathematics foundation course. By 1984 this network consisted of three Dec System 2040 computers at different sites, each of which had a number of ports enabling simultaneous dial-up access. Students taking a variety of courses were able to access the computer from one of 250 terminals in study centres, usually housed in local educational institutions. On Mathematics computing courses the computers were used to learn about computing; on other courses CAL packages were used as tools to enhance the learning of completely different subjects. On these courses, students used computers either at residential summer schools or at regional study centres and use was usually optional. A major aim of this kind of CAL was to address the limited immediate feedback available to students by providing diagnostic feedback, remedial and revision help through a computer terminal. However, Jones and O'Shea[1] found that for many students the effort and time required (which included booking the computer, time spent travelling to a study centre, learning to use the system, reading the documentation etc.) was greater than the perceived benefits.

On courses for which students needed continual access to a computer as they studied, purpose built machines were designed and developed by the university. These were loaned to the students for the course of their study. For other courses, students needed access to commercially produced microcomputers; for example, teachers using the "Micros in Schools" study materials used their own microcomputers, or those in their schools. When access to a machine could be guaranteed, student satisfaction with computing activities rose.

A HOME COMPUTING POLICY FOR STUDENTS

By the middle of the 1980s it was clear that a coherent policy was needed to address the issue of student computing. The rapid growth of information technology in the 1980s was paralleled by a growth in new courses for which computer access was essential. National surveys indicated an increase in ownership of personal computers, but of diverse and incompatible makes and models. This led to the situation in which different microcomputers were being used for different courses, whereas it was clearly desirable that students who were intending to buy a microcomputer should, as far as possible, be able to acquire a machine that they could use for their whole university career. The result was that in 1988 the Open University implemented a policy under which students on specified courses are responsible for arranging access to a computer system that meets the University's specification, basically an MS-DOS machine with a printer and mouse. Course teams who expect students to provide their own access are required to make the case that this access is an essential academic requirement. An important consideration was that this strategy should not put computing courses out of students' financial reach. A number of schemes were introduced to help students with the financial outlay, including fee reductions on specified courses, a bank loan scheme for acquiring machines, a rental scheme and discounts on purchases of specified machines which kept the price below £500.

There are few comparable innovations in the U.K. Gardner[2] reviewed developments in the U.S.A. and U.K. and divides the growth of the "electronic campus" into three phases. These progress from a period in which there is pervasive provision of cheap microcomputers to a more developed and sophisticated appraisal of the potential of information technology leading to a demand for a more coordinated approach and in many cases the appointment at a very senior level of what Gardner refers to as information technology "Czars". During the first phase of large scale provision of micros, several universities in the U.S.A. demanded mandatory microcomputer ownership by all or a substantial majority of their students, but this did not generally require any outlay of institutional resources or restructuring of the curriculum. In the U.K., there were no similar experiments during the early 1980s, although some institutions, such as the Information Technology Institute at Salford, do now require every student and member of staff to have a computer and they are connected to the local mainframe and to remote services. Such computing provision relies heavily on a network of industrial partners. At University College, Swansea, an experiment was carried out to provide clusters of terminals in student halls of residence[3]. Although there were difficulties setting up the project, long term advantages for the students were reported. These were: greater flexibility in organising working schedules, more economical and widespread use of computing facilities and a better working relationship between users and staff of the Computing Centre. At the University of Bradford there are similar plans and other universities are also monitoring and evaluating their own particular computing strategies.

The Open University is in rather a different position from these other institutions, both because of the very large number of students and because it is engaged in teaching at a distance. An evaluation study of home computing was started in 1988 to assess how well the strategy was working in practice and to consider what kinds of problems or disadvantages students might experience. This paper draws on the evaluation to consider the benefits and problems as perceived by the students.

EVALUATING THE POLICY: THE SCOPE AND APPROACH
OF THE EVALUATION

Methods of investigation

The main evaluation study used a number of different methods, including large scale surveys of students, smaller surveys of tutors, interviews with students, tutors and the course authors and journals kept by the students in which they recorded their progress and significant successes and problems.

Scope of evaluation and issues examined

The evaluation programme was set up to assess the effectiveness and impact of the OU's strategy for student-based computing and to inform future academic policy. A secondary aim was the evaluation of particular courses using student-based computing. Although evaluation findings were reported to course designers and authors, immediate changes to most materials were impossible since sufficient printed units, etc. are produced to last for the estimated lifetime of each course. However, modifications can and have been made to more ephemeral aspects of the course material such as tutor notes and assignment strategy.

Four particular areas of the evaluation will be discussed in this paper. The first of these is *access* to the home computing equipment in the broadest sense, including affordability, choice of means of access, reliability of equipment and ease of setting up the equipment. It was important to know whether, with the introduction of home-based computing, problems of access had been solved. The evaluation examined whether students were finding the system financially viable, what the take up was of the various options available; whether the administration of the discount or purchase scheme was working satisfactorily; how well the equipment worked; how easily it was fixed if it did malfunction and whether there were any particular groups of students suffering disadvantage. The second issue examined was the *spread of use* of the facility; i.e. the extent to which the system was used by students for other courses of study or for other purposes, or by other people. Did students perceive the equipment to be better value for money if it was being used more widely than just for the course and was there evidence of a spread of general computer literacy and IT awareness skills from the student to family and friends? A third issue was that of *workload, difficulty and organisation*: what impact had the equipment on how students organised their work, on the workload itself and on its perceived difficulty? Finally, the issue of *getting help*: as distance education learners, OU students are working on their own and there was concern that there should be as much help and support available as they needed when things went wrong. These issues are discussed further below.

The courses

The evaluation data for this paper relate to courses which were within the Home Computing Policy during its first 2 years. These fall into two main categories: those concerned with teaching about computing and/or information technology and those which use the computer to run prepared software to teach particular subjects and/or as an educational tool of a more general nature. The courses are shown in Table 1.

Student numbers ranged between 250 on a third level mathematics course and over 2000 on the Technology foundation course. A large percentage of these students took part in the evaluation. For example, Computational Mathematics had 255 students, of whom 61% completed a questionnaire at the end of the course and a further 6 students were interviewed. Programming and Programming Languages had 1258 students, and of these 206 students completed an initial questionnaire followed by a further 289 students returning a final questionnaire. Small numbers of students filled in detailed journals or were interviewed.

RESULTS OF THE EVALUATION

Access

There are four factors influencing the quality of access a student has to computing equipment:

—the decision a student makes about how to obtain access, e.g. purchase, rent, use a machine at work;
—the type of equipment the student has access to;
—the reliability of that equipment and the quality of service; and
—the ease the student experiences in initially setting up and getting going.

Table 1. Home computing courses 1988 and 1989

Courses teaching about computing/information technology:
An Introduction to Information Technology Fundamentals of Computing Programming and Programming Languages
Courses teaching with the computer as an educational tool:
Computational Mathematics Technology, a foundation course

The patterns of access and type of equipment differed for men and women. For example, on the Computational Mathematics course, 56% of the students did not already own suitable equipment but hired or purchased equipment in order to do the course (22.2% bought their equipment and 33.4% hired it). Others made their own arrangements (which includes already having suitable equipment or arranging access at work or elsewhere). However, the pattern was quite different for the two sexes, with well over half of the women hiring equipment as opposed to under 30% of the men. This trend was true for the other courses. On all courses [4–8] more men than women made their own arrangements for access (which includes already owning machines) and, overall, men had more powerful equipment. On some issues a pattern of difference was also found between other categories of student: e.g. computer novices also had less sophisticated equipment and tended to hire rather than buy. Most of the students used a PC with a dual disc drive, which exceeds the Home Computing Policy specification, but again, there were gender differences with fewer women having equipment of this standard.

The Programming and Programming Languages course differed from the others in having a higher number of students (60%) who made their own arrangements, although, as with the other courses, there were more men than women in this position. The general picture of home computing on this course is of many students having had a home computer for some time and its use therefore being well established. It should also be noted that this course was first presented in the second year of the home computing policy and took students who had obtained equipment for a course in the previous year.

Across all the courses the percentage of students who used a computer at work for their main access was relatively low, although it ranged from 8 to 27%. A slightly larger minority (30%) used work access in addition to their home access on some courses. Less than half of the students on any of the courses found the arrangement of having access only at work to be very convenient and, indeed, some students found using a machine at work so inconvenient that they made different arrangements part way through the year, usually obtaining equipment for home use.

There were relatively few faults reported in the equipment, but hirers were more likely to report faults and were not always happy with the way the rental firm dealt with their problems. The handling of computer purchase and hiring was contracted out by the University. Although purchasers did not report as many faults, they did have some difficulties with the suppliers and complained of delays and poor service and communication. The length of time it can take to get faults rectified has serious consequences for students' study schedule:

> "Computer returned . . . for repair—sent back still faulty. Lost by Securicor. Therefore without PC for vital period of time" and

> "Computer arrived in unserviceable condition; took 8 weeks to get three different faults corrected" [6].

These problems were worse in the second year of the policy when there were more courses and more students.

Students who had purchased or hired equipment in order to do the course were asked how they felt about the financial implications of buying their equipment or whether the rental option had been a good deal. The majority of the purchasers thought that the financial outlay had been worthwhile, although a small percentage of the students who had bought equipment for the course thought that it had been quite a financial outlay for the amount of use that had been made of the equipment. Slightly fewer of the hirers felt that it had been a good deal and students who did not think the hire arrangement was good value complained that the hire costs were too high, or too high given the amount of use made of the equipment. Although the majority of students felt they got value for money, the perception of the extent to which the financial outlay was justified differed between courses, with buyers more satisfied than hirers, men more satisfied than women, younger more satisfied than older students.

Various sources of guidance were available to students when setting up equipment, including manufacturers' instructions, a special OU booklet and course specific guides. Most students consulted at least one of these and smaller numbers of students also consulted other sources such as family members, friends, colleagues and the Academic Computing Service (ACS) Help Desk. Very few students reported significant difficulty in setting up their equipment and getting started. Those studying computing courses were less likely to need help in setting up the equipment than computer novices on other courses, e.g. the Introduction to Information Technology course, but even novices got the equipment up and running. A lot of thought had gone into the documentation that accompanied the software, and for some courses there were audio-cassettes that took novices through the detailed steps of getting the software running. The ACS Help Desk was kept very busy and some students clearly needed back-up support and help.

Spread of use

On all the courses except one there was very little use of the machine by other people at home; any significant use by others is by the partners of women students. Male students were more likely than women to use their computers for activities such as non-OU work and for pleasure. The exception to this pattern was the course Programming and Programming Languages where use of the equipment by other members of the household and for non-course work was much higher. On this course, over half of the respondents said that they intended that the equipment would be used by others. In the event, just under 30% reported that their spouse/partner used the equipment and 26% reported that the machine was being used by their children (which was higher than the 21% who said they expected it to be used by the children). Their own use for other courses and non-university work was also high at 68 and 59%. This usage by others in the household is considerably higher than was reported on the other home computing courses. Fifty-three per cent of students on this particular course had owned some kind of computer for more than 3 years; 18% had owned one for between 2 and 3 years; 20% for between 1 and 2 years and only 9% had had a computer for less than 1 year. For this population of third level students, then, it seems that the use of their machine for other tasks and by other people was already established before the course began and this presumably accounts for its wider use. Students on this course are generally much more experienced computer users and may also have more general software which is suitable for family use.

Workload, difficulty and organisation

Nearly 60% of the students taking the course Computational Mathematics regarded themselves as computing experts at the beginning of the year and 76% rated themselves as experts at the end. It is not an easy course for students and has a fairly high attrition rate. However, 34% of the students said that there were some exercises which took them an excessive amount of time. Nearly half of the students did the practical work when they had time, but a significant proportion (14%) said that they spent extremely long periods at the computer and over a third said that there were some exercises on which they spent much more time than they considered reasonable. Sometimes the problem was not the amount of time, but simply not knowing that the exercise was going to take so long. However, no students credited difficulty with practical computing as a direct cause of withdrawal. Students on other courses reported similarly that practical computing exercises took them much longer than they anticipated: for example, this comment was made by an Introduction to Information Technology student[6]:

> "The practical work took far longer than the '1/5 of the course' envisaged by the course team. Also, there were quite a few teething troubles. The combination of the inordinate amount of time required for the practical element and the various teething troubles made me fall behind with the remainder of the course work and forced me to withdraw from the course".

On the Programming and Programming Languages course students found the practical work difficult and time consuming and those students who gave detailed feedback through journals reported some severe problems with a programming language, Pascal, including technical or hardware problems. Most students sought advice when they had difficulties which they could not solve, but on all courses there were students who were fiercely independent and spent excessive amounts of time trying to make their programs work without ever seeking help or advice. This led to frustration and exasperation and a loss of confidence in both the computing and the course generally. Such behaviour was not confined to novice users.

The two mathematics courses described above had previously existed with practical computing activities designed to be done using networked terminals at study centres. Activities designed for this system are usually gathered together in the course material so that the student can plan a 30 or 60 min session once a week at a terminal. When a course team can presume unrestricted access to a computer by students, it is possible to integrate computing activities into the study material. Students can be expected to do short activities and perhaps a number of activities during an extended period of practical work. The result of this seems to be that students spend more time on the computing activities since they are not under pressure to log off at the end of a booked terminal session to allow access to another student or catch a bus home. This may be beneficial if the time is relaxed, but it also seems to mean that for some students the time spent expands to fill the time available.

Other courses, e.g. the Technology foundation course and the Introduction to Information Technology courses, had existed previously either with *no* practical computing or were newly conceived. Students on these courses were more often novice users on entry and they found that the time needed to get the equipment going, learn to use the software and complete the practical activities was much greater than they expected. Some students felt that the time necessary was excessive. Moreover, their practical computing work required them to be where the computer was! This meant that students who usually took their course work to do in places other than where their computer was set up (e.g. while commuting to work) were restricted in the study time they could devote to the course.

Getting help

The University's Academic Computing Service (ACS) which supports and develops computing facilities for students throughout the university, provides an advisory service which students can ring for help on any computing related problem. The Mathematics Faculty runs a Faculty Help Line and all students have their own regional course tutor as well as a tutor/counsellor to advise on more general university issues. Mathematics students needing help or advice, therefore, might be expected to consult one of these sources. In fact most (70%) of the students on the Computational Mathematics course did not need to consult anyone about their practical computing work, but those who did comprised two-thirds of the women respondents but only one-quarter of the men. Not surprisingly, less experienced students were more likely to consult someone than the more experienced students: 53% of the novices consulted as opposed to 24% of the experts. The students who did seek help were asked which of a number of sources they consulted. The most frequently cited were the tutor (60%) and the ACS Advisory Service (39%), followed by friends (22%), fellow students (20%), "other" (14%), Faculty Help Line and spouse/partner (both 10%). It seems likely, then, that most students consult more than one source.

On the Programming and Programming Languages course, about 20% of the students had needed advice on the first piece of practical work. Most of these students contacted their tutor (70%) or fellow students (18%). However, for more general queries which were not related to understanding the course content, 20% of the students had contacted the ACS Advisory Service and found the service to be friendly, efficient and helpful.

On other courses, where students were less experienced, a greater proportion sought help from various sources and, not surprisingly, it was the novices who sought most help. The number of enquiries did put some pressure on the ACS Help Desk, which received up to 130 calls per day in 1989[9], but nearly all the students reported that they had been able to solve their problems.

Computer conferencing

As part of the Home Computing Policy, the University began to use computer conferencing as a tutorial support medium in 1988. Students on the Introduction to Information Technology course were sent a modem by the University, on loan for the duration of the course. Students were able to use the University's dial-up network to connect to the host computer and the conferencing software, CoSy. With over 1200 students using the system each year, this is the largest ever educational application of this medium.

Evaluation of the first year[10] shows that students made disparate use of the system—about a third logged on under 5 times or not at all; another third used it more frequently, but usually only to read other participants' comments, and the final third made extensive and often enthusiastic interactive use of the medium. For this active group of students the benefits were great: increased access to help, very quick response to queries, participation in active exchanges with the course team, tutors and fellow students and much less isolation as distance learners. The third who used the system less often and less actively experienced some of these advantages, but were often deterred by the amount of material, the lack of structure and the irrelevant remarks of their fellow students. The final third either withdrew from the course or abandoned the conferencing aspect of the course.

In 1989 and 1990, a number of changes and improvements were made to overcome some of the difficulties of the first year "guinea pigs". Marks have been awarded on assignments for the use of conferencing, as was requested by students. A new structure of conferences has been devised to find the right critical mass of participants for conferences. Finally, significant improvements have been made in the maintenance and support of the system, both by ACS and also by the CoSy coordinator representing the course team.

Although the log-on times over the whole course remain roughly similar over the 3 years, there is evidence that students are making more efficient and effective use of their on-line time. Due to the improvements mentioned, students know where to go and how to get there and consequently are not wasting precious log on time in simple navigation problems. Furthermore, evidence from student questionnaires shows that many more students are reading and writing messages off-line than was the case in the first year[11].

Although computer conferencing does not appeal to all students and has a number of limitations as a teaching/learning medium, it has shown considerable promise as a means of capitalising on the experience and expertise of adult learners. By offering ideas and describing personal experience relevant to course issues, students are given the opportunity of integrating new material with their existing concepts. By following inputs from their peers, students are exposed to models of how others think and talk about course issues and how they draw conclusions from existing evidence.

Students who opt not to take home computing courses and students who drop out

Investigations have been undertaken of the drop-out of students from the home computing courses and of the reasons for deciding not to take home computing courses at all. In the first year of the policy, 380 students were surveyed[12], all of whom had intended to study one or more of the home computing courses and did not in fact complete their study. The University has a procedure whereby students conditionally register for a course and then confirm their registration a few months later when they are offered a place. Of these 380 students, most of them chose not to confirm their place on a home computing course. Others started the course, but withdrew during the first few months. The study was particularly interested in assessing whether the policy might indirectly undermine attempts to encourage more women into science, technology and computing courses. The study found that the group of students who finally opted not to take the courses did contain a higher proportion of women and these women differed from the men in terms of their occupation category, level of educational qualification and prior computing experience. For both sexes, the lack of access to a suitable computer at home was a significant factor in their decision not to study the course. The most significant factors cited by the students in changing their minds were changes of personal circumstances, the cost of either buying or renting equipment and the realisation that the equipment they owned was not suitable. Those students who withdrew from the course were also asked which of 10 factors influenced their decision. Here, the most significant factors were firstly difficulties with the course material, followed by study time being in excess of what was expected and finally lack of tutorial support. Each of these factors affected the women much more than the men. For example, a student on one of the mathematics courses said: "time and energy are in short supply for a fairly time consuming course. . . . Could not skip or skim through units, needed to fully understand each one to progress. Shaky foundations led to struggles later".

Clearly the reasons for deciding to study a particular course are complex and the requirement of a home computer is only one factor. A survey was conducted of students who had the prerequisites necessary for taking a home computing course, but had not yet registered for one. Their course profiles, therefore, were similar to those students who had taken one of the home computing courses. A significant proportion of the students (45%) cited the high cost of getting access to a computer as a reason for not applying for a home computing course and 23% of those who gave additional reasons specifically said that the cost of renting or buying a computer deterred them from pursuing a home computing course. Statements about the cost included comments such as:

"Additional price of hire of computer tips the scale against applying", and

"Last year I was accepted for the Introduction to Information Technology course, but later had to decline offer (costs). I am unemployed and applied to the OU for financial assistance but was unsuccessful. My final course in 1991 is again Introduction to Information Technology and once again financial problems are evident, but I believe I shall be able to proceed in 1991. I have arranged to buy second hand equipment".

DISCUSSION

The policy the OU has established for student-based computing has been successful overall: the administrative and planning consequences of moving up to 13,500 students from regionally based computing to home computing are, of course, enormous but the move has gone very smoothly. A number of lessons have been learned from the first years of student-based computing: several are discussed below, while some of the wider issues are considered elsewhere[13].

The original choice of MS-DOS is still considered to have been the correct one. The decision of which machine to adopt in a market that is changing so rapidly was one of the hardest choices in setting up the policy. If a student buys a machine for use on his or her first course, it needs to have a life of 8 years, which is the "standard" period taken to complete an honours degree. The price was crucial: the University could not maintain an open access policy if students could not afford to take particular courses, and the price of £500 was seen as the most that students could be expected to pay. There was also a view, which has not been borne out, that this price would decrease substantially over the next few years.

Access: implications and recommendations

An important aspect of access is cost, and students' perceptions of the costs involved in taking a home computing course were on the whole favourable, though those who rented a machine were slightly less favourable: not surprisingly, students who did not plan to take further home computing courses had the least favourable reactions. In practice, the subsidy scheme was most advantageous to students who bought equipment or already owned it[14]. However, although the students who completed their courses generally felt that the outlay was worthwhile, there is some evidence that cost was an important influence on those students who changed their minds about taking a home computing course and also a factor which dissuaded other students from considering home computing courses. It is also the case that there are groups of students for whom access is more problematic than others. The data indicates that women are more likely to hire and to need financial help than men; they are less likely to have access at work, and tend to have less powerful equipment. The same pattern is true for computing novices.

One implication of this pattern is that there will be a continuing demand for a pool of rental machines and that women will have a greater demand than men, as will those students with no expertise or relatively little. It is important, therefore, to continue to provide a rental service if such groups of students are not to be disadvantaged. However, lack of further financial support to the University has meant that the rental option no longer exists except for particular categories of disadvantaged students. Such alternatives gave students who were not intending to take a number of home computing courses (or did not know whether they want to) the option of trying a home computing course without committing themselves to the full expense. The effect of the withdrawal of the rental option has yet to be monitored.

Workload, difficulty and organisation: implications and recommendations

With the introduction of home computing, practical workload on a course increases: a majority of students commented that the computer-related practical work took considerably longer than they had anticipated or than the course designers had expected. Ironically, this was partly because course teams aim to integrate the home computing into the course and to make sufficient use of the computer throughout the course to justify both the time and money which students have invested in its use. Although students were keen to do the practical work and found it rewarding, the time required to do it sometimes conflicted with the demands of the rest of the course. Moreover, some of the practical work could only be completed in large chunks of time, which for some students required changes in their study habits.

One recommendation would be for the course teams planning future home computing courses to ensure that students on home computing courses are not burdened by an excessive workload. Given that the students' range of previous experience with computers is very wide, it is not easy for course designers to write material which is challenging but not overloading for some students.

Spread of use: implications and recommendations

For most students, their expectations of the wider, family use of the machine were not met except for students on the Programming and Programming Languages course, for whom family patterns of use were already established. We would expect family use to increase as more courses come into the policy, as students become more experienced users and as they acquire a greater range of software. The experience at the OU and elsewhere suggests that the acquisition of a computer by one member of a household does not mean that the machine will be used by other members. This "absorption" theory of the dissemination of computer literacy in households has no foundation. It appears that equipment acquired for a particular purpose and with software dedicated to that purpose will remain the tool of the individual for whom it was acquired. If games software is acquired too, then other people may "play" with the machine. However, if a machine is on loan, there is less likelihood that games software will be bought. Only a small amount of games software was written in the 1980s for MS-DOS machines. Children who might have been expected to transfer the school computing experience to their parent's machine are likely to have been discouraged because schools' machines have not been MS-DOS and, again, software is not transferable. If MS-DOS machines become standard at all levels of education then more general use of an OU specification machine may be made by other household members.

Getting help: implications and recommendations

On the mathematics courses the various help services were not very highly used, but those who did seek help were generally satisfied with the advice that they received. The lack of help sought on these courses is not surprising as most of the students were not absolute computing novices and on other courses where there was a much larger range of expertise, more students had problems and sought advice. Many students requested more face-to-face tutorials specifically for help with home computing difficulties and computer novices in particular often felt at a disadvantage, needing to spend much more time than those who were already computer literate in getting familiar with the equipment and getting the software running successfully. An audiotape-led approach to beginning to work with the computer was very successful for some students, although others found the tapes too slow or would have preferred the instructions on paper.

However, in the first year of introductory courses in particular (e.g. the Technology foundation course) the extra burden on tutors in terms of their own need to become familiar with the hardware and software as well as the requirement to respond to student demands for help made these courses very demanding of tutors[15]. Tutors are advised that they are not expected to have computing expertise on courses such as the Introduction to Information Technology and the Technology foundation course, since hardware and software queries should be addressed to the Help Lines. However, the evaluation shows that students turn first to their local tutor for advice. The extra demands on tutors must be recognised.

Some students would have appreciated local or regional help in addition to the central Milton Keynes based telephone help services. These requests could be met by having more regional induction sessions and day schools, but the cost of providing local advisers for all regions is too great.

Future possibilities

Future students will increasingly be more computer literate, but they will not necessarily have had experience of using MS-DOS, so there will still be a need for detailed step-by-step guidance at the appropriate level for the novice. The audiotape tutorial introduction is very suitable for the novice: it can take the student through the necessary steps needed to get a particular program running and to learn to use a particular piece of software in real time. However, it is very inflexible in that once the student has some expertise and either needs to be reminded of particular keystrokes or functions needed to use a particular program, or how using one spreadsheet differs from another, the linear nature of an audio cassette makes searching difficult. What may be needed are different optional routes through the material depending on the student's past experience and level of expertise. Providing basic computer skills courses which are separate from course material is difficult as most of the courses discussed here make different use of the computer, use different software and require different levels of skill, and it may not be possible to produce a self-contained pack that would serve as an introduction to all courses. However, there is already some indication that different courses can use the same material: the introductory materials used on the Technology foundation course have been produced as a pack consisting of a book and audiotapes and are being used by at least one other course.

There are implications for other institutions. Home-based computing is a distance learning activity even when it is part of a face-to-face course. It is likely, therefore, that the kind of the support services established by the OU will be necessary in other institutions, e.g. evening help lines, on-line help, conferences and guided audio introductions. Locating computers in students' homes also leads to a shift in responsibility and control: e.g. students are responsible for providing a suitable space where they can work with the computer for and ensuring that their house contents insurance covers the equipment.

For the OU this model of computing access has proved successful: in 1990 over 13,500 students had access to a computer at home or at work in order to take courses which require extensive computer use. The number of courses using computing, and therefore the number of students, is increasing rapidly. As more students become computer literate, academics in areas which are not concerned with teaching about computing, such as the Arts and Social Sciences, are becoming increasingly interested in the possibility of students using home-based computers as tools for a variety of purposes including CAL, statistical and modelling programs, accessing databases, using spreadsheets and word processing. While this enthusiasm is in part a measure of the policy's success, some caution is needed in looking ahead to the future.

There is a potential impact on the balance of the curriculum, with two very different "streams" emerging: one consisting of courses for which a personal computer is a necessity and another for which it is not. It could become very difficult for students ever to cross the divide: students without a computer would be unwilling to make the investment and students with one will want to optimise their investment. The more home-based computing is seen as the norm, the more disadvantaged will be the students who want to take one particular computing course without taking a series of such courses. The major challenge, therefore, is how to build on the success of the policy without disadvantaging some students and without decreasing access to the courses as a whole.

Acknowledgements—The work reported here was carried out as part of the Home Computing Evaluation Project at the Institute of Educational Technology, The Open University. The other members of the team are: Alison Ashby and Clive Lawless.

REFERENCES

1. Jones A. C. and O'Shea T., Barriers to the use of Computer Assisted Learning. *Br. J. educ. Technol.* **13,** 207–217 (1982).
2. Gardner N., The electronic campus: the first decade. *Higher Educ. Q.* **43,** 4 (1989).
3. Startup R. and Brady P., Widening student access to computer facilities. *Eval. Res. Educ.* **3,** 1 (1989).

4. Kirkwood A. and Kirkup G., Computing on DT200, M205 and M371. CITE Report No. 65. Centre for Information Technology in Education, The Open University, Milton Keynes (1989).

5. Kirkup G. and Dale E., M205 end of year report 1988. CITE Report No. 69. Centre for Information Technology in Education, The Open University, Milton Keynes (1989).

6. Kirkwood A. and Dale E., DT200 end of year report 1988. CITE Report No. 77. Centre for Information Technology in Education, The Open University, Milton Keynes (1989).

7. Kirkup G., T102 set-up, start -up and block one report on February 1989. CITE Report No. 80. Centre for Information Technology in Education, The Open University, Milton Keynes (1989).

8. Jones A. and Singer R., Report on the use of home computing on M353. CITE Report No. 110. Centre for Information Technology in Education, The Open University, Milton Keynes (1990).

9. Loxton C., The help desk. Academic Computing Service Report. The Open University, Milton Keynes (1989).

10. Mason R., An evaluation of CoSy in an Open University course. In *Mindweave: Communication, Computers and Distance Education* (Edited by Mason R. and Kaye A. R.). Pergamon Press, Oxford (1989).

11. Mason R., Computer conferencing: an example of good practice from DT200 in 1990. CITE Report No. 129. Centre for Information Technology in Education, The Open University, Milton Keynes (1990).

12. Saxton C., To compute or not to compute. CITE Report No. 84. Centre for Information Technology in Education, The Open University, Milton Keyes (1988).

13. Jones A., Kirkup G. and Kirkwood A., *Personal Computers for Distance Learning*. Chapman, London. In press.

14. Kirkup G., Equal opportunities and computing at the Open University. *Open Learning* **4**, 3–8 (1989).

15. Kirkup G. and Dale E., T102 tutors' use of the home computing facility 1989. CITE Report No. 107. Centre for Information Technology in Education, The Open University, Milton Keyes (1990).

Computers Educ. Vol. 18, No. 1–3, pp. 195–200, 1992
Printed in Great Britain

0360-1315/92 $5.00 + 0.00
Pergamon Press plc

COMPUTING FOR THE TERRIFIED

Steve Kennewell

Department of Education, University College of Swansea, Hendrefoilan, Swansea SA2 7NB, Wales

Abstract—With the current need in England and Wales to involve every teacher in the development of pupils' capability in Information Technology (IT), it is necessary to consider the training requirements of those teachers who are reluctant to come forward for courses in the use of computers or to seek the help of expert colleagues. This paper examines the notion of "computerphobia", its causes, symptoms and possible cures; and describes how a major in-service training initiative in one Local Education Authority attempted to change teachers from being frightened of new technology to having a desire to use IT regularly and to learn more—in just 9 h. Participants' perceptions before and after the course are analysed, and some conclusions drawn of the effect of this type of training and its implications for school based work.

BACKGROUND

Practitioners in the field of teacher training in IT have long been aware of "computerphobia" amongst many teachers. For several years, however, little attention was given to the problem by those designing in-service courses. Their aim was to develop the competence of those who were interested and who often had some experience. There was an unrealistic expectation that they would pass on what they had learnt to colleagues in school through a "cascade" model of training[1].

Various "Introduction to Computers" courses have been provided, but most courses at introductory level have been specific to an area of IT—Word Processing, Information Handling, Graphics, Spreadsheets, Videotex, Control Technology—or to a curriculum area, such as Mathematics or History. Although such courses do not assume any particular computing knowledge, they generally skip certain fundamental techniques (e.g. how to connect and start the machine) and also assume teachers have enough knowledge of the jargon to be able to identify what they want to be introduced to! Many prospective applicants must have suspected that their knowledge would be inadequate to gain full benefit from the course, and that there would be other participants who would know too much. These suspicions were often correct on both counts. Other teachers have actually resisted gaining knowledge of IT.

Thinking about INSET generally in the U.K. changed during the mid-1980s towards the idea of entitlement to staff development for all teachers, and to the value of school focused INSET. Schools and LEAs encouraged staff to attend courses and increasingly provided school-based INSET for all staff. From the point of view of those providing training, the market changed. This was particularly the case in the field of IT. Indeed, it is now a requirement for all initial teacher training courses in the U.K. to incorporate practical skills in IT and an understanding of IT's place in the curriculum. This followed the recommendations of the report of the IT in Initial Teacher Training Expert Group[2].

It is generally felt that computer use in schools will never be fully effective if taught only by those enthusiasts with sufficient tenacity to overcome all obstacles to classroom use. Most teachers will rely on those with greater expertise to manage the resources and ensure that they can be used fairly easily. They are afraid, therefore, not so much of the machines, but of their own ignorance. They are reluctant to approach the enthusiasts, because such people

—do not seem to have much time
—use unfamiliar jargon
—expect them to acquire knowledge and skills too quickly
—will probably not be on hand when something goes wrong.

All teachers, then, need to have enough competence in the use of IT themselves to be able to solve simple problems when they occur, to communicate with the "experts", and to understand articles and handbooks. This should give them the confidence to allow pupils to use IT in their classrooms.

These factors led to a consideration (by a group of advisory teachers in Birmingham) of how to overcome the problems of computerphobia in teachers. Studies of teaching Computing in Adult Education have examined various aspects of the phenomenon. Fisher[3] cites research which has identified possible causes, such as:

the rapidity of technological change;
the apparent relation with mathematics, which also induces anxiety;
the feeling that the field is a male preserve;
contact with software which is designed to be used only by experts;

Knowles[4] identifies some differences between adults' attitudes to learning compared with those of children:
they do not tend to "brush off" failure;
they are concerned that their experience, and hence their self-image, will be shown to be inadequate;
they do not readily learn and accept new ideas;
they are less likely to feel that there is time to succeed later if they fail at first.

Fisher[3] also lists symptoms of computerphobia, which include a fear of damaging equipment, and even a refusal to accept the existence of computers! For teachers, this latter symptom often manifests itself in the form of "philosophical resistance", that is the belief that IT cannot be of value to their particular subject or student age range.

Summers'[5] research using an opportunity sample of postgraduate trainee teachers (which may be considered representative of entrants to secondary school teaching) considered the relation between students' experience of computers and their feelings about them. This indicated that negative feelings are reduced by experience, but did not examine the type of experience that would best foster positive feelings.

THE SELF-PROCLAIMED "TERRIFIED"

The body of serving teachers which are the subject of this study are not representative of the profession as a whole. They were those who applied for a course with the title "Computing for the Terrified", and who were nominated by their schools. There was a very high proportion of infant teachers on the courses, though it emerged that this was partly due to a lack of more specific provision for this group at a time when the need for them to develop some IT skills was becoming clear.

Certainly, there were very few men. Not, I think, because men are all confident with computers, but it seems that fewer men are prepared to admit being frightened of using the machinery. Summers[5], for instance, also noted, significant gender differences in feelings about computers, which could be because males have greater familiarity with low technology equipment.

THE COURSE ITSELF

Fisher[3] reviews a number of strategies which have been found valuable in teaching adults about computers, particularly:

the use of problems from a familiar context;
group discussion of problems and fears;
identifying personal objectives for each student;
open learning arrangements (as long as some group work is possible).

Fisher also noted some standard conditions for successful teaching, such as interaction with individual students, easy learning stages with continual feedback, clear objectives, and an enthusiastic manner. Studies involving children (e.g. [6, 7]) indicate that there is another key factor in learning to solve problems with IT: the acceptance that learners will make mistakes while exploring the uses of a new tool. Hence it is necessary for teachers to give encouragement in learning from the mistakes.

The main elements of the course were chosen to give maximum practical use of the computer. The types of software chosen for initial use were generic—Word Processing, Graphics and Viewdata—followed by the use of "content-free" software (where the teacher and pupils can include their own material) and finally the browsing of a set of more specific programs from a menu of options.

In addition, some time was spent on the parts of the computer system and its assembly, as it was felt that this was a major barrier to computer use. With no technician support in schools and a need to take equipment home for any extended period of practice, it is essential that teachers know how to make the system work from a set of component devices. This problem was confronted early in the course.

After the standard welcome and course administration, the teachers were asked to write down any feelings they had about computers. It was made clear that these notes were for their own use (so that they could consider changes as they made progress in the course) and not for public display or discussion unless they wanted to raise points at any time. It was hoped that this would encourage them to talk to each other and to the tutors about their feelings, and to make positive efforts to talk through any conflicts or blockages that they recognised.

Each computer was ready for word processing as participants arrived. They were introduced to the idea of input, output, processing and storage and asked to move straight onto the keyboard and try typing in any text they liked. Important keys were pointed out—space, delete and shift—and as they progressed with the entry of text, aided by a brief sheet of notes, various ideas concerning the control of layout were introduced on an individual basis. Participants were not constrained by the objectives of performing specific Word Processing techniques, and different pairs achieved different results. Course tutors ensured that each participant saved a document on disk and achieved a printout, and suggested they typed a "Certificate of Bravery in the Face of Information Technology"—either from scratch or by editing one stored on disk. The style of this work was described by participants as "low stress".

Each new piece of software introduced was presented with very little explanation—just a few notes designed to be enough to help them explore in the supportive environment, but not too much to be bewildering. Specific tasks were suggested when they wanted to move on from "playing", but they were asked to set their own objectives and were not put under pressure for something concrete to be achieved. The aim was not to teach word processing or other generic skills, but to give sufficient confidence, experience and knowledge of jargon to be able to use a manual or start a specialist course.

Later in the day, they were introduced to a different style of input and processing—a graphics package using a "mouse" pointer input. No instructions were issued except those for starting the program, yet participants were immediately able to confidently explore the environment of computer graphics. As they moved the mouse around the desk, a pointer would move around the screen, marking out behind it a line whose size, shape, colour and texture depended on the option chosen by moving the pointer to a word such as "Draw" or to a block of colour, and pressing a button on the mouse. Further options—shapes, filling areas, typing text, and manipulating the colours—were explored easily. Although few saw the relevance of this to their personal work, many would have preferred to start with the graphics, and this change is one which was adopted for later sessions.

This generic type of software was chosen because it would be equally suitable for, and interesting to, a wide variety of teachers. Each participant would be undergoing similar experiences and would be able to discuss these. They would get used to the feeling that they could do what they wanted, not just what the computer told them to do, and would realise that they did not have to program the computer themselves in order to gain this freedom.

There was a 2-week gap before the second day of the course, in order to encourage the participants to experiment back at school. Hence, at the end of the first day they were issued with a disk containing material about computers and educational computing, displayed using local viewdata format. This, it was hoped, would provide a test of whether they could start up a new piece of software, whilst still giving the security of a user-friendly environment for exploration. The effects of this were mixed, however, mainly due to lack of access to machinery and the failure of some of the disks to perform as expected. This feature was subsequently dropped.

Apprehension about introducing the computer to the classroom is another level of fear, and it was considered originally as being beyond the scope of a 9-h course. However, it was recognised that the software used on the second day should be relevant to as many as possible of the participants' own classrooms. The course offered a choice of an "infant disk" or other popular sets of simple programs for browsing. The aim of this was to develop an appreciation of the range of approaches and topics available, and how to browse simple computer-based material by scanning the documentation, then looking briefly at the screen layout and style of control before interrupting one program and moving to another.

A simple version of the "Developing Tray" idea was chosen for considering content-free curriculum packages. "Developing Tray" involves working out the content of a passage of text which is initially displayed with only the positions of letters marked. This is achieved by requesting particular letters to be filled in, or (more rewardingly) predicting parts of the text, first using the length and position of woods, then using combinations of letters and finally looking for meaning in the slowly developing "picture". After developing a simple text, pairs were then able to type in a new piece of text of their own design, "hide" it, swap with another pair, and develop each other's texts. Again, they were given very little formal introduction to this activity, but there was time for some discussion of strategies for developing texts, and reasons why this would be a valuable activity for groups of children in the classroom. At the end of the course, participants were able to take away the software that they had used.

EXPECTATIONS OF THE COURSE

In most cases, participants had expected a complete course in educational computing, although the duration was only 9 h. Questions about expectations were not asked until the end of the course, however. It is likely that expectations at the start would have been very limited or very vague; also one of the aims was to enable participants to identify what else they wanted to do.

Participants had nearly all expected to learn to assemble the equipment, and had the following expectations concerning other aspects of the course:

Word processing	44%
Graphics	41%
Viewdata	24%
Software browsing	69%
Solving problems set by the computer	51%

A number of other interesting figures emerged. Although only one-third had never used a computer before the course, over two-thirds were initially frightened of damaging the equipment when they used it, and over half had not expected to understand any instructions concerned with the computer. Nearly two-thirds felt that most other teachers knew more than themselves, and over one-third felt that their pupils knew more—and most were primary teachers.

OTHER FEELINGS ABOUT THE COURSE

The approach taken to building confidence was successful: most found it helpful to write down their feelings initially and to review these later. Nearly everyone found it useful to have a partner of similar experience in their work with the machine. The majority found the gap between the first and second day valuable.

The level of confidence gained in each area which they explored was considerable and rose beyond the stated objectives, which were written in terms of being able to talk to the school "expert" and progress to more specific courses. For the generic software (Word Processing and Graphics), most were confident that they could use it by themselves. Very few were not confident by the end. Some questions were asked about points which were beyond the scope of the original objectives; nearly every participant felt that they could see the value of the computer in enhancing their pupils' learning, and were confident that they could use the computer in their classrooms. A smaller number, though still a majority, felt that they could use the computer in their personal work; clearly the course designers' aims did not match the personal goals of many participants. In fact, tutors gained the impression that a significant minority of participants were not "terrified", but felt that by declaring themselves so they were likely to receive the low-pressure tutoring style that would suit them best.

EFFECTS ON SCHOOLS

At the start of the second day, course members were invited to share their experiences with each other and with the group as a whole. The changes in general confidence and enthusiasm were pleasing, and the ability of many to interest and assist their colleagues was quite astonishing. At least one group of "terrified" teachers had provided a formal INSET session for colleagues within a month of the course. In fact, it is of some concern that several graduates of our course were immediately seen as their schools' experts!

There was no illusion that individual teachers attending centre-based courses would have a significant effect on their schools in general, but it was clear from a number of follow-up visits that the wider effects of Computing for the Terrified were much greater than was expected. This seemed particularly true when there was more than one teacher from a school on the course.

It would be pointless firing the enthusiasm of so many teachers for use of the computer if there was to be no effect on their pupils, however. The methods used on the course were intended to provide participants with a good model for the classroom introduction of computers, as well as for school-based INSET. In addition, for the effects to be felt, greater access to computing equipment will be needed in many schools. The government's Education Support Grant funding for equipment and advisory teachers was provided at just the right time. The LEA was able to offer extra hardware for the schools and to allocate advisory teachers to work alongside the newly interested staff, in order to help them gain confidence in classroom management as well as personal use.

THE NEXT STEPS

Many of those attending requested follow-up courses designed specifically for the same group of teachers (computing for the Still-slightly-apprehensive? or the Now-quite-confident?), but the needs of the group became so widespread that this was unrealistic. Besides, the centre offered many other courses which are designed for teachers at this more confident level, and the aim of Computing for the Terrified was to prepare participants for more specialised work. However, many of the Now-quite-confident teachers found a group of colleagues in school who could identify a common need for support.

It was clear that in a large number of schools, several teachers wanted to attend the Computing for the Terrified course, but this need was not given high enough priority within the school's staff development plan. However, many schools did give a high priority to IT during the INSET days that had been made a government requirement. The advisory team was thus able to work with the staff in many schools, providing primary teachers with a variety of computer-based activities related to a particular theme, and providing secondary school staff with a range of workshops that enabled Computing for the Terrified to be offered as an option for the day.

There have been a number of changes since Computing for the Terrified was conceived. The introduction of the National Curriculum [8] is clearly a major influence, not least because, in its spirit at least, it requires every teacher to have a certain level of competence and confidence. Another factor is the increasing number of teachers who have access to personal computers at home.

The principles behind the Computing for the Terrified course are no panacea for the problems of IT INSET for the majority of teachers, but the experience of those who have participated indicates that it provides a good foundation for further development, and that their enthusiasm for this style of introducing computing activities will have a long-lasting effect on the use of IT in their schools.

REFERENCES

1. HMI, *Aspects of the work of the Microelectronics Education Programme*. DES/HMSO, London (1987).
2. IT in ITT Expert Group, *Information Technology in Initial Teacher Training*, HMSO, London (1989).
3. Fisher M. Computerphobia in adult learners. *Computer Educ.* **69,** 14–19 (1991).
4. Knowles M., *The Modern Practice of Adult Education*. Cambridge Book Co. (1970).
5. Summers M. Starting teacher training—new PGCE students and computers. *Br. Educ. Res. J.* **16**(1), 79–88 (1990).
6. Hoyles C. and Sutherland R. Ways of learning in a computer based environment. *J. Computer Assist. Learn.* **3**(2), 67–80 (1987).
7. Straker A., *Children Using Computers*, Chap. 4. Blackwell Education, Oxford (1989).
8. DES/Welsh Office, *Technology in the National Curriculum*. DES/HMSO, London (1990).

Computers Educ. Vol. 18, No. 1–3, pp. 201–207, 1992
Printed in Great Britain. All rights reserved

A HYPERTEXT SYSTEM FOR TEACHING EMPLOYMENT-RELATED LANGUAGE TO HEARING-IMPAIRED SCHOOL LEAVERS

C. Bloor, D. A. S. Curran, J. Fowler, K. Manktelow,
W. Middleton and A. O. Moscardini

The Computer Aided Learning Centre, Sunderland Polytechnic, Langham Tower, Ryhope Road,
Sunderland SR2 7EE, England

Abstract—This paper reports the outcomes of a project sponsored by the Training Agency (now TEED) to produce CAL material to teach employment-related language to hearing-impaired school leavers. The tutorial content was decided after conducting a survey of teachers of the deaf, in order to determine which areas they felt were significant and where there was a shortage of existing material. A survey of the literature relating to language and the deaf produced a number of rules for the generation of the language content of the tutorials. In addition tutorials were written at two levels of language so that the material can be related to the needs of the student using the system. These needs are assessed by a computerised version of the SPAR reading test.

A management system guides the student through the tutorials and reports back to the teacher on the student's progress, what help has been requested, and the results of the tests which are included in the tutorials.

INTRODUCTION

There have been a number of studies of the reading levels of hearing-impaired children. Conrad[1] reports his own study in the U.K. and similar studies in Sweden, Denmark and New Zealand. There have also been several surveys in the U.S.A.[2–4]. These have generally shown a depressing pattern of poor reading skills. Conrad, for example, showed that the average reading age of a 16-yr-old deaf child was nine. Webster[5] considers that research has concentrated too much on measuring reading ability, and that insufficient attention has been paid to how deaf children approach the task of reading. He also criticises the use of tests developed for hearing norms for a different population. Indeed for these hearing norms the concept of a reading age may be questioned[6]. We will consider the question of reading in more detail later; for the moment we can accept that the reading skills of the hearing impaired are poor and that this must have an implication when it comes to employment.

Employment prospects

Various surveys of the employment prospects of this group of schools leavers have shown that their opportunities have been very restricted[7–10]. Those in employment were almost exclusively working at an unskilled or semi-skilled level. In the 1977 survey of Storer[10], 85% of males and 100% of females fell into this category. Wildig[11] also looked at the post-school vocational training opportunities available for the hearing-impaired. This study showed a "considerable variation in the provision and support services available" and concluded that "much still needs to be done to ensure that every hearing-impaired school leaver has the opportunity to fulfil his/her natural potential". At the time of the survey there was only one Technical and Vocational Education Institute course in England and Wales actually teaching post-school hearing-impaired students. Our own survey[12] shows some improvement on this latter situation but we would agree with the main conclusion.

There is a general recognition by educators that the hearing impaired have a potential for employment at much higher levels of responsibility than they are normally given[13]. This is implicit in the conclusions of Wildig and supported by a survey of one London Borough (Bexley) in 1984[14]. Only 47% of hearing-impaired school leavers in the period 1975–1983 went directly into employment and in the year of the survey, none were directly employed in contrast to a figure of 61% for all school leavers in the borough. Participants were evenly divided by their attitudes towards the help received at school in terms of career guidance (45% registered positive comments, and the same number negative comments). They were also split on the additional advice they would have liked between more practical experience and more career information. All participants felt that realistic employment aspirations had not been met. Wildig and Elphick[15] concluded that one of the major hurdles to this was low levels in basic skills.

Given that the language skills of hearing-impaired school leavers are poor, and that there is a need to remedy this situation, the Training Agency (now TEED) sponsored a project at the Computer Aided Learning Centre, Sunderland Polytechnic, to produce CAL material to teach language in a specific area, that language which relates to finding employment. A previous TEED project had developed a system to teach mathematics to First-Year Polytechnic students[16]. This assessed the students' weaknesses and then guided them through a tutorial system designed to remedy these weaknesses. It was decided to follow a similar approach in teaching language. There would be a diagnostic test at the beginning of the suite of tutorials. This would not identify specific weaknesses, as in the maths system, but would establish a level of language competence (measured as a reading age) which would be used to direct the student to one of two levels of tutorial.

A COMPUTERISED READING TEST

The system developed operates at two levels of reading ability. These were designated "high" and "low" with the language being assessed by teachers of the deaf. As the reading age of the average deaf school leaver is of the order of nine, it was decided to make the split at about this level. A sophisticated test is not required, therefore. We only want to know whether the pupil's reading age is above or below a given point. The SPAR test is easy to administer, and one which gives an estimate of reading age. It was thus decided to computerise the test.

The paper version of the test consists of a series of pictures, each of which has four or five words below it. The stuent has to identify the correct word. No feedback is given. In the later part of the test the pictures are replaced by sentences, each of which has a word missing. There is a list of possible words below the sentence and the student has to identify the correct word again. The pupil's score is obtained by noting the point at which ten wrong answers have been given. The reading age is then derived by using a look-up table. This test is thus ideal for our purposes. It is easy to computerise and the derivation of the reading age is fairly straightforward. In the paper version of the test the student circles the correct answer. In the computerised version, which is implemented in LinkWay, the student points at the correct word using a mouse and clicks on the mouse button. When ten wrong answers have been obtained, or the test is finished, the computer stops the test. In the paper version the student may continue to the end of the test but answers after the first ten wrong answers are ignored for scoring purposes. We believe that this is an advantage of the computerised version. The student only sees that part of the test which they can reasonably be expected to cope with. The harder parts are not seen. Conrad[1] has noted that deaf readers may use different strategies from hearing counterparts in approaching a test such as this. The computerised version may discourage this approach as the student will quickly be taken out of the test when the ten wrong answers are obtained. The student is not allowed to continue using an incorrect strategy. The computerised version could overestimate the reading age, however. The student is forced to attempt an answer for each question, and will only go onto the next question when an answer has been obtained. There is no "do not know" box. This was not felt to be necessary. It would introduce a difference between the two versions of the test and for our purposes, where we only want to grade to two levels a strictly accurate reading age is not necessary. The correlation between the two versions of the SPAR test is currently being investigated.

The reading skill of the hearing-impaired

Having established that we wish to write tutorial material for the hearing impaired, and at two levels of reading skill, we must establish some rules by which we write this material, and by which we assess its suitability. It is therefore necessary to look at what current literature tells us about the reading skills of the hearing impaired.

The acquisition of reading skills is not a unitary matter: several distinct types of performance have to be mastered before a person can become a skilled reader. Many adults never achieve complete proficiency in some or all of these skills, and the hearing-impaired are faced with particular difficulties. In the following section an ordered breakdown of the components of reading skill is given, together with an indication of the degree to which the hearing-impaired in particular are affected; the consequences of any such disadvantage for good practice in the design of reading materials for this group; and prospects for remediation of these difficulties. It should be borne in mind that this examination of the literature will be with respect to the particular age-group concerned in the current project, i.e. 15–16-yr-old school leavers.

A hierarchy of component skills

A convenient way to break down reading is to consider its component skills as a hierarchy. In order of appearance, these skills are:

(1) Decoding the visual symbols
(2) Vocabulary
(3) Syntax
(4) Pragmatics and inference

This analysis should not be pushed too far: while it may be true that children begin to acquire each of these skills in roughly this order, they will be refining them all in parallel as they get older. Similarly, these skills become interactive at quite an early age.

Decoding

The first stage in reading is to decode the printed marks so as to relate them to the content they are intended to convey. Very young hearing children can begin to do this. There is a basic division in educational practice between the phonic and look-and-say method of teaching decoding. The phonic method involves linking the letters and letter combinations of written language to the sounds of speech. The look-and-say method involves learning to perceive the meaning of words directly, without recourse to their spelling patterns.

Clearly, deaf children are going to have difficulty with phonics, given that they have best an impoverished repertoire of speech derived phonemes to begin with. Webster[17] makes the point that if phonic skills are not a prerequisite for reading for reading, there is little point in teaching them to the hearing-impaired. However, as with many such debates, it seems likely that both abilities are useful in reading; look and say techniques may work well with familiar, frequent words, but an ability to analyse in terms of small elements may be necessary when coping with novel or unfamiliar words. Naturally, it does not follow that ability to decode and speak a written word indicates that the word has been understood: there is plenty of evidence that some children who are good at reading aloud have very little understanding of what they have read[18]. At the age range we are dealing with, however, we can assume that basic decoding skills are already present, so we will not pursue this aspect of reading further.

Vocabulary

According to King and Quigley[19], vocabulary plays a primary role in reading skill: obviously, without knowing what words mean one is unable to compute the content of a text. Deaf children score significantly lower than hearing children on all tests of meaning comprehension, and their worst performance is on tests of the meanings of single words. This is most probably because there is a minimum of contextual information available in this situation which could be used as a cue to meaning.

Two more subtle aspects of vocabulary are also worth mentioning: polysemy and figurative meanings. Polysemous words are those which have more than one meaning, and it is a property of natural language that the most frequently used words tend to have the greatest number of possible meanings (the word "set" has over 150). The "true" meaning is determined by the context. Hearing students are better than deaf students at computing and selecting from these different meanings[19]; thus the context in which significant words appear should always be designed to disambiguate common words effectively.

Figurative language is a related phenomenon: not only are common words likely to have a large number of possible literal meanings, they also tend to be widely used in non-literal or figurative ways. In written language, the most common forms are metaphor (time flies), simile (time flies like an arrow) and idiom (the grim reaper). According to King and Quigley, deaf children do not, contrary to expectation, have a particular difficulty with these expressions, compared to hearing children, as long as they are embedded in a meaningful context. Comprehension of metaphors has been found to improve with practice. However, hearing children and adults find some of them obscure, and figurative usages will, because of the extra computational demands they make, possibly interact with other aspects of language to increase difficulty by increasing the load on working memory during reading (see below). One can feel this happening to oneself when too many figurative expressions are used in succession.

We can thus derive three rules for language production:

(1) Infrequent words should be avoided if a familiar substitute is available
(2) Figurative usages should be used with caution
(3) Context should be used carefully to aid understanding

Syntax

It is in the use of syntax that one finds some of the most characteristic and most damaging differences between the hearing and the hearing-impaired. King and Quigley[19] and Mogford[20] both report that the syntactic abilities of groups of hearing-impaired 18-yr-olds are only on a par with 8–10-yr-old hearing children. This is not a uniform deficit: King and Quigley give the following order of difficulty of common syntactic elements from greatest to least:

passive voice > relative clauses > conjunctions > pronoun > indirect objects.

In short, hearing-impaired readers tend to fixate on content words (nouns, verbs, etc.) and ignore the syntactic influence of function words (articles, prepositions, conjunctions, etc.), so turning most sentences into simple, active, affirmative declaratives. Thus "Jim was hit by John", "The man who hit Jim hit John", and "Jim might hit John" will all be read as "Jim hit John". Modal auxiliaries associated with deontic expressions (may, ought, should, etc.) cause particular difficulty, a factor compounded by phonetic similarities, e.g. between may/might, could/should. A fourth rule can hence be stated:

(4) Avoid unnecessary syntactic complexity.

Pragmatics and inference

An area of language understanding which has received less attention than the above, especially with regard to the hearing-impaired, is the role of inferential and metalinguistic factors in the pickup of information from text. Recent evidence, however[18], indicates that skill in these processes constitutes a major difference between good and poor readers. We shall consider two processes here, inference and the role of top-down knowledge.

Inference

The types of inference we shall look at here are those specifically to do with language understanding. Mostly they are to do with keeping track of the topic of a text, relating different parts to one another and realising when different expressions are referring to the same thing. On all such inferences, poor readers are measurably worse than good readers[18]. Hearing-impaired readers are similar to poor hearing readers in this respect: King and Quigley suggest that very few hearing-impaired readers become highly skilled at reading because of these factors.

Examples of these linguistic inferences are as follows:

Anaphora. Knowing that a later expression is co-referential with an earlier one. The two main varieties of this are pronoun anaphora:

I met John yesterday and he hit me

and definite noun-phrase anaphora:

A man called John came into the office. The man hit me.

Ellipsis. A device for saving one's breath by not repeating a prior expression completely when referring to it again, e.g.

The police asked me if I had seen Jim hit John. I hadn't (i.e. I hadn't seen Jim hit John).

Bridging. A "gap-filling" device for maintaining continuity of reference, e.g.

I met John yesterday. The bounder hit me. (We infer than John and The bounder are the same person.)

John died yesterday. The gun was found nearby. (We infer that he was murdered.)

Poor readers have great difficulty with these cohesive devices. These difficulties are not particular to reading, since similar mistakes occur when text is listened to as well as read. They are not due to a general memory deficit, since they also occur when readers have the text in front of them. According to Oakhill[21], mistakes such as these are most probably attributable to the restricted capacity of working memory. This is another reason why figurative expressions should be used with care. Syntactic complexity should also be avoided as it adds further computational demands which will make these problems worse. Thus the rules stated above are reinforced.

Top-down knowledge

In any perceptual task, including reading, there is an interaction between bottom-up knowledge (the data coming in through the senses) and top-down knowledge, which is what we already know. In reading, this relationship is between what is printed on the page and prior knowledge about the topic in question, as well as the purpose for reading the text and expectations about what will be gained from doing so.

Poor readers are more influenced by top-down knowledge than are good readers: skilled reading is predominantly text-based. This is true both of poor- and beginning-hearing readers and the hearing-impaired[17, 19], and a false impression of the reading abilities of the hearing-impaired can sometimes result from their reliance on top-down knowledge[22]. Webster[22] counsels against fighting this and instead urges that top-down components in reading be manipulated rather than too many modifications being made to the text itself: "cues for meaning in the context are much more powerful than modifications". This will have the advantage of preserving cohesive links in the text which might otherwise be lost by reducing it to "Janet and John" form. Hence we obtain a final rule:

(5) Do not reduce sentences to the simplest form at the expense of loss of textual link.

THE TUTORIAL SYSTEM

Content

In order to determine what areas should be covered in the tutorials, and which jobs should be included, a survey of teachers of the deaf was undertaken. The detailed results of this survey have been reported elsewhere[12]. Five areas were proposed for the tutorial contents, and teachers were asked to rate each on importance and the need for additional material. The five areas were:

(A) Deciding on a career; opportunities available; qualifications; restrictions; skills needed; courses
(B) Applying for a job; advertisements; application forms; interview techniques; aids to help you in your job
(C) Pay; pay structures; tax; national insurance; pensions
(D) Structure of the workplace; who you report to; how to obtain help; belonging to a union
(E) Promotion, career progression

Category (A) was considered to be very important by 93% of respondents, with 70% considering there to be a need for additional material. Category (B) was considered to be very important by

86% of respondents with 59% considering there to be a need for additional material. The remaining categories did not score significantly. The aim of the project was to produce CAL material targeted towards the language of employment, however. It was felt that this could best be met by covering area (B) (applying for a job, adverts, etc.) rather than area (A) which had received a slightly higher rating in terms of importance. It was also felt that area (B) lent itself to a CAL approach, whereas the other area was best approached by a discussion with the student as to their own aspirations.

Tutorials

Tutorials were written to cover three topics, namely job adverts and where they are found, the structure of job adverts, and applying for a job. All the tutorials written are at two levels of reading age. In addition help is available throughout each tutorial via the hypertext facilities of LinkWay v. 1, the language chosen to write the tutorials. This has some limitations, in particular it is only possible to navigate down one level, but LinkWay was the best of the PC-based hypertext systems available at the time the system was written. The first two topics have a series of short tests throughout the tutorial so that the understanding of the pupil is assessed. The third topic does not lend itself to this approach, so a tasks pack has been produced to aid understanding of the tutorial material. The tasks set are writing letters, preparing for a telephone enquiry, and filling in application forms. It is difficult to estimate the time taken for each tutorial. They were written with the intention that each tutorial should take about 20 min. The time taken depends on the help requested however, and may be only a few minutes if the student is already familiar with the material, or up to 1 h if the student is going through the material with the teacher and stopping to discuss points raised. The student may leave the system at any point and return to that point on a later occasion. Help in using the system may be obtained at any point. There is also a tutorial on how to use the system. It was found during the initial trials however that students had little difficulty in using the system after a simple explanation from the teacher. This tutorial was thus taken out of the path for the student, but left in the demonstration module so that the teacher can go through the system with a student (see below).

Students navigate through the system with the aid of five buttons: forward, back, quit, help and return to the beginning of the tutorial.

In order to ensure consistency between tutorials standards were established for screen layouts including the position and colours of the main text areas, adverts and the pop-up help. These standards also covered the font size, style and colours.

The language content of the tutorials was monitored by producing scripts which were agreed by two teachers of the deaf prior to each tutorial being written. As indicated above, although the SPAR test splits the students at a reading age of nine, the tutorials were written and assessed by the teachers as being high and low level judged by the teachers' experience of their own school leavers.

The management system

Access to the tutorials is controlled by a management system written in KnowledgePro. This system is the main interface presented to the student when they start the system. It presents a list of names to the user. Students choose their own name and the system then takes them to the appropriate tutorial at the level selected by the SPAR test. The management system may be entered by choosing the name Teacher, although this access is controlled by a password. There is also a demonstration option which allows any tutorial to be run should the teacher wish to do work with a pupil or group or pupils.

The management system records any help requested by a student, and the path taken through the system by a student. This information is available to the teacher to aid the preparation of language extension work. The responses made in the SPAR test may also be viewed, as may the answers to the questions in the first two sections.

Assessment of the system

The system is currently undergoing evaluation by teachers of the deaf, but no formal evaluation has been undertaken. It is not intended that this system be used in standalone mode, but as part of a programme of careers work. The evaluation planned is therefore a questionnaire to users to determine if the system is of use, what areas are particularly useful, and whether the language levels used are appropriate. The initial response from teachers who have seen the system has been positive. When sufficient data are available the correlation between the paper and computerised versions of the SPAR test will also be determined.

Acknowledgements—We wish to thank Hodder and Stoughton for permission to use the SPAR test. Thanks are also due to Sarah Wildig, of the Centre for Audiology, Teaching of the Deaf and Speech Pathology, University of Manchester, for much useful advice, and to Aidan Tasker, of the Unit for Hearing Impaired Pupils, Usworth Comprehensive School, Washington, for his commments on the tutorials and his time, and that of his pupils, taken in evaluating the system. Doncaster College for the Deaf, and Mary Hare Grammar School for the Deaf, Newbury, are also thanked. Financial assistance from TEED is acknowledged.

REFERENCES

1. Conrad R., *The Deaf School Child*. Harper–Row, London (1979).
2. Furth H., A comparison of reading test norms of deaf and hearing children. *Am. Ann. Deaf* **111**, 461–462 (1966).
3. Difrancesca S., Academic achievement test results of a national testing program for hearing impaired students. United States, Spring, 1971 (series D, No. 9). Gallaudet College, Office of Demographic Studies, Washington, D.C. (1972).
4. Trybus R. and Karchmer M., School achievement scores of hearing impaired children: national data on achievement status and growth patterns. *Am. Ann. Deaf Direct. Prog. Serv.* **122**, 62–69 (1977).
5. Webster A., *Deafness, Development and Literacy*. Methuen, London (1986).
6. Brooks G., Personal communication.
7. Stavers O., What happens to them . . . ? Congress on the education of the deaf, pp. 324–327. Gallaudet College Press, Washington, D.C. (1963).
8. Rodda M., *The Hearing Impaired School Leaver*. University of London Press, London (1970).
9. Montgomery G. and Miller J., Assessment and preparation of deaf adults for employment. *J. Br. Assoc. Teach. Deaf* **1**, 167–176 (1977).
10. Storer R. D. K., The vocational boundaries of deaf and partially hearing adolescents and young adults in the West Midlands. *J. Br. Assoc. Teach. Deaf* **1**, 134–136 (1988).
11. Wildig S., Post-school educational and vocational training opportunities for the hearing impaired in England and Wales. *J. Br. Assoc. Teach. Deaf* **11**, 118–126 (1987).
12. Bloor C., Manktelow K., Curran D. A. S., Moscardini A. O. and Middleton W., Using CAL to teach employment specific language—a research proposal. *J. Br. Assoc. Teach. Deaf* **14**, 80–88 (1990).
13. Agathangelou A. M. and Agathangelou L., The employment potential of the deaf school leaver. RNID, 105 Gower St., London WC1E 6AH (1982).
14. Woolgar J. and Sigston A., Consulting the client: the hearing impaired reflect on schooling. *J. Br. Assoc. Teach. Deaf* **12**, 16–23 (1988).
15. Wildig S. and Elphick R., The hearing impaired school leaver and after: education and employment. In *Education of the Deaf—Current Perspectives* (Edited by Taylor I. G.), pp. 1146–1162. Croom Helm, London (1985).
16. Curran D. A. S., Moscardini A. O. and Middleton W., Remedial mathematics for engineering students—evaluation report. Training Enterprise and Education Directorate, Department of Employment, Moorfoot, Sheffield S1 4PQ (1989).
17. Webster A., Deafness and learning to read 1: theoretical and research issues. *J. Br. Assoc. Teach. Deaf* **12**, 77–83 (1988).
18. Oakhill J. V. and Garnham A., *Becoming a Skilled Reader*. Blackwell, Oxford (1988).
19. King C. M. and Quigley S. P., *Reading and Deafness*. College Hill Press, San Diego, Calif. (1985).
20. Mogford K., Oral language acquisition in the prelinguistically deaf. In *Language Development in Exceptional Circumstances* (Edited by Mogford K. and Bishop D.). Churchill Livingstone, London (1988).
21. Oakhill J. V., Children's comprehension difficulties: the nature of the deficit. *Spiel* **8**, 27–49.
22. Webster A., Deafness and learning to read 2: teaching strategies. *J. Br. Assoc. Teach. Deaf* **12**, 93–101 (1988).

Computers Educ. Vol. 18, No. 1–3, pp. 209–221, 1992
Printed in Great Britain. All rights reserved

THE IMPACT OF NEW INFORMATION TECHNOLOGY ON YOUNG CHILDREN'S SYMBOL-WEAVING EFFORTS

JULIA BLACKSTOCK and LARRY MILLER

Faculty of Education, Queen's University, Kingston, Ontario, Canada K7L 3N6

Abstract—This article explores young children's symbol-weaving efforts from two perspectives. "Symbol-weaving" is an umbrella term for three mutually supportive systems of meaning-making: drawing, talk, and writing. First, we examine how children use traditional media in their symbol-weaving efforts. Examining children's talk, along with their traits, preferences, and styles of drawing and writing, with traditional media, we apply the lessons learned to how these undertakings might be influenced by new information technology. In some instances, technology may detract from the symbol-weaving process; however, newer, more sophisticated software may enhance children's endeavours. Far more influential than the technology is the guidance of teachers. The manner in which teachers permit children to use technology seems to be a crucial variable in terms of restraining or enhancing symbol-weaving. Finally, we suggest that new information technology may offer new ways of thinking about young children's story-making processes and products.

INTRODUCTION

Amy, a Grade 1 child, works intently on her latest narrative, occasionally putting down her pencil to look at the drawing. At the table are three other children, equally intent on creating pictures and stories. The conversation at the table is animated, with children sharing the tools of composition and offering comments about each other's pictures and stories.

Megan (*handing Amy a crayon*): Green, green, green. Make it green Amy.
Amy: But I'm not sure it was green.
Megan (*looking up briefly from her story*): Monsters are green.
Claire: Not always. Some monsters are black . . . or even purple.
Amy: This is a real story, not make-believe. I saw it.
Susan: But it's a sea monster. Real sea monsters are green. I know.

The conversation continues with deep seriousness for several minutes. Amy takes in the various opinions as to the correct colour for her sea monster. Most of the time, Amy is a concerned listener, but she asks questions of her informers as well. Finally, she announces, "It's green". Picking up the crayon offered earlier by Megan, she carefully colours an amorphous shape previously drawn on the right side of her picture. Then, to her attentive peers, Amy reads the story aloud.

WON DA We Wet TO The OShiN AND I WUS CLUOMING SOm RokS. AND Win I WUS ON The RokS I SOo SUPIHiG MooViG in The RoKS. AND I WUS SkirD.

(One day we went to the ocean and I was climbing some rocks. And when I was on the rocks I saw something moving in the rocks. And I was scared.) (Miller, unpublished case study, 1982).

Taking her pencil, Amy inserts a caret (an editing device taught by the teacher) between the words *something* and *moving*. "How do you spell *green*?" Amy asks no one in particular. Quickly, her classmates move on to a discussion concerning the spelling of the word *green*.

Overview

The goal of this paper is to examine the effects of new information technology on young children's symbol-weaving efforts, a term borrowed from Dyson[1] and elaborated upon by Newkirk[2]. In considering this issue, we will first explore the nature of young children's drawing and writing using traditional media. The lessons learned about this relationship using established media will be applied to the question of how new information technology may enhance or detract from the partnership. However, as we will point out in the article, it is inappropriate to look at children's efforts only from the perspective of their drawing and composing. Two additional variables, talk and children's perceptions of their meaning-making, must be considered in this equation. Finally, we will extend our discussion of children's symbol-weaving to explore the notion that new information technology may create new ways in which the union of drawing, writing, and talk may be conceptualized.

YOUNG CHILDREN'S SYMBOL-WEAVING ENDEAVOURS USING TRADITIONAL MEDIA

Authors of Pictures, Draughtsmen of Words is the instructive title of a fascinating new book by Ruth Hubbard[3] describing the efforts of young children in drawing and composing. This book, along with an equally important study, *Multiple Worlds of Child Writers: Friends Learning to Write*, by Anne Haas Dyson[4], informed our discussion of children's drawing, talking, and writing using traditional media. Both longitudinal studies used an intensive case study format within the larger context of the classroom. Hubbard concentrated on a Grade 1 class while Dyson observed children from Kindergarten to Grade 3. The categories examined in this section of the article do not exhaust all the topics discussed by Dyson and Hubbard. Instead, we extracted those issues that may be influenced most by new information technology. The key issues raised here are highlighted by vignettes gathered by the authors of this article as well as those presented in the writings of Dyson and Hubbard.

Newkirk[2], in Chap. 2 of his book *More Than Stories: The Range of Children's Writing*, uses the heading "Draw me a word—write me a picture" to highlight the contention that young children may not perceive the two mediums of drawing and writing as different. Specifically challenging the image of drawing-as-rehearsal for writing, a notion prominent in many school-based composing programmes, he states:

> "The idea of drawing-as-rehearsal is just one more example of the word-centered view that reigns in our educational system. The child's drawing is reduced to a preliminary, a kind of pre-writing, rather than being accepted as an important communicative system in its own right" (p. 37).

Newkirk's assertion presented a dilemma for us in composing this article. Moreover, the challenge of drawing-as-rehearsal does not exhaust the questions Newkirk raises about children's natural symbol-weaving tendencies and the teaching of the composing process in schools. For example, Newkirk shows us that once drawing and writing are accepted as equal partners in the meaning-making process, the relationship between picture and text may be examined from a variety of perspectives. Another icon of writing challenged by Newkirk is that young children prefer narratives to non-narratives. An examination of his daughter Sarah's early writing convinced Newkirk that non-narrative was the preferred mode of writing. Recent research by Coe[5], who studied three pre-school children writing in a home environment, supports this contention.

Do we examine children's drawing and writing attempts from a school-based perspective, where drawing often is seen as rehearsal for composing, or do we accept Newkirk's notion that one must view symbol-weaving from a child's perspective? Do we look mainly at narratives, the mode of writing fostered by many schools, or do we look beyond this form of writing? We decided, for the purposes of this article, to proceed from a posture of school-based symbol-weaving because this perspective represents, for the most part, what is happening in formal education. However, throughout the article, we also returned to the important questions raised by Newkirk[2] as they influenced our discussion of future formulations of technology's role in children's symbol-weaving endeavours.

Movement between text and drawing

There are two issues related to movement between text and drawing. The first issue involves the locus of meaning; is the story embedded mainly in the text or in the drawing? Both Dyson[4] and

Hubbard[3], along with observers such as Newkirk[2], Calkins[6], Graves[7] and Bartelo[8], recognize that children frequently move back and forth between drawing and writing for reasons described by Hubbard[3]:

> "The children shifted back and forth, sometimes relying more on words and sometimes more on pictures. There appeared to be two main influences on which symbol system dominated a literacy event: the nature of the task and the cognitive bias of the child" (p. 144).

Early on, young children may rely heavily on the picture to convey meaning. Indeed, entire stories maybe captured in one drawing or a series of drawings, without accompanying text. Talk, rather than print, is viewed by the young child as an appropriate vehicle for telling the accompanying tale. Dyson[4] tells a delightful story illustrating two children's views of the need for words:

Brian: Why do we always have to write words? *(Translation: Why can't we just write the pictures?)*
Teacher: Well, I like to see what you're going to write.
Sara: Why can't you just ask us? (p. 12)

As children mature, meaning tends to lean more heavily toward text, demonstrating an ability to decontextualize. However, although this trend may capture the general tendency of young writers, one must keep in mind Hubbard's caveat as well as Graves'[9] admonishment that the "behaviours of writers are ideosyncratic and highly variable" (p. 29). And one must not neglect Newkirk's[2] assertion that meaning—between text and picture—may reside in as many as seven different dimensions.

The second issue concerning movement between drawing and text relates to children's style in creating stories. As seen in the vignette presented at the beginning of this article, Amy believes the text must be consonant with the picture, so when she colours the sea creature green, the text is amended as well. Our observations of Kevin, a Grade 2 student, depict another common situation relating to movement between drawing and text. The following conversation took place at a time when Kevin was creating a fantasy story about a tornado and his rescue of a family whose house was about to be demolished:

Researcher: How's your story coming, Kevin?
Kevin *(Staring intently at the picture and ignoring the researcher's attempt to conference.)*: Okay.
Researcher: Have you written any of your story yet?
Kevin: I can't write the story until it's done.

Kevin's comment that he cannot write the story until it is done may seem cryptic, but, over time, he demonstrated a style where the words were composed only after the picture or a series of pictures accompanying the tale were complete. However, although he created the drawings first, perhaps using them as rehearsal for the text, Kevin frequently worked back and forth between picture and text, modifying both symbol systems. Like Amy, changes in the drawing sometimes prompted a modification in text, but the reverse situation also was observed.

Social aspects of writing

Dyson[10,11] showed that a richer understanding of the drawing/composing relationship was possible when another variable was considered—talk. And, in a later work[4] she expanded the idea of talk influencing drawing and composing to include the entire social fabric of the classroom. By examining the complete classroom structure, Dyson revealed how such variables as daily routines, curriculum, social interaction, the physical make-up of the room, and teacher expectations influenced children's drawing and writing in terms of both process and product.

To illustrate some of Dyson's points, especially the role of talk, consider the following situation, which occurred while one author of this paper was involved with a Grade 1 in New Hampshire. Each morning, after opening exercises, the children drew and wrote stories for approx. 45 min, a substantial amount of composing time for a primary class. Children knew the routine and immediately collected their writing folders after opening exercises. It was not uncommon for the children to talk for 15 min or more before drawing and/or writing. However, as a new observer in the classroom, the researcher was concerned about the "excessive" talk that went on at one table consisting of four girls. Guilty of the stereotype that a noisy child was not learning, numerous trips to the table were made to stimulate "productive work". This concern was shared with Donald Graves who suggested cryptically that the conversations of the children should not be stopped but be monitored more closely. Accepting the suggestion at face value, the following discourse, based on a Disney movie, was observed:

Janet: Oh, I loved it when they ate the spaghetti together.
Ruth *(giggling)*: Yea, and they ended up kissing.
Rose: I was scared when they got chased. I didn't think they would get away.
Amanda: Oh Rose, it's a movie. They always get away. Are you going to the movie next week?
Ruth: No, we're going camping. I love camping. Dad's going to take me fishing with him.
Janet: I'll go. Do you want to go with me?

So it went, a seemingly endless, disjointed exchange about the movie *The Lady and the Tramp* as well as the development of plans for the following weekend. Eventually, the children began drawing and writing. Talk was still evident, but now it was more focused on the task at hand.

Janet *(carefully adding a meatball to her plate of spaghetti)*: Look at my kissing dogs!

(The other students gather around Janet's picture and story, laughing.)
Amanda: Look, Lady has lipstick on. Oooolala.
Ruth: She didn't have lipstick on in the movie.
Janet: Who cares. It's my story.
Rose: Yea, it's your story.

(The children break into an animated discussion as to whether a writer can change a movie. After the conversation, Janet begins a conversation with the researcher.)

Researcher: Where do you get your ideas for your stories?
Janet: I just think them up in my head.
Researcher: Do your friends help you with your ideas?
Janet: No, I think them up all by myself.
Researcher: But you talk about your stories with Amanada, Rose, and Ruth, don't you?
Janet *(Looking puzzled.)*: Yea, but it's my story.

Janet, like many young children, retains her sense of ownership of stories even though she accommodates the suggestions and comments of peers. To Janet, talk is just talk, but classmates' ideas show up in her stories in both topic choice and content.

Dimensions and symbols

When young children create drawings and accompanying stories, they use a variety of devices to convey meaning. These devices include the dimensions of time and space as well as physical techniques such as movement and colour. Manuel, to show how much exertion his fisherman is expending, adds lines to depict perspiration dripping from his face. Jake draws lines leading from his plane to indicate the path of the bomb. Mitzi, perhaps taking a lead from the comics, adds a bubble to her picture to show a girl talking. Megan's addition of a pop-up dog to her circus story started a trend that was quickly borrowed by other children[3,4].

At times, children may unconsciously use time and space dimensions and symbols, but Amy, a Grade 1 student, showed a keen awareness of how these techniques supported her kite-flying story.

Researcher: How's your story coming Amy?
Amy: See my kite? It's flying. Do you know why it flying?
Researcher: No, why?
Amy: See the wind. *(Amy points to the smoke coming from a chimney on the house she drew. The smoke is heading in the same direction as the kite.)*
Researcher: Oh, so that's how I know the wind is blowing.
Amy: Yet, the wind is blowing really strong.

Colour also plays an important role in children's drawing, often supporting the total story, that is, both drawing and text. The sun is coloured a bright orange or yellow not simply because of its physical appearance in the real world but also because the author wants to show warmth and happiness. Manuel's snowman, also happy, is not white but yellow[4]. Hubbard[3] tells of Ming, a Grade 1 child, who gradually changed the colour of the car in her first published book to indicate that it was fading from age. Amy showed her awareness of how colour conveys meaning, albeit stereotypical meaning, in her "baby story".

Researcher *(Pointing to the picture.)*: Is that your neighbour's new baby?
Amy: Yep. *(Picking up a pink crayon.)* She's a girl.

Tangible aspects of traditional media

Although we know of no research that examines this issue, it is interesting to speculate about the impact of tangible aspects of traditional media on writing. Without making claims for kinesthetic styles of learning, one still may ask if there is a role for tangible tools in composing. A local artist told us she loved the feel of pastels in her hand: "They connect me with my work". Anthony Burgess[12], ever eloquent, spoke more directly to the role of tangible tools in his writing life:

> "As I write, an IBM word processor with daisywheel sits malevolently waiting for me in a customs shed. I am scared of making the transition from clattering Qwert Yuiop to his velvety successor, even though I am beginning to be warned that publishers will soon accept from the authors only floppy discs. I have not even made the hop from manual to electric typewriter. I do not like the low hum which says 'Get on with it, you're wasting power', and I do not like my hammering to be muffled. When you hear your own clatter, you know you are at work, as a blacksmith is. More, the rest of the household knows you are at work and does not suspect you of covertly devouring a *Playboy* centerfold" (pp. ii–xiii).

Is this attachment to the tools of art and composing a trait seen exclusively in professional artists and authors, or do children exhibit this characteristic as well? Consider this scene from the same New Hampshire Grade 1 described previously:

Rose: Janet, give me the pink one.
(Janet reaches into the large container, pickling up a thin pink crayon.)
Rose: No, no. My pink one.
(Janet puts the thin pink crayon back into the box and takes out a long, thick pink crayon. She hands the crayon to Rose.)
Janet: Thanks. *(Janet immediately begins work on her picture.)*

Neither child made an issue as to which pink crayon Rose would use, but clearly they shared an understanding about the need for a certain tool. The crayon was not just a pink crayon, it was "my pink one", even though it was provided by the school rather than the child. In an interview with Rose about the tools of drawing and writing, the researcher encountered a child who could not fathom his questions.

Researcher: Rose, why did you ask Janet for the special pink crayon?
Rose: What special crayon?
Researcher: You asked Janet to give you a special pink crayon, not the skinny pink one she gave you.
Rose: She did? *(long pause)* Yea?
Researcher: You seemed to want a special crayon.
Rose: I did? *(long pause)* What do you mean?

The conversation continued, but Rose never acknowledged any special attachment to her fat, pink crayon. However, many such incidents, where children clearly insisted on using certain tools in their drawing and writing, were evident during the observation period (Miller, unpublished case study). Perhaps young children share Burgess' requirement for tangible tools, but they may not possess his awareness of this need.

Ownership

"Write about what you know" is one of the dictums of good writing[13]. Originally a tenet of the professional writer, this notion now is becoming part of elementary school writing programmes. In many classrooms, children are no longer fed a steady diet of story starters, films without sound-tracks, and boxes filled with key words that must appear in a subsequent story. Instead, they write about topics related to their lives and interests, whether real or imaginary. Graves[7], in support of this idea, even went so far as to argue that children should choose approx. 80% of their own topics.

In the classrooms observed by Dyson and Hubbard[3,4], children wrote stories about their worlds, both real and imagined. In the real world, Graham drew and wrote about his swing accident; Kelly wrote about her birthday; Mitzi drafted a tale of her little brother while Regina portrayed herself as a brownie scout. Imaginary worlds produced stores of space, volcanoes, bubble cars, and sled dog stories. Of course, even so-called imaginary worlds relate to the real world of the child, and the mixing of the two worlds typically is seen in children's drawing and composing.

Conclusion

If we are to appreciate and nuture the symbol-weaving efforts of young children using new information technology, then we first must understand how they go about this process using traditional media in a formal school setting. Symbol-weaving is a complex process: to educators, revision and editing often appear to be the ultimate goal of writing; to children, prewriting activities such as talk can be as important as revision and editing. Variables as diverse as knowledge of the world, interaction with peers, understanding of the role art plays in composing, awareness of the stages of the writing, and children's familiarity with composing tools influence the total symbol-weaving process. Only with this global vision can we examine how new information technology may affect this process and how new conceptions of symbol-weaving may be imagined.

THE INFLUENCE OF NEW INFORMATION TECHNOLOGY

If one accepts the notion that drawing, talking, and composing are important, interlocking components in young children's symbol-weaving using established media, then an intriguing question emerges regarding the role of new information technology in this effort. Does technology enhance or detract from the interrelationship? To explore this question, we will examine the impact of new information technology using the lessons learned from children using traditional media as a focus for discussion. In recent years, technological innovations offered young authors the ability to insert art into their stories, revise and edit pieces as an integral aspect of the composing process, and publish pieces in a professional manner. However, the question raised above, related to the total symbol-weaving process, remain problematic.

Rather than refer to specific computer programs to highlight our discussion, we selected generic types of composing software currently used in schools. Specific programs may come and go, but the general types of programs depicted in our discussion tend to remain constant. Also, a program that exhibits a certain negative trait may be corrected in an updated version. Our goal is to raise issues related generally to the use of certain types of software in the symbol-weaving process.

Clip art and composing

Becky, working alone, moves the mouse to the animal collection in the clip art section of her computer program. "Shoot, there's no cat, only a dog. I don't have a dog. I have a cat—a girl cat", she complains aloud. Becky clicks on the dog, named Randy, reluctantly bringing him over to the picture and story on which she is working. "Stupid dog", she mutters. "Now I have to change my whole story". She moves down to the text and begins to rewrite her story to accommodate the unwanted male canine. However, Becky receives another shock as the program allows her only six lines of text. "My story isn't done", Becky wails. But the conspiracy isn't over. When Becky attempts to print her picture and text, she discovers the program has no print option.

The scene described here occurred when, several years ago, one of the authors of this article brought home a new computer program for his daughter to try out. Becky was accustomed to writing using traditional media as well as a word processor. This program appeared to offer her the best of both worlds, the opportunity to combine art and writing. But Becky was used to choosing her own topics, and both her cats—Tuffy and Miss Mew—appeared frequently in her stories. This program, using clip art, contained elephants, dogs, rabbits, birds, and myriad of other animals, but, for some strange reason, there were no cats. Ownership of the story was taken from the author and transferred to the program. Moreover, Becky was used to deciding the length of her stories, and, frequently, she composed two or even three pages of text to accompany the pictures. Finally, Becky was keenly aware of the final act of the writing process—publication. Some of her stories were put in hard covered books while others were placed on the refrigerator or bulletin board, but she knew that writing was meant to be shared with others.

What impact did these features, or the lack of features, have on Becky? She never used the program again, even though it sat on a shelf next to her computer. Becky had control over the decision to use or not use this program, but what about children in school where use of such a program may be dictated? If these children, like Becky, were accustomed to combining drawing and writing, selecting their own topics, working through the writing process in stages, and sharing their final products with others, they might find such technology detracting from rather than enhancing their efforts.

Fortunately, not all clip art programs suffer from the same lack of features as the one described here, but even the most recent software may restrict children's options in the drawing/composing process. It is difficult to imagine a data bank of clip art images so complete that it could accommodate the full range of young children's experiences, especially if children "write about what they know". Amy's story about her mom baking 36 pies for the Deerfield fair did not conform to the program's data bank, so who is in charge?

Clip art programs also raise questions about young children's artistic development, especially as it relates to illustrating their stories. Hubbard[3] showed that children use a variety of sophisticated methods for dealing with "flatland", a term she used for the two-dimensional world of the blank page. These techniques include organization of space, relationship of size, transparency, overlapping figures, mixed perspective, bird's-eye view, and the combination of pictures with words. And one must not forget that many young children use drawing and composing as integral aspects of the total story.

When we return to Newkirk's assertion[2] that young children may see the entire story contained in the picture, the role of clip art becomes even more obscure. Indeed, if one simply goes into a bank and selects an image, will children continue to see the picture and text as equals in the symbol-weaving process? Or will children revise their conceptions to fit the medium?

The description of clip art programs presented thus far depicts them as inhibiting young children's drawing and composing efforts. However, despite the limitations shown, there may be some use for this type of software, especially when ownership remains with the child. Image banks are increasing at a dramatic rate as computers become more powerful, thus enhancing the number of pictures available. Some recent programs permit the user to manipulate the image selected. Thus, a child may change the relative size of a house and the beanstalk to depict her Jack and the Beanstalk story. Further, newer clip art programs may overcome some of the past shortcomings, and, intriguingly, even offer new avenues for enhancing the art complementing children's stories. Some programs permit motion, real motion. In flatland, motion must be indicated by devices such multiple images. Of course, even if motion can be displayed onscreen, once the story is printed, these dynamics disappear. Finally, newer clip art programs frequently contain more sophisticated word processing programs, ones that allow the writer to work back and forth between text and picture.

Another value of clip art may relate to programs that permit children to produce newspapers, banners, cards, and signs. If Coe[5] and Newkirk[2] are correct about their contentions that young children prefer non-narrative to narrative forms of composing, these types of programs may provide an easy vehicle for accommodating this preference. In one Grade 3 class, where children had easy access to a print shop type program, and the freedom to compose, we observed far more non-narrative writing than found usually in a school setting.

Word processing

Perhaps no other aspect of technology has been praised as frequently as the potential of word processing to foster children's composing in schools. Word processing has been applauded because it holds the promise to relieve the tedium of rewriting, diminish the impact of handwriting, facilitate revision and editing, and allow fast and easy publication[14–17]. Such programs often are supplemented by computer-assisted writing packages that offer advice on spelling and grammar or even lead the writer through a series of activities designed to produce a certain type of writing (e.g. a character sketch or a haiku poem). Special programs for young children that simplify editing functions or offer large print are now common.

Clip art software stresses the image aspect of telling a story, with most programs offering only primitive text insertion or word processing capabilities. At the other end of the continuum, one finds word processing software designed especially for young children, but most of these programs provide few opportunities for the inclusion of both drawing and text. If clip art programs restrain ownership of children's stories because of their limited bank of images, word processing programs, designed for children, seem to restrict the symbiotic relationship of drawing and writing by focussing primarily on text.

Enamoured by the values of word processing, it is possible for teachers to ignore the relationship between drawing and composing. Even in situations where productive learning is occurring, the values of word processing, as related to text, may overcome one's perspective of the total creative symbol-weaving process. Phenix and Hannan[18] describe a Grade 1 student, Tim, who they believe overcame some of his writing difficulties because he wrote with a word processor rather than traditional media. The authors note that his computer-produced stories were longer and neater than those created using established media, and that he no longer had to be cajoled into writing. Two of Tim's stories, one on a new classmate (computer written) and one about the adventures of a walkie talkie (traditional media), are presented as examples. Without disputing the virtues of the computer-based piece, we found the walkie-talkie story equally interesting. The computer-based story was longer (approx. 102 words), but there was a great deal of repetition as the new classmate's name accounted for 22 of those words. On the other hand the walkie-talkie story was written in a comic strip form, a familiar artist's device that aided the flow of the tale. As well, the accompanying drawings lent personality and action to the adventures of the protagonist, a walkie-talkie.

In another example of contrasts, Cochran-Smith *et al.*[19] depict the differences between a 5-year old child's paper and pencil text and a word processed text on the same topic. Interestingly enough, by calling the first story a "paper and pencil" text, they ignore the accompanying drawing. Although the authors are cautious in their claims, they imply the word processed text is richer than the one produced by pencil and paper, but by neglecting the drawing, the authors may be missing a crucial aspect of the child's total story. Their analysis again asks one to return to Newkirk's[2] important question. From whose perspective do we analyze the composing process and subsequent products?

Just as clip art programs are beginning to accommodate the marriage of picture and text, and to permit more ownership, so too are word processing programs being adapted to permit the transfer of drawings and paintings to the text. Interestingly enough, in the real world of schools, some change is not emanating from modified word processing programs designed for young children; rather, it comes from teachers who are using more powerful and sophisticated programs, often designed for professsional authors, with children. True desk-top publishing programs may go a long way in providing the flexibility needed by young symbol-weavers.

While the movement of a drawing or computer-created painting into a text-based story seems to be an improvement over either a text-only word processing program or a clip art program that allows little or no text, neither type of software permits children to work in the same manner observed by Dyson or Hubbard[3,4]. Using traditional media, many children worked back and forth from drawing to text in a fluid manner. Only those children who prefer to work with one aspect of the total story-making process at a time will benefit by newer word processing programs, which permit the inclusion of drawings in text but still treat them as separate processes. Again, we may find children modifying their symbol-weaving, and their conceptions of meaning-making, because of the nature of technology. Would such a change be productive or non-productive?

Drawing and paint programs

Recently developed drawing and paint programs offer devices that, in the past, were available only to the professional graphics artist. Using this software, intricate pictures may be created that use combinations of patterns, geometric shapes, and lines in complex ways. Pictures within pictures can be generated, and some programs facilitate the editing of text, using various fonts and sizes or even spraypaint, within the drawing. Changes in pictures are facilitated with a handy eraser. Because the picture is created from scratch, much in the manner of the child beginning with a blank piece of paper, none of the obvious disadvantages of clip art is evident. Indeed, drawing and paint programs would appear to offer a perfect tool for your artists. However, as with word processing programs that permit the transfer of drawings into text, drawing and paint software may limit the ability of children to write and draw, moving easily between mediums.

Consider a program used by many children we observed during a 3-year longitudinal study of a Grade 1 classroom in a technology rich school[20]. The program was a marvel of technological achievement, far surpassing most available software. Children, using an icon environment, selected from a rich palette of colours, many types of brushes, patterns and stamps, and lines. Moreover, they accessed options such as "fill", "reverse background", "text insertion" and "add motion". Seemingly, this program represented the perfect technology for nurturing the drawing/writing relationship. Unfortunately, text could not be reselected for editing once the cursor had been moved and this small limitation created large problems for the children. Even though children tried to overcome this shortcoming with tricks such as blanking out the offending pasages with the background colour and then adding new letters on top, the cursor had to be positioned with such accuracy that the resulting attempts appeared as messy as handwritten copy unsuccessfully erased and rewritten. Many children experienced the same frustration on computer as they did on paper.

Colour: screens, printers and the symbol-weaving process

Susan, a Grade 1 student, working with the paint program described in the previous section, selects a wide brush. Dipping her brush into the indigo paint pot, Susan sweeps a line across the screen. "Oooh, come here", she calls to the researcher. "Come see my whale". Susan immediately initiates a conversation with the researcher about her forthcoming "whale story", but the text portion of the story never develops. Over the next 20 min, Susan makes a variety of choices concerning the colours, types of brushes, and patterns that will be included in her illustration, but text insertion is not one of her preferences. The result of this effort is a delightful picture showing Susan's blue whale frolicking in the ocean with several aquatic companions.

Because of his interest in Susan's original comment about the "whale story", as opposed to the "whale picture", the researcher initiated a conversation about the piece. However, Susan appeared to follow her own agenda as to whether or not the story should be published, as depicted in this exchange:

Researcher: Can you tell me your whale story?
(Susan launches into a rich, elaborate oral tale about her whale story, which is based loosely on a book she has been reading in the classroom.)
Researcher: Your story is really interesting Susan. Are you going to write it?
Susan: I don't have time.
Researcher: Well, we could save the picture and write the story later.
Susan: *(laconically)* Yea.
Researcher: Don't you want to write the story?
Susan: *(Ignoring the question)* My picture is really pretty, isn't it?

(Blackstock and Miller, to be published)

The researcher later brought the printout of Susan's whale story back to the classroom. However, Susan showed neither interest in the picture nor in producing the text to accompany it. She appeared to be too busy with her next composing effort.

Profuse colour clearly is a prominent aspect of children's drawing when traditional media is used, and the application of colour often complements the "telling of the tale"[3,4]. This same attraction to colour is evident in Susan's meaning-making efforts at the computer, but she demonstrates little interest in linking the picture with text. Why? One possibility is the nature of the printout, a stark black and white product that barely resembles the bold primary colours as well as the rich tints and tones of Susan's computer-produced painting. Another answer may be in Susan's conception of where the story lies. A third possibility lies in children's tendency to focus on the here and now. In our study, children seldom showed a great interest in past composing efforts even when prompted by an adult. Instead, they tended to focus on whatever task was at hand.

Notwithstanding children's focus on the task at hand, it is instructive to return to the issue of colourful pictures, as seen in paint programs, and the transfer of these pictures to black and white printers. To an adult eye, the difference is remarkable because the printer-produced picture bears little resemblance to the original. If, as Hubbard and Dyson[3,4] contend, colour traditionally is used by young children as an important vehicle to transmit detail, mood, culture, light, and feeling, and thus complement the textual aspect of their stories, then the reality of printer-produced black and white pictures may be an inhibiting factor in the story-making process. Of course, as colour printers become more common, these apparent barriers may be overcome.

Talk

The discussion concerning the potential impact of new technology on young children's drawing and composing efforts has, thus far, focussed on technology itself. However, as both Dyson[4] and Cochrane-Smith *et al.*[19] pointed out, the development of writing is influenced by many variables. Dyson showed that talk among children she studied created an impact on their topic choice, story content, and drawings. Cochrane-Smith *et al.* argue that another aspect of talk, that between teacher and child, is equally important in fostering the writing process, even in a technology-rich classroom.

Unlike the issues discussed previously, the quantity, quality, and nature of talk in the classroom is influenced heavily by the teacher. We have observed classrooms where there is only one computer, and throughout the day children are allocated a fixed amount of time to use the available technology. If the single computer is treated as a learning centre, and only one child at a time is permitted to use it, the facilitating influence of talk among children clearly would be absent. Even in technology-rich settings, we have observed situations where children are expected to work alone, and talk is discouraged. The amount of technology available does not seem as important as the teacher's vision of learning.

Conclusion

New information technology often is praised for its potential to help writers in the composing process, and some of these plaudits appear warranted. Technology may assist children in revising and editing, manipulating art, and in publication. Further, current software offers tools for symbol-weaving, such as air brushes, multiple fonts, and picture change options, that previously could be provided only through great effort and expense. Unfortunately, several factors cloud this positive view of technology's impact on young children's symbol-weaving. The first factor is the lack of integration in composing programs: many programs focus either on the creation and manipulation of text or on the creation and manipulation of art. Given our current understanding of how children work back and forth betwen the two mediums, some of these programs may detract from symbol-weaving rather than enhance it. Another factor is the discrepancy between screen product and print-out. A final factor relates to teacher's use of these programs: for the total meaning-making process to work, teachers must understand the role of variables such as talk, insuring a place for them as children compose.

TECHNOLOGY: NEW WAYS OF THINKING ABOUT THE RELATIONSHIP AMONG DRAWING, COMPOSING, AND TALK

The discussion thus far has described young children's traits in symbol-weaving and the effect new information technology may have on these endeavours. New information technology has been portrayed as either having an enhancing or detracting influence on children's drawing and composing efforts depending on how closely the technology mirrored endeavours using traditional media. But it may be that new information technology will permit us a new window on young children's story-making efforts. Consider three examples of new information technology that facilitate such thinking.

Hypermedia

As Burnett[21] points out, software such as HyperCard may be regarded as a form of data base or as a set of tools for designing. He sees HyperCard much as one might view a blank canvas, a medium ready for the creative touch of the artist, or artist/composer. But hypermedia add dimensions to the symbol-weaving process that may not exist in either traditional media or in software such as paint programs. The notion of a stack is different from the single canvas, and the opportunities this medium presents may offer children new ways of creating. And, as teachers and researchers, we may have to reconsider the fundamentals of children's symbol-weaving and our expectations of their abilities.

Hypermedia hold the potential to move one away from linear thinking. Where traditional forms of print such as books, greeting cards, and notes tend to be read from front to back, hypermedia encourage the user, or creator, to move about in a non-linear fashion within the medium. Young children, using hypermedia that permit the easy inclusion of clip art, drawing, painting, text, and music, may learn to think about symbol-weaving in more diverse manners. For example, vertical dimensions of meaning-making, as well as the horizontal, are possible. Indeed, simply adding the vertical dimension may not capture the full range of new conceptions of the symbol-weaving process one might develop from hypermedia.

One example of how hypermedia may provide new ways of thinking about the composing process is seen in a tool called Bubble Dialogue. Bubble Dialogue, created by O'Neill et al.[22], uses the familiar format of comic-strips to provide a symbol-weaving scaffold for young children. In a HyperCard environment, children are able to use graphics, sound, and text to create stories. Unlike traditional programs, where composing instruments must be consciously, and sometimes laboriously, selected from various sources, O'Neill et al. have provided immediate access to all requisite tools. The utensils of composing thus become invisible, much like traditional tools such as paper, crayons, and pencils when they are readily available and taken for granted by the composer. Equally important is the ease with which a young child may move about the story being composed, a feature that facilitates the important revising and editing components of the total symbol-weaving process.

Discis Books

Discis Books (Discis Knowledge Research, 45 Sheppard Ave. East, Suite 410, Toronto, Ontario, Canada M2N 5W9) are presented on CD-ROM using Apple Macintosh technology. These books are a radical departure from previous attempts to "put books on a disk". The books, representative of high quality children's literature, are reproduced using full page texts with accompanying high resolution colour illustrations. Exercising ownership over the book, a reader may page up and down using a mouse, click on illustrations for vocabulary, hear the human-recorded voice pronunciation of any word, listen to the story read aloud, or add music to complement the tale. Ownership of the reading process is placed in learner's hands through use of the available options. There are other features to this series, but suffice it to say that these books come as close to "real" books on a disk as any technology to date.

So what does this series have to do with young children's story-making? The answer lies in the engine that drives Discis Books. Although not presently available, one might consider how children's drawing/composing processes might change if they were given access to such a powerful tool. Currently, the engine may be too complex for their use; however, technology that begins as too complicated for young children has an astonishing propensity to become the norm over time. Just consider the nature of the word processing programs used today by young children vs those used 5 or 10 years ago. If young children had access to an engine that permitted them to illustrate, add reading help, label, compose text, and supplement their stories with music, how would these features change our notions about their symbol-weaving processes? Indeed, one sees here why the term symbol-weaving is such an appropriate term for children's meaning making as it would be inaccurate to call such efforts simply drawing and writing. Engines such as the one used in Discis Books offer a complete workshop where art, music, and composing may be combined in the symbol-weaving process.

Microworlds

Peter Whalley[23] has created an object-oriented control language for young children that offers fascinating opportunities for learning. When we observed a demonstration of his microworld, created by young children, we noted a small village that provided the environment for the train that is a part of this package. Although Whalley does not address the issue of symbol-weaving in his article, we saw labels, written signs, and other forms of print complementing the environment drawn by the children, who used traditional media. Interestingly enough, Whalley's microworld prompted the same type of non-narrative composing as seen in the Coe's study[5]. The potential for children to view this microworld as a natural place for symbol-weaving exists. Just as young children create written rules for games, cards, invitations, messages, shopping lists, and even traffic tickets as a natural aspect of their play, microworlds such as one described by Whalley may offer opportunities for combining technology and traditional media in unique ways.

CONCLUSION

This article has explored young children's symbol-weaving efforts from two perspectives. First, we examined how children use traditional media in their drawing and composing efforts. Next, using children's traits, preferences, and styles of drawing and writing with traditional media, we applied the lessons learned to new information technology as how it might influence these undertakings. Technology may enhance children's symbol-weaving efforts by facilitating the revision of both text and pictures, offering composing tools normally unavailable, and aiding in the professional production of final products. But in some instances, technology appears to detract from the symbol-weaving process. The difficulty children face in switching between drawing and writing on the computer is the most extreme example. We recognize the technical challenges of creating software that allows children to draw as they write; had the importance of the relationship between drawing and writing in young children's symbol-weaving been understood more fully by developers 10 years ago, however, we might be further ahead now than we are presently.

Although it is often admitted that the teacher is the key to success in any educational undertaking, in the face of the kind of limelight that technology tends to steal, it is well worth repeating this principle. The manner in which teachers select software, set up the learning environment, and guide children's use of the technology is an important variable in restraining or enhancing the symbol-weaving process. Moreover, it is the observant teacher who first will see the need to reformulate our notions of the symbol-weaving process in light of the influence of new information technology. But such reformulations are possible only if teachers have a sound understanding of young children's conceptions of symbol-weaving, and the manner in which children actually make meaning, using traditional media.

"We are on the brink of..." seems to be a phrase hackneyed in the realms of educational technology, in particular computing, but the educational applications of recent software seem particularly encouraging. Sophisticated software, such as Bubble Dialogue, based on the concept of hypermedia as well as newly developed microworlds may expand children's potential beyond current limits. Thus, new information technology may offer new ways of thinking about young children's symbol-weaving, both in terms of process and product.

Acknowledgement—Some of the examples presented in this article were taken from the Schools, Computers, and Learning Project in Kingston, Ontario. The authors acknowledge the support of The Ontario Ministry of Education in funding this project.

REFERENCES

1. Dyson A. H., Transitions and tensions: interrelationships between the drawing, talking, and dictating of young children. *Res. Teach. English.* **20**, 379–409 (1986).
2. Newkirk T., *More than Stories: the Range of Children's Writing*. Heinemann, Portsmouth, N.H. (1989).
3. Hubbard R., *Authors of Pictures, Draftsmen of Words*. Heinemann, Portsmouth, N.H. (1989).
4. Dyson A. H., *Multiple Worlds of Child Writers: Friends Learning to Write*. Teachers College Press, New York (1989).
5. Coe D., Emergent writing behaviour in young children: taking the task of writing to task. *Reading-Canada-Lecture* **6**, 186–204 (1988).
6. Calkins L. M., *The Art of Teaching Writing*. Heinemann, Portsmouth, N.H. (1986).
7. Graves D., *Writing: Teachers and Children at Work*. Heinemann, Portsmouth, N.H. (1983).

8. Bartelo D. M., The linkages across listening, speaking, reading, drawing, and writing. *Reading Improvement* **27**, 162–172 (1990).
9. Graves D., A case study observing the development of primary children's composing, spelling, and motor behaviours during the writing process. Final Report, NIE Grant No. G-78-0174, 1 September 1978–31 August 1981.
10. Dyson A. H., The emergence of visible language: interrelationships between drawing and early writing. *Visible Lang.* **16**, 360–381 (1982).
11. Dyson A. H., Unintentional helping in the primary grades: writing in the children's world. In *The Social Construction of Written Communication*. (Edited by Rafoth B. A. and Rubin D. L.). Ablex, Norwood, N.J. (1988).
12. Burgess A., *But do Blondes Prefer Gentlemen?* McGraw–Hill, New York (1986).
13. Murray D., *A Writer Teaches Writing*, 2nd edn. Houghton Mifflin, Boston (1985).
14. Chandler D., *Young Learners and the Microcomputer*. Open University Press, Milton Keynes (1984).
15. Miller L., Computers and writing: a theoretical perspective. *McGill J. Educ.* **20**, 19–28 (1985).
16. Balajthy E., *Microcomputers in Reading and Language Arts*. Prentice–Hall, Englewood Cliffs, N.J. (1986).
17. Strickland D. S., Feeley J. T. and Wepner S. B., *Using Computers in the Teaching of Reading*. Teachers College Press, New York (1987).
18. Phenix J. and Hannan E., Word processing in the grade one classroom. *Lang. Arts* **61**, 804–812 (1984).
19. Cochran-Smith M., Kahn J. and Paris C. L., Writing with a felicitous tool. *Theory Prac.* **29**, 235–245 (1990).
20. Blackstock J. and Miller L., Schools computers and learning project interim report No. 3 from the Kingston regional pilot test centre: yes, but are they learning anything? Ministry of Education, Ontario (1989).
21. Burnett J. D., Who's in the driver's seat? Technology, the arts and education. Paper presented at *CAL'91*, Lancaster (1991).
22. O'Neill B., McMahon H. and Cunningham D., Bubble dialogue within a language awareness support system. Paper presented at the *American Educational Research Association Conference*, Chicago, Ill. (1991).
23. Whalley P., HyperTechnic—a graphic object-oriented control language. In *Proceedings of the Seventh International Conference on Technology and Education* (Edited by Estes N., Heene J. and Leclercq D.), pp. 24–26. CEP Consultants, Brussels, Belgium (1990).

Computers Educ. Vol. 18, No. 1–3, pp. 223–229, 1992
Printed in Great Britain. All rights reserved

TOWARDS A METHODOLOGY FOR ANALYSING COLLABORATION AND LEARNING IN COMPUTER-BASED GROUPWORK

Stefano Pozzi, Celia Hoyles and Lulu Healy

Institute of Education, University of London, 20 Bedford Way, London WC1H 0AL, England

Abstract—This paper presents a methodology for researching effective groupwork within computer environments, developed as part of the Groupwork with Computers Project. The research involves eight groups of six mixed-sex, mixed-achievement pupils, undertaking research tasks using both the Logo programming language and a database program. Our aims are to identify factors influencing effective computer-based groupwork in terms of both group outcome and individual learning. Two groups working on a Logo-based task are described to focus attention on how our methods of analysis address the relationship between group processes, individual progress and group outcome, and some emerging considerations are discussed.

BACKGROUND

Educational research into groupwork and learning has adopted and developed a variety of approaches in order to address a range of factors and issues. Two approaches in particular have influenced our research: co-operative learning schemes and research into peer collaboration. Specifically designed learning schemes[1–3], based on the social-psychological theories of Deutsch[4], involve restructuring the learning environment to emphasise peer interaction in the context of cooperative goals rather than the individual or competitive goals of the traditional classroom. In general, studies indicate higher levels of achievement and social benefit for cooperative groups, compared to other groups or individuals. However, there is little description of the underlying processes which facilitate such benefits.

In contrast, research into peer collaboration attempts to provide a theoretical perspective of the process of learning within groups by giving an account on the role of language and discussion[5,6]. Further, the introduction of the computer into the groupwork provides a new context which, potentially at least, is different from the traditional one since the process of learning can be seen as mediated through interaction with the computer as well as any discussion with peers[7].

Given this complexity any methodology for analysing the processes underlying computer-based groupwork must, in our view, take into consideration the inter-relationship between the task, the computer and the communication between peers.

RESEARCH DESIGN AND DATA COLLECTION

The research described in this paper forms part of the "Groupwork with Computers" research project[8]*. Our aim is to identify factors influencing effective computer-based groupwork in the context of mathematics and programming—in terms of both individual learning and group outcome. Our methodology attempts to capture the relationship between the group processes, individual progress and group outcome.

The research takes place within seven classes from six schools. Eight experimental groups of six students (aged 9–12 years) have been selected—three girls and three boys from each of the achievement levels high (H), middle (M) and low (L), as assessed by their class teachers. Each group undertakes three research tasks, two involving Logo programming and one database work. During the research session the group is given one copy of the task and three computers are available for their use. A research session lasts about two and a half hours.

*Funded by the InTER programme of the Economic and Social Research Council 1989–1991, Grant No. 203252006.

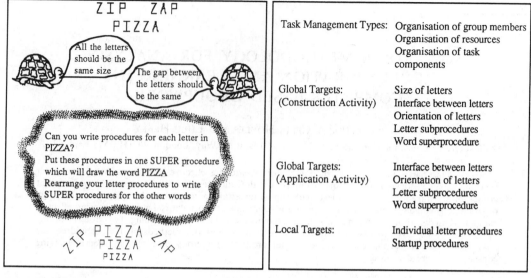

Fig. 1. The letters task.

The research tasks vary in terms of mathematical and programming content, but have a common underlying structure consisting of a construction activity and an application activity, each with an associated group outcome. The intention is that these group outcomes are appropriated by all group members. The tasks have been designed so that, to be successful in terms of group outcome, the following would have to be negotiated: Task Management—the organisation of people, task components and resources (including computers); Global Targets—the mathematical and programming ideas which underpin the group outcome; Local Targets—subcomponents of the task which can be legitimately allocated to subgroups.

Process data is collected through researcher notes, video recordings of the whole group and the screen output of one computer. During the administration of the research tasks the researchers do not intervene except in exceptional circumstances. Group outcomes are scored by reference to computer products and completed task sheets. Individual learning is measured by a series of pre, post and delayed post tests aimed at assessing some of the ideas on the basis of which the task has been constructed. The group is given a semi-structured interview after each task in which pupils are asked for their perception of the task, the group and individual learning. A further interview is conducted informally with the teacher in order to obtain background information about the group members, both individually and collectively, and the class.

WHAT HAPPENED

By providing an informal description of two groups from the same class on one task (the *Letters* task), followed by an outline of our methodology and preliminary analysis, we hope to give a flavour of how far our methodology goes in capturing the essence of the groups' approaches. The Logo-based *Letters* task is made up of the construction activity *Pizza* and the application activity *Zip Zap*. Figure 1 shows the task and associated management types, global and local targets. The tests associated with this task attempt to measure understanding of the programming ideas of procedure, modularity and subprocedure.

Group A

Group A was made up of Erica (L), Haley (M), Jenny (H), Steve (L), Guy (M) and Chris (H). The group had difficulty in getting started: Guy made some effort to get things going, but received no constructive response from the group. He suggested a move to the computers, but this was rejected by Steve, who argued that they should initially plan their work. This idea was taken up, and the group split into two distinct single-sex subgroups, who worked on separate group outcomes for the rest of the session.

Table 1. Scoring scheme for collaboration and involvement

Collaboration Scores

$$CS = \frac{\sum_{i=1}^{N} n_i}{N \times \text{group size}} \left(\frac{a}{b}, N \right)$$

for CS_m
n_i = No. of pupils party to task management episode i
N = total No. of task management episodes
a = No. of task management types addressed
b = total No. of task management types

for CS_g
n_i = No. of pupils party to global target episode i
N = Total No. of global target episodes
a = No. of global targets addressed
b = total No. of global targets

Involvement Scores

$$IS_m = \left(\frac{a}{N} \frac{c}{d} e \right)$$

a = No. of task management episodes in which pupil is involved
N = total No. of task management episodes
c = No. task management types in which pupil is involved
d = total No. of task management types

$$e = \frac{\text{No. of task management episodes in which pupil is active}}{\text{No. of task management episodes in which pupil is involved}} \times 100\%$$

$$IS_g = \left(\frac{a}{N} \frac{c}{d} e \right)$$

a = No. of global target episodes in which pupil is involved
N = total No. of global target episodes
c = No. of global targets in which pupil is involved
d = total No. of global targets

$$e = \frac{\text{No. of global target episodes in which pupil is active}}{\text{No. of global target episodes in which pupil is involved}} \times 100\%$$

$$IS_l = (f, g)$$

f = 0 if no local involvement
= 1 if no partial local involvement
= 2 if maximal local involvement

g = 0 if no active local involvement
= 1 if partial active local involvement
= 2 if maximal active local involvement

Table 2. Collaboration and group outcome scores (group A)

	Collaboration scores		Group outcome scores
	CS_m	CS_g	
Whole group	0.67 ($\frac{2}{3}$ 4)		
SG 1 (E, H, J) Construction		1 ($\frac{5}{5}$ 12)	30/30
Application		1 ($\frac{4}{4}$ 6)	17/19
SG 2 (S, G, C) Construction		1 ($\frac{3}{3}$ 3)	3/30
Application		N/A	0/19

Within the girls' subgroup (SG 1), Jenny took control of planning the letter procedures on paper, which were then copied by the other two. They discussed the letter size, but Jenny encoded* interface commands without discussing her strategies, even when Erica asked her to explain them. Haley on the other hand accepted Jenny's procedures without question. The other subgroup (SG 2) also only discussed letter size before Guy and Chris separately planned letter procedures. Steve copied Chris's work, although Chris was ambivalent about letting him do this, sometimes hiding his work. This led Steve to comment that they were "supposed to copy each other", indicating that there was some awareness that the group was expected to attempt the task together, but his suggestion was rejected.

SG 1 finished planning first and moved together to one computer. The girls carefully shared the roles of typing, dictating and monitoring screen output. However, as much as there were any problems to sort out, Jenny took over and suggested ways forward. She elaborated little, either changing the procedures herself or dictating changes for Haley or Erica to type. Haley was very quiet while Erica was more active. In particular she tried to maintain a degree of control over the keyboard, thus preventing Jenny from taking complete control. They managed to write a procedure to draw the word PIZZA, and went on to almost complete the word ZIP.

Guy went to a computer soon after the girls, having planned four letters. He had trouble with procedure syntax and received help from Chris. When Chris finished planning his letters, he and Steve joined Guy, although Steve wanted to work with Chris on the third computer. Guy's letters

*Formalised in the Logo language.

Table 3. Involvement scores (group A)

	IS_m		IS_g Construction	IS_g Application	IS_l
Erica (L)	$\left(\frac{2}{4}\frac{1}{3}\,50\%\right)$	SG 1	$\left(\frac{12}{12}\frac{5}{5}\,75\%\right)$	$\left(\frac{6}{6}\frac{4}{4}\,83\%\right)$	(2, 1)
		SG 2	0	0	
Haley (M)	$\left(\frac{2}{4}\frac{1}{3}\,50\%\right)$	SG 1	$\left(\frac{12}{12}\frac{5}{5}\,58\%\right)$	$\left(\frac{6}{6}\frac{4}{4}\,16\%\right)$	(2, 1)
		SG 2	0	0	
Jenny (H)	$\left(\frac{3}{4}\frac{2}{3}\,67\%\right)$	SG 1	$\left(\frac{12}{12}\frac{5}{5}\,100\%\right)$	$\left(\frac{6}{6}\frac{4}{4}\,100\%\right)$	(2, 2)
		SG 2	0	0	
Steve (L)	$\left(\frac{3}{4}\frac{2}{3}\,100\%\right)$	SG 1	0	0	(2, 1)
		SG 2	$\left(\frac{3}{3}\frac{3}{5}\,67\%\right)$	0	
Guy (M)	$\left(\frac{3}{4}\frac{2}{3}\,100\%\right)$	SG 1	0	0	(1, 1)
		SG 2	$\left(\frac{3}{3}\frac{3}{5}\,67\%\right)$	0	
Chris (H)	$\left(\frac{3}{4}\frac{2}{3}\,100\%\right)$	SG 1	0	0	(2, 2)
		SG 2	$\left(\frac{3}{3}\frac{3}{5}\,100\%\right)$	0	

were eventually abandoned in favour of Chris's. For the rest of the session, SG 2 flitted on and off task. When they were unhappy with their attempts, or someone in their subgroup commented on how well SG 1 were doing, the computer was reset and the group would start again. Chris made most attempts to bring the subgroup back on-task, either retyping his letters from paper or dictating to Steve to type. Guy made some constructive comments, but wandered away from the group on occasions. By the end of the session, SG 2 had only drawn P and I.

Group B

Group B was made up of Elly (L), Ann (M), Carla (H), Jim (L), David (M) and Tom (H). After the introduction, the group split into single-sex subgroups and went immediately to start work at the computers. Each subgroup worked on the letter P at a different computer, deciding on the letter size separately. After realising they were supposed to do the task together, David and Carla shared out the letters between the subgroups, with Tom and Ann recapping and making sure they understood what needed to be done. Carla initiated discussion about uniform letter size, while Tom brought up the issue of the size of gap between letters.

The girls went on to write the I and Z letter procedures—Elly typing, Carla dictating and Ann occasionally making suggestions. They tended to enter procedures directly into the editor without first trying them out in direct drive. Problems with their Z led to some discussion and argument between Ann and Carla over whether to use the PENERASE command or edit the procedure to debug their letter. This disagreement was left unresolved and Carla simply pursued her method—taking over the typing from Elly when any such debugging was necessary. David joined the girls' discussion of the length of the Z diagonal, which was eventually resolved by trial and error. He also asked them for the angles so the boys could do a similar Z. The girls extended the task by writing further letter procedures for other words as they waited for the boys to complete an A procedure.

Table 4. Individual learning scores (group A)

		Pre	Post	Delay			Pre	Post	Delay
Erica (L)	P	√√	√√	√√	Steve (L)	P	√	√	√
	M	√√	√√	√√		M	×	√	√
	S	×	×	×		S	×	×	×
Haley (M)	P	√√	√√	√√	Guy (M)	P	√√	√√	√√
	M	√√	√√	√√		M	×	√√	×
	S	×	×	×		S	×	×	×
Jenny (H)	P	√√	√√	√√	Chris (H)	P	√√	√√	√√
	M	√	×	√√		M	√√	√√	√√
	S	√	√√	√√		S	×	×	×

P, procedure; M, modularity; S, subprocedure; ×, no use; √, partial use; √√, full use.

Table 5. Collaboration and group outcome scores (group B)

	Collaboration scores		Group outcome scores
	CS_m	CS_g	
Whole group	0.83 ($\frac{2}{3}$ 7)		
Whole group Construction		0.66 ($\frac{5}{5}$ 20)	28/30
Application		NA	0/17

Table 6. Involvement scores (group B)

	IS_m	IS_g		IS_l
		Construction	Application	
Elly (L)	($\frac{4}{7}\frac{3}{3}$ 25%)	($\frac{7}{20}\frac{3}{5}$ 29%)	0	(2, 2)
Ann (M)	($\frac{5}{7}\frac{3}{3}$ 40%)	($\frac{17}{20}\frac{5}{5}$ 53%)	0	(2, 2)
Carla (H)	($\frac{6}{7}\frac{3}{3}$ 67%)	($\frac{17}{20}\frac{5}{5}$ 100%)	0	(2, 2)
Jim (L)	($\frac{6}{7}\frac{3}{3}$ 33%)	($\frac{13}{20}\frac{4}{5}$ 54%)	0	(2, 1)
David (M)	($\frac{7}{7}\frac{3}{3}$ 71%)	($\frac{15}{20}\frac{4}{5}$ 73%)	0	(2, 2)
Tom (H)	($\frac{7}{7}\frac{3}{3}$ 57%)	($\frac{10}{20}\frac{4}{5}$ 90%)	0	(2, 1)

In contrast to the girls, the boys planned their letters in direct drive before attempting to write procedures. Jim and David did all the typing, although Tom was involved in much of the discussion. When they had any problems, David would take control of encoding. He also typed when they were working in the editor. Their letter A ended up with a base width larger than the other letters. Ann and Carla joined the resulting discussion in which David wanted to improve the procedure to satisfy the group's decision about letter width. The rest of the group argued that the letter "would do", so David conceded, though he was far from happy.

Having completed the letter procedures, the group, with the exception of Elly, came together on one computer. Carla initially took control of encoding, with Ann, Jim and David making suggestions about how they could resolve the problem of interfacing the letters. The group then became fragmented, with Carla and Ann, and then David and Tom, going to other computers to pursue their own activities. Jim attempted to combine the letters himself, but to no avail. Carla took over again, drawing the attention of the other group members as she finally constructed a superprocedure to draw the word PIZZA.

ANALYSIS

We present here one part of our analysis which concerns the systematic data collection. The first level of this analysis begins with classifying the discussion and interaction of the group into a number of *episodes*—group interactions concerning task management, global and local targets. For each episode, the particular type of management decision or target is recorded, together with the pupils involved in the episode and the form of this involvement. At minimum, involvement means being party to an episode; simply attending to any discussion or interactions with a computer without necessarily contributing. This allows for the possibility that an individual can learn by observing what others do or say. The form of individual involvement in an episode is classified as either *active* or *non-active*: a pupil is *active* if she makes a contribution to any discussion or interaction with the computer, and *non-active* otherwise.

In order for comparisons to be made across tasks and across groups we aim to develop a *group profile*. At a base level this consists of group outcome scores, measures of collaboration on task management (CS_m) and global targets for both construction and application activities (CS_g), and the number and types of management and global targets addressed. To make comparisons across pupils and to assess the effect of the group and task on learning, we also plan to develop an *individual profile*. At the first level this consists of individual test scores and measures of involvement in task management, global target and local target episodes (IS_m, IS_g, IS_l). Table 1 shows the methods used for scoring collaboration and involvement.

Table 7. Individual learning scores (group B)

		Pre	Post	Delay			Pre	Post	Delay
Elly (L)	P	×	✓	✓	Jim (L)	P	✓✓	✓✓	✓
	M	×	×	×		M	✓✓	✓✓	×
	S	×	×	×		S	×	×	×
Ann (M)	P				David (M)	P	✓✓	✓✓	✓✓
	M	N/A	N/A	N/A		M	✓✓	×	✓✓
	S					S	×	×	×
Carla (H)	P	✓✓	✓✓	✓✓	Tom (H)	P	✓	✓✓	✓
	M	✓✓	✓✓	✓✓		M	×	✓✓	✓✓
	S	✓✓	✓✓	✓✓		S	×	×	×

P, procedure; M, modularity; S, subprocedure; ×, no use; ✓, partial use; ✓✓, full use.

Although the intention is that the whole group work on the global targets together, in cases where they split into subgroups to work on the task separately (e.g. group A), episodes on global targets are distinguished for each subgroup and independent collaboration and involvement scores are measured. Subgroup outcomes are also scored separately. Collaboration and involvement in management episodes is still measured across the six pupils as any subgroup management of limited resources has implications for the whole group.

RESULTS

Table 2 shows group A split into two single-sex subgroups, each of which were maximally collaborative on global targets. Collaboration on task management was restricted to four episodes, none of which involved organisation of task components. Despite obtaining identical collaboration scores, the subgroups achieved very different group outcomes. SG 1 achieved a high score for the construction and application activities working over a total of 18 global target episodes addressing all five targets. In contrast, SG 2 accomplished very little and only three global target episodes occurred.

From Table 3, involvement scores indicate that there was no intergroup communication on global targets. Boys were more actively involved in task management. High achieving pupils were actively involved in all the global target episodes within their subgroups, which was not the case with the other pupils.

With regard to individual learning, Table 4 shows that only the test scores of Jenny and Steve indicated improvement: Jenny improved with respect to her use of subprocedures and Steve improved in his use of modularity.

Table 5 shows group B worked together on a single outcome. There was less collaboration for global target episodes than for management episodes. They obtained a high group outcome for the construction activity in which they addressed all five global targets over 20 episodes, but they did not have time to address the application activity.

Table 6 indicates that high achieving pupils engaged more actively in the global target episodes in which they are involved. However, they were not necessarily involved in a high proportion of these target episodes.

Table 7 shows that Elly and Tom made some progress: Elly improved in her understanding of procedures and Tom improved with respect to his use of modularity.

Looking across the groups, group A was a multiple outcome group whereas group B worked on a single outcome, with collaboration on global targets being higher for each of the subgroups of group A (SG 1 and SG 2) than for group B. It is perhaps a consequence of group size that all the pupils in SG 1 and SG 2 were involved in all their global target episodes, given each subgroup stayed at the table or at one computer. In group B, interaction on global targets was unlikely to always involve all six members. In fact it here tended to occur within single sex clusters, with particular members managing cross-cluster communication. This may also partly explain the fact that although both group B and SG 1 addressed all the construction global targets, group B did so over 20 episodes, in contrast to 12 episodes for SG 1 of group A. Management episodes were also more numerous, with seven in group B as opposed to four in group A. Thus coordinating joint activity across six pupils required more activity and was more time consuming.

Both SG 1 and group B scored highly for the construction activity, but unlike SG 1, group B did not have time to attempt the application activity. However, group outcome for both activities cannot be simply attributed to the group size as SG 2 accomplished little.

Comparing individual profiles across groups, individual learning scores show no clear relationship with the level of individual involvement, active or otherwise. High achieving pupils tend to show high active involvement in the global target episodes in which they are involved—although they are not always involved in a high proportion of the global target episodes.

CONCLUSIONS

The analysis presented here necessarily simplifies group dynamics in order that comparisons can be made at some level about the processes and interactions. Within this framework we are able to describe a range of group behaviour—single or multiple outcome groups, the level of involvement on different aspects of the task and the level of collaboration on these aspects. It should be noted that this quantitative analysis forms just one part of the development of group and individual profiles which will also incorporate qualitative descriptors. In particular, the following themes are emerging as potentially important.

Forms of involvement and computer interaction

Developing an understanding of the relationship between involvement and learning suggests a need to examine the *form* of individual involvement in more detail than the account given here (see also Healy *et al.* [7] and Webb[10]). The *active/non-active* distinction goes some way in distinguishing between active engagement with peers or the computer and simply attending to such interactions. However, consideration of the patterns of involvement need to address the nature of child–child and child–computer interaction. We have begun to characterise a number of forms of involvement; encoding, planning and typing being three such forms. The extent to which such activities are shared or become roles exclusive to particular pupils may be significant in both group and individual progress. The nature of discussion within the group may also be affected by different patterns of sharing these activities. This in turn may influence the extent to which the targets of a task are communicated to and taken on board by different group members.

Background data

There is a need to give an account of the ethos of the school and the normal pattern of work in the classroom in order to provide a more complete picture of what groups bring to a computer-based task. Together with a description of the group members' past groupwork and computer experience, friendship, status, etc. this may provide some explanatory variables as to why groups work in the way observed. As Salomon and Globerson[9] point out, groups who know each other may yield different results from short experiments involving individuals who are unfamiliar with each other. The inter- and intra-personal variables within a group sharing a common school, classroom and group experience may therefore have a major influence on the dynamics which has to be considered. It also seems important to provide a view of the group members' perception of the task, the group dynamics and their individual learning. We are collecting such data through interviews with class teachers and groups, and hope to be able to synthesise these accounts with our group and individual profiles to give a more rounded characterisation of the functioning of the groupwork observed.

REFERENCES

1. Slavin R., *Co-operative Learning*. Longman, New York (1983).
2. Aronson E., Bridgman D. L. and Gellner R., The effects of a co-operative classroom structure on student behaviour and attitude. In *Social Psychology of Education; Theory and Practice* (Edited by Bar-Tal D. and Saze A.). Wiley, New York (1978).
3. Johnson D. and Johnson R., *Joining Together: Group Theory and Group Skills*. Prentice–Hall, Englewood Cliffs, N.J. (1975).
4. Deutsch M., A theory of competition and cooperation. *Human Relat.* **2**, 129–151 (1949).
5. Perret-Clermont A. N., *Social Interaction and Cognitive Development in Children*. Academic Press, London (1980).
6. Forman E. and Cazden C., Exploring Vygotskian perspectives in education: the cognitive value of peer interaction. In *Culture, Communication and Cognition; Vygotskian Perspectives* (Edited by Wertsch J.), pp. 323–347. CUP, Cambridge (1985).
7. Healy L., Hoyles C. and Sutherland R., *The Role of Peer Group Discussion in Mathematical Environments*. Institute of Education, University of London (1990).
8. Eraut M. and Hoyles C., Groupwork with computers. *J. Comput. Assist. Learn.* **5**, 12–24 (1988).
9. Salomon G. and Globerson T., When teams do not function the way they ought to. *Int. J. educ. Res.* **13**(6), 89–99 (1989).
10. Webb N., Microcomputer learning in small groups: cognitive requirements and group processes. *J. educ. Psychol.* **76**, 1076–1088 (1984).

Computers Educ. Vol. 18, No. 1–3, pp. 231–241, 1992
Printed in Great Britain. All rights reserved

DEVELOPING COMPUTER USE DURING A PRIMARY POST-GRADUATE CERTIFICATE OF EDUCATION COURSE

Susan E. Sanders

Coleg y Brifysgol Abertawe, Adran Addysg Hendrefoilan, Abertawe SA2 7NB, Wales

Abstract—A group of 42 students was followed through their Post-Graduate Certificate in Education (P.G.C.E.) course and their first year of teaching. They were assessed on their skills and confidence prior to the course, the course they received (constrained by lack of resources including staffing), the way they used computers on two teaching practices. They assessed their own confidence and needs at the end of their course, and their use of computers during their first term of teaching. Initially, only 10% had never used computers but 29% reported no confidence in personal computer use and 60% no confidence in using them as a teacher. There was a marked lack of practical skills. 29% could not load a program, 29% could not use a program that had been loaded and only 12% could connect hardware together. The use of computers varied over both teaching practices but the overwhelming use in both was of wordprocessing packages with the use of databases increasing during the second practice. 37% of respondents did not use computers on the first practice and 26% on the second. 47% reported an increase of confidence after the second practice. During the first term of teaching 87% of respondents used computers more often than on teaching practice. 94% reported that the college course had helped them with 44% mentioning (unsolicited) a gain in confidence. The paper concludes with a discussion of the practicalities of delivering the Council for the Accreditation of Teacher Education (C.A.T.E.) criteria to P.G.C.E. students training to teach in the primary phase.

INTRODUCTION

Prior to the start of the academic year 1989/90 we were faced with a dilemma. Forty-two students of varying ages and backgrounds had enrolled for an Upper Primary (age 7–11) Post-graduate Certificate of Education (P.G.C.E.) course. The staffing of the course was, to a great extent, on a part-time basis, there being only one full-time tutor whose sole teaching load involved this course. Available equipment (shared with all other courses run in the department) consisted in the main of Acorn BBC B and Master machines in a range of conditions. For the most part there were seven or eight working machines at any one time. These models predominated in the local schools. There was no designated Information Technology (IT) lecturer in the Department although there was a chemist who took overall responsibility for this area on the Secondary P.G.C.E. course and who had run a short course for the smaller Primary P.G.C.E. course in previous years. Commitments did not allow this arrangement to continue.

The Primary phase tutor had limited expertise with computers and very little with this type of machine. When asked at interview if she would be willing to undertake this element of the course she had replied with a categorical "No!".

As with any Primary P.G.C.E. course there was limited time available and although there was an excellent Local Education Authority (L.E.A.) support service that could have been bought in to deliver a course, this would have to have been presented between 18:00 and 20:00 h and would obviously have incurred additional costs. The challenge was to provide a course that would develop both confidence and skills appropriate to 42 students' individual needs in a limited amount of time (about 8 h) using seven machines and one tutor with limited expertise.

METHODOLOGY

The first task was to ascertain the confidence and skills of the students. This was done by means of an open-ended questionnaire (Appendix A) administered by the deviser so that any misunderstandings or queries could be dealt with during completion. The questionnaire was devised by the full-time primary tutor, who had experience with this technique, in consultation with an experienced researcher.

Apart from explanations of the meaning of technical terms such as hardware and software, there was no difficulty experienced by the subjects. Use in a subsequent year with another group of students (96 in number) has confirmed this. Two aspects have to be considered when examining the data from this survey. Firstly, if the students were to be grouped in any way they had to be identifiable despite Oppenheim[1, p.37], who points out the advantages of using anonymous questionnaires.

> "... respondents are usually given ... a guarantee of anonymity. This is often crucial in obtaining frank and revealing responses; indeed, anonymous mail questionnaires often produce a greater proportion of socially unacceptable responses than face to face interviews".

A very high level of return, from 100% for the first questionnaire to 88% for the third, was achieved. Oppenheim reports that even in studies of interested groups, 80% return on postal questionnaires is rarely exceeded. A straw poll gave the impression that the high return was due to the fact that the students felt they were benefiting from the questionnaires in terms of course provision.

Secondly, there was a complex relationship between the researcher who was also the main deliverer of the course, the only full-time tutor, and personal tutor to one-third of the students and respondents which is too complex to explore here but which would be informed by discussions of both the case study paradigm and the action research paradigm.

Because the lack of anonymity and the complex relationship could be perceived as weaknesses and because the number of subjects is relatively small, results are simply presented as percentages of total returns. No attempt has been made to determine statistical significance between responses. Similarly as the gender split was 5 male to 37 female no attempt has been made to explore responses in terms of gender differences.

Given the very open nature of the questions the coding was devised in all instances after the responses had been examined.

INITIAL QUESTIONNAIRE FINDINGS

The students' skills and competences prior to the course

- Only 4 students (10%) had never used computers. This is a lower figure than the 15% reported by Summers[2] with a group of secondary P.G.C.E. students.
- 29% of the students had used computers in school, 48% had used computers at university (compared with 46% in Summers' sample), 31% had used computers in employment and 38% had used computers at home. 29% of students indicated that they felt no confidence at all in personal computer use.
- A much larger percentage (60%) felt they had no confidence at all as teachers using computers. This was explained by the students in terms of lack of knowledge as to how teachers might use computers and lack of general confidence about teaching, neither of which are surprising given that the questionnaire was administered within the first month of the course.
- 29% of students could not load a program and 26% felt that they would not be able to use a program that had been loaded. Only 19% knew how to connect up hardware, e.g., keyboard, monitor, printer. This gives some indication of their experience at university and the use they had come across in employment.

One student reported

> "Some guy stood up and talked about statistics and then we were meant to use the computer to analyse some results. These had already been fed into the computer and every thing was set up. I don't think they were computers like this.
> I think they were all linked to some big computer somewhere else". (*Presumably this student was using a mainframe terminal.*) "I didn't know what to do, or what was going on. I didn't like to ask as everyone else seemed to be getting on. It put me off

Table 1. Initial skills and competencies. Data is presented as percent of all respondents

Never used computers	10
Used computers in school	29
Used computers at university	48
Used computers in employment	31
Used computers at home	38
Could not load a program	29
Could not use a program if loaded	26
Could not connect up hardware	81
No confidence in personal use	29
No confidence in use as teacher	60

computers completely. They seem to be mysterious things that you can either use or not. I obviously can't".

Only six of the students had access to a computer at home and five of these were women living in family environments. This represents 14% compared with 17% in Summers'[2] sample.

Information gleaned informally from students from the 1988/89 cohort had indicated that they had been overwhelmed by the large amount of software they had seen and the speed at which some deliverers had introduced skills. They had also found the timing of some parts of the course unacceptable (18:00 to 20:00 plus a 30 min coach journey to the venue). They had also felt that they could not really relate what they were learning to how they might use it in the primary classroom.

This information together with individual students' descriptions of their own skills and confidence provided the basis for course planning.

THE COURSE OUTLINE

Given this information it was decided to concentrate on contextualising any skill development by starting the course with a video of good practice. It was decided to use the M.E.P. video *Talking Point* (1984) although it was 5 years old, as the practice illustrated in the film in the main reflected local use. Four practical sessions of 90 min were set up. The students were split into two groups which were then organised into threes for working at one machine. The three comprised of one student who claimed to have good competency, one who had some competency and one who had no competency or who claimed to lack confidence. The lack of technical support, standard of skill of the tutor and group size (21) led to a decision that this mode of grouping would be beneficial. No student later reported any major difficulty with this arrangement.

Although one male student said he was aware of "hogging the computer" the other students in the group reported

"it was very useful to have A in our group as he knew what he was doing and we did not waste ages finding simple things like 'shift and break' out by trial and error".

One session was arranged after hours at the local L.E.A. Computer Centre to show a wide range of software and hardware, such as mouse, concept keyboard and floor turtle, that was not at that time readily available in the department. The four practical sessions concentrated on one use per session. One on wordprocessing and desktop publishing, one on databases, one on adventure games and simulations and one on a software review. Logo use was provided within the mathematics method sessions. It was intended to introduce the students to the software most commonly in use in local schools so that they would have the confidence to use it on teaching practice. The wordprocessing package available at the time was not the one at use in most local schools, which was PENDOWN, however it did become available later in the year.

The students used EDWORD which was available on chips on all machines although some difficulties were encountered due to different versions being in use. The assistance of a part-time colleague was invaluable and once again emphasised the need for good support. However, the fact that the tutor had to go and seek help was perceived as a good role model

> "S always seems to know what she's doing in the rest of the course so it made me feel confident when she had to go off and find J or C or H to help her. I thought well you can't know everything so you just ask".

In fact the tutor found this aspect very stressful and was relieved much later in the year to find this had been the students' perception. She had thought it made her look disorganised and not fit to lead the course. It is not possible to fully explore lessons about modelling practice here. Some students indicated that if tutors appear to be perfect they can make the students feel so inadequate that the task of becoming a competent teacher can appear to be too large. The database used was GRASS the one in use in local schools. Students used an existing database before constructing their own.

Six or so adventure games/simulations were available and the students chose to work on one that caught their interest. For the software review the students had free choice but were asked to record their impressions of any piece of software on a database. It had been intended to introduce desktop publishing as part of the wordprocessing session but time constraints made it more viable to include it in this session.

QUESTIONNAIRE 2: USE OF COMPUTERS ON THE FIRST TEACHING PRACTICE AND REACTIONS TO THE COURSE

At the end of the 6-week programme students undertook their first assessed teaching practice in local primary schools. At the end of the practice students were asked a series of questions (Appendix B) related to the introductory course and their first teaching practice. This time there was a 95% response rate. 92% of respondents reported an increase in confidence at a personal level and 63% reported an increase in confidence in computer use as a teacher. Seven students reported that they did not feel that they could respond as they had not had any opportunities to try incorporating the use of computers during teaching practice.

In all 37% did not use computers on teaching practice. This compares with the some 30% of the students in Dunn and Ridgeway's survey[3] of primary B.Ed students who did not use computers on teaching practice. Both these figures are higher than the reported 6% use by new teachers in the 1988 H.M.I. survey[4]. Reported reasons for non-use by the P.G.C.E. students were: the class teacher was afraid of the computer (4), the computer was not available (3), the computer was unreliable (2), the computer was not usually used in the classroom (1), there was no computer in the school (1).

Reasons given by Dunn and Ridgeway's subjects were personal lack of confidence/or expertise, lack of suitable software, absence of hardware and a belief that computer-based activities were not appropriate for the class. Of the students that did use computers the overwhelming use was of wordprocessing packages (usually PENDOWN), used in 16 instances, then desktop publishing (6) databases (3), short mathematics programs (3), and "games" (3). Individuals reported use of a music program/art program/adventure game or special needs program. These cases reflect student/teacher interest or termly theme or topic. One student had used the computer to "prepare discs for the teacher". The scale of these uses are similar to those reported in Dunn and Ridgeway with wordprocessing being the overwhelming use.

Support from teaching practice schools was encouraging with 83% of student users receiving help whenever they asked. Two reported that they did not like to ask for help. Reasons given for not using the computer included:

> "My teacher did not like using the computer and discouraged me from using it with the children".
> "The computer in our classroom was said to be 'unreliable' and I was advised that I might be making things difficult for myself if I had problems as a result. The computer 'expert' in the school had just left and no-one else seemed very keen. I took the advice—I had enough on my plate as it was!"

Table 2. Developing use of computers. Data is presented as percent of all respondents

	1st Teaching practice	2nd Teaching practice	1st Term of teaching
Response rate	95	88	43
School support	83	81	67
Computer use	63	74	75
Wordprocessor use	40	51	78
Desk top publisher use	15	19	17
Database use	7.5	27	22
Short maths program use	7.5	11	5
Games use	7.5	3	Nil
Other uses	10	11	11

"There seemed to be no interest in my 'Area' (open plan building) by either of two teachers, so I felt ill-placed to push for computers".

"Although my class teacher did attend a short computer course she was not competent/confident in the use of computers. Hours were spent attempting to set up activities with the children which often came to nothing".

QUESTIONNAIRE 2: FOLLOW UP PROVISION

Students were also asked to indicate what support they felt they needed during the rest of the P.G.C.E. year and also what professional development they would be looking for during their probationary year. Responses to the latter are reported later, allied to students' responses after the first term of teaching. The two main opportunities that students were looking for during the college-based section of the course were related to software. For the school-based part of the course it was access to computers.

COURSE PROVISION

To facilitate familiarisation and practice with software during the college-based section of the course three strategies were tried. Firstly, students were offered a tutor-supported option of four 90 min sessions the content of which was to be negotiated. Secondly, students were encouraged to try software in non-contact time using an Acorn BBC B machine in one of the teaching rooms. Thirdly, methods' tutors were asked to include the use of software in sessions wherever appropriate.

Those students who had not used computers on their first teaching practice were encouraged to make every effort to do so on the second.

Interest in the option was fairly high even though it was timetabled against sports options such as rugby football coaching! It was intended to repeat the option in the summer term to allow all students indicating an interest to take part but a change in staff duties did not allow this to happen. These sessions were well attended and students indicated approval for the style which once again included using a database to record programs reviewed.

A small number of students took advantage of the availability of the Acorn BBC B machine outside contact hours. Reasons for not doing so were mainly to do with the intensity of the course and lack of help if "things went wrong".

"You could sit there for hours trying to get a program to work when perhaps all you needed to know was one or two simple commands".

The need for easily-accessible well-informed advice, not necessarily from an academic, was mentioned informally by many students.

The third strategy had mixed success. Two tutors (English and Mathematics) gave computer use some prominence but the staffing of much of the course did not allow for much development.

Use of computers during the second teaching practice was once again patchy due to a variety of factors including commitment of teaching practice supervisor, accessibility and the class teacher factor.

QUESTIONNAIRE 3: USE OF COMPUTERS ON THE
SECOND TEACHING PRACTICE

Students were questioned (Appendix C) again along similar lines. This time there was an 88% response. 74% of respondents had used computers on teaching practice and of these 7 (19%) had not used them on the first practice. Reasons for using this time were varied: access (3) classroom organisation more conducive (1), teacher keen (1) more appropriate to work going on in class (1) hardware more reliable (1).

Once again wordprocessing dominated use with 19 cases. Use of database increased to 10 and desktop publishing to 7 and short mathematics programs to 4. Once again individuals used games, art and music programs. This time a science package and the Doomsday Project were used.

Reasons for not using the computer were lack of availability (4) no appropriate use (2), not allowed to use the program/computer (2).

> "The teacher of J1(Y3) would not allow the computer to be brought through her room".
> "The program I had hoped to use is used each summer by the third years (Y5) and so my fourth year class (Y6) had already used it".

Sometimes the class teacher led that part of the work (2) or there was no relevant software (1). 47% of students using computers on their second teaching practice said they had been much more confident. Once again support from the schools was encouraging with 81% students receiving help whenever they asked. Only one student reported that she was seldom given help. Once again students indicated a need to become more familiar with software during the rest of the college-based element of the course and strategies two and three were employed again.

QUESTIONNAIRES 2 AND 3: FUTURE PERCEIVED NEEDS

At two stages during their P.G.C.E. year students were asked what professional development they would be looking for during their probationary year.

After the first teaching practice the overwhelming desire was for an increase in confidence (11 responses) although no student indicated how they thought this could be achieved. However after the second teaching practice, when 12 students reported a desire for increase in confidence, 8 students were looking for a course and 6 students were hoping to increase their experience with computer use.

QUESTIONNAIRE 4: USE OF COMPUTERS DURING THE PROBATIONARY YEAR
AND SUPPORT PROVIDED

All students were written to in February 1991 requesting information about their first term in teaching (Appendix D). 20 of those that replied were teaching, 18 in the primary sector. The responses from those teaching in the primary sector are detailed below. 75% had used computers in the classroom during their first term. Once again wordprocessing dominated use (14 responses). Databases were used in four instances, desktop publishing in three instances and short mathematics programs, LOGO and a music program were used in one instance each.

Frequency of use varied widely, from every day (4), three times a week (1), once a week (2), three times per child per term (1).

87% of students were using the computers more than they had on teaching practice. Four students reported that they were using computers less due to breakdown of equipment or teaching an age range for which no suitable software was available. Two students had limited use due to supply work.

No clear reason for the increase in use emerged. Reasons given included more access (6), school attitude (3) more confident about classroom management (2), given responsibility for information technology (1), had more support from teachers (1), had more time (1), more confident about software (1), had been on night school course and one student reported "I had no-one watching me!". School support was slightly lower at 67%. One student reported in very positive terms on a lunchtime workshop organised by one of her colleagues.

L.E.A. support varied, 9 probationary teachers had already received an in-service training course, one had been accepted for a course next term, one had been unable to attend a course due to a clash with a L.E.A. organised probationers' meeting, two had worked with an advisory teacher.

Three students were working as supply teachers (common practice in this L.E.A.) and in-service training was not always available. Seventeen students reported that their college course had helped them, various ways were mentioned including raising of confidence (8) software related (9). When asked how they thought the course could be improved the strong emphasis was on more of the same. Other suggestions included a special project.

DISCUSSION

In 1989 the new C.A.T.E. requirements included the following statements related to the use of Information Technology.

"All courses should contain compulsory and clearly identifiable elements which enable students to make effective use of information technology in the classroom and provide a sound basis for their subsequent development in the field. They should be trained to:

(a) make confident personal use of a range of software packages and IT devices appropriate to their subject specialism and age ranges
(b) review critically the relevance of software packages and IT devices to their subject specialism and age range and judge the potential value of these classroom use
(c) make constructive use of IT in their teaching and in particular to prepare and put into effect schemes of work incorporating appropriate uses of IT and
(d) evaluate the ways in which the uses of IT changes the nature of teaching and learning"[5, p. ix].

This paper has looked at computer use and it is that aspect of IT that this discussion addresses. Dunn and Ridgeway[3] feel that these requirements are long overdue. There is no doubt that there should be specific mention of IT within such a document and as expectations for experienced teachers these aims are laudable. However they are more appropriate as long term goals for initial teacher training. My contention is that, given the lack of confidence and skills with computers alone on the part of a large number of P.G.C.E. students training to teach in the primary phase the task as it presents itself is too great to be undertaken successfully in the current 36-week course. A continuation of the 1989/90 survey with the current 1990/91 intake of some 96 students training to teach either in the early years (3–8) or upper primary (7–11) ranges gives little indication of any significant improvement in students' stated skills or confidence.

There is little flexibility within the course timings to provide extensive taught elements but anecdotal evidence exists from all three cohorts of primary P.G.C.E. students, that supported self-directed study is a preferred mode. This relies on student motivation and resources both human, hardware and software with obvious financial implications.

Student motivation may be affected by pressure of work, confidence and perception of the need for such skills as indicated by the current practice observed in school and modelled in the course.

Constructive use of IT and evaluation of the ways that the nature of teaching and learning can be changed requires experience and I would question whether or not the majority of students achieve such experience within a 36-week P.G.C.E. (primary) course. Students reported an increased use of computers when they felt more confident about their classroom management and organisation. For some this may come sooner, for some much later. Although most schools had computers available, access to students on teaching practice was not always possible. With the development of a profile of competences that will provide a basis for negotiation with schools for teaching practice placement it is hoped to make progress in providing optimum potential for students to explore both computer and wider IT use. This too will no doubt take time. Not all experienced teachers feel competent to support a student in this field.

Critical review of software requires both extensive personal use as well as experience of use with pupils of a range of ages, interests and abilities.

Before any judgement of potential classroom value of a particular piece of software can be made experience of similar software and similar classrooms has to be considered. How realistic is it too expect such a breadth of experience to be available after a 36-week course? It is possible to start to develop these skills particularly through a collaborative model with students sharing limited experiences. I have no argument with (a) as a minimum requirement for all students completing a P.G.C.E. course and reports from the 1989/90 cohort would indicate that this was successfully achieved in the majority of cases within the constraints outlined at the start of this paper.

POSTSCRIPT

In 1990/91 different constraints exist and a modified version of the same provision has been presented. Once again the students' progress is being reported. With a larger full-time course team it has been increasingly possible to use computers as part of method sessions and to encourage students to increase use on teaching practice due to the increased expertise of tutors in this respect. Teaching practice schools are also more aware of supervisors and students interests in the use of computers.

The appointment of a designated Information Technology Lecturer to the Department as well as a large investment in equipment during the year enhances the opportunities for subsequent years. More competent students have generously set up self help networks and cross-phase tutor supported curriculum development is beginning. It is hoped that within the next 2 years the use of computers will be fully integrated into the P.G.C.E. course allowing students whatever their needs to proceed towards the long term goals as suggested by the C.A.T.E. regulations.

This longitudinal study will continue to inform course developments. How representative this case study is of the situation in P.G.C.E. Primary Courses is not known. It is offered as a starting point for discussion.

REFERENCES

1. Oppenheim A. N., *Questionnaire Design and Attitude Measurement.* Heinemann, London (1966).
2. Summers M., Starting teacher training—new P.G.C.E. students and computers. *Br. educ. Res. J.* **16,** 79–87 (1990).
3. Dunn S. and Ridgeway J., Computer use during primary school teaching practice: a survey. *J. computer Assist. Learn.* **6,** 7–17 (1990).
4. H. M. I., *The New Teacher in School.* HMSO, London (1988).
5. D. E. S., *Future Arrangements for the Accreditation of Courses of Initial Teacher Training.* HMSO, London (1989).

APPENDIX A

INFORMATION TECHNOLOGY QUESTIONNAIRE

Name ....

1. Have you ever used a computer?
   at school ....
   at university ....
   in employment ....
   at home (including games) ....
   other ....
   If no go to 4.
   If yes briefly detail type etc. and then continue ....
   ....

2. Can you
   load a program ....
   use a program that has been loaded ....
   write a program ....
   connect up a keyboard/monitor/printer ....
3. How confident are you about using
   hardware ....

   software ....

4. Do you have access to a computer at home? ....
   Type ....

5. How confident do you feel about using a computer?
   personally ....
   ....
   as a teacher ....
   ....

6. Any other relevant information ....

APPENDIX B

PRIMARY IT QUESTIONNAIRE 2

Name ....

May I assure you that all your responses will be dealt with complete confidence and any writing on this subject by me will contain no references to individuals or schools.

1. Did the Introductory IT course increase or decrease your confidence
   Give reasons as appropriate.
   (a) at a personal level ....
   ....
   (b) as a teacher ....
   ....

2. If you worked in a mixed gender group would you have preferred to have worked in a male/female only group?
   If yes please give reasons.
   ....
   ....

3. Did you use computers during your first school practice? ....
   If yes describe type of work and frequency (also model) ....
   ....
   If no briefly outline reasons ....
   ....

4. How much support did you receive in your teaching practice school?
   (a) whenever I asked ....
   (b) occasionally ....
   (c) seldom ....
   (d) help refused ....
   (e) no competent person available ....
   (f) I did not like to ask for help because ....
   (g) other (please specify) ....

5. What further support do you feel is necessary during the rest of your P.G.C.E. year?
   (a) college-based ....
   ....
   (b) school-based ....
   ....

6. What professional development will you be looking for during your probationary year in the area of Information Technology?
   ....
   ....

Thank you very much for your help.
....

APPENDIX C

INFORMATION TECHNOLOGY QUESTIONNAIRE 3

Name ....

May I personally assure you that all your responses will be dealt with complete confidence and any writing on this subject by me will contain no references to individuals or schools.

1. Did you use computers during your second school practice? ....
   If you did not use them on the first practice explain briefly why you did on the second.
   ....
   ....
   ....
   If yes describe type of work and frequency (also model) ....
   ....
   ....

If no briefly outline reasons ....
....
....

How did your use on the second practice differ from your use on the first practice (in terms of confidence, competency, style etc.)?
....
....
....
....

2. How much support did you receive in your teaching practice school?
    (a) whenever I asked ....
    (b) occasionally ....
    (c) seldom ....
    (d) help refused ....
    (e) no competent person available ....
    (f) I did not like to ask for help because ....
    (g) other (please specify)
3. What futher support do you feel is necessary during the rest of your P.G.C.E. year?
    (a) college-based ....
         ....
         ....
    (b) school-based ....
         ....
         ....

4. What professional development will you be looking for during your probationary year in the area of Information Technology?
    ....
    ....

If there is any other comment you wish to make please note it here.
....

Thank you very much for your help.
If you would be willing to give me about half an hour of your time on two or three occasions during the rest of this year and complete a questionnaire in the Summer of 1991 please indicate below.
....

APPENDIX D

INFORMATION TECHNOLOGY QUESTIONNAIRE 4

Name ....

May I personally assure you that all your responses will be dealt with complete confidence and any writing on this subject by me will contain no references to individuals or schools.
1. Did you to use Information Technology during your first term of teaching? ....
    If yes describe type of work and frequency (also model) ....
    ....

    If no briefly outline reasons ....
    ....

2. Is this more or less than you did during your teaching practices last year? ....
    If yes briefly outline reasons ....
    ....

    If no briefly outline reasons ....
    ....

3. How much support did you receive in your school?
    (a) whenever I asked ....
    (b) occasionally ....
    (c) seldom ....
    (d) help refused ....
    (e) no competent person available ....
    (f) I did not like to ask for help because ....
    (g) other (please specify) ....
4. How much support has been available from the L.E.A., e.g. Advisory teachers, courses etc? Please give details ......
    ....
    ....

    If you have not been able to take advantage of this support please explain why ....
    ....
    ....

5. In what ways has your college course helped you in your use of Information Technology? ....
....
....
If you could turn back the clock what would you have changed about the Information Technology input to the course? ....
....
....

Thank you very much for your help.

Computers Educ. Vol. 18, No. 1-3, pp. 243-250, 1992
Printed in Great Britain. All rights reserved

0360-1315/92 $5.00 + 0.00

TECHNOLOGY AND MUSIC: AN INTERTWINING DANCE

Rena Upitis

Faculty of Education, Queen's University, Kingston, Ontario, Canada K7L 3N6

Abstract—In this paper, ways in which new information technology (e.g. computers, synthesisers and hypermedia) offer educators the opportunity to revise music teaching are discussed. These include emphasizing the creation of original works over performance, and finding ways to use music and its associated technology so that the teaching of "traditional subjects" is also enhanced. These changes in music teaching are considered in light of a specific teaching and research setting, where children were observed as they composed music, using computers, traditional materials and movement to create mixed media presentations. An analysis of this setting indicates the importance of (1) providing opportunities to manipulate raw materials, (2) learning through social interaction, (3) treating technology as a new tool in relation to old crafts and (4) creating activities where subjects are naturally integrated. It is argued that such an approach will lead to a deeper understanding of both music and the supporting technology.

INTRODUCTION

One of the most interesting outcomes of introducing new technology to traditional music teaching settings is that educators are thereby frequently jarred into thinking differently about the nature of music and music teaching. In particular, introducing synthesisers and computers to school music programs often results in teachers thinking about the role of performance and reproduction of other people's works vs the creation of original works. Also, the role of music in relation to other curriculum subjects is highlighted with the emergence of new technology. Finally, many educators are drawn into discussions of what makes technology "good", or in a more general way, what makes some tools of the trade more useful than others, and in what settings such tools might best be used. In this paper, an attempt will be made to consider each of these issues in such a way as to emphasise the interdependence of all of the above-named factors: the teachers and their expectations of their students, the relationships amongst various disciplines or subjects, features of the learning environment, and tools and technology employed in creatively exploring a subject domain—in this case, music. As such, this paper is primarily a position paper rather than a report on research. To illustrate the approach taken, however, an example of an environment where computers are used as music composition tools is described in the latter portion of the paper.

Music technology

In describing and thinking about the technological tools of music, or any other discipline for that matter, it is important to remember that all old technology—like the piano—was once new technology. As such, they all once had a special place as new developments, and were met both with enthusiasm and skepticism, as are the new tools of this century. Some new tools endure, some do not. But what makes some tools last so that they become integral to a discipline?

Often new tools are invented because there is a need to do a faster job—it is much quicker to produce a score by computer than by laborious copying by hand. Sometimes new tools enable the composer to create effects with timbre that could not be produced before, forming new instruments in the process. But there are also times when the old tools, like pencil, manuscript paper and piano, are best. While in recent years the most significant new tools for music improvisation and composition have been computer-based, these new music tools, and the digitized instruments that go along with them, do not and should not replace the old. Each has its own strengths and constraints.

I am indebted to many colleagues and students for supporting the Dungeon, and for the numerous discussions which have enriched my thinking and helped me see familiar things in new ways. In particular, I thank Hugh Allen, Mark Danby, Bill Egnatoff, Bill Higginson, Larry Miller, John Olson and Gary Rasberry of the Faculty of Education at Queen's University and Seymour Papert and Aaron Falbel of the Massachusetts Institute of Technology.

Which tools, both computer-based and otherwise, are good tools? There are two features which I find myself considering when choosing tools for myself and for children: flexibility and an aesthetic dimension.

Good tools are flexible. By flexible, I mean that the tool should have many possible uses, both imagined and unimagined. For this reason, music software that is intended solely for the purpose of drilling elements of music theory, has limited use as a tool. The opposite is true of what might is often called open-ended or creative software—software that allows the user to play with a motif, experiment with different arrangements for acoustic instruments, or compose a new piece of music.

Flexibility also means that one is unlikely to outgrow the tools. A woodworker will never outgrow the need for a plane. Nor do I ever expect to outgrow the need for a piano, even though I also have a synthesiser and computer, both of which I use a great deal. Computer software and computer-based instruments simply allow us to expand our collection of useful tools. While the woodworker does not outgrow the need for a plane, he or she may well accumulate new tools—adding a special drill or sabre saw to the collection of useful tools.

Another feature of good tools is that they have an aesthetic quality that makes them pleasurable to use. Good tools are not merely useful objects, they are aesthetically pleasing objects. I far prefer my Heintzman grand piano to the old clunky 1920s bright orange upright I once owned. It is not only because the sounds are richer on the grand, although that is aesthetic reason enough. It is simply because there is more pleasure in playing an instrument that looks and feels beautiful.

So too, should computer tools offer aesthetic appeal. Computers can be inviting, so that experimenting seems natural. This is especially important in music, for many people, even children, do not view music as something for experimentation. Computers, on the other hand, are often regarded as "something to mess around with" and can therefore offer the opportunity to begin exploring sound and form, almost through the back door. The same is true for synthesisers. I have lost count of the number of times where I have observed those who are slightly timid of music walk straight to the synthesiser, walking by, around, or away from a piano that is in the same room. An example of an environment where this kind of observation has been made repeatedly is given later in this paper. Because we are allowed to make mistakes with computers and their relatives like synthesisers, computers offer a way for people to begin engaging in those processes that enrich their musicianship, processes that may well later be transferred to more traditional instruments and settings.

Computers can also be used to increase the range of sounds that can be produced by the user, especially if the computer is linked to a synthesiser or some other instrument through a MIDI (Musical Instrument Digital Interface). Sound, after all, is central to all of this, and any tool that offers opportunities to create new opportunities for playing with sound goes a long way towards enhancing the music experience. By sound, I do not mean only instrument sounds—I also mean all of those special effects sounds—ice blocks, stars, a dentist's drill, and the sound of someone knocking at the door. And finally, there is indisputable excitement experienced by people when they see their compositions presented in an elegantly printed form. Just like children are thrilled when their books are printed, published and with wallpaper cover bindings, placed in the library, so too do we all thrill to seeing our compositions in print. An excerpt of a 10-yr-old child's composition produced in this way is given in Fig. 1.

What can be learned by using computer music tools?

(1) Multiple representations. One of the important features of creative arts environments is that of providing ways for participants to make more than one representation of an idea or object. In using computer software to aid in music composition, the notational forms used by children can be both enhanced and limited. Most software programs provide a single pre-determined notational system, often standard music notation [e.g. the *Deluxe Music Construction Set* (for the Apple, Commodore, etc.)]. A few exceptions such as *MusicLand* (for Apple and ICON, from the Ministry of Education of Ontario), *Concertware* (for Macintosh, from Great Wave Software in California) and *LogoMusic* (for Apple, from Terrapin) use modified systems. *MusicLand* and the Music Player application of *Concertware* use rectangles to depict duration, where the length of the rectangle is directly proportional to the duration of the note. *LogoMusic* uses numbers and lists to show pitch and duration—another non-standard form. Regardless of the choice of notation, however, when

Underwater World

For Flute, Clarinet, and Piano -- Full Score

Fig. 1. An excerpt from a child's composition produced on a Macintosh computer music writing system.

using a piece of software, the child is immediately confronted with the dynamic interaction between the notation on the screen and the sounds he or she hears. Much is to be learned through this confrontation. For it is through the process of relating one's own system of understanding to another's that knowledge grows. Ideally, a child should be given the opportunity to compare his or her notation with notations used by other children, by adults, and in computer programs as well.

Using computers also makes it possible to mix music with text and pictures, both still and moving, thereby opening up the possibilities for other kinds of multiple representations. Consider, for example, a few routes that a child can take with a piece of music he or she has played on a synthesiser connected to the computer through a MIDI interface. He or she can manipulate the notation on the screen using the mouse, or through the synthesiser, revising the music until ready to produce a "final" copy. But the piece of music may also be as a "paint" file, allowing the child to add illustrations and text to his or her piece through an application like MacPaint on the Macintosh. The child may in fact combine any number of representations and ideas, linking music with graphics, text and movement. The music can be performed by the computer or on other instruments, and the computer can be made to perform conditionally and predictably in a way that live performers may not.

(2) Pattern and form. A second issue which arises in using computers as composition tools is that of the importance of pattern and form. In every composition, there is usually pattern and an overall form. Children naturally write music with pattern, using devices that have been employed by composers across cultures and time. Consequently, it is very important that teachers draw attention to pattern and various devices used to create pattern, such as repetition, retrograde, inversion, diminution, augmentation and transposition. This should be the case with and without computers. The use of these devices can be enhanced by using one of the many computer programs allowing such manipulations. Here the computer often does a better job than other tools. It is relatively easy for a child to take a short motif, say of four or five notes, and play it upside-down (inversion) or even backwards (retrograde) on a simple acoustic instrument. It is much more difficult to play the same motif upside-down and backwards, at least without some trial and frustration. The computer can be made to perform such a manipulation with ease, and of course, any other combination of manipulations the child may desire.

It is possible that the immediacy of computer notations also makes it easier for children to grasp a larger sense of form. It is difficult to hear form as one is playing the piano or an Orff instrument, as so much needs to be retained in aural memory to do so. On the other hand, it is quite a different thing when one can see form by watching patterns emerge and relating them to one another as a graphic score is created on the screen while a piece is played.

(3) The process of composition. In the preceding discussion, I considered some of the processes of composition that children engage as they use computer tools, such as manipulating motifs to generate patterns. There are many other processes. An important one is that of revision.

Teachers are now much more aware of the importance of revision in children's prose—revision in the truest sense, as opposed to mere re-copying. Computers can play an extremely useful role in sweetening the editing process to produce a handsome and well articulated final product[1]. The same can and should occur with children's music compositions. It is not easy to revise compositions of prose or of music by hand. It is much easier to do so with computer editors. Just as children are more likely to revise their prose with a word processor, they are more likely to revise their compositions with a music editor. Even better, many music programs incorporate editing features with the others already described, so that children can not only edit, but make manipulations and see the dynamic changes in graphic notations that accompany the changing sounds. Sometimes it is the promise of seeing their own work in a final printed form that provides the impetus for children to learn to read standard notation if they have not cared to before. This is often the case if the child has crafted a piece on a digitised instrument which the software has translated into standard notation.

Perhaps the most important issue related to process is that by having both adult and child composers using the same computer tools, children come to understand that the composition process is similar for adult and child, and for professional and amateur. Further, the active searching for sound and pattern, and constant revision-making on the computer, serves to remove much of the mystique which, in the past, has separated composers from mere performers. I have also observed that once children regard themselves as composers for computer-based instruments, they begin to see that they can compose for traditional acoustic instruments as well[2–4].

Moving back and forth between new and traditional instruments, and seeing oneself as a composer in relation to other composers, are both related to a third realisation: that process and product are part of an infinite chain. In the past, children have tended to assume that published works are somehow finished, whether story books or printed music. However, when they enter the process of composition, they begin to see products as evolving rather than established entities.

The learning environment: an example

Many of the notions developed in the present paper arise from observations made over the past few years in an Arts Playground, where participants, both adults and children, have been encouraged to create original works using both new tools and traditional materials. The Arts Playground or the "Dungeon", as it was named by some of the children involved in its creation, is located in the basement of the Faculty of Education at Queen's University in Kingston, Ontario, Canada. The Dungeon was intended to provide an environment where local children and teachers could work alongside one another in exploring arts materials and media. While some of the materials and activities in the Dungeon are clearly associated with a particular discipline (e.g. the synthesisers and music software are related to music, while the paints and paper are related to visual arts), others are not (e.g. making an animation film, while art related, also incorporates mathematics, movement, and sound). Even those tools and materials that are more obviously linked to a single discipline, like the synthesiser, are nevertheless used in mixed media creations (e.g. using the synthesiser to produce special effects for a puppet show). As a result, traditional subject boundaries bend and break.

The Dungeon was also meant to be used as an alternate practicum setting for students in the Bachelor of Education program. Since it was created, however, the Dungeon has become much more than an alternate practicum setting and a place for local students and teachers to frequent. Within a few years, the Dungeon has attracted considerable demand—by the local schools, as expected, but also by distant schools, arts festivals, local artists, and as a setting for teaching music and visual arts courses, and courses on technology and education, both at the undergraduate and graduate levels. Graduate students have carried out research projects in the Dungeon. Administrators from local, neighbouring and distant boards have visited the Dungeon with the view to creating a similar environment in their own boards. By word of mouth, news of the Dungeon has spread far beyond what was initially anticipated. Why?

At first glance, there is little that might be deemed as extraordinary in the Dungeon. In fact, in many ways, it looks much like a crafts room—initially one is aware of the large work tables, and of the shelves cluttered with boxes and containers full of bits of wood, fabric scraps, newspapers, bottle caps, paper and egg carton. But on looking around, one sees that there are also rhythm instruments, a guitar, an Apple IIe and two Macintosh computers, Lego/LOGO and a Yamaha synthesiser. There is an old square grand piano, and near it, a large trunk overflowing with costumes. In a corner hangs a giant's head, large enough (5 feet tall) to crawl inside to manipulate the eyes and mouth. There are also many tools—hammers, screwdrivers, a soldering gun, saws and the like. None of these tools are unique in themselves. Nor is there an overabundance of technology in evidence. What is unique, however, is the combination of these tools, and moreover, that the tools are used in ways that the participants choose to use them—participants as young as 4 years of age, right through to adulthood. What follows is a brief description of a day in the Dungeon with a full class of children and their teacher. Of all of the uses of the Dungeon, this one is the most analogous to the school situation, at least in terms of numbers of children and teacher:student ratio, and the number of computers likely to be available in a classroom setting (three or fewer).

When a class full of children and their teacher arrive for a day in the Dungeon, they are given only a few brief instructions before their day begins. Introductions are made (usually a university student is there to help out, and possibly a parent volunteer), places where materials can be found are pointed out, and a few examples of works might be shown (e.g. a pair of paper earrings or a plaster mask). The children are then invited to find something to do. They are not assigned to groups, nor are time limits placed on how long they can stay with one activity. Children and adults immediately disperse to one activity or another. It is almost uncanny to see, every time, that the children able to choose whatever they would like to do, without conflict or incident. Teachers have often commented that they find it surprising that there are rarely disagreements regarding the use of materials and tools, pointing out that in their classrooms, given the choice, many more children would flock to the computers and synthesiser, and argue about fair computer time. Perhaps it is because it is because all of the activities and materials are somehow on equal footing, and that time is not limited as it typically is in a classroom environment, that children see the computer and other enticing technology in a different way. Over the course of the day, some children try many activities, spending less than 30 min at each. Others may spend the entire day engaged in one undertaking. Throughout the day, a moment is taken here or there to share something someone has created, either with a few others who happen to be close at hand, or with the entire group.

While the children are working, the adults (teachers and researchers) are similarly engaged. Rather than teaching, they too are creating Lego/LOGO artifacts, paper jewellery, computer graphics, music improvisations and compositions. As indicated earlier, there are no boundaries in terms of these creations. Thus, a child may make a plaster mask in the early morning, use it with other children as part of a dramatic improvisation later in the morning, and then, along with yet another group of children, write a script for a short play on the computer later in the afternoon, making use of the earlier improvisatory material, and perhaps incorporating the other children's musical improvisations as well. Similarly, a child who has spent considerable time making a helicopter out of Lego may later use it as part of an animated film. In this environment, children and adults learn from each other, and help each other, not in a contrived way, but in a way demanded by the creation of the work at hand. People use materials and tools to enrich their creations. Conversations are peppered with moments of concentrated silence. People eat when they are hungry—and at the end of the day, the Dungeon is cleaned up and everyone gathers up their completed creations to take home.

Features of the Dungeon as a learning environment

While many have observed over the past few years that "good things happen in the Dungeon", there are, predictably, numerous levels at which the good things that happen can be examined. For instance, some have commented on the quality of the products created by the children, showing how simple materials are combined in unique ways with new technology (McRae, pers. commun.). Others, particularly classroom teachers, comment on the absence of discipline problems when children spend time in the Dungeon. Still others have been drawn to the richness of the language used by children involved in drama and music improvisations. What features of this environment contribute to its richness?

What follows is a description of features seen as critical this type of learning environment, generated by a group of graduate student researchers who had spent a 6 week period participating in Dungeon explorations. In making these observations, the researchers did not comment on specific tools or technology, for they argued, the technology and tools would continue to change, but the features which allow for the smooth integration of new tools were more likely to remain fixed. Therefore, the work was guided with the view that new technology would continue to come and go, but that children and environments should be equipped not only to deal with rapid change but to take advantage of it. There were eight features identified. They range in character from the kinds of learning expected of children, to features of the physical environment. The descriptions below were reached by consensus, after many hours of discussion. They are presented in no particular order.

(1) An emphasis on methods. Many have stressed that it is important for children learn to make sense of the world so that they can deal with the new situations they are likely to encounter. This comes in part, one suspects, because of the rapid growth of information technology and with it the realisation that one can no longer hope to teach facts, but rather ways, so that new information can be integrated with the old. Of the various ways of making sense, the following were identified as being most important, and all possible in the learning environment described in the present paper: problem solving, reflection, patterning, questioning, developing a love for the earth, creating and re-creating, reading, making investigations, linking aesthetics with function and making transformations of objects and ideas. Cooperation was also regarded as a critical kind of learning. The researchers defined cooperation as including the ability to adapt and change, to see and communicate different points of view, to respect others, and to learn to resolve conflicts. Finally, "love of self" was seen as a central kind of learning. By this, is meant the importance of developing confidence in one's abilities, becoming self-motivated, experiencing success and developing self-respect.

(2) Nurturing atmosphere. In order that the kinds of learning identified above might take place, the atmosphere must be an inviting one. By inviting, this meant not only physically attracting, but a place where questioning is encouraged, where it is appropriate to take intellectual risks, where there is safety in physical, social and intellectual terms, and where there are opportunities for talk, sharing and discussion. Again, all of these things are embedded in the Dungeon as a learning environment.

(3) Ownership. In order for participants to feel "ownership" in a learning environment, and therefore, arguably, in their own learning, personal choice must be encouraged, activities and materials should be such that any student can find success on his or her own terms, negotiation of activities should be possible, and people should be encouraged to work together.

(4) Physically inviting. To be inviting physically, an environment needs comfortable meeting and working areas, ample space for unexpected needs, and many open-ended materials both in terms

of raw materials like paper, wood, plastic, paint, and in terms of sophisticated tools like computer programs which allow the child to build and create (e.g. Lego/LOGO, graphics programs, music composition programs). Further, these tools and materials need not, and perhaps should not, be differentiated. That is, if all of the tools are presented on an equal footing, rather than drawing attention to computer tools, children will be more likely to search for the tool as needed whether that tool is a xylophone or computer composition program. This kind of environment is not unlike many kindergarten and primary classrooms. We are suggesting that some of the same physical features be extended to environments for older learners as well.

(5) Integrated activities. The activities of the environment should be such that different learning styles can be accommodated, that ways of linking subjects are provided, rather than being subject bound (e.g. linking mathematics, design, computer programming and sound in a Lego/LOGO creation), that the activities are learner-directed, and that activities are presented which speak to our innate desire to create. Many teachers already do this by organising their curricula by theme, and the Dungeon environment is an extension of this notion in that there is an expectation that original works will be created as well.

(6) Teacher as "learned friend". Adults in a creative arts environment learn along with children, and are thereby active participants and models of the kind of learning that can take place. In so doing, they show themselves to be open and receptive to new ideas, ideas that they can then incorporate in their own explorations and learning. The term "learned friend" is used, because in this role, teachers are in some sense learning colleagues with the children, and as such, friends. They also, however, possess knowledge that the children have not yet acquired—hence, the term "learned". For when teachers are learning alongside the children, they should be learning at their own level, not the kind of "learning" where the teacher pretends to discover something along with the children (e.g. "let's discover" game) where the teacher obviously already knows what is to be discovered by the children.

(7) Allow children to create structures for learning. Children can create their own structures for learning by their choices of materials, the time spent on any given undertaking, and the people they choose to work with. Further structuring on the part of the children may occur through the activities themselves, where the skeletal structure is provided by the teacher, but the children give life to the structure with their own content. An example of a music activity like this would be limiting the number of elements (e.g. only four notes on the piano or synthesiser) while allowing any kind of operation on the elements (e.g. you can do anything you like with the four notes [3]).

(8) Multiple representations/modalities. In order for children to learn in a style that suits them best, and to recognise links amongst different representations, modalities and subjects, tasks should allow people to use multiple ways of interacting with the material, both intellectually and physically, so that people can make sense of things visually, aurally, kinesthetically, and so on. Recall that in the previous section, where specific attributes of technological tools are discussed, the possibility of using technology to present notation through multiple representations was addressed.

The teachers

Thus far, my comments and observations have emphasised the children's reactions to the Dungeon, researchers' interpretations of their work, and features of the learning environment that make possible the kinds of interactions and learning reported. But what of teachers' reactions? How does the teacher, as a learned friend or in some other role (e.g. researcher, explorer, composer, participant), fit into an environment where subjects are integrated and technology is used to help produce original works? I would like to return now to the first two issues outlined at the beginning of the paper, namely (1) performance vs creation, and (2) the role of music in relation to other curriculum areas.

It is obvious to most teachers that the Dungeon is not a place where music performance is emphasised. Rather, children are primarily involved in creating their own music—improvisations on the synthesiser and traditional instruments, soundscapes, accompaniments for dramatic improvisations and compositions. This emphasis on creation is in stark contrast to most school music programs, where performance of other people's work forms the core of the program[5, 6].

This can be in the form of choirs, instrumental groups, or a mixture of the two, but in all of those cases, children are involved in reproducing the works of others, rather than in creating their own.

The notion of having children actively engaged in improvisation and creation can be threatening to many teachers. Countless times, I have heard teachers say that they cannot have children composing if they themselves are not composers. While it would take much more time to address this argument than is possible in the present context, suffice it to say that by using computers as composition tools as outlined above, it is much easier for teachers to accept the idea of children as composers and nurture the process.

When children are involved in composition, this does not mean that performance is neglected or eliminated. Rather, different kinds of performance become important. Often children have the need to perform their works informally, trying out their latest on the nearest available audience. But also, there is still a place for performing the works of others alongside the works of children. In this way, their performance and appreciation of other composers is heightened.

The second issue, namely that of the music in relation to other disciplines, has already been dealt with in the present paper through a number of different contexts. In approaching the teaching of music through composition, other original works, and technology, one is already breaking traditional boundaries. In environments like the Dungeon, where subjects are not taught *per se*, but rather, activities are introduced and materials and tools are provided, subjects are not seen as separate from one another, but inseparable. I am not, however, advocating the total integration of subjects at all times. As Whitehead[7] observed, in the building of knowledge, there should be an endless cycle of specialisation and integration. Whitehead actually identifies three ways of interacting with the material in this cycle; romanticism (a form of integration), precision (what I call specialisation), and generalisation (another form of integration). By introducing music through technology and traditional materials as described in the present paper, a rich context for integration can be achieved, integration which is often missing as subject teaching becomes more and more specialised.

CONCLUSION

It is my belief that in looking at the effects of technology on children's participation in and understanding of music, it is critical to consider far more than just the technology. The technology does not stand alone. Rather, there is a endlessly changing dance between teachers, students, the subject matter, the technology and the environment. Some parameters for considering this intertwining dance have been provided in the present paper. In the kind of environment provided by the Dungeon, where technology is part of a seamless and changing whole of materials, ideas and tools, I believe that children are much more likely to concentrate on creating and learning about music and other related subjects, than on the tools that aid in such creations. By using technology as an integral tool in the kind of learning environment described in this paper, I am sure that participants in such an environment will emerge with a deeper understanding of both music and technology, and the interdependent relationship between them.

Acknowledgement—The research reported here was supported in part by financial assistance from the School of Graduate Studies and Research, Queen's University, Kingston, Ontario, Canada.

REFERENCES

1. Miller L., Computers and writing: a theoretical perspective. *McGill J. educ.* **20**, 19–28 (1985).
2. Upitis R., The craft of composition: helping children create music with computer tools. *Psychomusicology* **8**, 151–162 (1989).
3. Upitis R., *This Too is Music*. Heinemann, Portsmouth, New Hampshire (1990).
4. Upitis R., *Can I Play You My Song?: The Compositions and Invented Notations of Children*. Heinemann, Portsmouth, New Hampshire. In press.
5. Borstad J., But I've been pouring sounds all day: an ethnographic study of music composition by young children. Unpublished Master's Thesis, Faculty of Education, Queen's University, Kingston, Ontario (1990).
6. Wilson J., Implications of the Pillsbury foundation school of Santa Barbara in perspective. *Council Res. Music Educ.* **68**, 13–25 (1981).
7. Whitehead A. N., *The Aims of Education*. Macmillan, New York (1929).

Computers Educ. Vol. 18, No. 1–3, pp. 251–257, 1992
Printed in Great Britain

0360-1315/92 $5.00 + 0.00
Pergamon Press plc

THE ALTERNATIVE CONFERENCE:
AN EVALUATION OF CAL91

MURRAY SAUNDERS and JOYCE BISSET

Centre for the Study of Education and Training, Lancaster University, Cartmel College, Bailrigg,
Lancaster LA1 4YL, England

Abstract—The paper analyses the responses to two evaluation instruments used to assess the experience of participants in CAL91. The evaluation was particularly concerned to chart how some innovations in symposia organisation were received by participants. Arguing that CAL91 was attempting to change the culture of the experience, the paper demonstrates the difficulties in preparing people for these changes in advance. The conventional expectations of a substantial proportion of participants were challenged by the introduction of a more participative and negotiated framework for action. Paradoxically, this more organic structure required significantly more organisational control than in the conventional case. The paper concludes with some general observations about planning events with a similar format in the future.

INTRODUCTION

CAL91 was the title of an international symposium on information technology in support of learning. While the symposium had been running biannually for 20 years, it had not developed a style or ethos which differed markedly from conferences or symposia in other areas of practice. It is apparent, perhaps even to a casual participant, that, given the domain indicated by the title (one of the fastest moving in terms of innovative pace) its biannual get together had not been characterised by a similar free ranging innovative spirit. In 1991, the programme committee attempted a radical departure from convention and initiated a symposium which had a number of innovative characteristics.

As the early communication to intending participants in CAL91 stated unequivocally, the event was not a "conference". Its intention was to stimulate interactions between people in small groups, certainly no more than 20. The vision was of individuals coming together over a period of 3 days to set up and pursue negotiated agendas on the basis of the stimulus of posters, seminar input, workshops or demonstrations.

In interactional terms the scenario was intended to be essentially organic rather than mechanistic. Procedural behaviour was highly specified, in that the framework and administrative support was prescriptive, while the process, goals and knowledge exchanges within this procedural framework were left unspecified. If the word "conference" has any clear meaning, in the sense of the set of cultural conventions it evokes, i.e. formal presentations, keynote speakers, reactive responses, then the organisers of CAL91 attempted a self conscious departure from these activities.

NEGOTIATION AS A CORE PROCEDURE

The central idea for CAL91 was that there would be a process of negotiations and discussions between people who wished to "run" a session and those that were to participate. Phase one of these discussions began with an indication to the programme committee of a broad intention to participate and the kind of session which might be run. Essentially, these would be in the form of a seminar, a demonstration, or a workshop (each of these was defined precisely). The content of these events, while unspecified, was to provide an opportunity for new areas of work or research to be presented, discussed or developed with interested colleagues.

The next phase of negotiation and discussion involved a poster display which might act as a prelude or shop window to the session. At the beginning of the symposium, all session leaders were asked to provide a poster display at which participants could "sign up" or discuss the ensuing event with session leaders.

The final phase of discussion or negotiation would be at the event itself during the presentation of ideas/demonstrations etc.

Thus we have a structure held together with three phases of discussion with a large number of potential experiences from which to choose. Sessions were unlikely to be for less than 3 h each, although many more spontaneous interactions were intended.

The central paradox in all this was that in order to promote an organic flow of interactions during the event itself, the organisation and framework, including help and support during the 4 day period of the symposium, required a tighter frame than in a more conventional context. Its success also depended on two other variables. First was the extent to which participants understood the cultural shift that CAL91 was intending to promote and did not have conventional expectations which clearly would not be met. Second, as in the conventional scenario, was the capability of the session leaders to sustain and stimulate discussion and interest over a long period.

EVALUATION DESIGN

In order to assess the experience of participants of CAL91, in the light of its innovative features, a two-stage evaluation was constructed. The first stage attempted to gauge the experience of participants of the pre symposium documentation and guidance (see Appendix 1 for the instrument). The second stage involved a feedback questionnaire which participants were asked to complete and return at the end of the symposium (see Appendix 2 for the instrument).

PRE-CONFERENCE EXPERIENCE

In the light of the innovative characteristics of the symposium, the pre-conference explanations and procedure guidance became particularly important. It was extensive. Table 1 gives responses to questions asked of all potential participants. 56 replies were received at the start of the event giving an indication of views.

It is clear from Table 1 that there was ambivalence about the idea of a symposium without formal presentations, although a slightly higher proportion of respondents were attracted by the idea. A high proportion of respondents considered the structure over elaborate, but the idea of a large number of parallel sessions was overwhelmingly supported. The documentation was considered too complex by nearly two-thirds of respondents and a high proportion of respondents did not have time to read all the material. Overall, the administration of the preparatory phase was considered efficient.

From a session leader's point of view, they were in general reasonably clear about their role, felt slightly over directed and did not want any more help planning their sessions.

While some respondents may have had some misgivings about the innovations in CAL91, it is difficult to see how the programme committee could have improved their preparation without burdening them still further with advance documentation.

Table 1. Pre-conference preparation

	Strongly agree	Agree	Disagree	Strongly disagree
The initial flyer calling for participation was clear and informative	11	16	12	4
The initial flyer gave clear instructions for potential contributors	8	17	8	10
Detailed information (Aug. 1990) on the styles of sessions was too complex	6	20	13	1
I didn't have time to read all the explanatory material	12	13	16	3
Enquiries to the CAL91 organisers were treated promptly	21	21	3	2
Enquiries to the CAL91 organisers were answered clearly	19	15	11	1
I am attracted by the idea of a symposium without formal presentations	7	20	12	12
The Symposium structure seems over-elaborate	8	21	17	7
I like the idea of so many parallel sessions	21	22	7	—
Four days involvement with the symposium is too long	13	16	21	1
Enough information was given to me to make a reasoned choice of which sessions to attend	8	33	7	5
Information was distributed in good time	19	21	9	2
Session Leaders/Co-Leaders				
The role of session leader was clear	10	9	4	5
The role of session leader seems difficult	5	7	12	3
I would have liked more help in organising my session	2	3	17	2
I was over-directed in planning my session	2	14	9	—
Overall preparation for session leaders was good	6	10	7	1
I am disappointed that alterations were made to my original session proposal	—	3	11	7

CONFERENCE EXPERIENCE

This section is organised around the responses to the questionnaire items with a brief comment under each item drawing attention to key features of the table. The latter part of the section pulls together all the open ended comments for inspection with a brief summary of the main features. There were 94 questionnaires completed, of which 62 were male and 32 female.

From Table 2 it is clear that the majority of participants thought the symposium well run, had a relaxed and informal atmosphere and that there was sufficient time to think about issues and consolidate ideas. A relatively high proportion of respondents had difficulty keeping track of what was going on.

The wide choice of sessions was appreciated although some found this a difficulty. A high proportion of participants considered the sessions too long. Overall, there was some agreement that there were too many sessions.

The large number of parallel sessions and the length of time for each is clearly an issue here. While choice was valued, it also presented some participants with a difficulty. However, choices do. Presenting difficult choices might be a positive dimension of the symposium experience and should not necessarily be seen in a negative light. The length of time of the sessions, however, presents a different problem. In that around 60% of respondents indicated they thought the sessions too long, future organisers may consider more flexibility here. The design of the symposium overestimated participants' ability to sustain "organic interaction" over a 3-h period.

Table 2. Practical organisation of conference

	Level of agreement				Nil
	1	2	3	4	0
It was hard to keep track of what was going on	14	20	38	19	3
Everything seemed to run very smoothly	22	47	18	4	3
We rushed from one thing to the next without time to think about issues	6	15	40	28	5
We could have done more than we did in the time available	26	26	24	15	3
The atmosphere was very relaxed and informal	49	35	5	2	3
We had all the resources and materials that were needed	30	37	15	4	7
I felt that the sessions were too long	40	23	23	7	1
People moving between sessions was a distraction	1	8	36	43	6
I appreciated the wide choice of sessions	26	31	21	12	4
Support from sessions stewards was valuable	49	31	6	1	7
Finding my way to sessions was easy	25	32	30	5	2
I found participation in sessions hard work	3	19	40	24	8
It was hard to make a choice between	44	29	11	6	4
There were too many sessions	23	22	28	15	6

Table 3. Types of sessions

	1	2	3	4	5	> 5	None	Total No. sessions attended
Workshops	27	23	1	4	—	—	39	92
Seminars	6	13	25	22	7	5	16	264
Demonstrations	21	6	4	1	1	6	55	106
Total time spent poster browsing	282 h 10 min							

Table 4. Quality of sessions

	Level of satisfaction				No
	1	2	3	4	response
Workshops	22	30	7	1	34
Seminars	13	51	17	3	10
Demonstrations	8	33	3	0	50
Poster quality/information	32	42	8	0	12

Table 5. Satisfaction of informal interests

	Very well	Fairly well	Not at all	No response
Having the chance to meet and talk with colleagues	52	37	4	1
Learning about current concerns	31	49	12	2
Sharing experiences	32	53	7	2
Other	8	3	7	76

The results of Table 3 suggest a well rounded use of the various sessions. The poster display provided, at least using time spent browsing as an indicator, a well used backdrop to the other sessions.

Table 4 investigates the general quality of sessions. Unfortunately the demonstrations were less popular than other forms of input, being attended by only half of the total participants.

Again posters came out on top followed closely by seminars which also had the lowest number of nil responses. The workshops proved very satisfactory to two-thirds of participants but a suggestion for improvement might be to create "Workshops for Beginners with more specific titles for experienced people".

The satisfaction of informal interests was high and value was placed on having the chance to meet and talk with colleagues working in similar areas and sharing their experiences. This is reflected in the results of Table 5. In that a fundamental aim of the symposium was to generate interaction and discussion, these data suggest a strong message to organisers concerning success in this respect. What is less certain, however, is the extent to which these positive responses were greater than would have been the case with a more conventional structure.

OPEN COMMENTS

As part of the evaluation, participants were asked to comment openly on their experience by identifying the best and worst aspects for them, suggestions for future symposia and any general observations.

The worst

Some comments reflected a dislike of the parallel sessions which competed in interest.

"There was no escape from badly chosen sessions"
"There was an over concentration of parallel events leading to a clash of choice"
"It was difficult to make informed choices"
"Too many sessions to choose from"

Some comments reflected a need for themes, threads, unifying ideas or keynote speakers to "pull" things together.

"No keynote addresses"
"Lack of central theme"
"No focus, no main thread"

The best

Some comments valued the informal environment and the time to engage in measured discussion.
"Meeting colleagues informally"
"The chance to meet and mix"
"Easy to get involved in discussions and demonstrations"
"Informal nature and stimulation/interaction of ideas, themes and events"
"Time for understanding"
Comments reflected an appreciation of the way the symposium was organised and stewarded.
"Helpful shirts and porters"
"Extremely helpful people on the reception desk"
"Friendly local support"
"Well organised, efficiently run, friendly coaching and reception"
The poster display generated a number of positive comments.
"The continuity of the poster display"
"The exhibition hall"
"Genuinely interesting posters"
"The way the posters generated debate"

CONCLUDING REMARKS

The evaluation gives the programme committee and others who may be considering innovating in the way CAL91 has, some mixed messages. The preparedness participants have for this alternative style varies considerably. For some, the length of sessions, the wealth of choice and the lack of a unifying theme or address were serious problems. For others these were precisely the factors identified as positive. This type of symposium requires a set of expectations which are more process than product oriented, a culture which is discursive and forms of interaction which are more participative than passive.

To some extent the range of comment on the degree of focus reflects a range of expectations one might have predicted. The "unresponsive" text is probably the least effective mode of communication to prepare participants for a culture shift in an event like this. However, conference organisers are left with few alternatives. What this evaluation does suggest is that the administration of the symposium worked well, the quality of the sessions varied but within acceptable limits and the degree of interaction and discussion was high.

Future symposia which use this model may consider some "anchor points" like recurring themes or keynote speakers which will address a number of the points made by the more critical observations, without substantially eroding the organic structure. The physical environment should be carefully considered to encourage and enhance the interactive dimension not act as an irritating distraction. Finally, if informal processes are to be stressed then serious design work should be incorporated into session preparation to avoid unfocused or rambling experiences stretching over long periods.

APPENDIX 1

Build-up and Preparation for CAL91

Your responses to the items will inform the style and planning of future Symposia in the CALxx Series.

Please take a few moments (perhaps during your journey to Lancaster) to answer the questions by circling a number which most closely represents your view.

Please hand your completed form to the Secretariat as soon after your arrival at CAL91 as possible.

Thank you for your help.

You will be given a second short questionnaire which will ask for your actual experiences of the CAL91 symposium.

	Strongly agree	Agree	Disagree	Strongly disagree
The initial flyer calling for participation was clear and informative	1	2	3	4
The initial flyer gave clear instructions for potential contributors	1	2	3	4
Detailed information (August 1990) on the styles of sessions was too complex	1	2	3	4
I didn't have time to read all the explanatory material	1	2	3	4
Enquiries to the CAL91 organisers were treated promptly	1	2	3	4
Enquiries to the CAL91 organisers were answered clearly	1	2	3	4
I am attracted by the idea of the symposium without formal presentations	1	2	3	4
The symposium structure seems over elaborate	1	2	3	4
I like the idea of introductory poster displays	1	2	3	4
I don't like the idea of so many parallel sessions	1	2	3	4
Four days involvement with the symposium is too long	1	2	3	4
Enough information was given for me to make a reasoned choice of which sessions to attend	1	2	3	4
Travel information and joining instructions (March 1991) were easy to follow	1	2	3	4
Information was distributed in good time	1	2	3	4
Session Leaders/Co-leaders				
The role of session leader was clear	1	2	3	4
The role of session leader seems difficult	1	2	3	4
I would have liked more help in organising my session	1	2	3	4
I was over-directed in planning my session	1	2	3	4
Overall preparation for session leaders was good	1	2	3	4
I am disappointed that alterations were made to my original session proposal	1	2	3	4

APPENDIX 2

CAL91 Evaluation of Participants Experience

We hope that you will have already completed the pre-Symposium feedback questionnaire. Now, we would like feedback on your actual experience and the content of CAL91.

Please fill in this questionnaire and return it to a Session Steward, to a member of the Programme Committee or the CAL91 Secretariat. Analysis of the questionnaires will enable organisers to improve the quality of future CAL Symposia. Many thanks for your co-operation.

Please circle the appropriate answer for each question

1. Gender   Male   1
             Female   2

2. Please state your main occupation or position: _____

3. Please state whether you were a
             Session Organiser   1
             Participant   2
             Non-resident participant   3

4. Please indicate how you feel about the following statements which people have made about the practical organisation of conferences.
   (Please circle *one* number on *each* line.)

	Strongly agree			Strongly disagree
It was hard to keep track of what was going on	1	2	3	4
Everything seemed to run very smoothly	1	2	3	4
We rushed from one thing to the next without time to think about issues	1	2	3	4
We could have done more than we did in the time available	1	2	3	4
The atmosphere was very relaxed and informal	1	2	3	4
We had all the resources and materials that were needed	1	2	3	4
I felt that the sessions were too long	1	2	3	4
People moving between sessions was a distraction	1	2	3	4
I appreciated the wide choice of sessions	1	2	3	4
Support from session stewards was valuable	1	2	3	4
Finding my way to sessions was easy	1	2	3	4
I found participation in sessions hard work	1	2	3	4
It was hard to make a choice between sessions	1	2	3	4
There were too many sessions	1	2	3	4

5. We would like to know more about the types of sessions you attended.
   Please state how many of each category of session you attended.
   Workshops   _____
   Seminars   _____
   Demonstrations _____
   Please state approximately how much time you spent Poster Browsing
   Time browsing   _____ h.

6. On balance what did you think of the general quality of the sessions.
   Please circle *one* number on each line.

	Very satisfactory			Very unsatisfactory
Workshops	1	2	3	4
Seminars	1	2	3	4
Demonstrations	1	2	3	4
Poster quality/information	1	2	3	4

7. How far did the Symposium satisfy your more informal interests?
   Please circle *one* number on each line.

	Very well	Fairly well	Not at all
Having the chance to meet and talk with colleagues	1	2	3
Learning about current concerns	1	2	3
Sharing experiences	1	2	3
Other _____	1	2	3

8. Please indicate how you feel about the general arrangements for the Conference. Please circle *one* number for *each* line.

	Very satisfactory			Very unsatisfactory
Food	1	2	3	4
Catering arrangements	1	2	3	4
Accommodation	1	2	3	4
General environment	1	2	3	4
Working facilities	1	2	3	4
Social events	1	2	3	4

9. CAL91 has been organised differently—a limitation on individual presentations, an attempt to stimulate interaction. We would like your open comment on how your experience of CAL91 compares with your experience of more traditionally organised symposia.

_____

_____

_____

_____

_____

_____

_____

_____

10. In conclusion, please identify the best and worst features of CAL91 from your own point of view.
The best feature of CAL91 was:

_____

_____

_____

_____

_____

_____

_____

The worst feature of CAL91 was:

_____

_____

_____

_____

_____

_____

Thank you for helping us.

AUTHOR INDEX

INDEX